The Politics of Surviving

The Politics of Surviving

HOW WOMEN NAVIGATE DOMESTIC VIOLENCE AND ITS AFTERMATH

Paige L. Sweet

UNIVERSITY OF CALIFORNIA PRESS

University of California Press
Oakland, California

© 2021 by Paige Sweet

Library of Congress Cataloging-in-Publication Data
Names: author. Sweet, Paige L., author
Title: The politics of surviving : how women navigate domestic violence
    and its aftermath / Paige L. Sweet.
Description: Oakland, California : University of California Press, [2021] |
    Includes bibliographical references and index.
Identifiers: LCCN 2021015702 (print) | LCCN 2021015703 (ebook) |
    ISBN 9780520377707 (hardcover) | ISBN 9780520377714 (paperback) |
    ISBN 9780520976429 (ebook)
Subjects: LCSH: Victims of family violence—Services for—United States. |
    Abused women—United States—Social conditions. | Abused women—
    United States—Psychological aspects.
Classification: LCC HV6626.2 .S95 2021 (print) | LCC HV6626.2 (ebook) |
    DDC 362.82/920973—dc23
LC record available at https://lccn.loc.gov/2021015702
LC ebook record available at https://lccn.loc.gov/2021015703

Manufactured in the United States of America

25 24 23 22 21
10 9 8 7 6 5 4 3 2 1

For all the women whose stories are told here
and for those who can't or won't tell stories

And for "Susan," a.k.a. Sunshine (1983–2020)
Thank you for your light

Contents

Acknowledgments

I've relied on the generosity of so many to write this book. My deepest gratitude goes to the domestic violence survivors and anti-violence advocates who tolerated my intrusions into their homes and workplaces, who told me their stories with such candor and wit. Thank you.

I developed these ideas under the guidance of faculty and graduate students in the sociology department at the University of Illinois at Chicago, a program that nurtured my political commitments as deeply as my sociological ones. Claire Decoteau has been a true mentor and ally the whole way through. I'm sure I never would have made it without her, and I hope to be as committed and generous to students as she has been to me. To have a mentor I admire so much as a scholar and as a person is a real gift, and I'm so grateful.

Beth Richie has been a thoughtful advisor on this project and on my career—her scholarship, her warmth, and her passion never fail to amaze me. Many thanks also to Lorena Garcia, Sydney Halpern, and Annemarie Jutel, who served on my dissertation committee and provided invaluable feedback. At UIC, I also benefited from the mentorship of Barbara Risman, Nadine Naber, Laurie Schaffner, Andy Clarno, Maria Krysan, and Barbara Ransby. I'm incredibly grateful to all the graduate students at

UIC who helped and inspired me along the way. To my good friends Jody Ahlm, Michael De Anda Muñiz, Tünde Cserpes, and Meghan Daniel, thank you, thank you, I wouldn't be here without you. My work and spirits have been boosted at critical times by Kate McCabe, Erin Eife, Eric Knee, Emily Ruehs-Navarro, Anna Colaner, Lain Mathers, Sarah Steele, Sangi Ravichandran, and Piere Washington.

I've been lucky to be a part of several reading and writing groups that have made me love this job. Claire Decoteau's reading group at UIC was an indispensable part of my education. To Kelly Underman and Danielle Giffort, I owe so much. Such good friends, such excellent sociologists—to get their feedback on my work and their support on *whatever* is a privilege. To Heather Welborn, thank you for making me smarter and happier in graduate school. To my dear friend Katelin Albert, thank you for your intelligence, for being there, for making me laugh. I'm so grateful to Maryam Alemzadeh, Anna Skarpelis, Hanisah Sani, Moira O'Shea, and Sneha Annavarapu for giving me a lovely virtual community while writing this book.

My thanks to the family of Susan Schechter for allowing me access to her archives, as well as to the archivists at Smith College, Harvard's Schlesinger Library, and DePaul University. I'm so grateful to the National Coalition Against Domestic Violence for allowing me to scour their storage units in search of historical materials. Key insights were also offered by the staff at the National Center for Domestic Violence, Trauma, and Mental Health, especially Heather Phillips and the incomparable Dr. Carole Warshaw. Thank you to the generous people at Mujeres Latinas en Acción and Sarah's Inn for guidance on this research. I thank Valeria Velazquez, Jasmine Maldonado, and Hector Dominguez for their excellent assistantship during fieldwork. The National Science Foundation, ACLS/Mellon Foundation, the Rue Bucher Memorial Award at UIC, the Alice J. Dan Dissertation Award, and the Chancellor's Award at UIC all provided valuable funding for this project.

I was lucky enough to find myself at the Inequality in America Initiative at Harvard University for two years while working on this book. To Claudine Gay, Larry Bobo, and Jennifer Shephard, thank you for not only leading a program that gave me time and space, but for offering real encouragement and guidance. Jocelyn Viterna has made me a better scholar and has taught me what it means to carry oneself with grace and care in this profession. I certainly wouldn't be where I am today without Jocelyn's encouragement and careful reading of my work. I owe thanks to Jocelyn's graduate students, who welcomed me into their community and contributed important feedback to this project. My gratitude to Caroline Light for taking me under her wing, and to the sociology faculty at Harvard for creating a welcoming space in the department. Julia Weiner, a brilliant student and an anti-violence advocate herself, provided excellent research assistance on this project. A warm thank-you to the fellow postdocs who made my time in Cambridge so special, especially Anthony Johnson: I couldn't have done it without your kindness and camaraderie. Anna Skarpelis provided ongoing encouragement and feedback, as did Michael Aguirre, Miao Qian, David Mickey-Pabello, Charlotte Lloyd, Talia Shiff, and Shai Dromi. To the Cambridge Women's Center, where I spent afternoons answering hotline calls and talking with members while writing this book, thank you for reminding me that it *is* possible to provide care and community to those who need it, without demanding anything in return.

While at Harvard, I had the incredible experience of convening a book manuscript workshop with some of the scholars I admire most. Enormous thanks to Lynne Haney, Cecilia Menjívar, and Catherine Connell. This book is only what it is because they took the time to read and comment. The first time I read Lynne's work, I knew I had found a place in sociology, and I thank her for supporting me. Cecilia's scholarship is a constant guidepost for me, and she is—unsurprisingly—also a very generous advisor. Cati Connell's support has meant so much, and I hope to be the kind of mentor and scholar she is. A huge thank-you, as well, to Naomi Schneider and Summer Farah at UC Press. Gratitude to Michelle Pais for emergency design advice and to Donna Ferrato for allowing me to use her remarkable photograph on the cover.

Since coming to the University of Michigan, I've had the warm support of Karin Martin, Elizabeth Wingrove, and especially Elizabeth Armstrong and Anna Kirkland, who both took the time to support me long before I landed at U-M. My department has been so welcoming, despite the strange and isolating period during which I started this job. My love to Robert Manduca, Roseanna Sommers, Luciana de Souza Leão, Neil Gong, Kate McCabe, and Apryl Williams—thank you for helping to make Ann Arbor home.

Who knows where I'd be without my chosen family. Such love and gratitude to Jody Ahlm and Meghan Daniel—truly, my "support group"—for keeping me laughing and always being on my side. To Anna Skarpelis, whom I can't believe I didn't meet until we got to Harvard, since we were meant to find our way to each other. To Ati Rahimpour and Michael Levin, for making Chicago home and for taking care of me. And of course, to Ayla Karamustafa, all my gratitude and admiration. Thank you for sharing your sharp sociological imagination and for believing in me. I'm unreasonably lucky to count you as a true constant in my life. My heartfelt thanks to the whole Karamustafa-Keshavarz clan for their love and guidance throughout this journey.

My family has always given me that deep kind of energy and support that is difficult to put into words. To Ross Sweet, Lizzie Nolan, and of course Ollie—thank you for always being there, for feeding me and listening to me and making me so happy. To Becca Kehm and Nick Brady, thank you for your unconditional support and for giving me so much to look forward to—I wouldn't survive a day without you. To Dave and Diane Kehm for being the best bonus parents. Thank you also to David Brundage and Susan Stuart for being so supportive and for giving me a new place to call home. I thank my grandmother, Barbara Prior, who showed me what it means to be proud of your work and who always encouraged me to write and write. To Reed Prior, whom I love and admire. And of course, to my parents, Laurel Prior-Sweet and Dave Sweet, who have always been unwavering in their support, and who really are just the best. I'm so lucky to be your kid. Thank you for giving me everything I needed to be able to write a book.

And lastly, my love and gratitude to Jonah Stuart Brundage, my partner, friend, editor, champion, critic—my favorite. Thank you for everything. I hope this book makes you proud. What a dream to be on this road together.

Parts of chapter 4 are adapted from Paige L. Sweet, "The Paradox of Legibility: Domestic Violence and Institutional Survivorhood," *Social Problems* 66, no. 3 (2019): 411–27. Parts of chapter 5 are adapted from Paige L. Sweet, "The Sociology of Gaslighting," *American Sociological Review* 84, no. 5 (2019): 851–75.

Acronyms

AA	Alcoholics Anonymous
ACEs	Adverse childhood experiences
APA	American Psychiatric Association
BPD	Borderline personality disorder
CBT	Cognitive behavioral therapy
CETA	Comprehensive Employment and Training Act
DCFS	Department of Children and Family Services
DOJ	Department of Justice
DSM	*Diagnostic and Statistical Manual of Mental Disorders*
EMDR	Eye movement desensitization and reprocessing
FVPSA	Family Violence Prevention and Services Act
ICADV	Illinois Coalition Against Domestic Violence
LEAA	Law Enforcement Assistance Administration
MPD	Masochistic personality disorder
NCADV	National Coalition Against Domestic Violence

NIMH   National Institutes of Mental Health
OVW   Office on Violence Against Women
PTSD   Posttraumatic stress disorder
VAWA   Violence Against Women Act
VOCA   Victims of Crime Act

Introduction

DOMESTIC VIOLENCE AND
THE POLITICS OF TRAUMA

Things only seemed to get worse after she left him. That's when he started
going after her for custody of their child, using her mental health records
against her to try to convince the courts she was an unfit mother. Nevaeh's
ex-partner abused her for years.[1] Though they are no longer together, like
many abusers, he continues to harass her through the family court system.[2] "He uses the kid now to try to regain his control. . . . His target is
me. I clearly have a big, red bullseye on my back. . . . And the kid is like
the bow and arrow. Any means necessary, he's gonna hit that target." Like
many women who have experienced domestic violence, Nevaeh was not
allowed a reprieve upon leaving her abuser—no breath of fresh air, no
sense of unshackling.[3] Rather, leaving him has led to extended custody
battles and public accusations that she is "crazy," exaggerating about the
abuse, and unable to parent on her own.

In response to these accusations, the judge in Nevaeh's case recommended that she get counseling at a domestic violence organization.
Nevaeh found an agency for victims nearby and went in for individual and
group sessions, fearing what would happen to her child if she refused. At
first, Nevaeh was resistant to attending counseling at the judge's behest.
But she came to like the therapists and the other women at the domestic

violence agency where I met her. In group, she practiced deep breathing, processed out loud her battles in family court, and learned about the biology of posttraumatic stress disorder (PTSD). Throughout our interview, Nevaeh used the language of trauma and psychological victimization with practiced confidence. She described herself as "strong," as someone who has "overcome": she felt she was a *survivor*.

But Nevaeh also questioned whether she had *really* "overcome," since she regularly relives the abuse in court: "It had to take ... strength to come through it. You know that much. But allowing all these things to happen and having to go through all these things [again]? It's like, at what moment did I get enough?" Nevaeh also worries that attending counseling is risky because it might make her appear "crazy." She does not believe she *needs* counseling and resents being pushed into it—pushed by the very systems that did nothing to help her recover financially from the abuse or to parent her child safely, away from her abuser. It isn't as if the court actually forced her to go to counseling—she is a *victim*, after all. Nevertheless, the court's "recommendation" that she get counseling felt like punishment to Nevaeh. And it felt mandatory: "It was 'suggested' through court order that I seek [therapy] ... even though I had already been through therapy." Nevaeh felt that her lawyer colluded with the courts to make it seem like she needed counseling: "[My lawyer] said, 'It's just protocol.'" Even though she liked her counselors at the domestic violence agency, Nevaeh was upset about being pressured into attending therapeutic programs in order to show the courts that she is a credible victim, a responsible mother, a good survivor. "It wasn't even my fault in the first place. *I* was being abused by *him*." Going to counseling came to feel like *one more thing she had to do* in order to actually survive.

Domestic violence agencies pitch their services as "optional" and premised on "self-determination." However, I found through my fieldwork that women who experience domestic violence are regularly pressured or required to attend counseling by child welfare agencies, judges, and social workers. Most of the domestic violence victims I interviewed for this book were attending several kinds of therapy simultaneously when I met them. Most were pushed into counseling at domestic violence agencies because they *needed something*—from family courts, from child services, or from the immigration system—and attending therapeutic programs became an important way to demonstrate to state agencies that they were worthy of those resources. Trauma language pervades these programs, teaching women the medicalized terminology of victimization and recovery. It turns out that for women like Nevaeh, proving that you fit the definition of a good, legal victim is not enough. Women must also show that they are in "recovery" from domestic violence, as if it were a disease: they must show that they are transforming from "victims" into "survivors."

Today, the idea that people seeking social services have suffered *trauma* and should engage in psychological *recovery* is taken for granted. The language and therapeutic logics of trauma suffuse social service programs in the United States, from addiction services to child welfare to HIV care to homelessness, and, of course, rape and domestic violence programs. Domestic violence services—the topic of this book—are an important part of this infrastructure, with over seventy-seven thousand people using them in an average twenty-four-hour period in the United States.[4] Domestic violence agencies have changed dramatically over the past forty years. Not only are they more professionalized than ever before, but they are also increasingly medicalized, staffed by clinicians rather than feminist advocates, clinicians who use "trauma" as the vocabulary of victimization.[5] Domestic violence victims are also more likely than ever to be labeled with PTSD when they access services.[6] When someone like Nevaeh enters a domestic violence agency, chances are she will be offered "trauma-informed" counseling and asked to write a recovery plan. Through participating in therapeutic programs, Nevaeh learns how to talk about her experiences in the language of trauma and recovery.[7] She understands that she should become a "survivor" at a revelatory moment in the therapeutic process.

This book examines the complex, contradictory, and unequal process of creating "survivors" out of women who have experienced domestic violence. It exposes the pressures that domestic violence victims face to attend therapy as a condition of receiving aid *and* the labor-intensive processes by which women are expected to become "survivors" in order to be seen as responsible and worthy. As such, this book forces us to wrestle with questions about the gendered nature of the welfare state—and the unintended consequences of feminist mobilizations for these programs. What happens when state resources like visas and child custody are made contingent on

participation in therapy? How and why are victims of gender-based violence expected to show that they are "recovering"? Is "recovery" imbued with
social expectations around gender, sexuality, race, and class? Throughout
this book, I show that women's citizenship at the margins is increasingly
medicalized through the language and technologies of trauma. Through
this process, new norms of deservingness enter into the therapeutic state
and shape women's lives: you don't have to be innocent or self-sufficient to
be deserving of social services, but *you do have to be resilient*. You have to
become a survivor.

The pervasive expectation of a victim-to-survivor transition emerged
inductively from life story interviews I conducted with women who have
experienced domestic violence, creating a connective thread across their
stories. I noticed that domestic violence victims conceived of their relationship to nonprofit organizations, to their families, and to the social
world itself through their success (or not) in becoming a survivor. This
success was to be *achieved* through attending therapy; but the identity
"survivor" was also perceived as a *natural state of being*, the right way to
be a respectable woman who deserves care. Attending therapy and becoming a survivor operate as a shorthand for worthiness. Surviving violence
requires that women make medicalized claims for personhood and state
recognition based on experiences of psychological trauma, a process that
I refer to—following anthropologists Vinh-Kim Nguyen and Erica Caple
James—as *traumatic citizenship*.[8]

"Trauma" has emerged, in far-reaching ways, as the state's answer to
the question of why women need help to get by. Federal policy increasingly
identifies "trauma" as the source of women's and children's "dependency"
on state resources.[9] This pervasive interpretation of victims as "trauma
survivors" has implications for women's symbolic and material relationship to the state.[10] I trace those relationships throughout this book, exposing therapeutic transformations in governance and anti-violence politics,
showing how state programs attempt to "civilize" marginalized women
through therapy.[11] Indeed, *governance*—how external powers such as
the state shape our behaviors, our relationships, our identities, our consciousness—is a central thread throughout this book. I am concerned
with how therapeutic norms become intertwined with mandatory and
quasi-mandatory programs for women on the margins, diminishing their

autonomy while claiming to empower them.[12] As such, I'm interested in governance as a gendered process—as gender intersects with race, class, sexuality, nationality, and ability—and in exploring how the lessons of coercive institutions become embodied.

But at its core, this book is about how women who have experienced domestic violence come to feel like they belong in the social world. I go beyond a unidirectional approach that focuses only on how women are "seen" by the state. Instead, I offer a relational framework that highlights how women *make themselves legible* to systems, forging attachments to therapeutic programs and refashioning their identities in order to survive program requirements and make meaning about violence.[13] After all, as Nevaeh's story reveals, domestic violence is not a discrete event. *Abuse is processual*, full of bureaucratic entanglements and legal pressures—characterized by ongoing attacks on victims' credibility, sanity, and respectability. In this harmful configuration, as Nevaeh explains, the survivor identity feels aspirational, associated with a better life. Trauma and survivorhood are the capacious discourses through which women interact with service providers, explain abuse to friends and family, and find camaraderie with other women. These are the terms through which women who have experienced domestic violence become legible to the state, to professionals, and to each other. Throughout this book, I explore the struggles and contradictions of this labor of legibility.

Nothing about these struggles and their history is inevitable. As Nancy Naples reminds us, survivor discourse is individualized and tethered to psychological expertise—but it did not start out that way.[14] The medicalization and institutionalization of survivorhood raise questions about feminist politics and the state, about the privatization of suffering, questions about whose trauma we are really invested in addressing. Throughout this book, I ask questions about survivorhood as a therapeutic category, a discourse of state recognition, and a lived identity. Why must we make victims *redeemable* through the expectation of survivorhood?[15] What do victims need to be redeemed *from*?[16] The politics of redemption, I show, increasingly sets the terms for women's social inclusion after violence. Survivorhood transforms anti-violence work into recovery work: an internalizing discourse of suffering obfuscates the diffuse, pounding structure of male violence. But we can do better. We can offer victims more than the labor of psychological redemption without the material supports of real recovery. We can offer healing without using psychological improvement as a criterion of deservingness. This book is not a polemic against trauma and survivor narratives, but an *attempt to begin extracting survivorhood from an exclusionary politics of worthiness.* Listening carefully to women's stories—and placing those stories in the historical context of the anti-violence movement—is a good place to begin.

MANDATORY HEALING

Most contemporary domestic violence agencies emerged from feminist anti-violence organizing in the 1970s and 1980s. These are nonprofit organizations that rely on a combination of federal and state funding, donations, and private foundation dollars. They offer a range of direct services to victims, including case management, legal advocacy, and emergency housing. Some also offer psycho-educational groups for perpetrators. Despite this diversity of services, domestic violence organizations increasingly specialize in the kind of quasi-clinical therapy that Nevaeh attends. Today, spending time in a domestic violence agency means becoming conversant in the language of hypervigilance and flashbacks. Running a domestic violence agency means demonstrating quantitative program outcomes based on "reduction in trauma symptoms." Women who attend support groups may be shown diagrams of their brains, learning the effects of posttraumatic stress on cognitive function. They are likely to encounter "trauma-informed" yoga or mindfulness classes as part of their curriculum.

Domestic violence agencies' orientation toward clinical therapy mirrors other social services and reflects the increasing imbrication of punitive and therapeutic systems.[17] Often, women come to domestic violence programs through a kind of therapeutic extortion. The Department of Children and Family Services (DCFS) may require her to attend a support group in order to get her children back from state custody.[18] A judge in a custody case may request that she take her children to therapy in order to demonstrate parental fitness. An immigration lawyer will likely tell her that she needs to attend domestic violence counseling before she can apply for a visa. Victims of domestic violence learn from other women in support groups that they should get proof of therapy attendance so that their custody cases will go better. Domestic violence counseling becomes a "cure" for violence and related problems in this institutional configuration. The message is: get yourself "healed" or you won't get what you need.

Still, attending counseling is not usually "mandatory" in the strict sense of the word. Domestic violence programs *seem* softer and nicer than other kinds of services like addiction treatment, which is typically a penal system requirement. Nevertheless, as I conducted interviews with survivors, I came to feel that scholars and policy makers have focused too much on distinguishing mandatory from nonmandatory programs. Women themselves make very few distinctions between services that are "required" and those that are "suggested." They usually do not know the difference. Domestic violence victims often approach feminist-based therapeutic programs the same way they approach compulsory parenting classes or psychiatric evaluations. Starting with survivors' own narratives tells us a new story about this web of programs: therapy feels and often *is* compulsory, a condition of accessing critical resources—even in feminist-founded organizations that pride themselves on offering "optional" services premised on self-determination.

Domestic violence agencies manage this tension in a variety of ways. For example, the types of counseling offered in domestic violence organizations are different from what you might find in a traditional mental health agency. Yoga and other somatic therapies are popular because counselors see them as "soft" interventions, less pathologizing than other types of therapy. On an unseasonably warm February weekend in Chicago, I attended a trauma-informed yoga workshop recommended to me by several therapists in the anti-violence field. A mix of counselors, yoga instructors, social work students—and one researcher and novice yogi—sat in a semicircle on yoga mats as the instructor welcomed us with a series of "self-care" and breathing exercises, reminding us that we should lie down, twist, stand up, and stretch throughout the day. The instructor articulated precisely the kind of ambivalence about neuroscientific trauma theories that I found in domestic violence agencies, telling us, "There's a lot to say about the brain, but I'm not a neuroscientist. I came into this through my own experience. Now I'm developing the vocabulary to describe what I went through." Like domestic violence counselors, the instructor combined neuroscientific language with lay theories of trauma and personal testimony.

As the workshop progressed, we learned that trauma is "held" or "stored" in the body. The instructor explained the role of the limbic system, discussed theories of the "reptilian" brain, the way the hippocampus "goes offline" during trauma. She described trauma victims as "lost animals in the wild." We heard about how our bodies are designed to help us run away from tigers, and victims' trauma reactions mirror this "vulnerable prey" response. Speakers insisted that trauma is about the loss of relationship to one's body. For this reason, somatic approaches like yoga are ideal, reteaching the body how to "regulate." Throughout the workshop, we were asked to practice mindfulness by acknowledging how our bodies felt in space. All day long, the language of neuroscience blurred into the language of evolutionary biology which blurred into empowerment language, landing finally on mystical discourses of yoga and mindfulness. At first, trained as I am to identify boundaries, I found the discussion dizzying, moving in too many directions at once. However, I soon became accustomed to these vertiginous moments: this kind of hybridity—a blend of neuroscience, feminism, pop psychology, and "Eastern" philosophies—characterizes the trauma paradigms used in domestic violence agencies.

Often, domestic violence counselors attend trainings like this in order to learn stretching and breathing techniques to implement in support groups. The idea that trauma is stored in the body—and therefore that the body should be a site of therapeutic work—is widely accepted. Almost every domestic violence counselor I interviewed endorsed somatic theories of trauma and used body techniques in counseling. The uptake of trauma in domestic violence agencies encourages a focus on victims' bodies as a site of disequilibrium. Trauma thereby institutionalizes a new regime of embodiment and a new type of therapeutic labor into domestic violence agencies, one premised on unconscious suffering and body-based recovery.

Trauma is contradictory in that it brings together "soft" interventions like yoga with the "hard" requirements of attending therapy in order to get critical resources from the state. It is through these kinds of hybrid interventions that women are thrown into an intimate relationship with a distant therapeutic state.[19] When women engage in these kinds of therapies, they may not *feel* like they are interacting with the state at all.[20]

That's because the welfare state is privatized and operates through non-profit organizations like domestic violence agencies. The US welfare state governs indirectly, through a "cascade of political and administrative relationships."[21] This allows for "governing at a distance," such that nonprofit agencies use state funds to operate seemingly *outside* of the state, and programs are "submerged" in private networks.[22] There is an illusion of "distance," then, between state institutions, experts, and citizens themselves.[23] Even when state policy requires arduous and intimate transformations in people's lives, it seems far away and irrelevant.[24]

Further, the state enacts its policies through domestic violence organizations that have complex commitments embedded in second-wave feminism and in their local communities. Just like the yoga workshop, domestic violence agencies are hybrid. Workers fulfill state funding requirements while pursuing their own aims, which are often explicitly feminist. Domestic violence workers interpret their situations and respond to problems in diverse ways.[25] Part of understanding the contemporary welfare state, then, is explaining how its goals—in this case, reforming "problem subjects" through therapy—get filtered through agencies with their own histories, practiced by professionals with different aims, and thereby reconfigured.[26]

After all, the ascendance of trauma therapy in domestic violence agencies is peculiar. When feminists founded domestic violence hotlines, shelters, and political coalitions in the 1970s, medicine and psychiatry were serious enemies of the movement. Male psychotherapists were likened to battering husbands. Doctors and their diagnoses were cast as misogynistic and coercive. Feminists argued that battered women needed political, not clinical, interventions. In chapters 1 and 2, I explain how feminists' opposition to traditional therapy motivated them to develop their own models of therapeutic expertise. Today, domestic violence agencies operate on the borderlands of medicalized "treatment" goals and feminist philosophies of care—through an *articulation* of these disparate logics, which I explore in chapter 3.[27] The transformation of domestic violence work into *trauma work* is not a wholesale reinvention but is constituted by "interlocking structures and strategies that are themselves composed of old and new elements."[28] Trauma work is a site of struggle between feminist politics and medicalized social service logics, a struggle that domestic violence workers themselves embody.

While it is difficult to "see" the dispersed, privatized, and "trauma-informed" state, then, what *does* connect services to each other is the expectation that victims attend therapy and work on becoming survivors. Though the state is "retrenched and fragmented, [it] also provides powerful cultural representations."[29] As women who have experienced domestic violence are funneled through systems, they learn to speak the language of therapeutic progress, to demonstrate psychological improvement through racialized and classed norms of feminine embodiment, sexuality, and motherhood.[30] Becoming a survivor in these institutions sometimes allows women to access resources that they lost as a result of abuse, or to gain new resources altogether—but not always. The rub is that achieving survivorhood feels like individual, psychological work, when it is actually embedded in complex state and institutional requirements.

THE VICTIM-SURVIVOR BINARY

The labor of navigating bureaucratic systems after abuse is intensified by the fact that women enter into a symbolic economy of "victim" and "survivor" when they name their experiences in the public sphere. These terms determine much of what it means to endure rape or domestic violence, both in popular culture and in social programs. "Victim" and "survivor" are powerful "public narratives" that have institutionalized a bifurcated understanding of what it means to endure gender-based violence.[31] But those categories are also made and remade through women's stories and actions. As Rose Corrigan and Corey Shdaimah show, a woman's ability to become an "ideal victim" does not *just* depend on characteristics like race and class, but on how she *mobilizes those characteristics in interactions* with legal authorities.[32] A relational approach is therefore necessary for understanding victim and survivor categories: these are intimate categories of practice.

Importantly, the victim/survivor binary is also hierarchical. Survivorhood is *better than* victimhood.[33] Linda Martín Alcoff and Laura Gray have written about the historical transition in anti-rape work from "passive victim" to "active survivor."[34] Popular feminism has been particularly obsessed with the "binary of passive, innocent victimhood pitted against active, responsible agency."[35] Rather than a victim saturated in feminine dependency, we now prefer a therapeutically engaged "survivor" figure. The survivor figure, according to sociologist Poulami Roychowdhury, is someone who can become a "savior" of herself: she is better than women who are stuck in a "victim mentality."[36] Chanel Miller, who was sexually assaulted by Stanford student Brock Turner, wrote in her memoir that Stanford University pressured her to commemorate her experience on a plaque with "uplifting" words, rather than words that spoke to her rage and devastation.[37] The "pernicious dichotomy" of victim/survivor pressures victims into becoming "heroines," giving us gendered archetypes in place of the complicated realities of human suffering, anger, and social action.[38] Further, the temporal sequence presumed by the progression *from* victim *to* survivor belies the reality of domestic violence, which is processual—characterized by ongoing struggles with abusers and coercive systems that may extend years after "leaving."

Nevertheless, the term *survivor*, evocative of a "courageous struggle," has largely replaced the term *victim* in professional anti-violence work.[39] Understandably, organizations prefer to represent women as capable agents rather than as victims in need of saving.[40] In her historical analysis, Nancy Whittier shows that feminists created the "survivor" label to ally with conservative policy makers and other skeptics in the 1980s and '90s, creating a "positive" language for public-facing work.[41] Survivor discourse is legitimating for the field. Further, psychological experiments reveal that people ascribe more positive attributes to women perceived as "survivors" than to those perceived as "victims."[42] Survivors are seen as "optimistic," "brave," "confident," and "active"—*and as people who attend therapy.* Victimhood can be overcome, it is thought, through testimony of trauma in professional settings.[43] In this way, "survivor discourse" facilitates psychotherapeutic evaluation, making "survivor" both a moral and a medicalized category.[44]

On the one hand, then, the "victim" is a failed figure who must be expelled from the boundaries of successful survivorhood. In Rebecca Stringer's words, the victim is a "reviled subject" who has "questionable fitness for the rigors of citizenship."[45] On the other hand, the victim is a desirable figure before the law: she is a victim *of crime*. Imagine the white woman with the black eye who shrinks in fear at her husband's approach. This racialized, hetero-gendered figure of helplessness offers valuable currency in legal systems. Anthropologist Cristiana Giordano writes that "helplessness" is essential to the production of this state-recognized "victim"—but one must be *either* helpless or empowered, never both.[46] "Victim" and "survivor" are tethered to state bureaucracies, legal procedures, and expert economies of care, which often make them appear as mutually exclusive categories.

Author Lacy Johnson writes about the failings of this binary in her 2014 memoir, *The Other Side.* After leaving an abusive relationship, Johnson's abuser kidnapped and held her hostage in his basement, raping and assaulting her. She writes:

> In the final police report, dated August 14, 2000, I am identified as Lacy Johnson: VICTIM. I read this and feel certain it is true. I see myself as the officers saw me.... I am a subject to be questioned, a story to be investigated, the victim of a set of illegal acts.... And yet, when I close the file, I remember how the truth is more complicated than this. I remember, for example, making choices. I look into his eyes while I undress. When it is done he apologizes and finds me something to eat. I tell him everything is *fine, just fine* and stroke his hair while he cries into my lap. He begs me to come back. Outside, in the hallway, his rifle leans against the wall. At any moment, he may or may not kill me. I remember how the two possibilities can coexist: I am both alive and dead in every room but this.[47]

In this passage, Johnson reveals a devastating multiplicity—a multiplicity that takes shape in the face of the legally definitive category, VICTIM. The last line is a reference to Schrodinger's famous cat experiment, meant to illustrate a paradox in quantum physics: a cat shut in a box with a vial of poison is both alive and dead—both of those realities coexist—until we open the box and observe what is there, at which point reality collapses to one side or the other. Johnson draws brilliantly on this thought experiment to comment on the failings of institutional categories to capture the deep ambivalences of intimate violence. The categories of object or agent, victim or survivor, will never capture Johnson's coexisting realities: that when she was powerless, she strategized and made choices; that the intimacy of her relationship with her abuser complicated her identification as victim. Her agency and powerlessness were forged together, unyieldingly entangled, producing multiple realities simultaneously.

Johnson's writing speaks to the inability of the victim/survivor binary to reflect the lived realities of abuse, despite its dominance in institutions and popular discourse. She shows that the victim/survivor binary—like all binaries, perhaps—actually works to conceal the complexity and ambiguity of lived experience. For example, a recent survey of college students who experienced sexual assault reveals that almost half of the students identify as *both* "victim" and "survivor" and almost 20 percent identify as neither.[48] In a survey of abused women, respondents reported feeling that the pressure to identify as *either* "victim" *or* "survivor" eclipsed opportunities to talk about other problems in their lives.[49]

The victim/survivor binary is omnipresent in women's lives—but this binary is also constantly undone, made untenable, as women put their lives back together during and after abuse. Usually, women who have experienced domestic violence have to perform their worthiness *across* the binary. Despite the desirability of the "survivor" label, the women whose stories appear in this book cannot eschew "victim:" to do well in the legal system, they have to convince powerful authorities that they are legitimate victims. Navigating these contradictory pressures requires embodied and narrative labor that can easily slip. As Jennifer Dunn writes, "The 'true' or 'worthy' victim loses some of her halo if her presentation falters."[50] This "presentation" of worthiness, I show, includes demonstrating one's commitment to psychological recovery, a commitment to the temporal sequence *from victim to survivor*. Legitimacy as a victim is often contingent on proving that one attends therapeutic programs and is working toward psychological betterment. The categories of "victim" and "survivor" are linked and layered, both key to the distribution of social and political power.[51] This book exposes how the victim/survivor binary shapes the messy institutional labor and identity work that women must accomplish in order to survive domestic violence.

LEGIBILITY

As is clear through the institutionalization of "victim and "survivor," domestic violence policies and programs are examples of how the state governs in *gendered* ways. From the construction of the ideal victim in court to the implementation of self-esteem exercises in carceral programs, states "position and produce" masculinities and femininities.[52] Drawing from Michel Foucault's work on governmentality, Lynne Haney defines governance as the "patterns of power and regulation that shape, guide, and manage social conduct."[53] Feminist scholars have been particularly interested in how social service programs produce and reinforce norms related to gender, sexuality, race, class, and ability.[54] Historically, resources have gone to "good women" and their children.[55] This makes the welfare state a key site of gendered and sexual norms in Western democracies.[56]

In contemporary state programs, gendered norms are often constituted through *therapeutic* norms. As sociologist Allison McKim explains, men are expected to work on problems of "maturity" and impulse control, whereas women need "self-esteem."[57] Further, good feminine-citizens should "resist the pitfalls of lower-class, racialized womanhood" by taking up performances of the middle-class therapeutic self.[58] Haney describes women in correctional programs being encouraged to eat Luna Bars rather than cheap snack foods—to embody, in other words, "healthy," middle-class femininity.[59] As I show throughout this book, women who have experienced domestic violence are required to improve themselves psychologically—to become "self-managing feminine subjects" who can make claims to "reasonable" citizenship.[60] Empirically, this book contributes to literature on gender and governance by exposing the increasingly central role of trauma therapies and medicalized discourses of victimization in this state infrastructure.

But also, as Wendy Brown reminds us, states do not execute "one type" of power: they operate through a range of techniques, discourses, rules, and practices that are often in tension with each other.[61] Tracing gendered governance requires attention to the tangled relationships between state policy, local programs, street-level bureaucrats, and clients' intimate lives. In this sense, women's constitution as gendered subjects is a *negotiated process*, rather than a top-down process directed by the state.[62] Women may deeply desire the categories to which they are subjected. To capture the multi-sited and often contradictory nature of gendered governance, this book offers "legibility" as a theoretical tool. As I see it, legibility is concerned with active and intimate *relations* of governance.

Our need to be recognized and acknowledged binds us to each other, to social structure, to institutions, and to performances of self. We are all awash in the pleasures and perils of legibility. Feminist and queer theorists have been prolific on this topic, with their interest in how categories interpellate and produce gendered, sexual, racialized, and national subjects. When I say "interpellate," I am referring to the ways in which people are called forth as particular kinds of subjects—how the state and other systems ask each individual to participate, actively, in ideology.[63] We may be harmed by but also desire interpellation. As Judith Butler writes, "The very possibility of subject formation depends upon a passionate pursuit of recognition."[64] Recognition is necessary for social life but is also constraining and exclusionary.[65] Giordano calls this the "double bind of recognition."[66]

James C. Scott famously underscored this tension: the same tactics that allow states to "see" citizens and provide them with services may also undergird policies that surveil citizens, allowing states to "round up undesirable minorities."[67] For Scott and other theorists, legibility is about *what states do* to categorize citizens, to render them visible.[68] My interest is more dynamic, reflecting queer and feminist theorists' interest in *how and why subjects turn toward power*. Legibility refers to a relationship—often a dissonant one—between state categories and people's practices of belonging.

After all, state categories and service programs do not produce uniform kinds of people from the top down. Becoming legible as a good subject is a social practice. This is not just about *complying*. Rather, legibility involves desire, pleasure, loss, and contradiction—a *relation* between subject and system. The process of becoming legible pulls us into relationships with experts, with institutions, with ideas. We sometimes desire a category like "victim" because it helps us name something confusing or because it gets us access to material resources. In this book, legibility is about the hard work that women have to execute in order to access resources and belonging in powerful systems. But it is also about the inequities and stratifications of legibility, and about the alternative kinds of labor women execute when institutions fail to provide for them. In this way, legibility is always about matching *and* not matching—about striving for an idealized fit from precarious foundations *and* about pushing back against institutional norms that require dangerous and impossible contortions.

Legibility therefore captures the profoundly ambiguous nature of "fitting in," which can't be summed up neatly as either passive capitulation or clear-eyed participation. I cannot separate women's actions into distinct categories of "authentic" or "strategic"—to distinguish between genuine performances of survivorhood and superficial ones. A survivor may attend therapy reluctantly in order to appease a social worker on Monday, but by Friday she uses trauma as a deep language of sensemaking in a support group. Authenticity and strategy are entangled: there are "vast overlaps between these states of being" because subjectivity is always "a source of both submission and rebellion."[69] However, as I will show, some women have more resources than others—such as middle-class backgrounds—that allow them to perform survivorhood with ease. Middle-class women are ideal therapeutic subjects: they are "quintessentially bounce-backable."[70] Poor women, on the other hand, may be embroiled in ongoing material struggles that disallow them from the appearance of having "recovered" at all. The ability to perform survivorhood "naturally" is not equally distributed.

In this book, legibility refers to how social actors interact with symbolic and material systems—such as norms around therapeutic recovery—that they "make work." This may involve sitting in an uncomfortable chair and signing an attendance slip at a support group so that the child welfare office will allow you to continue parenting your child. It may involve driving to two therapy appointments each week so that a judge will look favorably on you as a good victim. Or it may involve describing your experiences as "brain-based trauma" so that friends and family see you as a sympathetic victim. Making oneself legible requires the uptake of existing symbols, as well as the possibility of using those symbols to belong in a new way. It is this duality of legibility—violence plus the desire for social belonging—that makes it such a useful sociological concept, refusing dichotomies of structure/agency and activity/passivity. As Butler writes, "I am led to embrace the terms that injure me because they constitute me socially."[71] What Pierre Bourdieu names *symbolic power* makes us want to fit in, and we work (in spite of ourselves, perhaps) to achieve that fit.[72] My point is that becoming legible as a victim or a survivor is risky, complex, and active—a *striving* rather than simply a *strategy*.

Further, just because categories are imposed and individuated does not mean they cannot also become *collective*. For Raewyn Connell, identities are not about individual performance or state discipline, but about the practice of social belonging.[73] "Doing gender" in a recognizable way, she argues, may be constraining and disciplinary but may also be "an active invitation to recognition and solidarity."[74] We may embody categories that feel imperfect, even harmful, so that we can draw others into our social worlds. Legibility is in part about collective identification. But it is also—always—about accessing the resources of survival.[75] Being "seen" is therefore part survival and part yearning.

When women use the categories of "victim" and "survivor" to access resources or to make sense of a terrifying experience, they are seeking material survival *and* striving for a new language of sensemaking about violence. I do not want to suggest that there is something romantic about legibility. Becoming legible may be violent and distorting. But perhaps there is also nothing romantic about *illegibility*, about suggesting that people would do better to live outside categories that have the shape of normativity. As Nevaeh reminds us, regimes of trauma make survivor identities possible—generating meaningful attachments between women and state programs—even as they introduce new obstacles into women's lives.

After all, for most of the women I interviewed, it was not "domestic violence" that took place. It was something more amorphous and confusing to name. Many women felt stunned the first time someone called their relationship "abusive." Domestic violence usually only "occurs" when women enter into institutions that use it as an expert category. It is not easy to place the reality of abuse in any one location, since women read and reread their experiences through such categories as they move through institutions. Becoming a survivor requires a labor of legibility that is distorting, but that also generates new attachments to the state, to family, to self and other.

THE CONTEXT: INTERSECTIONAL VIOLENCE

Throughout this book, I show that intimate violence violates women's citizenship—severing them from community and social networks, from a sense of being autonomous and rights-bearing subjects.[76] These ruptures affect women's relationships to the state, to social roles like motherhood, to communities, and to family and work. That's because the experience of intimate violence is not "private" at all: it is forged through intersecting systems of race, class, gender, sexuality, nationality, and ability—as well as by inequalities in housing, legal systems, and mental health systems. This is what I mean when I refer to intimate violence as *intersectional,* following the foundational work of Kimberlé Crenshaw—and it's also what Beth Richie refers to as the "matrix of violence."[77] This violence is shaped by gendered power relations and by other forms of violence in everyday life—sometimes called structural violence—such as racism, homophobia, and poverty.[78] Intimate abuse is a multi-sited, immiserating force that exploits existing social inequalities in victims' lives.

Domestic violence is defined as a pattern of coercive and violent behaviors exercised by one intimate partner against another in order to maintain power and control.[79] Victims of domestic violence endure multiple forms of social restriction, isolation, and control.[80] As many as one in three to one in five women in the United States have experienced physical violence, stalking, or sexual assault by an intimate partner.[81] Although domestic violence is relatively common among LGBQ+ couples, and men may experience abuse from women partners, *domestic violence is overwhelmingly perpetrated by men against women.*[82]

Intimate abuse involves gendered forms of entrapment and control: depriving victims of the liberty to speak, to work, to see family, and to determine the course of everyday life.[83] These dynamics create a "condition of unfreedom" that crosses multiple realms of social life.[84] Even when women "leave" abusive relationships, they are often forced to remain attached to their abusers through shared social networks, child custody disputes, and coparenting arrangements, and/or because they are stalked. In fact, women face the most physical danger when they leave abusive partners.[85] Because financial abuse is a common aspect of domestic violence, victims often face financial devastation even after "leaving" abusive relationships, including problems with credit, problems accessing welfare benefits, and disruptions to paid employment.[86] Further, victims are regularly forced into punitive systems precisely because "survival action is often criminalized action, including . . . strategies such as self-defense, migration to a safer location, or avoiding violence by submitting to coerced illegal activity."[87] In this sense, the harms of domestic violence cannot be captured by an irregular punch, hit, or slap between partners. Rather, domestic violence is about control, disorientation, and degradation—it deprives victims of social resources and autonomy in a context of inequality and isolation. These dynamics likely exist for victims of all genders, but structural inequalities make it more likely that women (cis and trans) will experience them.

Structural/Interpersonal Violence

Jenn, a thirty-five-year-old mixed-race woman, told me her domestic violence story through a story about housing. Housing might seem like a strange narrative structure for a story about her husband's manipulative, isolating, and controlling behavior. However, housing insecurity is a major component of domestic violence and often keeps women trapped in abusive relationships.[88] Domestic violence is one of the leading causes of women's homelessness nationally.[89] A truism in the anti-violence community is that when you tell a woman to leave an abusive relationship, you are asking her to become homeless. Multiple types of housing instability are tied to domestic violence, including unwanted moves, skipping meals to pay rent, "doubling up" with family or friends, threats of eviction, and living in motels or shelters.[90] Almost all the women I interviewed were forced to flee their homes upon leaving abusive relationships, either temporarily or permanently.[91] Some women escaped to Chicago from other cities. Others moved to neighborhoods far from their families. Women who stayed, who were able to kick out their abusive partners, were more likely to have middle-class backgrounds and full-time employment.

That Jenn told me her story through housing demonstrates her profound grasp of the structural contexts of abuse and abandonment. Like many of the women I interviewed, Jenn is savvy about working within and around systems in order to get by. Jenn earns $600–$900 per month working as a patient care technician at a hospital in Chicago. She prefers to work at night because the hourly pay is higher. She also has some income from food stamps and $20–$150 per month in child support. Jenn's rent—in a tidy basement apartment on the outskirts of Chicago—is $800/month. The cost of rent leaves little money for Jenn's car and childcare. She relies on upstairs neighbors to watch her two youngest daughters while she works in the evenings.

In many ways, Jenn's life was easier when she was with her abusive partner. They lived in a spacious first-floor apartment in a more affluent neighborhood and relied on two incomes. When Jenn left her husband after a violent episode that their children witnessed, she lived on friends' couches for a year and a half while she searched for housing.[92] When she found her current apartment, Jenn told me that she began, piece by piece, to rebuild her life into something resembling "independence" and "stability." When I saw her at support group a few weeks after our first interview, Jenn proudly displayed her new nose ring and explained that her husband never would have let her have one.[93]

This was not Jenn's first scrape with homelessness. Her mother left when she was seven and she lived with her grandmother for nearly ten years. Eventually, Jenn had to leave because her grandmother's boyfriend became abusive. She lived in a shelter for girls while she finished high school. She had her first child in her late teens and moved around between friends' apartments while her daughter was an infant. Despite her lack of permanent housing, Jenn secured a medical card, food stamps, and cash assistance. She began living with a boyfriend who became abusive. Jenn wanted to leave, but she stayed with him until she could save enough money to rent her own apartment. She lived for two years in the new apartment until she could no longer afford it. She then bounced around to friends' apartments until she met her husband. Jenn describes falling in love with him during their first conversation. Over time, though, he became violent and controlling. He isolated her from friends and family, called her "crazy," "bitch," and "whore," and followed her when she went out with friends. He also expected her to cook, clean, and provide all the childcare. He regularly left bruises on her arms from grabbing her when she tried to leave. They broke up several times, but Jenn got back together with him so that they could combine their incomes and afford a nicer place to live.

For Jenn, living in a dangerous relationship was better than being on the streets. In fact, most of Jenn's experiences of homelessness were connected to male violence. The dilemma she faced was not violence or no violence, but violence *where* and *from whom*? The structure of the housing market and the strength or weakness of her social networks were key to each of Jenn's decisions about whether to "stay," "go," or do something in between.[94]

Though housing is the central thread in Jenn's story, she also used other languages to explicate her experiences. For example, Jenn sought therapy many times and told me she had "low self-esteem." Jenn also referred to her ex as a "chauvinist." She is currently attending group counseling at a domestic violence agency. If she goes to counseling for a while, she believes, the agency will help her find a pro bono lawyer. Like many of the women I interviewed, Jenn understands legal and other resources to be contingent on therapy attendance.

Jenn's story typifies the savvy systems work that women regularly master in order to survive abuse. Jenn pieces together resources from domestic violence agencies with food stamps, police reports, and legal services, making herself legible as a victim/survivor across institutional sites. Through this process, Jenn deploys what Celeste Watkins-Hayes calls "experiential capital," a "hard-won credential" rooted in her experiences of poverty and homelessness *and* in the labor she executes to patch together the resources of survival.[95] To get those resources, Jenn becomes a client of several institutions simultaneously. She knows she must *do things*, comply with guidelines, in order to receive help. To comprehend the violence that Jenn faced, the structural obstacles that kept her in dangerous relationships, as well as her hustle to secure resources, we must understand domestic violence as *processual* and as *embedded in intersectional systems of power*. Like Jenn, I take a structural approach to theorizing domestic violence, refusing to separate material inequalities and structural violence from the intimate violence that women experience in their relationships.[96]

Domestic Violence and Intersectionality

Though people like to say that domestic violence crosses social and economic boundaries and affects all women equally, we know that's not true. Black women are more likely than any other racial/ethnic group in the United States to be murdered by an intimate partner.[97] Like other social harms, vulnerability to abuse is concentrated in particular social locations.[98] Domestic violence disproportionately affects low-income women.[99] Victims of domestic violence are more likely than other women to receive state assistance, to be unemployed, and to have high health care costs.[100] It is more difficult for marginalized women to leave abusive relationships; this is because they may be dependent on their partners for material survival or because they are reluctant to involve racist systems like police.[101] Poverty and racial inequality are, quite simply, dangerous for women.[102]

Domestic violence is a symptom of "male violence" on a structural level, produced with and through other forms of gender-based, racialized, and state violence.[103] Social inequalities create dangerous intimate conditions for women of color, queer women, poor women, immigrant women, and disabled women.[104] Studies demonstrate that women with annual incomes under $25,000 are more likely to experience life-altering abuse, that a majority of women experiencing homelessness have been abused by partners, and that women receiving cash assistance and living in subsidized housing programs are at increased risk of abuse.[105] As Beth Richie explains, dangerous social positions create the conditions for dangerous intimate relationships.[106]

Unsurprisingly then, the women I interviewed experienced abuse in the context of other social deprivations. For many of them, domestic violence was not the worst thing happening in their lives: it was just the thing for which they could get services. Maria L. was separated from her children, who were stuck in a detention center at the border. Nanette's son, recently released from prison, was shot to death outside a payday loan store just months before our first interview. Though Brenda was haunted by her boyfriend's brutal violence, what she really cared about was getting her children back from state custody. For Tina, endless court dates fighting for child custody meant that she was forced to leave her job, jeopardizing the financial stability she had achieved to get away from her abuser. Several of the women I interviewed dropped charges against their abusers because they needed them to provide childcare. For many of the undocumented women I interviewed, access to health care and good jobs was more urgent than the abuse itself.[107] Women's experiences of harm in their intimate relationships are compounded by racism and poverty, as well as lack of health care, childcare, and social supports.[108]

Further, researchers have found that criminal solutions to domestic violence—such as mandatory arrest policies—disadvantage women of color, who are more likely to be penalized by police and legal systems when they seek help.[109] As Brenda, a thirty-four-year-old Black woman told me, "They put me in jail because they said they're tired of coming back and forth. And I keep letting him out [of jail]. So, they're gonna take me this time. They took me to jail. I stayed there for two days." The police had to arrest *someone* when they showed up. And they were annoyed at Brenda for calling them too many times. Eventually, then, she was the one who got locked up. Like Brenda, women may be fined or arrested for refusing to cooperate with police, even if their reason for noncompliance is that they will suffer financial hardship, homelessness, or loss of childcare if their partner is incarcerated.[110] Researchers have shown that Black women in particular are subject to police violence in ways that exacerbate the harms of intimate abuse.[111]

Further, Black and other marginalized women may experience what Richie calls the "trap of loyalty:" reluctance to involve police since the men in their lives are already surveilled and disproportionately punished by criminal systems.[112] As Rosalyn explained to me, "My family did not agree with my choice to press charges. [They said], 'Don't put him in the system cause it's already hard for a Black man. Why are you adding this type of pressure to him?' So, I didn't really get any support from my family. . . . Don't bring the police in, don't bring no outsiders in, our struggle is already hard enough." Rosalyn was put in the position of trying to stay safe without "putting him in the system," a contradiction that left her guilt-ridden and isolated from family. Systems that are supposed to help women gain autonomy and resources often end up eroding their social networks and placing them in more danger.

Further, as Roberta Villalón shows, harried workers regularly deny victims access to certain resources—such as visas—when they lack the markers of heterosexual, middle-class respectability.[113] This is what I mean when I talk about intimate violence as *processual*: systems like police, family court, immigration, and child services often exacerbate women's lack of control over their lives. The women I interviewed knew— as did their counselors—that this array of problems could not be solved by therapy alone. They needed housing, they needed jobs, cash, childcare, a car, and legal representation. As Leigh Goodmark reports, "Women who receive assistance in securing . . . material resources are significantly less likely to experience physical and psychological abuse after leaving shelter and report greater improvements in their quality of life."[114] Nonetheless, almost all the women I interviewed were hurrying between therapy appointments, trying to "cure" themselves of abuse. Perhaps "something is better than nothing."[115] And yet, through therapeutic programs, women often come to blame themselves—their own "self-esteem" problems— for the ongoing harms they suffer. For many women, the imperative to become a "survivor" is just another thing, in the long list of things, that they must survive.

STUDYING DOMESTIC VIOLENCE

One of the central contentions of this book is that we can better synthesize the interpersonal, institutional, and structural dynamics of abuse if we view them through women's stories. In order to do this, I conducted eighteen months of fieldwork, including life story interviews with women who experienced domestic violence, interviews with domestic violence professionals, months of archival research on the history of anti-violence organizing, and participant observation in professional meetings and domestic violence agencies.[116] I met survivors through their support groups, to which I had access as a volunteer and a state-certified domestic violence crisis advocate myself. In the first three chapters of the book, you'll meet some of the activists who built the anti-violence movement and the trauma workers who are busy providing services to abused women and their children. Woven throughout the book are also survivors' personal stories. I'll take a moment now to introduce you to a few of those women.

I interviewed Emma, a twenty-four-year-old white woman, in the small front office of the domestic violence agency where she had recently begun attending a support group. Her infant daughter slept soundly in her car seat throughout our conversation. After her boyfriend's abusive behavior caused her to lose her job, Emma had to move back home with her parents. Relying on her parents for money left Emma feeling dependent all over again. Still, she was relieved to be single because it meant she did not have to call or text her boyfriend constantly to "check in." Emma hopes to be with him again one day, though, once he's gotten help. She wants her daughter to have two parents at home. Emma was one of the few women I interviewed who wanted to get back together with the man who abused her, and she'll show us later in the book how that desire imperiled her performance of good survivorhood.

Emma helped me remember that women struggle to define their partners as "abusers," to shift their vision of the relationship to be about "domestic violence"—rather than about coparenting, shared backgrounds, community, and young love. Rubi, a thirty-four-year-old Mexican woman, told me, "There were lots of really beautiful times. Not all of it was ugly. There were moments when he was in good spirit. He'd caress me and indulge me. But there were bad times as well." Rubi's experience of domestic violence was complicated by the fact that she was undocumented while her abuser was a US citizen, a power imbalance he leveraged against her constantly. Like Emma, Rubi agonized over her ex-husband's role in her children's lives. She told me that when her husband was arrested, she "felt like dying" because she believed it was her fault that her daughters had a father who was in jail.

Not all the women I interviewed were concerned about their abusers' freedom. For example, Emily, a sixty-two-year-old Black woman, wanted her abusers in jail. I interviewed Emily in a comfortable armchair in her subsidized apartment. The first time I went to Emily's apartment, it was tidy and she was sprightly. The second time, she was on a bender: there were trash bags scattered around the apartment and Emily struggled to keep her eyes in focus while we talked. She told me that domestic violence had driven her to drugs and alcohol. Abusers want you to "lose your mind," she said. Despite years of counseling, Emily can't get rid of the nightmares. It's like a tape in her mind, playing and sticking. Talking with Emily forced me to remember that often, for women who have experienced domestic violence, physical distance from an abuser—and even access to resources like housing and decent health care—does not equate to safety. For Emily, a straightforward trajectory of improvement would remain out of reach. Throughout her life, something like "recovery" came and went, came and went, and went again.

These are just a few of the women whose stories structure this book. You'll also get to know Adriana, a twenty-two-year-old Latina woman who had recently become the first person in her family to graduate from college at the time of our interview. You'll meet Betsy, a sixty-eight-year-old white woman who spent most of her life raising six children at home while her husband worked a high-paying corporate job. With the $2,000 per month she now receives from him, Betsy is able to afford a studio apartment as well as acupuncture and other "self-care" services. You'll meet Carla, a thirty-year-old Latina woman I interviewed in her basement apartment while her kids played rambunctiously around our feet. Though Carla is currently out of work, she managed to open a bank account to save money for her son's education, an account she keeps hidden from her current partner in case he starts to exhibit the "red flags" of an abuser. And you'll meet Rosa, a forty-one-year-old Latina woman who works two fast food jobs and recently found new meaning in her life through local activism to raise the minimum wage.

These diversely situated women all have things to teach us, from the conflictual desire to restart a formerly abusive relationship to the effects of immigration on abuse. Demographically, the women I interviewed are more or less representative of domestic violence victims who seek services in urban areas in the United States. All the survivors I interviewed were women whose abusers were men, and all were constrained by low and/or unpredictable incomes. All lived in Chicago or nearby suburbs. There were eleven women who identified as Black, seventeen Latina, twelve white, one mixed race, one Arab, and one South Asian woman. Sixteen of the women were immigrants to the United States, and twelve were undocumented at the time of the abuse. Most of the women were from poor or working-class backgrounds, though some grew up middle class and experienced new forms of economic precarity because of domestic violence. Most relied on public assistance and child support to pay their bills, though some also worked full-time jobs or, more commonly, unsteady part-time jobs.

Data from the Illinois Criminal Justice Authority, which collects demographic information from all domestic violence programs in Illinois, confirms that the women in my study reflect key characteristics of Chicago service users.[117] Of nearly fifteen thousand victims who used domestic violence services during 2015–2016, 43 percent were Latinx, 39 percent were Black, 14 percent were white, and 4 percent were other categories. The majority rented apartments, about half used food stamps, and over half reported a monthly income of less than $1,000. Less than 20 percent had a college degree. Almost half were unemployed, which may indicate that work was interrupted when they left abusive relationships. My point is that domestic violence services—free, community-based programs—primarily serve poor and low-income women of color facing housing insecurity and chronic underemployment. As such, domestic violence services are part of the infrastructure of urban poverty governance, though urban poverty scholars rarely acknowledge them. As I'll show, paying attention to these programs changes our understanding of what it means to interact with the state and to forge identities using its gendered logics.

ORGANIZATION OF THE BOOK

Taking a feminist sociological approach to the study of intimate violence requires understanding abuse as interwoven with structural, institutional, community, and psychological dynamics—pushing back against legalistic frameworks that focus on incidents of physical violence.[118] In this book, I challenge the temporal structure through which domestic violence is typically characterized. Abuse is a social process: it may be felt most profoundly in the moment of a slap or slur, in a therapist's office years later, in a courtroom fighting for child custody, or when someone asks a victim to name her experiences in a new language. State systems are central to the process of abuse, and women's labor of legibility within institutions must be understood as part of intimate violence. This type of violence does not have bookends—women remain entrenched in the social structures and networks that have variously harmed and helped them.[119] Further, violence is not about victimization only, but about making choices within imposed conditions.[120] I am not interested in constructing heroines or fearless resisters, but in exploring how women get by—and the terms through which they reach for different futures.

This book is organized into two parts. "Survivorhood" explores how and why we find ourselves in the midst of a medicalized trauma revolution in anti-violence work. This part of the book takes a historical approach, exploring the relationship between feminism, the psy sciences, and the welfare state. It also makes its way into contemporary domestic violence agencies to reveal what trauma work looks and feels like. The second part of the book, "Surviving," focuses on how women who have experienced domestic violence interact with these structures of care, claiming rights and resources through narratives of psychological trauma and recovery. This part of the book shows how women's performances of survivorhood are structured by race, class, gender, and sexuality—and how those performances strain, fail, and/or pivot when women encounter disorienting forms of abuse such as gaslighting.

Chapter 1, "Building a Therapeutic Movement," explores the history of feminist anti-violence activism and its relationship to the state. Early years of feminist organizing witnessed the rise of neoliberalism alongside the rise of a new social conservatism. In this hostile climate, feminists managed to pass the two most comprehensive pieces of anti-violence legislation ever seen. Feminism entered the state unequivocally during the 1980s and 1990s, redistributing millions of federal dollars to feminist organizations. How did they do it? This chapter draws on original archival research to show that feminists transformed the state by creating the victim/survivor binary. The "victim" category responds to the carceral arm of the state, while the "survivor" category responds to the therapeutic arm of the state.[121] The chapter refuses any simple notion that feminists were "co-opted," revealing instead that feminists have been challengers *and* collaborators in neoliberal state projects—ultimately helping to create a gendered, trauma-saturated "victim services" branch of the welfare state.

Chapter 2, "The Trauma Revolution" explores the rise of PTSD and trauma theory in domestic violence work, showing how a movement for women's equal citizenship transformed into a movement for trauma services. The language of trauma is now the primary language of victimization across welfare state programs. This chapter reveals that trauma has been central to *quantifying* and *professionalizing* domestic violence work, key to feminist efforts for state legitimacy. The rise of "trauma" signals the emergence of a new style of health governance in anti-violence work that satisfies the technocratic policy sphere *and* makes domestic violence workers into health experts. The unfolding of the trauma revolution, however, is pockmarked with tensions between feminist care work and medicalized "treatment" goals.

Chapter 3, "Administering Trauma," is located inside contemporary domestic violence agencies. Through the words of policy leaders and workers, this chapter explores the epistemic and political struggle between clinical trauma frameworks and feminist politics. I show how domestic violence workers are tasked with translating quantitative demands for trauma symptoms into actual care work. Workers struggle over how to define trauma, negotiating their conflicting aims by administering interventions through "soft" techniques like yoga and deep breathing. Survivors and workers alike are asked to engage in "self-care," revealing the embodied and relational dynamics of trauma work.[122] As I show, importing trauma into the domestic violence agency relocates the effects of abuse *inside* the body, prompting survivors and workers to regulate themselves in new ways.

Next, I move to women's stories of abuse and help-seeking in this landscape of expertise and service provision. Chapter 4, "Becoming Legible," asks how women access recognition and resources in the increasingly therapeutic institutional configuration surrounding domestic violence. Domestic violence agencies, I show, teach women how to use trauma narratives to recover their children from state custody, to comply with court mandates, and to apply for visas. In order to win much-needed resources, women learn to *perform psychological wellness through racialized and classed tropes of respectable motherhood.* In this chapter, I reveal how gendered therapeutic norms shape women's efforts to become legible to institutions.

However, one of the challenges women face when they try to become legible as survivors is that only *some* of their experiences are visible to institutions and experts. Chapter 5, "Gaslighting," shows how experiences of invisible violence—specifically gaslighting, or "crazy-making" tactics—constitute the central axis of power and control in domestic violence, constructing women as fundamentally irrational. Gaslighting shapes women's efforts to become legible to institutions, since this type of abuse is invisible and distorts victims' sense of reality. In this chapter, I document women's strategies to combat this invisibility, such as describing trauma through its physical effects on the body, making abuse "real." In broader strokes, then, this chapter explores what it means to survive in a body marked by irrationality.

The final chapter, "Surviving Heterosexuality," takes a queer approach to domestic violence by asking how survivorhood shapes women's relationships to heterosexuality as an institution.[123] To borrow sociologist Jane Ward's words, I ask what happens when heterosexuality is experienced as "tragic" rather than as safe and normative.[124] Surviving violence requires that women orient themselves *away* from the ideological promises of heterosexual romance and the nuclear family. But this reorientation is fraught. Women face ongoing cultural pressure to find a male partner and achieve familial "success," while they also learn—through therapeutic programs—to feel suspicious about men, to stop dating, and to refrain from sexual relationships. This chapter considers how sexual and reproductive citizenship become sites of struggle for women after they survive male violence.

At the end of the book, I take up the question of citizenship directly, theorizing what I call *traumatic citizenship*: telling stories about trauma and performing recovery in order to become legible in powerful systems. My goal is to show how citizenship has undergone a therapeutic turn for women who have experienced domestic violence.[125] Therapy may not seem like a cruel obstacle to put in women's ways. But I find that only the most vulnerable women face these requirements. Women who can escape abusers without losing homes and bank accounts, without losing legal status, who can hire private lawyers, who are not at risk of being deemed "bad mothers," are unlikely to face intensive therapeutic demands.[126] Money buys privacy.[127] Even though privileged women must also perform as good survivors, their labor of legibility is less onerous, the stakes less steep. Marginalized women face higher-risk therapeutic requirements, and they are judged more harshly for failures in their performances.

Traumatic citizenship does *not* offer what Charles Tilly would call "thick" citizenship, then, wherein the benefits of citizenship are robust and secure.[128] Through domestic violence services, women are granted barebones resources that are contingent on performances of psychological wellness—a "thin" citizenship with limited entitlements.[129] Further, because survivorhood feels like a therapeutic achievement rather than a *right*, women perceive their "failings" as individual rather than structural.[130] This book addresses the ways in which women are forced to use vocabularies of trauma and survivorhood to "struggle against their [own] exclusion."[131] In so doing, women sometimes make new meaning beyond expert discourses. Since becoming a survivor is about forging *relationships* to systems, new desires, identities, and forms of belonging may emerge. Through the muck of institutional claims making and systems navigation, women make clear demands for repair, again and again. Let us listen.

PART I Survivorhood

1 Building a Therapeutic Movement

During the 1970s, feminists established an extensive network of domestic violence shelters, hotlines, and drop-in centers. Their aims were radical: to dismantle the patriarchal structures that allowed domestic violence to occur and blamed women for the abuse inflicted upon them. They marched, they demanded funds, they published the names of suspected rapists in underground newspapers, they hid battered women in their homes and churches.[1] Shelters were meant to act as "physical and symbolic" boundaries separating women from male violence.[2] Early documents from the National Coalition Against Domestic Violence (NCADV) reveal that many of the first domestic violence shelters served queer and trans women and that the shelter movement was "born in [the] gay bars" of cities across the country.[3] One of the first shelters in the country (in Cambridge, Massachusetts) was started by two queer mothers on welfare who opened their apartments to women fleeing their homes.[4] Activists met in donated rooms and stayed in sleeping bags on the floor while they hustled for money to develop training materials.[5] Feminists faced harassment from authorities—the Portland police even tracked them for suspected "terrorist acts" thought to be coordinated through a mysterious "underground" shelter network. By the mid-1970s, there were already between three hundred and five hundred grassroots shelters operating across the United States.[6]

Through community projects, protests, and public testimonies, feminists called on the state to assume its responsibility for protecting women from patriarchal violence. Feminists argued that "private" violence was in fact a *public* issue of women's citizenship. Their claims therefore necessarily involved the state. However, activists relationship to the state was ambivalent. It was common for activists to hold genuine commitments to both resisting and using the state.[7] No stark line existed between state-averse feminists who knew government cooperation would be their death knell and more "practical" feminists who sought to influence policy and change institutions.[8] While scholars are often nostalgic for a pure, grassroots feminist past, the truth is fuzzier. And in fact, such a distinction between pro-state and anti-state activists is anachronistic, a reflection of contemporary rather than historical realities. The shelter movement could be described as *revolutionary* in its approach to redefining and expanding the welfare state—or perhaps as anti-state in its infancy, following the goals of movements that operated *outside* the state such as the Women's Health Movement and the Black Panthers.[9] Nevertheless, activists quickly saw the benefits of applying for federal funds.

When they built the first wave of shelters, hotlines, and drop-in centers, feminists won resources from Johnson-era programs like the Comprehensive Employment and Training Act (CETA), Law Enforcement Administration Assistance (LEAA), and Title XX grants for economically underserved women.[10] By 1976, 65 percent of shelters relied on CETA funds.[11] NCADV organizers spent much of their time teaching local organizations how to apply for federal grants.[12] Activists were optimistic about using these distributive federal policies for their own aims, and that optimism formed the basis of their approach to the state.[13] Activists coordinated White House meetings and sought to establish domestic violence as a "top priority social problem" for state policy.[14] Even feminists who were trepidatious about state involvement saw it as a necessary site of agitation because *they addressed what they thought was an expanding welfare state—and sought to expand it further.*

However, another revolution was afoot. This movement, which would come to be known as neoliberalism, sought to undo the Johnson-era projects

that had (unintentionally) galvanized feminism and other liberation projects.[15] Neoliberals—intent on installing market logic in all arenas of social
life, including the state—stripped the welfare state that had provided the
seeds of the shelter movement, dissolving entire funding sources (such as
CETA) and moving money into block grants to be administered by states.[16]
Neoliberalism, as it aligned with neoconservatism, sought to replace the
idea that "women" deserved unique state protections with the ideology that
"families" and "victims of crime" should be the locus of state support, albeit
limited.[17] With Ronald Reagan's election in 1980, funding for domestic violence programs was immediately under threat—both by a restrictive anti-
welfare ideology and by "family values" advocacy groups. Reagan quickly
abolished the fledgling Office on Domestic Violence after his election.[18]
Under this new regime—in which neoconservatives and neoliberals were
allied—feminists were forced to make their claims to a new state.[19]

The neoliberal revolution would come to dramatically reshape, though
not forestall, the work of the anti-violence movement. It might seem
strange that domestic violence services actually *gained* ground in the 1980s,
the height of neoliberal retrenchment. This was in part because "victims of
crime" became a new category of state investment during these years, as
activists and federal policy makers found common cause by zeroing in on
the figure of the innocent victim. In a landmark federal report in the 1980s,
Assistant Attorney General Lois Herrington wrote that victims are "forgot-
ten citizens" who have been "blamed and ignored" rather than assisted by
courts.[20] This policy report would come to have significant influence over
victim policy in the coming years, helping to pass the Victims of Crime Act
(VOCA) in 1984, which provides millions of dollars annually for domestic
violence services. The Task Force was led by Herrington, who had a long-
standing interest in domestic violence, but also included key figures of the
rising conservative right, such as Pat Robertson. Notorious segregationist
Strom Thurmond helped usher the bill through the Senate. Progressive
policy makers, anti-violence activists, and neoliberals and conservatives
forged a joint effort around the innocent victim: a powerful figure who
was used to justify a stronger, "protective" penal state *and* to create a new
"victim services" branch of the welfare state.[21]

On the heels of state interest in "victims of crime" came an even more
targeted interest in "family violence." Anti-violence activists had been

laboring in shelters and drop-in centers for over a decade before federal policy makers passed legislation specific to their efforts. Over the course of the next fifteen years, the federal government would pass two key pieces of legislation addressing violence against women—the Family Violence Prevention and Services Act (FVPSA) in 1984 and the Violence Against Women Act (VAWA) in 1994—funneling millions of dollars into feminist organizations.[22] It's nothing short of stunning that this happened in the 1980s and 1990s during the roll-out of the neoliberal and neoconservative revolution. The discourse of innocent victimhood helped pass these bills, but it wasn't enough. Feminists also had to convince policy makers that *they* were the experts, that their agencies could provide effective services. Just as importantly, they could do so in *private* organizations far from the state, providing in-kind services rather than direct cash assistance to victims.[23]

I'll make the case in this chapter that feminists became legitimate state experts by investing in the figure of the psychological victim (the trauma sufferer) *and* inventing the "survivor" (the figure of therapeutic recovery). The expertise they developed in order to satisfy policy makers was *therapeutic* expertise. Therapy promised to heal the family's "dependency" on state programs, a concern of neoconservatives and neoliberals alike.[24] For this reason, the human services infrastructure premised on therapeutic rehabilitation in private organizations remained intact even during Reagan's dramatic 1980s funding cuts.[25] Further, neoconservative fears about the "crisis of the family" were bound up in public health discourses about social "illnesses" and violence as "disease," popularizing treatment and recovery models for violence.

Feminists were prepared to offer therapeutic services because their organizations were already quasi-therapeutic, premised on "lay therapy" models including feminist peer counseling and consciousness-raising.[26] Feminists were good at convincing policy makers that their organizations should be the locus of new federal funds because they had already developed successful counseling models for abused women and children. The emphasis on therapeutic recovery was evident from the beginning of feminist collaborations with the state, even in the name of the first proposed FVPSA bill in 1977, presciently called the Domestic Violence Prevention and *Treatment* Act. The models of therapeutic governance that would come to pervade the welfare state throughout the 1980s and 1990s, then, drew from feminist therapeutic expertise *and* from discourses of women's psychological "dependencies."

So, how did feminists manage to implement a large-scale federal response to violence against women during the 1980s and 1990s, years characterized by neoliberal retrenchment and the rise of "family values"? They convinced policy makers that they could respond to the "crisis of the family" and they made themselves into the experts who could "treat" victims— who could, in fact, *make victims into trauma survivors*. As scholars have pointed out, the victim is an ideal figure for state intervention.[27] She sets the foundation for a stronger punitive response—to save her—as well as a clinical infrastructure geared toward her recovery.[28] In this way, activists became, as political scientist Kristin Bumiller has argued, part of the carceral state *and* the therapeutic welfare state at the same time.[29]

Existing research on the anti-violence movement focuses overwhelmingly on its participation in expanding the carceral state.[30] However, I find that the *medicalization* of domestic violence has been equally consequential—and in fact, a necessary condition for criminalization.[31] Feminists combined their philosophies of care with penal and therapeutic discourses in order to secure funds and execute complex direct service work. In order to become indispensable to the state, feminists developed unique counseling models; they constructed women as psychological sufferers and bearers of "family" health; and they created stable, therapeutic organizations that became integral to a burgeoning "trauma industry" in the 1990s.[32] In this way, feminists did not simply adapt to neoliberalism—they helped *enact* it.[33] As I show through original archival research, feminists helped generate the "shadow state," or the "parastate apparatus" of voluntary organizations that would come to deliver welfare services under neoliberalism.[34] As Melinda Cooper argues, neoliberalism did not dismantle the welfare state but reconfigured it in order to regulate "needy" families through social obligations and therapeutic interventions.[35]

By satisfying the demands of both neoliberals (who wanted to send social problems "down" to families and to the states) and neoconservatives (who were obsessed with the "crisis" of the family), feminists used federal funds to build their own brand of therapeutic expertise. They promised that they could treat "victims of crime" and heal families—and they promised to do that in organizations *far from the state* that seemed not to be part of it at all. Feminists forced the state to redistribute federal dollars to services for women fleeing their homes—but they did so by submerging their more radical politics into theories of traumatic victimization and by investing in the figure of the survivor, someone who can recover from violence, rebuild a "healthy" family and "break the cycle of violence." This chapter tells the story of the anti-violence movement's contested investments in the therapeutic state, a terrain of struggle that feminists have shaped and been shaped by.[36]

FEMINISTS POSE THE PROBLEM

> States and their component parts undoubtedly embody
> several sets of interests, only some of which intentionally or
> unintentionally serve women well. However, the precise sets
> of interests that dominate at a particular moment are not
> given a priori, but rather are formed out of struggle and
> negotiation within a political field.
> Ray (2000, 14)

The feminist anti-violence movement is arguably one of the most "successful" social movements in US history. Domestic violence and rape services—though still chronically underfunded—are firmly incorporated into the state and into public expectations of aid. There are nearly two thousand domestic violence programs operating in the United States today.[37] Almost all of them rely to a significant degree on federal funds. Three big pieces of federal legislation fund domestic violence services. The federal Office on Violence Against Women administered a budget of close to half a billion dollars in 2018. Domestic violence is defined as a crime in all fifty states and in federal law. There are over two hundred specialized domestic violence courts with trained judges and legal advocates in operation in the United States.[38] Domestic violence is a publicly recognized social problem with a large, complex state infrastructure attached to it. There are few such resolute examples of feminism entering into and transforming the state.

Many second-wave feminists were interested in *using* the state to expand the boundaries of women's citizenship.[39] Anti-violence work was part of a broader effort to make women into legitimate political subjects—and to force recognition of the "private" sphere as central to social and political life.[40] Indeed, the anti-violence movement never could have avoided a relationship with the state—even the retrenched, punitive, medicalized welfare state we now associate with neoliberalism—because it aimed to make domestic violence victims into recipients of social services and state protections.[41] Still, such efforts were delimited because, as Ann Orloff argues, women's claims to citizenship are usually based on their familial roles.[42] Because claims for state incorporation are premised on aid in marriage and motherhood, social forces like "male dominance" can only be partially challenged through such efforts.[43] Further, feminists' efforts excluded poor women, queer women, and women of color—both implicitly and explicitly.[44] Though feminists argued for women's citizenship, they did so in a way that was partial and stratified.

For example, anti-violence feminists challenged the state's neglect of the private sphere by depicting white, suburban homes as spaces of women's imprisonment. Consider the images from domestic violence organization brochures in figures 1 and 2. Anti-violence activists deliberately disrupted the ideal of suburban, heterosexual, domestic sanctuary. They recast women's home lives as dangerous spaces of unfettered patriarchal power. Women's equal protection as citizens, feminists argued, required the state to intervene in the "private" sphere on women's behalf. The cry "Help Me," scrawled on the inside of the window, suggests the responsibility of some authority to "save" the battered woman, or at least to intervene and protect. Even activists who were skeptical of the state insisted—often with ambivalence—that police training, orders of protection, and legislation were probably necessary. At the US Civil Rights Commission, for example, activists told stories of women's egregious mistreatment by police, collusion between police and abusers, and prosecutors refusing to file charges. They demanded better protections. But feminists also insisted that "relationships with the criminal justice system" are inherently dangerous.[45] This push-and-pull between calls for legal reform and distrust of legal systems characterizes anti-violence work.[46]

Figure 1. Woman trapped in front yard with broken arm, domestic violence shelter brochure, c. 1970s. Courtesy of Smith College, Sophia Smith Collection, Violence Against Women Collection, Northampton, Massachusetts.

Despite demands for state intervention, feminists worried about co-optation and depoliticization from the beginning.[47] Activist Susan Schechter wrote and spoke extensively in the 1970s about a divide between professionals who were concerned with "family violence" and the more radical feminists who catalyzed the movement, activists who she feared would soon be sidelined.[48] Early movement documents are replete with calls to tread lightly with state funds so as to not allow conservative policy makers to overtake feminist aims. Women of color and lesbian activists warned their allies about the dangers of losing critical analyses of class, race, and sexuality as they applied for state funds. The Woman of Color Task Force of NCADV argued continuously against overreliance on the state. As early as the 1970s, before feminists felt the sting of neoliberal retrenchment, Judith Stevenson of NCADV wrote that reliance on the

Figure 2. Woman trapped in home writing "help me!" on the inside of a window, domestic violence shelter brochure, c. 1970s. Courtesy of Smith College, Sophia Smith Collection, Violence Against Women Collection, Northampton, Massachusetts.

state would mean the "kiss of death" for the movement.[49] She told stories of women calling shelters only to be offered counseling. Women responded in frustration, asking, "But will you help me find an apartment?" This, Stevenson argued, is the story of the "co-optive state," wherein material needs are recast as psychological problems. Domestic violence work was particularly vulnerable to such a recasting because it had *always* engaged in therapeutic politics via consciousness-raising groups, feminist

Figure 3. Prescription pad with "Grin and bear it" written by "John Doe, MD," from activist materials. Courtesy of the National Coalition Against Domestic Violence.

counseling, and the like—and, ironically, through its struggles *against* professional psychiatry.[50]

In fact, concerns about the *medicalization* of domestic violence galvanized anti-violence activists from the outset. Feminists deliberately set themselves up against psychiatry and psychology when they developed anti-violence programs. NCADV founding documents include a 1977 newsletter written by Mary Metzger that lambasted psychiatrists for labeling abused women "masochists."[51] The article features an advertisement for Deleuze and Guattari's classic anti-psychiatry tome, *Anti-Oedipus* and a cartoon with a prescription pad reading "Grin and bear it," signed by "John Doe, MD" (figure 3). Flyers about patients' rights in therapy are scattered throughout early NCADV documents (figure 4). Also included is a 1975 article written by activist Betsy Warrior, who claimed that masochism was the central patriarchal myth used to keep women subjugated.[52]

YOUR RIGHTS IN THERAPY

1. The right to interview your therapist.

2. The right to ask for what you want.

3. The right to confidentiality.

4. The right to question and disagree with your thera-
    pists' assumptions and perceptions about you.

5. The right to decide which areas of your experience
    will or will not be an issue in therapy.

6. The right to confront your therapist with griev-
    ances.

7. The right to refuse medication and shock treatment.

8. If you decide to take medication--the right to know
    what condition it's prescribed for; it's composition,
    action (how it effects your body), complications,
    side effects and safe usuage.

9. The right to give your therapist feedback on her
    effectiveness.

10. The right to terminate at your discretion.

Figure 4. "Your Rights in Therapy," from activist materials.
Courtesy of the National Coalition Against Domestic Violence.

She called psychiatrists "mind-butchers." Included is also a 1978 statement
from the Network Against Psychiatric Assault, asking for battered women
to join the anti-psychiatry movement in its fight against "the therapeutic
state." As psychologist Janice Haaken has argued, psychology was the "bad
object" of the women's movement—as bad as the batterer himself.[53]

These forceful statements against psychiatry were the foundation of
1970s anti-violence work. Personal testimonies included in policy documents and organizational brochures focus on the violence of psychiatric systems, showcasing stories about therapists colluding with abusers
to make women seem "crazy," "frigid," and "hysterical." Feminists sought

to keep domestic violence funding out of mental health systems, and throughout the 1970s and 1980s, they made public statements against the National Institute of Mental Health (NIMH) and the American Psychiatric Association (APA). They even protested at APA meetings. At the US Commission on Civil Rights in 1978, Yolanda Bako of Women's Survival Space in Brooklyn spoke against NIMH funding, arguing that "NIMH ... cannot adequately address the extensive needs of battered women" and would be "detrimental" to public education efforts.[54] "Self-improvement" for battered women, she argued, should *never involve therapy*. While scholars have paid nearly exclusive attention to feminist collusion with criminal and legal systems, the antagonistic position of feminist activism toward psychiatric authority is one of the most defining scenes of the movement. For activists during these years, the authoritative male psychiatrist was even more of a bogeyman than the state.[55]

Betsy Warrior produced the first national directory of domestic violence organizations in 1976, and it began with a woman's story of mistreatment by a therapist: "When I said that I was so afraid of my husband because he had tried to strangle me the night before, the therapist answered: 'But ma'am, do you ever think how terrible it is for your husband that you're so afraid of him?'"[56] Permeating the archives are stories about women being committed to psychiatric institutions, being made to apologize to their husbands during couples counseling, or prescribed pills for their "nerves." These stories were shared informally through a growing network of domestic violence shelters, and later more formally through NCADV. Handwritten notes accompanied these stories, often with instructions for fellow activists on how to open safe houses *without* mental health system involvement. Opposition to professional psychiatry unified feminist organizers. As Illinois activists stated, "Instead of therapists to analyze women's problems, we wanted women who believed in each other's abilities."[57] NCADV even disallowed shelters from joining the coalition if they asked victims to see psychiatrists.

Despite this strong anti-medical positioning, the feminist anti-violence movement—over the course of the next fifteen years—would become a key player in the therapeutic state. After positioning themselves so resolutely against psychiatry and psychology, why did feminists adopt a role within the state as therapeutic professionals? As feminists negotiated the terms of abused women's citizenship in the 1980s, they were forced to respond to two dominant state discourses: (1) a "victims of crime" discourse that advocated strong penal solutions; (2) a "families in crisis" discourse that was concerned with the "disease" of family violence. Feminists responded to these discourses by convincing policy makers that they could manage the "crisis" created by crime and family violence. They could do so, they argued, by providing safe houses and therapeutic services, making "victims" into "survivors" who could rejoin the world. Counseling would ensure that children would not continue the "cycle of violence" when they became adults. In their private organizations, seemingly far from the state, feminists were tasked with "breaking the cycle of violence." It was no longer "women" who would be the beneficiaries of their efforts, but "victims of crime" and "families." The state outsourced the problem of "family violence" to feminist organizations, so long as feminists *medicalized women's dependency.*

Feminists' opposition to psychiatry and psychology did not hinder them from engaging with the state—quite the opposite. Feminists used their critique of masculinized, medicalized therapy to advocate for their own role as "experts" who could serve battered women properly. Because the state had no idea how to respond to "family violence," the field was extremely porous. Federal policy makers *listened* to feminist organizers because they were some of the only stakeholders who could provide testimonials about domestic violence. In the late 1970s and early 1980s, feminists participated in dozens of congressional hearings and federal task forces, traveling with survivors to speak about their experiences in front of federal bodies. In these hearings, feminists argued forcefully that *they were the ones* who could provide effective services. They were the ones, in fact, who already knew how to do it, and could keep the government's role limited and distant—an ardent desire of conservative policy makers.

For example, Everett Koop became surgeon general under Reagan and took an interest in "family violence."[58] He organized an influential 1985 meeting that included physicians, police officers, academics, and feminist activists. Many meeting participants were neoconservatives who used the language of "epidemic" to describe violence against women, casting abuse as a crisis of the American family *and* as a public health issue in need of a "treatment" approach. "Our nation must feel as comfortable controlling its violent behavioral urges and practices as it does in controlling bacterial, viral, and physical mechanisms of morbidity and death."[59] Public health discourses were explicitly linked to neoconservative language about the crumbling edifice of the American family. Physicians spoke about "preserving" and "securing" the "traditional American family" through victim services. Clinical, therapeutic interventions were explicitly prioritized. Feminist organizers, on the other hand, spoke about "sexist social structure." They talked about their counseling models and peer-support approaches. While feminists never *themselves* engaged in neoconservative language during these meetings, they benefited from it. Feminists entered the arena of federal policy making through bizarre collaborations with conservatives, and they were able to do so because they had built a network of shelters and counseling programs that were already quasi-therapeutic and therefore legible to policy makers as "rehabilitative" institutions.[60]

Entering the state through task forces and coalitions premised on the language of "disordered families," "epidemic," and "breaking the cycle of violence" was a conscious, contested, and controversial strategy. As sociologist Nancy Whittier reveals about the child sexual abuse movement, feminist activists reframed their work to focus on serving and saving children, rather than combatting power and inequality inside the home.[61] A similar story emerges for domestic violence organizers, who were already reliant on CETA and Title XX funds by the early 1980s and needed to keep paying their electricity bills. Scholars have documented anti-violence organizers' increased use of "clinical," "de-gendered" language throughout the 1980s in order to appear more legitimate, as well as a decreased emphasis on women's material needs.[62]

Some feminists saw these efforts as a way to "steal" money from the state and use it for radical aims, while others insisted that the movement was losing its political edge.[63] Archival evidence suggests that when feminists and other activists presented structural explanations for abuse—such as economic inequality, sexism, and racism—they received negative pushback from lawmakers.[64] On the other hand, clinical presentations about improving women's low self-esteem with "recovery" services received favorable, even enthusiastic responses from politicians.[65] Sometimes feminists participated actively in constructing women and children as "helpless" and "passive" in order to justify funding.[66] Feminists also drew on the language of the federal government's "duty" to protect women's lives.[67]

What's more, since lawmakers were reticent to provide public dollars for "private" issues, feminists reassured them that anti-violence organizations would not become too dependent on state money.

One of the anti-violence movement's most lasting strategies to survive in this political climate was to use language about professional counseling and "families," though they almost never used this language in their own organizational materials or meetings. For example, NCADV promised funders that volunteers would be "trained to be professional and effective in their work."[68] Feminists sought to keep their work volunteer-led by ensuring policy makers that volunteers could produce professionalized "outcomes." *Self-esteem* became another popular term of state negotiation, and feminists used it frequently in federal hearings throughout the late 1970s.[69] In 1976, a Seattle shelter described part of its mission as providing "self-esteem workshops" and "lifestyle alternatives" to living in violent homes. In 1978, a Cincinnati shelter run by activist Lois Hake reported in the newspaper that its purpose was to provide a safe place for women with "low self-esteem" who have nowhere else to go.[70]

Feminists saw "self-esteem" as safe, quasi-medicalized language for explaining women's suffering, preferable to language like battered women's syndrome and masochistic personality disorder—the latter a favorite of the APA in the mid-1980s. Feminists drew from "family violence" and "self-esteem" discourses in order to protect their services from takeover by more conservative forces. And takeover threats were real. NCADV archives reveal evidence of state efforts throughout the 1970s and 1980s to push CETA and LEAA funds into the hands of NIMH, rather than toward feminist organizations. Movement leaders also feared that conservative women's groups (led by Phyllis Schlafly) would swoop in and steal federal funds out from under them if they did not conform to professional standards.[71]

These types of concessions to conservative state discourses became more common in the 1980s.[72] Movement leaders feared that engaging in political activism would threaten the tax-exempt status of their organizations, since the Reagan administration tried repeatedly to enact laws barring political activity in service organizations.[73] By the mid-1980s, most shelters used a model that combined feminist philosophies (empowerment, peer support, self-help) with more professionalized therapeutic services.[74] This model of service provision, wherein grassroots advocacy blended into clinical approaches, would become widespread across nonprofit agencies in the 1980s and 1990s. As Steven Smith and Michael Lipsky point out, these kinds of transformations are central to the operation of the privatized welfare state: "The regulations and requirements of the contracting regime make it difficult for . . . social workers to sustain an alternative, nonprofessional model of service delivery."[75] In this sense, it is not really the case that feminists were co-opted—swallowed up by a carnivorous state. Rather, anti-violence organizers participated actively in creating the privatized, medicalized welfare state infrastructure that is still in operation today. Many were reluctant to professionalize, but feminists also saw the benefits of developing their own therapeutic expertise and making their organizations secure.

In part, then, feminists entered the state by convincing authorities that they could handle the "epidemic" of family violence, that they were the ones who could respond—therapeutically—to the suffering of victims trapped inside their homes. Feminists continued to offer structural analyses of violence in conservative policy spaces even as they conformed to new professional standards.[76] Conservative policy makers were meanwhile mired in discourses of the American family "besieged" by violence and were eager to hand off its "treatment" in a way that would appear as though they were not interfering in men's private lives. Through coalitions like the surgeon general meetings, feminists helped create and implement a federal response to abuse, but they did so in a way that allowed the federal government to appear small and family oriented—while actually expanding the state and funneling money to feminist organizations. In this way, feminism became part of the state by helping to construct a privatized, therapeutic welfare state premised on "the family" as a site of intervention.

FAMILIES IN CRISIS

> Because the strength of the nation depends upon the health
> of the country's families, the federal government also must
> play an important role in addressing the national epidemic
> of family violence.
> US Department of Justice (1984, 99)

What kind of state *was* it that feminists addressed during the 1980s? As the epigraph above suggests, the relationship between the state and the anti-violence movement was forged through discourses of the crumbling, violence-riven family; policies propping up the private, patriarchal family as a locus of economic and political life; and contestations over the size and role of the federal government.[77] In other words, the twin rise of neoliberalism and neoconservatism was the primary force with which anti-violence feminists had to contend. These collaborations and contestations would create a new sphere of *therapeutic victim services* in which feminists and the state became jointly invested.

Neoliberalism refers to a political and economic revolution that reorganized society according to the principles of the market and encouraged upward redistribution.[78] Rather than shrinking the state, as it purports to do, neoliberalism *reorganizes and decentralizes the state* in order to expand the reach of market ideologies. It is this reorganization of the state and its social welfare functions—premised on the individual's "freedom" to participate in the market—that primarily concerns me here.[79] Domestic violence agencies are an excellent example of what Kimberly Morgan and Andrea Louise Campbell call the "delegated state," wherein responsibility for social welfare is "contracted out" to private, nonprofit organizations.[80] This "delegation" of social welfare responsibilities to private entities was a response, scholars have argued, to "the changing gender and racial composition of the workforce, the civil rights and welfare rights movements, and rise of student radicalism."[81] The "delegated state"—enmeshed in but not reducible to neoliberalism—was therefore a reaction to feminist and civil rights gains, to fears that the government had become too large and distributive. Neoliberal and neoconservative state actors worked together to repeal liberation movement goals by dismantling and privatizing social welfare.[82]

The privatization of state resources matters enormously for service organizations like domestic violence agencies, both practically and ideologically. In this configuration, the state "purchases" social services from the voluntary sector, which means that nonprofit organizations become entangled with racialized and gendered state discourses of dependency.[83] The "delegated state" forces funds down into private organizations, often with arduous inclusion criteria, where social needs are derided as "dependencies."[84] As Joe Soss and his colleagues have argued, when the state is privatized, so are the social problems of its citizens.[85] These shifts there-fore remake the type of *person* deemed worthy of such services, since citi-zens are supposed to pursue "non-reliance" on the state. Anthropologist Aihwa Ong argues that neoliberal values constitute each person as a "free" subject who must rely on private, autonomous action to confront eco-nomic and social insecurities.[86] The neoliberal citizen, then, should not make a claim on the state at all lest she be read as "dependent" and "lazy."[87] Because dependency is associated with femininity and racial otherness, this also means that misogynistic goals to stomp out social welfare rights for women—especially women of color—are embedded in state policy.[88] Neoliberalism is fundamentally about using state policy to pursue oner-ous social welfare exclusions along the lines of gender, sexuality, ability, and race.[89]

Reconstructing citizens in the image of entrepreneurs also means investing in social welfare models that seek to *rehabilitate* the poor.[90] By the 1980s, needing help from the state—if you were non-white and non-male—meant that you had a "problem of dependency." As Andrew Polsky explains, the premise of therapeutic state programs is that "some people are unable to adjust to the demands of everyday life or function according to the rules by which most of us operate. If they are to acquire the value structure that makes for self-sufficiency, healthy relationships, and posi-tive self-esteem, *they need expert help.*"[91] Archival documents from the anti-violence movement indeed suggest that neoconservative obsession with the "crisis" of the American family became associated with a public health approach to treating "disordered families." Responding to violence against women—once it became part of the state—morphed into a project of targeting the family for therapeutic intervention.

Various "epidemics" of poverty and violence, policy makers imagined, could be solved through what Ellen Herman has called "mass treatment programs," or therapeutically inflected social welfare programs.[92] Joe Soss and his colleagues call these innovations "neoliberal paternalism."[93] They take old models of paternalistic social work and combine them with neo-liberal strategies aimed at encouraging the poor to regulate themselves.[94] It isn't that neoliberalism invented therapeutic and rehabilitative social programs. Rather, punitive neoliberal policies and discourses "overlaid" social welfare programs with restrictive means-testing, efforts to control citizens' conduct, the limiting of rights claims, and obsession with the pathologies of "dependency."[95] Psychological expertise and social scientific surveys became important to neoliberal policy shifts, creating "legible profiles of populations to be managed."[96] Domestic violence agencies were ideal places for the cultivation of this kind of medicalized, disciplinary logic because they were *already* quasi-therapeutic and founded on the more expansive social welfare ideologies of previous decades.

Anti-violence activists were forced to respond to the "recovery" model promoted by neoliberal policy makers *and* to the "crisis of the families" discourse promoted by neoconservative policy makers. As Melinda Cooper argues, neoliberalism and neoconservatism were a match made in political heaven because both sought to restore the private, white, patriarchal family as the locus of political and economic life.[97] Further, according to Loïc Wacquant, blaming crime and other social problems on "family breakdown" was always key to neoliberal rule.[98] What's left of the welfare state can then provide support *only* on an individualized basis for those deemed "worthy."[99] These restrictive, stratifying logics dramatically shaped the kinds of claims that feminists could make on the state, as well as the kind of services they could offer with federal funds.

Still, however, feminists consistently challenged state efforts to discipline their work and curtail their politics. In the mid-1980s, for example, NCADV voluntarily returned over half a million dollars to the Department of Justice (DOJ). Problems arose when the Eagle Forum and other conservative groups complained that NCADV should not have the money because they were a bunch of "pro-lesbian, hard-core feminists."[100] Conservative groups convinced twenty-four members of Congress to sign a letter castigating DOJ for awarding funds to NCADV. In response, DOJ insisted on reviewing all the résumés of NCADV board members to ensure they wouldn't use the money for "lesbian-related advocacy."[101] NCADV refused. DOJ then demanded they remove the word "lesbian" from their mission statement. NCADV called a board meeting and debated the request well into the night. The group voted to return the money rather than capitulate to DOJ's terms. This decision prompted the chair of NCADV's board to resign and form her own organization in Illinois to apply for the money without any "radical" language in the mission statement. The Illinois strategy worked. By 1987, DOJ was a top funder of the Illinois Coalition Against Domestic Violence (ICADV), which had removed itself from NCADV's membership.[102]

This battle over DOJ funds is illustrative of a larger struggle in the 1980s between the state and the feminist anti-violence movement. Federal policy makers, though newly committed to providing funds for domestic violence, were not interested in serving "women"—much less *lesbians*. Rather, state actors sought to place funds in the hands of groups that would use federal dollars to (privately) handle "the crisis" of the family and treat "victims of crime." Though feminists resisted state efforts to discipline their work, the movement was large and diverse enough by the 1980s that less radical groups seized funds on more conciliatory terms. By the late 1980s, for example, ICADV had developed "self-esteem" assessments for children in domestic violence programs.[103] ICADV also launched a "successful survivor stories" section in their newsletter. These shifts in ICADV's work are evident across a range of agencies in the late 1980s, even as groups like NCADV struggled to retain their radical roots. As feminists negotiated an increasingly complex relationship with state policy, their services inclined toward "victims" and "survivors" and their children—easier, more sympathetic figures of state aid.

These struggles suggest that the topic of domestic violence itself posed a problem for policy makers. Domestic violence occurs in the *private* sphere, a zone of protected patriarchal control. The figure of the domestic violence victim calls into question the boundary between public and private that neoconservatives and neoliberals were invested in sustaining. Should the state enter into the private home and regulate what happens between husband and wife? Between parents and children? Neoliberals and neoconservatives, new and powerful in the 1980s, shared an interest in protecting the white, patriarchal family from state regulation.[104] A central contradiction emerged with the victim figure, then: the state sought to protect the innocent victim (delimited by race, class, ability, and sexuality) without violating the sanctity of the private family. Congressional hearings throughout the early 1980s indicate policy makers' deep anxieties about the role of the federal government in creating *any* policy about family life, even if it was to protect "women and children."[105] This contradiction produced a series of political contestations over the boundaries of the state and its resources. These struggles, in which second-wave feminists were key players, generated new zones of inclusion and exclusion around the twin figures of the "victim" (a criminal-legal citizen) and the "survivor" (a therapeutic citizen).

Take, for example, the report from the Attorney General's Task Force on Family Violence, released in 1984. Philosophically, the document is incoherent—a befuddling mix of feminist calls to respond to women's needs, neoconservative discourse about the sanctity of the American family, and neoliberal distaste for federal intervention. The document starts with a thank-you to the YWCA, NCADV, and the National Coalition Against Sexual Assault—all feminist-identified organizations. NCADV was pivotal in organizing the task force hearings, bringing dozens of survivors to testify. The task force report then calls for the creation of "family life centers" to respond to victims, agencies that would foster "self-sufficiency," "preserve marriages," and "promote family stability." The mention of these centers is confounding, since such places did not exist. What *did* exist were feminist shelters, drop-in centers, and hotlines—none of which supported marriages "staying together."

But policy makers didn't seem to care that federal dollars would never fund anything like "family life centers." What mattered was that private organizations would be doing the work, not the federal government. Neoliberals' obsession with privatizing state aid saturates the document, which goes on to argue that despite widespread calls for federal support for family violence services, such support should come from *private* organizations: "Today, the American tradition of private initiative in the public's service is stronger than ever."[106] Volunteerism and corporate funding were preferable to federal support, the report insisted.[107] In this way, neoliberal concern with getting services out of federal hands, into private agencies, allowed feminist organizations to become funding sites. Feminists, after all, were already adept at combining private and public dollars to execute their work.

But then another pivot. The policy document goes on to argue that it's the federal government's job to prop up the American family, to save it from the disorders of violence. "The family" must be protected. A suggestion follows for an increase in federal income tax deductions for children. Here, federal support is acceptable if it sustains the patriarchal family.[108] After a story about a woman's husband beating her for not cooking dinner, the document states, "We found that Americans are *family people*. . . . We found a growing commitment to *family values*."[109] Women's suffering is briefly acknowledged, but only alongside a deeper investment in "keeping families together." The violent family, not the battered woman, is carved out as the preferred locus of state support.

The policy report seems to advance a series of contradictory arguments. On the one hand, the federal government should intervene to protect victims; on the other hand, these interventions should take place through private organizations. On the one hand, violence is widespread in families; on the other hand, families are serene, sacred spaces that are the center of national identity. Anti-violence feminists participated actively in the task forces that produced policy documents such as these, engaging with the state through a dizzying array of ideologies that seemed to contradict one another at their core.

Second-wave feminism therefore entered the state through conservative discourses of the private, violence-riven family, which also paradoxically required federal policy makers to admit that, in fact, the private cannot be separated from the public at all: *managing the "private" sphere requires public policy*. The state became a critical terrain of feminist struggle as activists helped generate the privatized, "delegated" welfare state through collaborations such as these.[110] Even as feminists transformed the public's understanding of violence against women during the 1980s, they also participated with neoliberals and neoconservatives in *reinventing* discourses of "family responsibility."[111] "Family violence," it turns out, links neoconservatism with neoliberalism more strongly than ever: both ideologies, as Cooper argues, offer up the private family as *the alternative* to a redistributive welfare state.[112]

Feminists were aware of the bizarre ways in which their organizations benefitted from these reactionary forces. Fittingly, Nancy Whittier argues that feminists and conservatives have long been "frenemies" in anti-violence work.[113] As activist Susan Schechter stated in a speech to anti-violence activists in Chicago in 1983, the state created the category of "needy victim" to which feminists have been forced to respond, pushing anti-violence work toward therapeutic solutions.[114] Feminists also sensed that the neoliberal emphasis on individual therapeutic solutions for structural problems was aided by a neoconservative emphasis on the private family. Activist Lois Ahrens wrote, "With the new federal emphasis on the nuclear family, the Center chooses to look at battered women as a 'family violence problem,' but refuses to consider the societal, cultural and political implications of why women are the ones in the family so often beaten."[115] Activists understood that feminist agencies would be increasingly forced to operate as respectable therapeutic institutions serving families. As early as 1981, Illinois activists suspected that the pushdown of social service grants to states would mean that they would have to focus more on children, since grantors in Illinois preferred "children" to "women" as a locus of aid.[116] By the late 1980s, children had become a major focus of ICADV's work, for the explicit goal of "fundraising" efforts. Pages and pages of instructions for filling out child intake forms were sent to organizations. This focus on child therapy is a far cry from ICADV's founding mission statement only a decade earlier in 1978, which read: "To expose the roots of domestic violence, with primary emphasis on the institutionalized subservience of women."[117]

Consider also the passage of FVPSA in 1984. Passed as part of the Child Abuse Prevention and Treatment Act, FVSPA was the first federal law to explicitly address domestic violence, with a strong focus on shelters and programs for children. Definitions of domestic violence under FVPSA refer to "family violence" rather than "violence against women" and the bill provided significant funding for local domestic violence programs.[118] The "families in crisis" agenda, then, became the cornerstone of the state's response to domestic violence in the 1980s, and local programs were forced to rely on the depoliticized language of family violence—including counseling, rehabilitation, and intergenerational cycles of violence—in order to satisfy policy makers. These compromises allowed feminists into the policy making arena and, as we will see, legitimized their counseling models.

THERAPEUTIC EXPERTS

Through legislation such as FVPSA, feminists shaped the state's response to violence against women in incredibly durable ways. Importantly, feminists convinced policy makers that *they* could provide "recovery" services for abused women and children. By the early 1980s, federal policy makers

agreed that they had to do *something* about the problem of "family violence." While congressional hearings from the late 1970s were dominated
by researchers and service providers trying to convince members of Congress that "family violence" was *real*, those hearings shifted in the 1980s
toward a language of both "recovery" and "protection." In other words,
what should the state *do* about it?

Lawmakers expressed unease about local organizations becoming too
"dependent" on federal funding. Feminists were prepared to assuage such
concerns: they already knew how to do this work. Expert testimony in the
early 1980s reveals a strong focus on "rehabilitation" and making victims
into "useful citizens," despite their "emotional scars."[119] Feminists demonstrated that in their private organizations, distant from the federal government, they could respond to women and children with recovery models,
interrupting the "cycle" of violence.[120]

But feminists did *not* agree that "recovery" should mean psychotherapy.
Feminists became powerful in these policy making arenas because they
had their *own* brand of counseling that was already working. The very
process of demonstrating the efficacy of their models, however, helped to
professionalize the work. For example, Susan Schechter began trying to
publish results demonstrating the efficacy of feminist counseling models
in the 1980s.[121] Her goal was to increase the legitimacy of feminist models
so that activists could prove to policy makers that funds should be directed
toward their organizations, rather than to NIMH.

As feminist self-help models became more sophisticated and training materials circulated between geographic regions, organizers began to
codify their brand of peer counseling by publishing and testifying to federal bodies about it. A presentation to the US Commission on Civil Rights
stated, "Many mental health practitioners have been exclusively trained
in psychoanalysis and, accordingly, are not comfortable with other types
of counseling that would be more effective for . . . abused women."[122] In
statements to the Commission, feminist organizers outlined the value of
"peer support models" that would explicitly counteract psychiatry's "masochism hypothesis." Despite the movement's critique of traditional therapy, every statement that feminists made to the US Commission in 1982
was about counseling, revealing the centrality of therapeutic techniques
to feminists' agenda.

In the 1980s, then, anti-violence activists formalized their counseling models. How-to manuals for domestic violence counseling—which drew explicitly on the techniques of clinical social work and psychotherapy—circulated widely (figure 5). Volunteers were instructed to paraphrase women's experiences back to them, validating and helping them find the "essence" of their story. Feminists began an explicit process of developing knowledge and protocol around feminist counseling that still shapes the field today.

Early materials are also imbued with the rhetoric of self-help: "There is help for you, and support and understanding from other women who have been through painful and degrading experiences. But you must take the first step, and you must be prepared to help yourself."[123] Women were to be the makers of their new lives, rather than allowing therapists to "rescue" them. Feminist counseling was also supposed to be delivered by community volunteers and survivors rather than credentialed experts. This DIY counseling model was marked by its (ostensibly) equal allocation of knowledge across the counselor and the victim. Even as domestic violence agencies developed sophisticated training materials to be disseminated across programs, they continued to insist that their counseling models were therapeutic *but not psychotherapeutic*, that they were counselors *but not therapists*.[124]

Training materials in the 1970s discuss the women's movement as the foundation for these counseling models, but already by the 1980s, "the movement" was distant. One set of training materials discussed the "debt owed" to the feminist movement, as if the agency in question were not part of the movement itself.[125] Even as activists admitted among themselves—at conferences and in written correspondence—that the movement was no longer "radical" by the mid-1980s, their explicit goal was to keep their counseling models anti-professional, to develop their own curricula that would keep domestic violence work out of the hands of clinicians.[126] Domestic violence counseling was a loose form of expertise, but feminists created guidelines around it nonetheless. Domestic violence organizations—it was hoped—were becoming increasingly legitimate as therapeutic organizations and therefore publicly legible as the only suitable sites for the provision of "family violence" dollars.

As part of this agenda, organizers from NCADV attended academic psychology conferences in the 1980s in order to present their materials—

HERE ARE SOME PRACTICE EXERCISES TO HELP YOU FEEL MORE CONFIDENT ABOUT
YOUR COUNSELING SKILLS, PLEASE COMPLETE THESE AND BRING THEM TO THE LAST
SESSION-COUNSELING TO FURTHER DISCUSS ANY QUESTIONS YOU HAD :

HELPEE: I think I've been raped, and I don't know if I should call the
        police...maybe they would think I asked for this rape...I don't
        know...
HELPER: (PARAPHRASE)-_____

HELPER:(OPEN QUESTION)_____

HELPER: (REFLECT FEELING)-_____

HELPEE: My husband beats me up, he just beat me up a few days ago, I know
this is wrong, and I know that he does this be cause his dad beat his
mom up, we're considering counseling, but hes not too thrilled about
the idea, I know he needs to change, but I don't know how to help him...

HELPER: (PARAPHRASE)_____

HELPER:(OPEN QUESTION)_____

HEKPER: (REFLECT FEELING)_____

HELPER: (DISCLOSE)_____

HELPEE: I'm calling because I have a problem, I don't know how to talk
about it...it's real personal...my girlfriend said you help people with
that stuff...it's real ah wierd...

HELPER:(PARAPHRASE)_____

HELPER: (OPEN QUESTION)_____

HELPER: (REFLECT FEELING)_____

HELPER: (DISCLOSE)_____

HELPEE: I have a daughter with a problem, she got molested by her teacher
at school and she is a very upset young lady, how can that kind of man
be allowed to teach in the schools ?
HELPER:(REFLECT FEELING)_____

HELPER:(OPEN QUESTION)_____

HELPER:(PARAPHRASE)_____

Figure 5. Counseling Skills document, from activist materials. Courtesy of the
National Coalition Against Domestic Violence.

focused on empowerment advocacy and feminist counseling—in the hall-way between sessions.[127] They also planned to "disrupt" presentations by traditional psychotherapists. Activists wrote letters to academic confer-ences asking that feminists be included on victimization panels, rather than clinicians and academic researchers.[128] Despite drawing on psychological models, then, feminists continued to mark professional psychiatrists and psychologists as "bad experts."[129] Lenore Walker, a feminist psychologist, was a frequent speaker in Congressional hearings about "family violence" throughout the late 1970s and 1980s, and she insisted that clinical models and "recovery" were important for abused women—but that these should take place in feminist shelters and drop-in centers, not therapy offices.[130] Throughout the 1980s, activists debated how to avoid federal rules around "how many counseling sessions" women should have to attend.[131] Even as they received federal dollars, then, they attempted to subvert professional-ized therapeutic guidelines.

As feminists responded to the "family crisis" and "recovery" discourses of the state, they also built up their own therapeutic expertise, distinct from mainstream mental health models. But this type of therapeutic expertise would not remain volunteer-led, informal, and grassroots for long. The very process of interacting with the state forced anti-violence activists to transform "lay therapy" into official models of service provision oriented toward "rehabilitative" goals for women and children.[132] The therapeutic expertise present in domestic violence agencies in the 1970s therefore merged with neoliberal and neoconservative policy goals. Domestic vio-lence agencies had to demonstrate "outcomes," making women recov-erable. As Evan Stark argues, domestic violence agencies began to look increasingly like homeless shelters and mental health programs in the 1980s.[133] That's because feminist activists had become important players in the therapeutic state, reshaping their grassroots counseling models into official models of service provision for victims. Legibility was not only con-ferred to victims through this process, but simultaneously to the move-ment itself.

As feminists built a movement, they also created new models for appre-hending and intervening in women's lives, a new configuration of expert knowledge and practices that was increasingly focused on the figure of the domestic violence survivor, the psychologically recoverable victim.[134]

This figure was forged at the intersection of feminist activism and the "delegated state"—and she became increasingly scientized during the 1990s as feminists began to play a key role in the emerging "trauma industry," a history I take up in chapter 2.

FROM FEMINISM TO TRAUMA

The conjuncture of anti-violence feminism, neoliberalism, and neoconservatism has led us into a new era of domestic violence politics characterized by a focus on women and children as psychologically vulnerable subjects in need of therapeutic recovery. As Kathleen Ferraro argues, the Reagan years were a turning point for domestic violence discourse, as concern for "battered women" morphed into interventions for "criminal families"—interventions that I argue also became increasingly therapeutic.[135] Domestic violence services were born through this interface of powerful forces but also remain embedded in the second-wave feminist language of empowerment and self-help, in a commitment to providing free, community-based services. It does not make sense to say that the therapeutic state "co-opted" feminism, exactly. Rather, feminist anti-violence organizers participated actively in building up the privatized, medicalized therapeutic state so that they could offer such services. They have been successful at this, but at the cost of an increased focus on "recovery," therapeutic discipline, and professionalization. The possibilities for feminist activism shifted over the course of the 1980s because the expansive welfare state that feminists initially addressed was pulled out from underneath them. The contemporary structure of care surrounding domestic violence—premised on traumatic suffering and psychological recovery—is an outcome of second-wave feminism *and* the "delegated" therapeutic state, a state to which feminists did not simply *react*, but helped create.

In many respects, this is a troubling story. Feminists entered into and changed the state, but they did so by transforming themselves into service providers rather than radical agitators. I do not mean to suggest that these are mutually exclusive categories: providing direct services for abused women in marginalized communities *is* social change work. However, the kinds of politics that can be executed in such spaces are limited.

As Marie, a national domestic violence policy leader, explained to me, "trauma" should operate the same way "feminism" does for domestic violence work: by providing an overarching framework for justice and care. In a context in which domestic violence workers are therapeutic experts, "feminism" loses sway to the capacious language of "trauma," and both words take on new meanings.

The shift to "trauma" that Marie articulated matters enormously for the kinds of rights-claims that abused women and their advocates can make. The relationship between feminism and the state is characterized by this double bind, wherein abused women are included as rights-bearing subjects only when they are redeemable figures embedded in a criminalized family. Second-wave feminists made abused women legible as *certain* kinds of citizens: therapeutically redeemable victims of crime. Feminist activists helped construct victims this way, even though they also consistently rejected oversimplified, pathologizing, sexist representations. Neoliberal social policy is in fact deeply multifaceted: it constrains radical politics and disciplines women, while also generating new spaces of social citizenship that sometimes save women's lives. In this sense, the "delegated state"—though it privatizes and depoliticizes social services—also has effects *beyond* the intentions of neoliberal and neoconservative policy makers. Indeed, the very growth of the neoliberal "state sub-apparatus" of nonprofit organizations means that this sector comes to wield significant political power in its own right.[136] Domestic violence advocates who hold feminist commitments are responsible for administering state programs, thereby complicating any straightforward understanding of neoliberal policies and their afterlives.

The contemporary social service infrastructure—wedded to frameworks of traumatic suffering and therapeutic recovery—bears the brand of this uneasy collaboration between state-phobic neoliberals, Christian conservatives, and second-wave feminists. As I will show in the next chapter, in the case of domestic violence, the twin figures of the "victim" and the "survivor"—and their attendant penal and welfare state infrastructures—are outcomes of these historical negotiations between feminism and the state. Though she seems natural and neutral, the trauma survivor is a historically specific political figure who has emerged from the conjunctures outlined here. And while "trauma"—as a psychiatric condition—would seem to prioritize the individual sufferer above all else, I have shown that domestic violence expertise focuses on "the family," and specifically on children. Trauma requires that domestic violence agencies offer children's therapy and focus on clinical "recovery." State funding language emphasizes the family as a locus of state support, recasting women's experiences of abuse as psychologically traumatic in a way that requires interventions to reestablish the healthy family. The public health approach to domestic violence, exemplified through legislation like FVPSA, is inextricably tied to a "crisis of the family" discourse that constructs the domestic violence victim as the bearer of the family's recovery.

The goal of domestic violence services under the politics of trauma is to transform the victim into a survivor, into someone who can recover and take responsibility for "breaking the cycle of violence." Such a logic is appealing to conservative state actors who like to profess *some* concern for violence against women. Consider Attorney General John Ashcroft's remarks at a domestic violence event in 2002: "We must work together to ensure that each victim has the opportunity to escape violence and to transform her life and the lives of her children. One victim of domestic abuse who found help described this transformation better than I ever could. She said, 'I finally realized the truth, that I was hurting not only myself, but I was hurting my children even more. I was teaching them by example that they deserved to be abused and that violence was acceptable.' *This victim found help and is a victim no more.*"[137] This is the lesson of trauma and survivorhood: an abused woman must make the temporal transition from "victim" to "survivor" lest she teach her children bad lessons about dependency. Her trauma is her responsibility, and it definitely requires therapeutic labor on the terrain of motherhood. While anti-violence leaders use trauma in an attempt to *overcome* victim-blaming narratives, it is far too easy for blame to be recast on victims using those very same frameworks. After all, trauma *installs* pathology within the self and the family. In the next chapter, I show how "trauma" has infiltrated social services, remaking the victim-subject and transforming feminist politics.

2 The Trauma Revolution

"Let's talk about trauma." This is how Jill, a domestic violence policy leader, begins her trainings. She patiently walked me through the steps of her training, which—as a "trauma-informed" program specialist—she has conducted for several hundred frontline domestic violence workers across several states. Jill begins her training by talking about the Adverse Childhood Experiences (ACEs) study, which quantifies children's level of exposure to "traumatic experiences" like domestic violence in order to assess later social and mental health outcomes. Jill then instructs workers in a series of trauma paradigms, mostly created for addiction programs, meant to help explain why victims act the way they do: "I try to bring them back to: anything [they see] is not a *symptom* but a *reaction to trauma.*" The purpose of the training is to help workers understand that victims are not "behaving badly" when they refuse to follow shelter rules or when they spank their children—rather, they're "dissociating" and having "anxiety attacks." According to Jill, "We *don't* have to be clinicians. We just have to look at everything through a trauma lens." Her training includes a crash course in the neurobiology of trauma, as well as suggestions for "self-care" exercises such as adult coloring books. Jill wants workers to help victims learn how to "manage their bodily responses to being triggered."

Like Jill, most advocates and policy leaders in the domestic violence field are committed to "trauma" as the new vocabulary of victimization. As Nima, a young therapist in a Chicago domestic violence program, told me, "Trauma is the theory of how you conceptualize a client." For Nima, trauma shows that a victim is not "crazy"—she's responding to something that was done *to* her. If a victim wants to find housing, Nima explained, she first has to address her trauma: "If I'm dissociating, I can't really focus on an application for housing. In order to do their daily functioning, they would have to work on that." Nima's organization has transformed to become "trauma-informed": they hired a cadre of clinical therapists, bought comfortable couches for their offices, painted the waiting area in "warm colors," and installed lamps in place of overhead fluorescent lights. When I walked in, I felt the warmth of the rooms' soft lighting and comfortable seats. The intake room, Nima explained, should mitigate "trauma triggers."

Jill and Nima's approach to domestic violence work is a significant departure from previous eras. The widespread use of biological theories of trauma to frame and respond to gender-based violence is a new phenomenon. Jill and Nima are remaking domestic violence work, rewriting the logics of victimization using language developed by mental health experts. Rather than a crime or a type of patriarchal harm, anti-violence workers increasingly conceptualize domestic violence as a "traumatic experience" for which victims need professional therapeutic intervention. Even Nima's reference to a victim as a "client" would have been controversial twenty years ago, since anti-violence leaders have long rejected the idea that they are "professionals" serving "clients."

But for Nima, using the word "client" just reflects her professional training. She, like the hordes of young workers in domestic violence organizations today, is a clinical therapist. Domestic violence agencies— liminal spaces at the crossroads of legal systems, therapeutic systems, and feminist advocacy—face increasingly medicalized demands to *quantify* victimization and to professionalize their interventions. "Trauma" has emerged as the dominant language of this credibility project. This chapter traces the rise of trauma as a new style of health governance in anti-violence work that satisfies the technocratic policy sphere *and* makes domestic violence workers into health experts. This style of health governance presumes that bodily and emotional dysfunction are the bedrocks of victims' problems—and it targets their bodies and affect for regulation.

The ubiquity of "trauma" in the anti-violence field reflects trends in adjacent welfare state service programs such as addiction, homelessness, and child services—making this something of a "trauma revolution."[1] Trauma offers service providers and policy makers a pervasive theory of harm and suffering that transcends any given experience and allows them to medicalize and legitimize suffering. Well beyond the context of social services, "trauma" is a powerful genre of self-understanding and identity in contemporary life. As medical sociologists have taught us, medicalizing a problem can bring legitimacy to it—especially in the case of "women's issues," which are chronically minimized and dismissed.[2] "Trauma" is clearly an attempt at this type of legitimization. And it is also bureaucratically useful. As sociologist Armando Lara-Millán shows, state programs "summarize" clients by filtering them into categories suitable for being "shuffled" between systems.[3] Today, trauma is the paradigm that executes this kind of summarizing and translation work in domestic violence agencies and adjacent programs. A belief that traumatic experiences cause enduring psychological and social problems is *the* conceptual framework that guides social service workers' visions.

The adoption of "trauma" in domestic violence work has allowed feminists to transform their movement: what was once about women's citizenship is now about victimization and recovery and resilience, which are more palatable offerings. At issue here is not just how victims' needs are represented. Rather, the trauma revolution results in what Nancy Fraser calls "acts and interventions" into women's lives.[4] In what follows, I show how feminists imported psychiatric theories of posttraumatic stress into the domestic violence field, and I trace their diffusion across programs as the demand for "evidence-based services" ramped up. More generally, I expose the mechanisms through which "trauma" has replaced "feminism" as the central paradigm of domestic violence work. In turn, abused women become bearers of new forms of internalized risk and responsibility.[5]

FROM MASOCHISM TO TRAUMA

> The Administration on Children, Youth and Families (ACYF)
> is committed to facilitating healing and recovery and
> promoting the social and emotional well-being of children,
> youth, and families who have experienced maltreatment,
> exposure to violence, and/or trauma. This funding
> opportunity . . . [is] designed to ensure that effective
> interventions are in place to build skills and capacities that
> contribute to the healthy, positive, and productive
> functioning of families.
>
> US Department of Health and Human Services (2013, 21371)

The border that feminists drew early on between politics and therapy, or between feminist empowerment and clinical intervention, is key to understanding the history of domestic violence politics. Like any border, it works both by dividing worlds and by bringing them into close contact. No object straddles this border quite as well as "trauma." Trauma has emerged since the mid-1980s as "*the* principal model for thinking about the interpretation of psychological injury . . . on behalf of victims."[6] Feminists used trauma models—engaging the mental health field as a site of struggle—in order to secure legal recognition for victims *and* to gain recognition for their counseling models in state-funded programs.[7] After convincing neoliberal and neoconservative policy makers that they could solve the "crisis" of the family, anti-violence feminists helped develop the trauma frameworks that have shaped social services over the past three decades. Reimagining women's suffering, pain, needs, rights, and demands as "trauma" has ushered in a medicalized era of domestic violence politics that reverberates across the welfare state infrastructure. As the FVPSA language in the epigraph shows, "trauma" aligns public health frameworks with neoconservative calls to restore "function" to "the family" *as well as* with neoliberal efforts to internalize families' social needs.

The assimilation of a psychiatric concept like trauma into domestic violence work has not been straightforward. By the 1990s, feminists already had a complex and contested relationship with trauma. This relationship is perhaps best exemplified in the 1985 debates over the proposed inclusion of masochistic personality disorder (MPD) in the DSM-III-R, the revised third edition of the *Diagnostic and Statistical Manual*, the APA's official manual of mental disorders. In the 1980s, psychiatrists were intent on including MPD in the manual, resulting in widespread feminist outcry at what was (correctly) perceived to be an attempt to slap a personality disorder on domestic violence victims. The first criterion of the disorder was written this way: "Remains in relationships in which others exploit, abuse, or take advantage of him/her." Making official what had long been unofficial practice, psychiatrists managed to invent a diagnosis for the experience of being trapped in a violent relationship. The proposed inclusion of MPD ignited a storm of opposition in the women's movement, enabled by the fact that activists had already spent a decade sharpening their blades against psychiatry. The APA claimed not to know "what all the fuss was about."[8]

Feminists lobbied to be allowed into the DSM meetings in order to contest the proposed disorder.[9] Two feminist clinicians were allowed entry, including Lenore Walker, a feminist psychologist who became one of the loudest voices of opposition to MPD. Walker published about her experiences in the DSM meetings, reporting that the "scientific" method used to create a nosology for MPD was to ask psychiatrists to shout out traits of masochism while the lead psychiatrist wrote them down.[10] Walker reported that one "symptom" for MPD was left out because one psychiatrist responded, "Hey, I do that sometimes!" The trait was discarded. Not only did the proposal of MPD embolden the anti-violence movement, but it also received national media attention and helped spur efforts to keep the treatment of abused women out of the hands of psychotherapists.[11] Importantly, however, Lenore Walker and other mental health experts insisted that rather than MPD, *we should understand abused women's experiences through the framework of trauma*. She offered her own theory of battered women's syndrome (BWS) as a subtype of PTSD. The domestic violence movement defeated "masochism," then, by adopting a trauma framework.

Why trauma? The history of trauma has come in waves, appearing first in the work of Charcot, Janet, and Freud in the 1800s, resurfacing as "shell shock" during World War I, and surging again—with staying power—after the Vietnam War.[12] Following Charcot, Freud located the origins of "traumatic hysteria" in the *psyche*, which departed from dominant theories of the time that focused on physiological shock.[13] Freud's original theory, published in the 1890s, laid out a "seduction theory" of trauma in which women's hysterical symptoms were traced back to memories of sexual assault.[14] Not long after he developed this theory, however, Freud renounced sexual assault as a traumatic event and instead theorized hysteria as emanating from psychosexual fantasies. Freud's repudiation of his patients' experiences of sexual abuse makes him an especially reviled figure in feminist anti-violence work.

Freud returned to theories of trauma during and after World War I, a time when "traumatic memory" became important to psychiatric practice.[15] In this "second-wave" conceptualization of trauma, the memory of an experience could trigger symptoms that looked like hysteria or neurosis. However, army doctors focused on distinguishing real sufferers from "malingerers" and they used the diagnosis to indict soldiers for failed masculinity.[16] According to anthropologist Allan Young, interest in trauma declined after World War I and would not surface again until the Vietnam War, when veterans, anti-war activists, and victims' advocates agitated for inclusion of PTSD in the new DSM.[17] Through its official designation as a psychiatric disorder in 1980, trauma gradually came to be seen as a legitimate way for veterans to claim compensation for the atrocities they suffered in war. Unlike other disorders listed in DSM-III, which intentionally dismissed the question of etiology, PTSD specified an "etiological event" from the outset, such that a traumatic event had to precede the symptoms of disorder.[18]

Because of its inclusion in the DSM, an increasing array of experts became tied to the concept of trauma in the 1980s and 1990s. The professionalization of trauma, and its diffusion across a range of new stakeholders, had officially begun. Trauma was quickly incorporated into psy fields *outside* of psychiatry's official ranks, expanding its reach.[19] As "the victim" transformed into a sympathetic subject, an increasingly vast professional network surrounding trauma was deployed.[20] Further, Veterans Affairs–funded research bolstered the legitimacy of PTSD in mainstream psychiatry.

In the case of domestic violence, the professionalization of trauma was important because anti-violence advocates and policy makers were then able to use trauma theory to construct a sympathetic victim in court. During the 1980s, expert psychiatric testimony became increasingly central to abused women's ability to claim victim status in legal settings.[21] Lenore Walker's career tells this story: "My evolution from clinical psychologist to legal expert witness . . . [allows me] to stand firmly as [battered women's] psychologist-advocate whether in the privacy of a psychologist's office or the public domain of a packed courtroom."[22] By 1989, Walker had testified in over 150 murder trials on behalf of battered women, arguing that women killed their abusers because they were traumatized.[23] As trauma theories were picked up across an increasingly eclectic range of experts, those theories also found a new home in the legal system, transforming victims' claims-making prospects. The success of trauma in the legal system also made feminists more amenable to professional counseling.[24] As sociologist Arlene Stein shows, feminists—once staunchly opposed to professional therapy—quickly became key players in the expansion of the trauma industry.[25]

In their negotiations with the legal system, then, anti-violence feminists relied on psy expertise to make the figure of the battered woman worthy, binding theories of trauma to the legal, rights-bearing subject. However, the importation of trauma theory also breathed new life into fantasies of lovesick, self-destructive women—consistent with earlier mythologies of masochism that feminists had worked so hard to repudiate. In popular accounts and anti-violence literature throughout the 1980s, the battered woman was represented as *split* by the twin forces of violence and love (see figures 6 and 7), causing irreparable harm to her capacity for rational action. Legal and popular interest in battered women as *split selves* encouraged psychotherapeutic explanations of her actions.

Rather than rejecting this quasi-masochistic thesis, anti-violence leaders in the 1980s drew on its themes to construct battered women as helpless victims in need of legal intervention. While activists were often internally critical of these discourses, they also used them to get women out of prison for killing their abusers, to enroll police in protecting women, and to convince prosecutors to act on women's behalf. BWS is the most classic example. Lenore Walker established something of a "cult of true victimhood" with BWS.[26] It was centered around the language of learned helplessness: "Terror of her abuser is a seed that is planted in the psyche

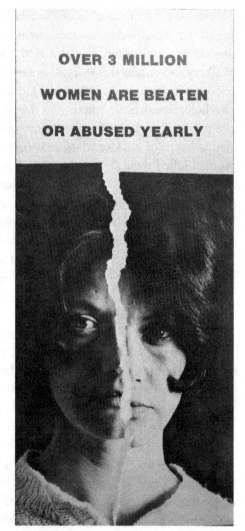

OVER 3 MILLION WOMEN ARE BEATEN OR ABUSED YEARLY

Figure 6. Woman with split face, domestic violence brochure. Courtesy of Smith College, Sophia Smith Collection, Violence Against Women Collection, Northampton, Massachusetts.

of the battered woman by repeated subjection to psychologically sadistic manipulation and physical bullying; it grows and grows until she is incapable of believing in the effectiveness of taking positive action on her own behalf, until she has become a true victim of learned helplessness."[27] While Walker identified as a feminist, she drew heavily on psychotherapeutic theories and NIMH funding to push her theory.

Figure 7. "Are you a victim of violence in your home?" Illustration of woman with half her face blank, domestic violence brochure. Courtesy of Smith College, Sophia Smith Collection, Violence Against Women Collection, Northampton, Massachusetts.

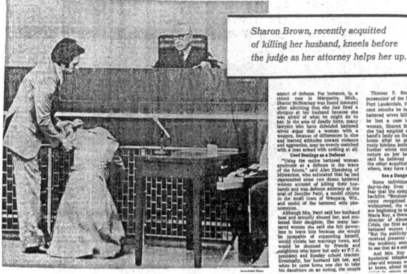

'ho Kill Their Spouses: The Causes, the Legal Defen

Sharon Brown, recently acquitted
of killing her husband, kneels before
the judge as her attorney helps her up.

Figure 8. Newspaper clipping, woman bowing before a judge while her lawyer tries to hold her upright. *New York Times.*

Walker's typical battered woman had low self-esteem and self-image, cared about being a good wife and homemaker, and behaved in traditional ways to please her husband. According to Walker, the battered woman is passive and susceptible to psychosomatic ailments and depression. She is conditioned into submission, quite literally like a dog.[28] According to legal scholar Leigh Goodmark, Walker's theory reflected larger trends in the anti-violence movement that constructed the ideal victim as a "passive middle-class white woman cowering in a corner as her enraged husband prepared to beat her again—a vision consistent with the . . . conception of subordinated women in fear of all-powerful men."[29] Walker's theory goes even further by emphasizing psychological vulnerability as central to femininity: women are by constitution helpless and passive, nonviolent, and in need of expert explanation.[30] In figure 8, a *New York Times* article depicts an abused woman in a quintessential position of feminine helplessness exemplified by BWS, bowing before the judge in a show of submission and regret for killing her batterer.

While this description of abused women may sound regressive and out-dated, Walker's theory can still be found in the brochures and pamphlets of domestic violence agency waiting rooms. BWS continues to find success in courtrooms. Anti-violence advocates' justification for using trauma theories like BWS was that the *event*, rather than the victim's psyche, became the problem: "There was no longer any need to delve into the depths of the soul or to seek out predisposing factors in the subject's personality or history. The event had become the sole cause of the pathology."[31] Thus, trauma theories like BWS drew on the "objective" authority of science to cast victims as blameless, while implicitly reifying feminized tropes of passivity and self-annihilation.

Further, while BWS has been used to help *some* women, many women continuously fall outside the bounds of such defenses. Sharon Allard has shown, for example, that Black women have been denied BWS and related defenses in court—they are always already guilty, violent, impervious to pain, never true victims.[32] Evan Stark writes that according to BWS, "Women must represent their actions one-dimensionally through their 'victim self,' making a fetish of weakness, passivity, and subordination that further impugns their claims to full equality as a class."[33] This fetishization of feminine weakness sets up white femininity as the primary beneficiary of trauma theory, highlighting the racialized and classed character of ideal victimhood. As Beth Richie has argued, when Black women or gender nonconforming people experience intimate violence, the abuse is typically cast as *a different type of violence* altogether, because they are not considered vulnerable enough.[34] In this sense, the anti-violence movement's success in the legal system depended on diffusing trauma expertise across a range of powerful institutions and experts, recasting masochism as an externally caused psychological helplessness (trauma). One of the most important effects of this has been to further center white femininity in the legible construction of victimhood.[35]

After this surge of expert trauma testimony in courtrooms in the 1980s, the anti-violence movement began to collaborate more actively with medical and mental health systems. These collaborations have had lasting effects on anti-violence work. As Samantha Leonard argues, the domestic violence field's capacity to act as "feminist" is constrained by its entanglements with conservative neighboring fields like mental health.[36] "Collaboration" sounds progressive but is often depoliticizing. In the 1980s, psychiatric professionals had become increasingly important to anti-violence efforts in the legal system. By the 1990s, domestic violence organizations drew actively on psy experts' construction of "the victim" via trauma theory.[37] Activists, researchers, and policy leaders adapted theories of psychiatric victimology and applied them to abused women, developing theories of "complex trauma."[38] By the time VAWA passed in 1994, domestic violence agencies faced increasing pressure to adopt professional standards to demonstrate "outcomes"—and the field of psychiatric victimology provided a ready resource with its symptoms and scales.

FROM WOMEN TO VICTIMS

> [We] definitely changed from being a women's rights
> organization to being a victims' rights organization.
> Emma, domestic violence organization director

Throughout the 1990s, anti-violence workers and policy leaders created their own models of therapeutic expertise that allowed them to professionalize, satisfying state funding requirements. In part, they built up this expertise by drawing on classic works such as Judith Herman's 1992 book *Trauma and Recovery*, which straddled feminist theory and trauma theory. Feminists worked hard to push this kind of gender-based trauma expertise outward across a network of other professionals, especially mental health providers and nurses. Domestic violence organizations began to train mental health practitioners about intimate abuse in the 1990s.[39] In so doing, they began for the first time to catalog abused women's behaviors and emotions into a psychiatric inventory. Speaking to health care providers, activist Susan Schechter created such a list: "37% [of abused women] have a diagnosis of depression, 10% psychotic episode, 16% alcoholism, 47% PTSD, and 46% anxiety."[40] She also handed out photocopies of a trauma textbook. By the 1990s, anti-violence activists were officially involved in the production of quantitative psychiatric profiles of abused women.

Additionally, health care–related services for abused women expanded in the 1990s as organizations like the American Medical Association (AMA) took an interest in domestic violence.[41] There were new CDC funds available for tracking "family violence" and developing "effective interventions"—complete with the public health language of "risk"—making domestic violence an attractive issue for health care providers, especially those looking to secure "women's health" grants.[42] Feminist clinicians who had been influenced by the anti-violence movement began to gain power in and shape their medical subfields, spurring these transformations.

In fact, feminists have contributed enormously to the rise of trauma paradigms across mental health, biomedical, and social service fields. By the 1990s, domestic violence leaders agreed that PTSD "was the primary mechanism by which violence was converted into psychological dependence."[43] Even activists who resisted the medicalization of domestic violence saw "trauma" as a safe language for discussing women's suffering. Schechter, for example, was suspicious of medicalization and resisted hiring clinical professionals in local organizations. However, she used the language of trauma and PTSD in trainings and public speeches throughout the 1990s. An explosive interest in "victimology" across psy professions made PTSD *the* diagnosis of the 1990s.[44] Trauma achieved the status of a universal "truth" about human suffering—a condition that also happens to demand expert therapeutic intervention.[45]

Organizational brochures, coalition newsletters, national meeting minutes, and communication among activists in the 1990s reveal the increasing diffusion of trauma across the domestic violence field. As Schechter trained other professionals about domestic violence during these years, she offered diagnostic profiles of abused women. She distributed handouts of official PTSD criteria, creating inventories of victims' "dysfunctional" symptoms: panic attacks, psychotic episodes, suicide/homicide, and drug/alcohol addiction.[46] Schechter also began attending trauma conferences and collaborating with organizations like the Center for Victims of Torture. The anti-violence movement's relationship to the psy professions therefore shifted during the 1990s—toward collaborative professional relationships built on shared therapeutic expertise.[47]

In the early 1990s, domestic violence policy leaders also began adapting PTSD measurement scales to assess women's experiences. "Stages of abuse" models circulated widely. These models lumped victims' emotional reactions into categories such as "dissimulation" and "withdrawal."[48] Domestic violence leaders created handbooks for doctors to "identify" domestic violence in their patients, complete with "illness profiles" for abused women.[49] Trauma frameworks were popular because they allowed for the inclusion of a "bewilderingly large range of symptoms," such that essentially any behavior or emotion could be interpreted as a trauma reaction.[50] By the late 1990s, domestic violence policy leaders were interacting regularly with an array of adapted PTSD scales such as the one shown in figure 9, as the language of traumatic sequalae and symptomology was normalized in anti-violence spaces.

Over the course of the 1990s, then, the domestic violence field became—rather definitively—part of a larger professional apparatus focused on the psychological effects of victimization. This shift did not occur without contestation, and there is evidence that professional psychologists sometimes complained about anti-violence workers because they were not "professional" enough.[51] Nevertheless, the language of trauma was ubiquitous in domestic violence work by the late 1990s. Documents circulating between domestic violence agencies reveal the increasing use of language focused on "healing" and "trauma survivors."[52] Agencies began scheduling trademarked PTSD trainings intended for clinical professionals.[53] These trainings emphasized clinical skills but also taught "soft" interventions like mindfulness, as well as techniques for service providers to avoid "vicarious traumatization." This language—along with victimization profiles—mirrored shifts in addiction programs, as these kinds of service programs developed a common language of traumatic victimization.[54]

Trauma is a convenient language for explaining suffering, since it *medicalizes* women's and children's dependency on service systems and state resources. The victim "has" trauma, so she needs help. Further, trauma solidifies abused women's status as "true victims," creating what Joseph Davis calls a "victim person-type" who is deserving of sympathy.[55] Trauma has the added benefit of carving out women *and* children as the same kind of deserving victim, allowing the state to continue its focus on "the family" as a locus of aid, rather than simply "women."[56] Marie, a national domestic violence policy leader, explained to me that trauma is popular in domestic

MODIFIED PTSD SYMPTOM SCALE

The purpose of this scale is to measure the frequency and severity of symptoms in the past two weeks that you may have been having in reaction to a traumatic event or events. Please indicate the frequency, how often you have the symptom, to the left of the item. Then indicate the severity (how upsetting the symptom is) by circling the letter that fits best on the right side.

FREQUENCY   SEVERITY

0 = NOT AT ALL   A=NOT AT ALL DISTRESSING
1 = ONCE A WEEK OR LESS   B=A LITTLE BIT DISTRESSING
2 = 2 TO 4 TIMES A WEEK   C=MODERATELY DISTRESSING
3 = 5 OR MORE TIMES A WEEK   D=QUITE A BIT DISTRESSING
                                   E=EXTREMELY DISTRESSING

FREQUENCY   SEVERITY

_____1. Have you had repeated or intrusive
upsetting thoughts or recollections of the event(s)?........A   B   C   D   E

_____2. Have you been having repeated bad dreams
or nightmares about the event(s)?.............................. A   B   C   D   E

_____3. Have you had the experience of suddenly
reliving the event(s), flashbacks of it
or acting or feeling as if the event were
happening again?.. A   B   C   D   E

_____4. Have you been intensely EMOTIONALLY
upset when reminded of the event(s), including
anniversaries of when it happened?............................. A   B   C   D   E

_____5. Do you often make efforts to avoid thoughts
or feelings associated with the event(s)?...................... A   B   C   D   E

_____6. Do you often make efforts to avoid activities,
situations, or places that remind you of the event(s)?.... A   B   C   D   E

_____7. Are there any important aspects about the
event(s) that you still cannot recall?........................... A   B   C   D   E

_____8. Have you markedly lost interest in free time
activities that used to be important to you?.................... A   B   C   D   E

Figure 9. Modified PTSD Symptom Scale, excerpt. Courtesy of Sherry Falsetti.

violence work because it emphasizes the "neuroscience of traumatic injury in children," allowing agencies to build highly fundable programs for kids.

By the late 1990s and early 2000s, federal funds through DOJ and DHHS became available to facilitate official collaborations between mental health professionals and domestic violence agencies.[57] And indeed, this came about through an explicit focus on "children" and "families." Domestic violence materials from the late 1990s are replete with language about the "child witness" to domestic violence, about organizations' responsibility to provide therapeutic services to that child. A 1998 statement from the executive director of ICADV reads, "Some of my saddest images are those of children who learn violence at home as a way of life they may later replicate."[58] Alongside the surge in trauma language in the late 1990s came a surge in references to the child's therapeutic needs, as well as the role of the domestic violence agency in "breaking the cycle" of violence. The centrality of the child professionalizes the work in a new way, since it is presumed that the child's needs must be addressed by a *licensed clinician.*

In this sense, while *trauma theory was central to the development of legal personhood for battered women in the 1980s,* the field took a more explicit approach to trauma in the 1990s and 2000s, drawing on and contributing to the growing field of psychiatric victimology. Feminists helped embed trauma frameworks into the victim services branch of the state, securing federal grants to make their programs "trauma-informed." Rather than abandoning their feminist aims, anti-violence policy leaders sought to resolve the boundary between political and psychological logics by using trauma as a grand narrative of political and psychic harm. Domestic violence conferences in the late 1990s and early 2000s regularly featured anti-racism workshops alongside presentations about PTSD. Domestic violence policy leaders frequently insisted that trauma frameworks would help address abused women's mistreatment in mental health systems. Their goal was to counter the mental health system's "pathology-inpatient model" by highlighting the structural *causes* of traumatic *effects.*[59] In this way, trauma promises a synthesis between external, socially produced harms (racism, sexism, war, domestic violence) and internalized psychic reactions (hypervigilance, flashbacks, anxiety, depression).

Critically, feminists' use of trauma theory helped secure funding, as demand increased for credentialed professionals who could bridge mental health "treatment" goals with feminist-founded advocacy work. It was hoped that trauma could suture across these worlds, providing such a capacious discourse of harm, injury, and suffering that both politics and individual psychology could reside there. And indeed, domestic violence agencies are now firmly part of what Allan Horwitz calls the "trauma industry," which includes schools, hospitals, government, police, mental health systems, and medical research.[60] This industry would not exist without anti-violence feminism and its negotiations with the therapeutic state. "Trauma" itself would not exist as the dominant discourse of social services if it weren't for the conjuncture of second-wave feminism, medicalized state program requirements, and federal funding for "victim" services.

Trauma has also helped usher in a new era of empowerment politics. In the 1970s, feminists imagined "empowerment" to be about women gaining independence and self-determination with and through a community of other women. The meanings of empowerment shifted over the course of the 1990s, however, as domestic violence policy leaders used this language as part of trauma frameworks to talk about "recovery." The empowered survivor figure today is saturated in trauma, but she can be rehabilitated through quasi-clinical interventions. As Bumiller argues, anti-violence services became oriented toward teaching women how to become "successful" survivors.[61] Empowerment comes to mean therapeutic "success." Indeed, this is the basis of trauma theory: victim accounts should move toward "empowered survivor" accounts, wherein the survivor is the "possessor of the inner resources that enable victims to persevere."[62] The survivor self must, of course, be cultivated in collaboration with a professional therapist.[63] What early activists imagined as a community of women helping each other has morphed into an infrastructure of therapeutic professionals in nonprofit organizations. "Telling" and "listening" are about expert evaluation. As Susan Schechter warned in 1982, "Even self-help, a liberating model for assisting women, can move in dangerously apolitical directions."[64]

Trauma has emerged, then, as a powerful explanation for women's needs, this time in medicalized guise. As scholars of gender and the welfare state have argued, policy makers invented discourses of "dependency" in order to justify shifting welfare away from income redistribution toward behavioral modification and discipline.[65] Trauma amplifies this shift, medicalizing dependency by locating an enduring pathology inside the victim—the harm came from outside, sure, but she must *do things* in order to recover. Trauma is the language of suffering but *also* of self-work and recovery. It is now commonplace to assume that all bad events have a pathological effect.[66] Critics argue that trauma also focuses our attention on psychological suffering rather than on victims' rage or rights-claims.[67] Overall, then, trauma mobilizes a gendered dependency narrative—but this narrative comes packaged in neuroscientific research with the promise of an empowered survivor figure who will (eventually) be free from service system needs, able to prevent her children from "repeating the cycle."

MEASURES AND OUTCOMES

As I've explained, research about and popular interest in trauma and PTSD exploded in the 1990s.[68] At the same time, domestic violence leaders began to collaborate with medical practitioners, and new emotional measurement techniques and psychiatric profiles for assessing victims were developed. Rather than a self-reflective woman hiding in shelter, or a victim of crime in need of legal help, the 1990s saw the rise of the domestic violence victim as a psychological survivor-subject, a woman who has been tortured and requires psychological intervention. The 1990s also witnessed the professionalization of the domestic violence field, as new federal funds shifted the field toward services delivered by licensed clinicians.

Interest in trauma mushroomed again in the early 2000s, as clinical social workers trained in trauma flooded into anti-violence organizations and policy leaders received grants to promote "trauma-informed" programming. Somatic and gender-based approaches to trauma therapy accumulated a research base, particularly via the addiction field, providing domestic violence policy leaders with a new set of "evidence-based" trauma tools. Today, "trauma" signals two sets of meanings in domestic violence work: (1) psychiatric definitions associated with flashbacks and intrusive symptoms such as hypervigilance and triggers; (2) feminist meanings associated with the harm of living under conditions of structural violence such as poverty, racism, and sexism. Trauma is itself hybrid. While policy leaders in the domestic violence field tack back and forth between both sets of meanings, usually it is the first, more clinical meaning that is found in the everyday work of the domestic violence agency. Clinical definitions translate more easily into "measurable program outcomes." They are quantifiable. Trauma sounds professional. Domestic violence workers told me that being "trauma-informed"—an increasingly common stipulation of grants—means hiring more and more clinical therapists.[69]

The structure of funding in the domestic violence field facilitates the shift toward clinical interpretations of trauma. Almost all domestic violence agencies rely on federal funding, typically through a combination of monies from VAWA, FVPSA, and VOCA.[70] The arrangement of these funding sources means that shifts in one funding mechanism affect entire networks of services. FVPSA began incorporating requirements that services become "trauma-informed" in the mid-2000s as a way to promote standardized assessments of programs. Typically, organizations are asked to demonstrate that they are "trauma-informed" with little instruction. Language may suggest something as vague as demonstrating how clients are made to feel safe in "body and brain."[71]

Due to this lack of clarity, the federal Office of Violence Against Women (OVW)—part of the DOJ and the grantors of VAWA funds—commissioned a study in 2013 of "what trauma-informed means" in the domestic violence community. Lindsey, a manager for the study, told me how the project came about: "They got all these [grant] proposals and they were like, oh, we don't really know how to assess whether what they're proposing is 'trauma-informed' or not." As Lindsey points out, there is significant disagreement in the field over the definition of *trauma-informed*. Eventually, OVW is expected to define and standardize what *trauma-informed* means. Currently, however, language remains vague. FVPSA requires domestic violence agencies to demonstrate that they are "trauma-informed" in order to receive funding; however, *trauma-informed* is defined as: "Understanding and responding to the symptoms of chronic interpersonal trauma and traumatic stress . . . as well as the behavioral and mental health sequelae of trauma."[72] The definition of *trauma-informed* seems to be, quite unhelpfully, that something is informed by "trauma"—quite a tautology.

Nevertheless, the incorporation of "trauma" in federal grants suggests the staying power of this paradigm for the larger welfare state infrastructure. In fact, trauma connects domestic violence services more strongly than ever to adjacent services—addiction, child welfare, courts, and mental health—that, as part of the therapeutic state, also speak the language of therapy, cure, and recovery. Trauma helps translate domestic violence victims' suffering across the institutional sites that construct them as problem subjects.[73] In this sense, trauma operates as a kind of "boundary object" that allows domestic violence counselors to collaborate with other professionals.[74] As an expert discourse and set of program measures, then, trauma binds feminist politics to therapeutic epistemologies and interventions, creating powerful new institutional links across the welfare state apparatus.

Since the publication of the Adverse Childhood Experiences study (ACEs) in the late 1990s, which demonstrated that traumatic experiences in early life translate into negative psychosocial outcomes later, federal policies have been moving explicitly toward trauma as a "common framework" for social services.[75] Federal committees have described trauma as an "awakening" for social services.[76] According to a federal policy report on trauma released in 2013, being "trauma-informed" means recognizing "signs and symptoms" of trauma in clients, reducing the risk of re-victimization, and being "recovery-oriented."[77] This widely cited report also insists that trauma-informed programs are about "gender-specific psychosocial empowerment" and that they should use "neuroscience-based resilience techniques" such as yoga, mindfulness, and meditation. The federal push for "trauma-informed" social services is shaped by research about the effects of traumatic stress on the brain. Reports regularly cite gender-based violence as a justification for neuroscientific approaches, suggesting that PTSD rates after sexual assault can be as high as 94 percent—a truly staggering claim.[78] By 2017, there were forty bills in eighteen states under consideration that included trauma language from the ACEs study. Some bills include requirements that people applying for Medicaid and entering juvenile programs first undergo a trauma screening. As of 2017, forty-nine such "trauma-informed" bills had been introduced at the federal level.[79]

This "trauma-informed" push is especially strong in domestic violence and rape services. Some domestic violence agencies comply with "trauma-informed" requirements in a minimal way—for example, by hiring one clinical social worker to lead a trauma support group. Other agencies have undergone wholesale reinventions. Irina's agency has to provide data to over fifty funders each year, an enormous task, and she told me that the only way they can do so efficiently is by demonstrating that they are reducing clients' "trauma symptoms." Lina's agency implemented twelve support groups per week focused on trauma. They also adopted a copyrighted "trauma-informed" organizational model intended for mental health agencies, which requires them to offer a weekly trauma workshop *and* to redesign their physical space to be "healthier" for trauma survivors, including a yoga room for employees and a water feature for clients. Holly, a trauma-informed specialist for her state, used federal grant dollars to develop collaborations with the mental health and addiction boards so that domestic violence workers could receive more mental health trainings. She told me this is important because trauma, unlike feminist advocacy, has "science and biology behind it."

Jill, whom we heard from at the beginning of this chapter, paid a national leader in trauma and addiction to conduct a series of trainings for domestic violence workers in her state. Agencies across Jill's state have started to look more and more like "addiction recovery" centers, replete with diagnostic language. Still, Jill explains that the trauma push does not mean that every domestic violence worker has to understand neuroscience—rather, agencies can implement a "trauma-informed yoga class" instead. These "gentle" implementations of clinical frameworks—usually through yoga, deep breathing, and body work like reiki—are common in domestic violence agencies. As Tess, an art therapist, told me, these strategies are about "helping people connect to themselves" through addressing trauma's effects on the physical body.

Despite this diversity in trauma implementation, every domestic violence policy leader and counselor I interviewed recognized trauma as the central, rising paradigm in the field. The shift toward trauma satisfies *and* amplifies funders' insistence on quantitative program outcomes. As scholars have demonstrated, quantification is an important tool of legitimacy, forcing policy makers, scientists, and lay-persons to "think and act differently" about social problems.[80] Quantifying domestic violence through trauma symptoms scales is powerful because it transforms confusing life experiences into a number.[81] The quantification of trauma also makes different kinds of social "things" (i.e., flashbacks, panic attacks, feeling nervous or sad) *commensurable* by transforming them into composite numbers that can be ranked.[82] When knowledge becomes quantified and standardized—in checklists, for example—the politics and professional struggles that produced those standards often disappear from view.[83] In

OUTCOME MEASURES DATA COLLECTION		
CLIENT SERVICE GROUP: COUNSELING	Our agency has a funder that requires us to report data on what you feel you have learned as a result of receiving counseling services from our agency. Please complete this form as instructed by the staff person that provided it to you. **Check YES OR NO for each question.**	
YES	NO	QUESTION
		I know more ways to plan for my safety.
		I know more about community resources.
		I feel more hopeful about my future.
		I have a better understanding of the effects of abuse on my life.
		I have a better understanding of the effects of abuse on my children's lives.

Figure 10. Outcome Measures Data Collection checklist from domestic violence organization. Photo by author.

this sense, quantitative protocols allow for trauma to be "performed" into being by experts in the domestic violence agency as if it were a "natural" category, innate to women's and children's experiences. Sally Engle Merry calls this "evidence-based governance."[84] Still, program leaders do not necessarily take quantitative assessments seriously, and they frequently use the feminist histories of their agencies to resist these transformations. For example, Denise showed me the checklist that her organization administers to clients (figure 10). The checklist is non-technical, avoiding numerical scales and symptoms language. When writing it, Denise chose to use "yes" or "no" questions and to measure nonclinical categories such as "feelings of hopefulness" or having a "better understanding" of abuse. Denise explained, "We'll tell you whatever you want to hear. Just give us the money." She also said, "Ninety-nine percent of the people who respond to that questionnaire have said that we're a thousand percent successful. So, where's my money? Does this advance the movement?"

Denise does not "believe" in trauma measures or outcomes scales. At the same time, she attends trauma workshops and trains her employees in trauma theory and the basics of neuroscience. She explained to me that trauma theories help workers understand victims, to see that victims are suffering from external harm. Denise's professional practices are indicative of a common ambivalence about trauma in the domestic violence field: she believes that quantified program outcomes corrupt feminist-based services, but she uses "trauma" nonetheless. Judges and DCFS caseworkers send clients to Denise's organization specifically because she has this checklist on hand to measure support group attendance and learning objectives. She resents that she had to create such a checklist to comply with punitive institutions, but she wants women to come to her organization. "[We] respect her enough that she is being believed for the first time in her life. Is that an important thing to do? Absolutely. Is it measured on that stupid questionnaire? Not at all." Denise critiques the quantification of her work even as she actively uses quantified tools to provide services. This quantification project enmeshes her agency with welfare and judicial systems more strongly than ever.

Domestic violence leaders often view trauma as "safe" because it allows for the quantification of symptoms while locating the source of harm outside of the victim: she is reacting to abnormal circumstances in a rational way. In this sense, domestic violence workers use symptom checklists, but they reject the idea that those symptoms reference *pathology*. Who *wouldn't* have trauma after experiencing domestic violence? Kim explained that trauma should not be used to "therapize" people, but to provide proof of "evidence-based" interventions to funders. Therapeutic interventions are simply easier to quantify than is case management, which involves helping women find housing or apply for food stamps. As Rosa told me, her organization is "stuck" because they cannot "prove" to funders they are having an impact on their community—as a result, they have been coerced into creating mental health outcome scales in order to justify their community-based education projects.

Quantification projects are taken up ambivalently and unevenly, then. Domestic violence workers, because they also draw from feminist philosophies of care, actively negotiate the trade-offs of quantifying their work. Amanda put it bluntly: "Advocacy is not easily measurable. The ways in which we work do not lend themselves to high-level, randomized control trial, research-based outcomes." Amanda's organization was recently forced to import a copyrighted trauma curriculum from a chain of addiction treatment centers. The trauma curriculum is intended for people with "compulsive" behaviors. She imported this curriculum in order to show that her organization is drawing from an "evidence base" for its services. The language of addiction now hovers over her agency even though she believes, as Sara, another program director told me, "What really works and makes a difference in people's lives *cannot be measured*." Domestic violence policy leaders seek to satisfy funders' increasingly clinical requirements even as they critique quantification and work to mitigate its negative impact on clients.

Though workers and policy leaders may feel ambivalently about such measures, women accessing services are nonetheless required to quantify and *symptomize* their own behaviors. For example, in Alexandra's agency, clients are required to complete anxiety and depression symptom questionnaires upon intake and to develop a treatment plan by the second session. Lina's organization asks that clients take stress evaluations, which staff are also asked to fill out. Cristina's organization recently hired an "evaluator" to develop mental health assessments for all the children receiving services in her agency. And Natalie's organization requires clients to fill out a twenty-item PTSD checklist upon intake. Having clients complete such an assessment allows her organization to pitch their services as "medical" in order to bill her state's health insurance program for reimbursement. As soon as they walk in the doors, women are asked to shuttle their experiences into diagnostic categories, ranking their behaviors and feelings in numerical order of severity. The uptake of PTSD in direct service organizations means that women are asked, routinely, to quantify their own "risk" for various kinds of psychological vulnerabilities and to write them down on paper.

"WHAT DOES FEMINISM EVEN MEAN?"

When I interviewed Amanda, the leader of a statewide domestic violence coalition, I asked her what she thought about the feminist history of domestic violence work. She responded with a series of rhetorical questions: "What does feminism even mean? In what ways do we see that feminism benefits people of all genders? How do we quantify that as 'work'? And how do we quantify that as success?" For Amanda, the pressures of quantification—and the political complexities of "feminisms"—make feminism irrelevant to her work. But the case for trauma is clear: trauma offers a way to think about symptoms as both "prior and ongoing," and to help frontline workers understand that women are not choosing to behave badly in shelters or in support groups—rather, they are "responding to trauma." As Amanda went on to explain, trauma is where the "good energy and research" can be found in social services today—unlike feminism, which is outdated. Using trauma and PTSD helps domestic violence agencies satisfy quantitative funding guidelines to show that their programs are "working"—for example, by requiring that women fill out PTSD checklists upon intake and exit. Trauma has become the primary language of harm in anti-violence work, as well as the language of program efficacy.

Still, some policy leaders are distressed about the trauma revolution. They feel a deep disjuncture between victims' material needs and the medicalized, therapeutic frameworks that increasingly saturate domestic violence work. Jane, a movement veteran, had the strongest response: "I think that 'trauma-informed' is morally bankrupt. . . . It's telling [victims] that they should focus on something that is basically upper-middle-class, privileged, navel-gazing. . . . It's not what [victims] need. It's a luxury to sit around and do therapy. We should [all] have access to whatever we need. And if that is therapy, then we should have access to it. . . . But, mostly it's probably childcare, cars that work, food, and shelters that don't have lead in the pipes." As we will see, Jane is right that the rise of "trauma-informed" has helped to professionalize and medicalize domestic violence services, shifting the work away from women's material needs toward therapeutic interventions aimed at reducing trauma symptoms.

But for Marie—a domestic violence policy leader who also identifies as a feminist—the "trauma-informed" framework is more promising than Jane will admit. "[It's a] social justice framework that bridges advocacy and trauma work. [It] allows people to . . . hold a human-rights, social justice piece around accessibility with mental health and substance use–related needs. . . . [Trauma-informed] is a kind of welcoming, inclusive, accessible culture." For Marie, trauma frameworks link the harm that women experience in their interpersonal relationships with the harm they suffer structurally. Marie admits that trauma paradigms *also* help agencies comply with "evidence-based" funding requirements. But she believes that trauma-informed programming can radicalize the field and build empathy among workers. In the next chapter, I explore how Jane's fears and Marie's hopes coexist in the everyday work of the domestic violence agency, where workers are asked to be "feminist" and "clinical" at the same time, asked to turn the therapeutic gaze of "trauma" and "self-care" on themselves—and where victims are offered trauma frameworks that regulate their bodies and emotions in new ways. Even as trauma transforms domestic violence work, quantifying women's suffering and making workers into health experts, the field remains unsettled: both politicized and a-political, gender-based and curiously de-gendered, both professionalized and invested in "lay" therapy models. Without clarity or purity, the trauma revolution unfolds.

3 Administering Trauma

Emma, a longtime leader in domestic violence work, led me through the twisting halls of her domestic violence agency as we talked about the history of the shelter. Photos of the organization's many construction projects lined the hallways, documenting its evolution from a single hotline in 1976—calls were routed through the local Planned Parenthood office—to the massive, maze-like structure we meandered through that day, complete with educational, counseling, and residential services. The edifice of the new therapy center envelopes the shelter, surrounding and concealing it from public view. Emma explained that this setup is intentional, so that donors can visit the therapy center without trespassing into the woman-only shelter. While the shelter sits at the core of the complex, it is literally subsumed by therapy offices, the feminist history of domestic violence work shut behind the doors of the clinic. Still, the shelter is crowded, shabby, and loud, alive with the women and children who call it home—it is undeniably *there*, despite the walls that obscure it. As we wound our way into the shelter, I thought about how the building's configuration mirrors epistemic, political, and institutional shifts in the domestic violence field: the woman-only space, packed with children's toys and the chaos of dozens of women living together, is concealed behind the forward-facing, clean therapy offices with cushioned chairs lining the waiting area.

Emma's organization is not unique. Most domestic violence agencies face pressure to shift away from the empowerment-based feminist service models developed during the 1970s toward professional trauma therapy for women and children. As Irina, one of Emma's employees, told me later that day, "What we do here now is primarily therapy. . . . [Our] resistance to [therapy] early on [in the movement] was misguided." Emma agreed, telling me that anti-violence activists' antagonism toward the mainstream mental health field has "softened" over the years. Emma has been a leader in the organization since 1989, helping it grow from a domestic violence shelter to a multi-service agency that now includes elder abuse programs. During this time, the organization took the word "woman" out of its name—they wanted something more "positive-sounding." This kind of reorientation is common. As I was writing this chapter, one of the oldest anti-violence organizations in Chicago, Rape Victim Advocates, changed its name to *Resilience*—the politicized language of "rape" and "advocacy" jettisoned in favor of the positive language of psychological overcoming.[1]

At first, Emma told me, the feminists who ran her organization were suspicious of her because she had a business background: "I wasn't a formerly battered woman, and I wasn't a counselor, and I almost didn't get hired because of that." But ultimately, the board needed someone to manage the "bigger dollars" that began flowing in during the 1980s. "[At] that time it was a women's rights organization. That really appealed. It was a really good fit. But I have to admit, I've been a part of shifting it [to become] a victim's rights organization." Emma went on to explain, with some regret in her voice, "I'm a strong feminist inside, but you know, you can't hold that banner too high." For Emma, being able to serve more "victims" by getting rid of the feminist label has been worth it. The agency is proud of its feminist roots and touts its work as "survivor centered," but as Irina confessed, what the organization "really does" is clinical therapy. In contrast to the organization that she joined in the 1980s, the agency Emma runs now is oriented toward victims of crime seeking therapeutic rehabilitation.

Emma's agency has clearly embraced the therapeutic turn in domestic violence work. The language of "trauma" is central to the organization's grants, service plans, and program language. When I asked Emma why they use trauma language, she told me bluntly: "We use it for fundraising." Emma has been doing this work for nearly thirty years and has seen buzzwords come and go, but she thinks *trauma* is special because it bridges mental health and domestic violence paradigms, allowing workers to address things like "depression." The use of trauma frameworks also helps her employees appear more legitimate to funders and to other service providers. Even though Emma and many of her employees identify as feminists, when it comes to grant language and hiring notices, they use the language of traumatic victimization. In Emma's agency, like many others, domestic violence work has become *trauma work*.

As one policy leader told me, "This is the trauma train and we're all already on board." Like a train with its linked cars, trauma is an *articulated* formation: a set of discourses and practices that connects the feminist history of the field to shiny new clinical paradigms. On the one hand, *trauma* reflects mental health logics associated with symptoms and quantifiable outcomes. On the other hand, *trauma* refers to women's diffuse experiences of harm, a kind of medicalized shorthand for structural violence. Policy leaders shift between both of these definitions in any given statement about "trauma." Connecting these paradigms is an ongoing political and epistemic struggle, a process of articulating contradictory frameworks together into some kind of coherent whole.[2] Trauma is a powerful system of meaning in domestic violence work, one designed to respond to funding pressures and an institutional environment premised on therapeutic recovery—but one that also attempts to preserve feminist ideas about structural harm.

This chapter shows how "trauma" introduces new political and epistemic conflicts in domestic violence work, transforming the way workers do their jobs and intervene in women's lives. I am not interested in deciding whether trauma is *really* feminist or *really* medical. Rather, governing through trauma requires *articulating* clinical expertise to feminist expertise.[3] When I talk about feminist expertise, I am referring to models of care focused on systems advocacy, empowerment-based and non-hierarchical counseling, and definitions of abuse that focus on gender inequality. That the concept of trauma can seemingly capture this feminist framework *while also* satisfying clinical funding requirements is what makes it a compelling object of inquiry. The story of trauma is the story of how anti-violence leaders have cultivated a new form of expertise at the crossroads of feminist politics and medicalized service systems. It is also the story of how domestic violence workers now have to do their jobs in this tenuous intersection. Like victims, trauma workers have to embody resilience, using "self-care" to demonstrate their professional commitment to wellness—"administering trauma" to themselves.

"Trauma" finds an enthusiastic home among domestic violence professionals because, as I explained in chapter 1, they have long combined psychological interventions with social change work.[4] We might even think of domestic violence organizations, in sociologist Thomas Medvetz's terms, as "constitutively hybrid," such that they engage feminist politics alongside therapeutic politics.[5] Domestic violence agencies tend to reject mainstream mental health approaches even though they have become *part of* the mental health field themselves. This tension between clinical and feminist logics does not forestall the work, but animates it, pushing it forward.[6] The domestic violence agency is a fascinating space in which to study knowledge production and expertise because it is a "world divided against itself."[7]

Throughout this chapter, I show that trauma work is a dense, complicated sphere of action and struggle.[8] Though trauma paradigms are increasingly powerful, feminist ideals have not disappeared into the waste bin of history. Domestic violence leaders regularly talk about feminism and profess social justice goals in public spaces.[9] Workers use clinical language on official forms even when they reject therapeutic protocols while helping women in one-on-one meetings. The feminist orientation of the work proves stubborn and resistant to erasure. In Emma's agency, after all, the music coming from the shelter's courtyard—vibrant inside the walls of the therapy center—beats loud and rhythmic, like a heart.

THE THERAPEUTIC GAZE

Trauma workers in domestic violence agencies are tasked, uneasily, with translating a quantitative demand for trauma symptoms and recovery outcomes into actual care work. This produces a layered expertise that refuses to "settle," to be *either* feminist *or* biomedical *or* technocratic. After all, processes such as quantification and medicalization are shaped by the political contexts in which they unfold, and feminism has been an important context for the development of therapeutic expertise since the 1970s.[10] When I talked to trauma workers, I found that they attempted to retain feminist goals by "softening" clinical interventions, using techniques like yoga and deep breathing. These "soft" interventions locate traumatic suffering and recovery inside the body, asking women to regulate their embodiment in new ways. Though such interventions are open-ended and flexible, the use of somatic trauma techniques actually *extends the reach of professional evaluation deeper inside women's bodies and lives.*

As such, installing clinical expertise in the domestic violence agency creates new responsibilities for women who have experienced domestic violence, new investments in bodily and psychic "recovery." Women's bodies and behaviors are reinterpreted through the expansive lens of trauma, which constructs them as psychological sufferers who should engage in therapy to become survivors. While survivor language has roots in feminist activism, it is increasingly enmeshed with professional therapy.[11] Women's behaviors become "reactions," their nervous systems reservoirs of trauma, bundles of "triggers." These reinterpretations are meant to make victims more comprehensible to professionals—*to redeem them.*

Trauma work is reorganizing the professional gaze in social services more generally. In *The Birth of the Clinic*, Foucault describes a massive epistemological shift in eighteenth-century Western medicine, wherein surface-level models of medical practice were replaced by a deep probing of the bodily organism.[12] Foucault describes this as a shift toward the "clinical gaze," a way of seeing the patient as embodied by disease, such that the physician learns to investigate the inner depths of the body with a penetrating eye. As doctors began dissecting cadavers, the patient was remade: "The patient is the rediscovered portrait of disease; he is the disease itself."[13] The medical gaze objectifies the patient's body as doctors discover the secrets of pathology hidden beneath the skin. The body is imagined as "an opaque mass in which . . . the very mystery of origins lie[s] hidden."[14] This makes the patient into an object of medical knowledge. But more than that, the clinical gaze inscribes the body with "a whole system of communications" that the physician, with training and skill, can decipher.[15] The invention of the clinical gaze therefore helps consolidate and institutionalize medical expertise, making doctors into truth seekers.

As in medicine, trauma frameworks introduce an epistemic shift in the domestic violence agency. Just as the body reveals the truth of disease under the clinical gaze, trauma reveals the *truth* of domestic violence victimization. Under the therapeutic gaze, the victim's body declares the truth of its suffering.[16] Trauma emerges as the "bearer of unspeakable truths" about the human condition.[17] As anthropologist Miriam Ticktin argues, human rights organizations actively promote the idea that suffering is universal and can be found, measured, and understood by looking at the body using medical techniques.[18]

In this way, the introduction of the clinical gaze in the domestic violence field—despite its ostensible neutrality—performs an almost religious conversion of the victim: she is redeemed by the expert's recognition of trauma as *that which acts inside of her*. It is "trauma" that makes her take opiates or stay with her abusive boyfriend or yell at her children or refuse to attend the substance use group. The victim who is judged for her bad decisions becomes the survivor whose decisions—"bad" or otherwise— are recast as "trauma reactions." As Foucault writes, "The essence of disease . . . is articulated upon the thick, dense volume of the organism and becomes *embodied* within it."[19] In this way, the therapeutic gaze saturates the domestic violence victim with trauma, remaking her into a traumatized subject. The hope is that this conversion will make her more sympathetic, *just as it makes programs more fundable*.

But while Foucault's clinical gaze was absolute, omniscient, and precise, the therapeutic gaze found in domestic violence agencies is ambivalent. That's because the gaze captures medical and feminist epistemologies together: both ways of knowing are present in the way recovery and wellness are imagined, in the way women's bodies are observed and discussed, and in the way therapeutic interventions are executed. The therapeutic gaze is itself a site of struggle between feminist and clinical meanings, a "complex contestation."[20] Workers and policy leaders develop creative ways of handling this ambivalence, rewriting the rules of clinical therapy to fit the feminist history of domestic violence agencies.

For example, Angela, a program director for a suburban Chicago shelter, explained that her organization integrates *advocacy* into therapy, rather than offering "pure" therapy. By advocacy, I mean working with clients to find housing, food, jobs, civil court remedies—help navigating systems, which is sometimes called "case management." Angela explained that unlike most therapists, domestic violence workers know women's day-to-day routines, their struggles to get to the train, to prepare food, to look for housing. "We've been working with her on establishing a nice bath time, bedtime routine, read the story. Because she's really harsh and really close to the edge there. We know that right away. [A traditional] therapist doesn't know that.... We have a lot more knowledge." For Angela, domestic violence counselors are *better therapists* because they understand women's concrete needs. Still, she says, unlike the early days of the movement when everyone was suspicious of therapy, now "we might as well embrace the term 'treatment' because what we really do is CBT [cognitive behavioral therapy] anyway."

While Angela's agency integrates women's concrete needs into their therapeutic services, in many agencies, *advocacy* is separated from *therapy* in organizational structure. Shelley, a trauma worker in another agency, explained: "[We] don't talk too much about case management needs. I do some. That's not my preference. I'm not all that good at it.... You have to come in and be a client; otherwise, I can't see you." Shelley knows that victims need systems advocacy and material resources, but she does not provide that—survivors must engage in deep emotional work if they want to see her.

Shelley's position is increasingly common. She is a trained clinician and simply does not know how to "do" systems advocacy: to help women apply for food stamps or find housing. Other agencies, like Natalie's, have separated their advocacy department entirely from their therapy department, creating a clear professional and philosophical boundary. Managing the tension between *systems advocacy* and *therapy* by segregating them also creates new class and educational divides between workers, making the organization itself more hierarchical.[21] Increasingly, advanced-degree workers with salaries are doing the "elite" therapeutic work in domestic violence agencies, whereas less educated workers with hourly pay are doing case management. Workers with degrees and status are more educated about the science of trauma and therefore presumed to be more skilled at working with victims. As Rhonda, the director of a large clinical team, told me, "When you're dealing with trauma, you really need to change a person's brain. You know their brain changes because of trauma. We know that from the research available. If we don't address that immediately when you're in the safe haven, how do we help put you on the road towards healing?" In Rhonda's agency, every client must complete a trauma assessment upon intake. The goal of her organization, she told me, is not necessarily to help women navigate social service systems, but to "interrupt trauma . . . so they can heal better." This is clinical work to be executed by clinical experts.

Still, agencies with strong feminist leadership tend to remain less clinical—they might hire master's-level workers, but they do not allow those workers to medicalize clients' behaviors. Like Angela, they integrate advocacy *into* therapy. On the other hand, organizations with a stronger mental health influence—for example, Amy's agency, which has recently been subsumed into a mental health facility—focus squarely on clinical therapy. The line between these organizational models is not always clear, however, and both models may be found within a single agency. For example, I interviewed Helen alongside her boss, Lina. Helen is a trauma therapist who has been in the field since the 1990s. Lina, on the other hand, is a survivor who has been doing the work since the 1970s. Lina told me, "[Helen] is not allowed to practice therapy here, because I'm still suspicious." Battered women are not "crazy"—they do not need "therapy."

Helen chuckled when Lina voiced those prohibitions and waited until Lina left the room to tell me that the line between therapy and advocacy is blurrier than Lina will admit. She confided, "While Lina says we don't do therapy, they've given me permission to do some Eye Movement Desensitization and Reprocessing Therapy (EMDR)."[22] Helen wanted me to know that the boundary between clinical therapy (like EMDR) and the anti-clinical approach that Lina champions is actually quite messy. Clinical therapy sneaks into the domestic violence shelter even when a powerful leader voices opposition, in part because the staff is made up of *clinicians*. Clinical models of behavioral intervention exist alongside feminist distaste for those models, in this case within a single building. These kinds of tensions—at once generational, epistemological, practical, and political—increasingly define domestic violence work.

STRUGGLING OVER THE THERAPEUTIC GAZE

Trauma and its therapeutic gaze are transformative but do not appear in the domestic violence agency without conflict and hybridization. Sociologists often theorize the historical relationship between social movements and powerful institutions like biomedicine as one of co-optation. In this formulation, what were once radical, grassroots discourses and organizations are usurped by forces that depoliticize the work in order to serve the interests of the status quo. This takeover may be ushered in by authorities such as doctors, or it may be brought about from below, agitated for by activists in order to gain resources.[23] The co-optation model makes sense, especially for biomedicine, which is good at "capturing" social problems.[24]

And yet, as I have shown, feminist anti-violence work grew up alongside neoliberalism and neoconservatism and has *always* engaged therapeutic politics. While co-optation provides a starting point, the analytic scheme of a homogenous takeover is too simple.[25] The history of domestic violence politics—its long-standing hybridization of feminist and therapeutic aims—belies co-optation.[26] Further, as I show throughout this chapter, domestic violence workers often use quantified tools and technical expertise in strategic and selective ways. Medicalization does not necessarily equate to depoliticization: getting expert, especially medical, attention for a problem is often precisely a political act, and this process may transform feminist politics without obliterating them.[27]

Part of my goal in this chapter, then, is to move beyond an understanding of medicalization as co-optation. Any form of expertise is itself a complex of meanings, objects, and practices that is only ever partially fixed and is always at risk of challenge by oppositional knowledge.[28] We should attend, therefore, to the sites in which competing knowledges encounter and shape each other.[29] I suggest understanding the rise of trauma in the domestic violence field as a process of *articulation*, or a set of connections between seemingly antagonistic meanings and practices. Stuart Hall and Laclau and Mouffe's concept of articulation insists that oppositional discourses, under certain conditions, can be organized together into something that appears unified, creating something new and productive.[30] Theorizing something as articulated—in the way of a multi-car bus with an accordion connector—helps avoid reductionism, encouraging a focus on the links between disparate discourses and practices.[31] Articulation requires that we think of structures as relational, endowed with meaning through their association with adjacent structures. Jennifer Slack writes that articulation is a process of *creating connections*, which is precisely what trauma does by drawing together clinical and feminist forms of expertise.[32]

As in Emma's organization, where the counseling center faces outward and the shelter hides from view, the biomedical model dominates domestic violence work today. Medicalized frameworks face outward— trauma's outcome measures and quantitative assessments have become indispensable. But the feminist history and philosophies of anti-violence work remain in play. If trauma is a "train," as Jackie told me, it is made up of both feminist and clinical cars, all of which seem to operate together. There is no ultimate takeover, no vanquishing of feminist philosophies of care. Trauma is an articulated formation that draws forms of expertise together and then *does things*: trauma invents a new way of apprehending and intervening in women's lives, extending the reach of domestic violence expertise, going deeper inside women's bodies and selves.

In order to understand this process of articulation, we need look no further than how trauma is wielded as a diagnosis—or not—in domestic violence agencies. Diagnosis is a key site of struggle over the therapeutic gaze. Trauma workers and policy leaders use symptoms language in their work, but they resist the official practice of diagnosis, paying homage to the feminist histories of their organizations, which were vociferously anti-diagnosis. Diagnosis is a generational flashpoint in anti-violence work, as newer workers trained in clinical therapy use diagnostic language enthusiastically, while older movement leaders tend to remain steadfast in their opposition to diagnosis. "Trauma" is an attempt to suture over the ideological divide between the activist generation (feminist founders of the movement) and the trauma generation (recently trained clinicians) by being *like* a diagnosis but *not quite* a diagnosis.

Shelley's professional dilemma provides a useful example. I interviewed Shelley in her small, comfortable office on the second floor of a suburban Chicago shelter. A clinically trained therapist, Shelley facilitates a domestic violence support group and sees individual clients for domestic violence counseling throughout the week. Shelley is sympathetic to feminism and cares about domestic violence as a social problem, but she identifies primarily as a clinician. She told me, "When you're with a victim, you can see that she's been traumatized. We don't diagnose, but . . . [*trails off*]." Shelley draws a line between her work as a therapist and her work as an employee of a domestic violence organization, which has historically positioned itself *against* diagnosis. Because of her clinical training, Shelley "sees" trauma in her clients. And yet, the PTSD label is intentionally withheld because "we" do not do *that kind* of work.

For second generation workers like Shelley who are trained as clinicians, the distinction between mental health work and domestic violence work is wobbly.[33] Shelley confessed later in the interview that she thinks it might be harmful *not* to diagnose, because "you have to know what you're working with." She thinks diagnosis might help clients "make healthier choices." Shelley's boss, Amy, who has worked hard to protect the domestic violence program from takeover by its parent mental health center, agreed that diagnostic language is helpful: "We don't diagnose people, but we need to look at how some of their behaviors . . . get acted out, to help them see how they can do something different. I think it's important to tell people . . . how it looks to you as the therapist." Therapy, according to Amy, can help women deal with "their own trauma." Still, Amy feels conflicted because she is nervous that the mental health organization will overtake the domestic violence program. Amy recently lost 25 percent of her staff and was forced to cede control of client supervision to the mental health team. She fears that even if she uses "trauma" language to collaborate with the mental health team, they will nonetheless take control of the work because they have more money and power. She is worried that they will pathologize victims and deny them control over their service plans. Even though Amy uses trauma models and hires clinical therapists, she sees mainstream mental health practitioners as enemies of anti-violence work, and she faces real organizational battles around the autonomy of her feminist-founded program.

For Shelley and Amy, the contradictions pile up. As I was leaving her office, Shelley pulled a sheet of paper from a stack in her drawer and slid it to me furtively. The top read "BORDERLINE," and the document listed traits associated with borderline personality disorder (BPD). For example, "They are unable to maintain a consistent concept of the self," and "Unable to differentiate within themselves a feeling, impulse, a body sensation." Shelley told me that a lot of domestic violence victims suffer from BPD. As soon as she handed me the paper, Shelley motioned for me to put it in my bag. She asked me not to show the paper to Judy, a domestic violence policy leader in Chicago whom we both know. She laughed nervously and told me that Judy "hates this sort of diagnosis thing." Shelley motioned again for me to put the paper inside my bag before I left, even though there was no one else in the small hallway of the shelter.

Shelley's simultaneous embarrassment and desire for me to understand BPD highlights the tensions of doing domestic violence work under the pressures of the therapeutic gaze. Domestic violence counselors are in the seemingly untenable position of providing a type of counseling *that is not technically therapy* under cultural and organizational conditions that bombard them with psychiatric language, tools, and labels. Performing diagnosis makes sense to Shelley as a therapist. For example, Shelley regularly meets with clinical colleagues in a neighboring mental health agency where she supervises interns. While Shelley's clinical orientation allows her to use labels like BPD, applying such a label would be a major offense in a domestic violence agency—it would be seen as pathologizing and patronizing. The line that Shelley treads between her role as a domestic violence worker and her role as a clinical therapist is a fragile one, one that makes her nervous and requires her to speak the language of disorder in a whisper.

I discovered over the course of my fieldwork that most trauma workers manage these contradictions by importing trauma language *while refusing to diagnose*. Despite trauma workers' overwhelming embrace of PTSD language, there is general agreement that, "We don't label women." Rejecting diagnosis allows trauma workers to connect themselves to the feminist history of the field. Stating their opposition to "labeling" allows trauma workers to make space for themselves in feminist-founded agencies while also presenting as clinical professionals, using symptoms language and theories of the traumatized brain.

This ambivalent relationship to diagnostic labels is further complicated by domestic violence organizations' position vis-à-vis other service agencies. Trauma workers are often asked by other agencies to "deal with" domestic violence, as if it were a disease.[34] Danielle, the director of a Chicago domestic violence agency, told me: "For years, DCFS would call and say, how many sessions does a woman need to go through before she's cured of domestic violence? [*Laughs*] I love that question. I was thinking about putting it up on my wall. And so, we would tell them . . . there's nothing that she needs to be cured of. . . . But we were concerned about women falling through the cracks . . . so we decided to put together a DCFS group." Here, Danielle speaks to the difficult role that domestic violence agencies play in their network of services, where "cure" and "treatment" are the norms. Adjacent organizations actively use diagnostic language and think of domestic violence as a kind of addiction. Domestic violence agencies are typically the only organizations in this network of services that have feminist roots and resist diagnosis. Danielle coolly rejects a labeling and treatment approach to domestic violence; in practice, however, her agency must take up this role. They created a group for DCFS-mandated women to comply with requirements, checking boxes off a list of problems as if domestic violence were a symptom of disease.

While trauma workers constantly encounter the language of diagnosis in their work, *diagnosing* is typically barred.[35] In Alice's words, "We don't care about diagnosis. . . . What are *your* particular things that are affecting *you* . . . ? Not, do you have PTSD or do you have oppositional defiant disorder? That doesn't matter." Thus, trauma is successful in domestic violence work precisely because it *need not involve diagnosis*. The victim's psychological state is offered up for professional evaluation, but official labeling is unnecessary. Carla, a therapist in a suburban Chicago agency, explained: "It's not like we aren't [diagnosing] in our heads. [*Laughs*] It *is* happening. But it's important not to have it down on paper. . . . I mean, the person can be depressed, and it's not like we're going to put 'major depression.' But in our notes, we might say, 'Client feeling depressed this week.'" Carla makes a relatively superficial distinction here: diagnostic language is used, but the official label is withheld from paperwork. Emma agrees: "We don't want [the diagnosis] on their record. . . . And yet, quite honestly, how do we also help the people that we work with to understand that while [the perpetrator] chose to do this, you need to take care of yourself better, take care of the kids better?" For Emma, the diagnosis should not be documented. On the other hand, diagnostic language should instruct survivors on how to "take care" of themselves, how to adjust their behavior according to expert knowledge.

Not everyone in the field feels comfortable even with the unofficial use of diagnostic language, however. Kim, a policy leader, told me that she has seen a surge in diagnostic language in the funding paperwork she reviews for programs across the state: "[Diagnosis] doesn't belong in our work. . . . Even if you're a licensed clinical social worker, if you're employed by a domestic violence agency, you are employed as an advocate, not as a licensed clinician. You want to do that work? Go work at a mental health agency. You can do your fifty hours and you're paid to diagnose." For Kim, even the informal use of diagnostic language is troubling. She draws a clear boundary: if you want to diagnose, you should leave. Still, Kim has been in the field since the 1970s. She remains stalwartly anti-clinical. Most domestic violence workers toe a much fuzzier line.

For example, Alexandra's agency in the Chicago suburbs no longer even has an advocacy program—aside from an administration and prevention team, *all* the employees are clinicians who see clients in one-hour time slots in a building that looks and feels like a clinic. Walking into the agency is disorienting. A glass reception window, waiting area, and hallway with closed office doors made me feel like I was in a doctor's office—a contrast to the "homey" feel of many agencies. I came to find out that the organization was recently redesigned to resemble a clinic. It even smelled like a doctor's office. Alexandra keeps therapeutic exercises scattered throughout her office—rock gardens and stress balls and the like. Sitting there, I could have been in any therapist's office.

Alexandra explained that even though she works in a domestic violence agency, she's not a domestic violence *advocate*; rather, she's a mental health service provider with a specialization in domestic violence. New clients that come to her agency are automatically assigned to a therapist. Clients don't have any contact with volunteers, since volunteers—according to Alexandra—do not have enough mental health expertise to work with victims of domestic violence. New clients complete four written evaluations upon intake: one for anxiety, another for depression, the ACEs checklist, and an abuse severity tool. Many of the agency's clients are mandated to attend the program by DCFS, and Alexandra explained that using "deep breathing," "guided relaxation," "self-care," and "positive thinking" is especially important for these women. Rather than teaching women about the dynamics of domestic violence, Alexandra and her colleagues delve straight into therapeutic work. In fact, the only education that clients receive about domestic violence is a short video they're asked to watch during intake. Alexandra explains that this is because her primary goal is to help women "change their behavior."

I commented to Alexandra that her agency does not seem to retain many of its feminist roots, that it feels like a mental health agency. Alexandra explained, however, that the real distinction between domestic violence work and mental health work is not feminist history, but diagnosis: "We don't diagnose. We're all trained. I'm a licensed clinical social worker. I *can* diagnose. But we don't formally diagnose in any of our records. We just say, there's symptoms of PTSD or symptoms of depression. . . . Now, with the client, I have no problem saying I think you have many symptoms of this particular disorder." Alexandra establishes a technical but not a philosophical boundary. The only difference between mental health and domestic violence work is the act of diagnosing for insurance reimbursement—diagnostic language, on the other hand, is allowed. Trauma is ideal here because a PTSD label is not necessary in order to interpret women's behavior through the lens of trauma. Victims' psychologies and embodiment become objects of professional observation, but those "problems" do not become official labels.

Diagnosis captures the tension between domestic violence organizations' new and old models of expertise. The old model created an absolute boundary between feminist and clinical expertise. The new model—the trauma model—forges an alliance between feminist and medical frameworks. Trauma is successful because it is better adapted to the institutional pressures of the therapeutic state in which domestic violence organizations are currently embedded, allowing trauma workers to maintain their professional credentials as clinicians. Whether or not diagnosis is official, the circulation of diagnostic categories in these organizations remakes victims into psychological sufferers, rewriting their bodies and behaviors through the powerful scientific discourse of posttraumatic stress.

EXPERTISE AND REDEMPTION

In this way, trauma introduces a new knowledge base and a new politics of the body into domestic violence work. As I was conducting interviews, trauma workers and policy leaders—even those who were critical of trauma frameworks—regularly insisted that the neurological sciences provide the key to understanding domestic violence. Neuroscience *has finally caught up* with what domestic violence advocates have always known: victims cannot help the way they behave. Women's "bad" or confusing behavior has been hardwired by trauma. The feminist claim that victims should never be blamed for their problems has moved inside the brain, achieving credibility at long last. Nearly every program leader I interviewed sent her employees to trainings on the neurobiology of trauma. Rape crisis activists frequently use brain images to teach police officers, judges, and lawyers about why rape victims have unreliable memories or tell nonlinear narratives. In this way, trauma is a legitimizing expert discourse that is purported to reveal the "truth" of victimization, a truth that feminists have always known.

Because trauma has neuroscientific credibility, it is mobilized to explain a bafflingly vast range of behaviors. Indeed, victims' whole lives are available for expert interpretation via trauma. Debra, the clinical director of a shelter, explained that while domestic violence victims usually want help with concrete needs such as housing, you can tell that, "they just have a lot [of] trauma." This rendering of trauma as a thing that women "have," the amount of which is *quantifiable* and which overrides their other needs and rationales, is pervasive. Women's trauma can manifest in any number of behaviors, including becoming aggressive or angry, ignoring children and staff, feeling lethargic and not participating in group activities, refusing to apply for food stamps or medical cards, overeating or using drugs and alcohol, and being "non-compliant" with shelter rules. All of women's complex reactions to domestic violence are pulled under the rubric of trauma. Further, women's responses to the often coercive institutional environment of domestic violence agencies are explained away as "traumatic responses." As policy leaders told me over and over again, shelter workers are less judgmental when they understand trauma, since it gives them an empathetic language for explaining victims' "bad" behavior.

Debra went on to tell me that they teach about the brain in their support groups: "That's on Tuesday nights . . . our life skills group. So, [the therapist] will bring the diagrams of the brain and explain literally . . . okay, that's because someone is responding with their, whatever the part is called." Debra's nontechnical implementation of neuroscientific

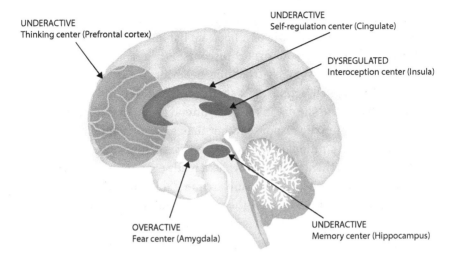

Figure 11. Illustrated diagram of the brain, regions identified. Shutterstock.

knowledge is common and points to the hybrid nature of trauma in the domestic violence agency, to the ways in which scientific knowledge can be applied in a loose, semi-expert way. Another agency I visited offers a weekly informational series about the neuroscience of trauma in which diagrams like the one in figure 11 are used to illustrate the effects of trauma inside the body. In both cases, women are asked to reflect on their behaviors through an image of the brain and its impaired regions.

Despite this scientific construction of trauma, trauma workers' explanations of trauma focus almost entirely on women's *behavior*. According to Cassi, "One of the reasons why there's so much drama in [the shelter] is because of the trauma they experienced. Anyone who's experienced any type of trauma in their lives . . . they have a lesser ability to engage. . . . Something has happened to you, and it is affecting you. You are still living as if you are in danger. . . . Your body still remembers what it's like to walk around the house and be on eggshells all the time. . . . We tend to recreate some of that stuff, because that's the only way that we know how to live." Cassi's explanation is full of empathy, as she uses trauma to describe the everyday struggles of living in a shelter. But trauma is an expert discourse, so it also assumes a great deal of knowledge that clients themselves are expected *not* to have. In her description of the body remembering, Cassi quotes directly from the title of a book by Babette Rothschild, a trauma clinician and author. As an expert discourse, then, trauma explains the source and logic of women's troubling behavior, regardless of women's own reasons for their actions. If a shelter resident tells a trauma worker to go to hell because she doesn't want to attend group that week, we are to read this as a traumatic response rather than as an actual invitation to go to hell, or rather, a rational critique of coercive shelter rules.

Professionally, then, trauma provides a ready explanation for "problem" clients. Debra continued, "Some staff are more tolerant about being yelled at than others, but that's because they understand more about trauma. . . . We do not expect people to behave like angels. . . . If somebody is not listening, are they trying to ignore me, or are they disassociating? . . . They're actually not trying to be difficult, but their emotions and their thinking [are] impaired." Trauma offers a language for explaining a woman's behavior as something that is happening *to* her, something inside her body, beyond her cognition. For trauma workers who are burned out, who have low pay and meager training about gender and victimization, sympathy for victims is a problem that trauma attempts to solve. Of course, domestic violence victims' own agency and decision-making capacities are also evacuated through this trauma-as-actor framework.

Angela explained further, "If you look at the neuroscience of this, someone whose frontal lobe is impaired, cannot be making the very best decision-making." Women don't intend to act badly—they can't help it, because their brains are off balance. And as Joan told me, "I don't care what name you put on it. What I care about is that we understand that this is something that people have experienced, that has decimated their ability to function well and to be safe and that we need to help them recover from that impact." Here, domestic violence victims become *reservoirs of trauma*, hollowed from the inside out by their traumatic experiences. While I was conducting these interviews, I often imagined Trauma as a puppeteer pulling women's strings. The trauma-as-actor model relocates action and capacity in trauma itself. When the victim's brain is hardwired to respond this way, when victims' emotions are linked to an involuntary bodily reaction, their actions become legible and redeemable. The victim's behaviors are *happening to her*. She becomes comprehensible to us but only once her own agency is replaced with trauma. Despite this hollowing out of women's agency, biologized discourses of trauma also suggest that women need to *do something*, such as participate in therapy, in order to overcome their trauma. Workers attempt to redeem domestic violence victims' ostensible failings through the capacious lens of trauma, setting them up for therapeutic absolution as "survivors."

As an expert mode of interpretation, then, trauma produces survivors. Joanne, a trauma therapist, taught one of her clients a deep breathing exercise to use while applying for social security benefits: "[Deep breathing is] something she could use *to not be a victim of her circumstance.* And that's when I realized the power of yoga.... People need tools.... [They] don't want to sit and talk about their experience." Here, trauma ostensibly "empowers" women by pushing them past their victim status, making them into survivors. *Victim* is a bad word, since trauma therapy provides the resources for becoming an active participant in one's wellness: a survivor. Trauma offers a new kind professional legitimacy, while it also offers a new discourse of redemption for victims by blaming their "bad" behaviors on their brains and bodies.

INVESTING IN THE BODY

Even when official diagnosis is not on offer, then, trauma is an incredibly powerful analytic. Trauma opens up such an expansive space of expertise that the victim seems to disappear behind it: *all* of victims' behaviors and bodily actions become available for reinterpretation. Trauma workers use trauma language to invest in, comment on, analyze, and intervene on the victim's body, her past, and her future. This dissection of the victim via trauma, in the context of evidence-based program requirements and quantified assessments, results in therapeutic interventions that target the body for regulation. As Tess, an art therapist, explained, "Maybe certain parts of their body ... don't want to *feel* ... because there is trauma residing there physically." Trauma is embodied, she insists—trauma is not "verbal." As a therapist trained in sensory techniques, Tess finds this understanding of trauma to be liberating for clients, since they don't just have to "tell stories." Rather, they can "focus on their breathing" and do "body scans" to "reconnect to their self." Indeed, therapeutic options have expanded with somatic theories of trauma. Speech is not the only mode of intervention. But the downside is that domestic violence victims now have risky bodies, bodies capable of reproducing traumatic injury at any moment, bodies that must be regulated at an ever-deeper level.

As many therapists explained to me, the body "stores" trauma. Somatic trauma theories are founded in the work of Bessel van der Kolk and others, who locate trauma reactions in the "flight-or-fight" response of the para-sympathetic nervous system.[36] When someone is exposed to trauma, her flight-or-fight instinct becomes overactive and "off balance." Joanne, a therapist, explained: "The heartbeat speeds up and the bronchi dilate.... This is preparing you to defend yourself. And this, evolutionarily, was sup-posed to be a temporary system.... What happens with trauma is that this normal cycle gets disrupted ... and people tend to spike outside of what they can tolerate. This is the classic borderline presentation. Zero to sixty in a heartbeat.... People are stuck on 'on.'... Their bodies are tight, their muscles are tight, they're not breathing very well because the abs are tight." This somatic framework, used widely in domestic violence work, empha-sizes bodily dysregulation ("muscles are tight," "not breathing well") and frenetic emotions. These theories of trauma do not call for pharmaceutical intervention—though they can—but rather, for interventions premised on "mindfulness" and "grounding" techniques, such as yoga, deep breathing, and art therapy, as well as variations of CBT and "self-care." Therapists describe the body as an access point to bring women "down to ground level." Interpreting women as trauma survivors therefore encourages body-centered interventions aimed at "regulation" as a form of recovery.

Through these frameworks, women's bodies are constructed as *jumpy* or *on-edge* or *anxious*. For example, while on a tour of a domestic vio-lence agency, the director pointed out a poster labeled "Emotional Energy Centers of the Body," a diagram of the torso with circles around the chest, head, stomach, and groin—"chakra" regions (figure 12). These kinds of diagrams highlight the role of the body and brain in victimization, asking women to reflect on their emotions through bodily sensations—feelings in their chest, tightness in their stomach.

Grounding their approaches in these embodied theories of emo-tion, domestic violence agencies increasingly combine talk therapy with

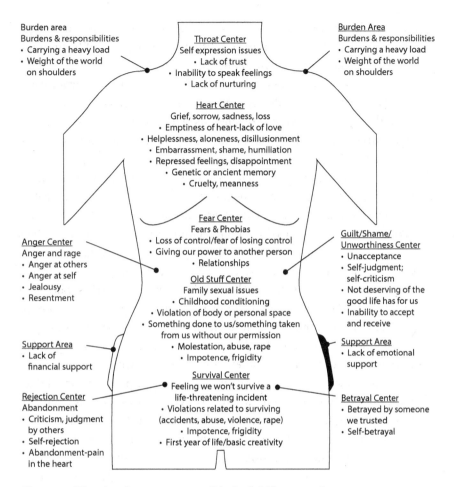

Figure 12. "Emotional energy centers of the body." Shutterstock.

mindfulness exercises, deep breathing, and gentle yoga, all to encourage "self-regulation." Lucy explained, "A lot of my clients like to use a ritual together at the beginning and end of each session.... We do deep breathing together.... I count out loud for them: one, two, three, and holding for one, and then exhaling one, two, three, four." Trauma workers discussed deep breathing as an essential practice of support groups and individual therapy. Some trauma workers also use yoga techniques such as seated stretching. Lucy and other trauma workers seek what they call "regulation" in women's bodies through such exercises, aimed at changing the patterns of the body's internal systems. These kinds of techniques posit trauma as both immanent in and disruptive to the body.

Domestic violence agencies of all kinds are quickly incorporating somatic practices—especially yoga, dance, reiki, and EMDR. Body-based trauma, therapists explained, teaches us what "talking" cannot. Most trauma workers agree that women may need talk therapy and medication, but that domestic violence agencies should provide a softer intervention. As I've shown, trauma is successful in the domestic violence field because it makes women's "bad" behavior professionally comprehensible *and* it allows trauma workers to use diagnostic language without diagnosing. While trauma therapies do not offer a uniform set of techniques, they do suggest that "healthy" modes of embodiment are calm, "regulated," and predictable. As Lynne Haney argues, *feminized* therapeutic models are usually aimed at teaching women "healthy" ways to relate to their bodies.[37]

Lucy believes that targeting the body through therapy educates clients about "human behavior and the way the brain works." Or as Amanda put it, therapeutic interventions should teach clients how to "understand their own experience." Reteaching women how to interact with their own bodies is an explicit goal of these approaches. Amanda and Lucy insisted that body techniques come in handy when a woman has to sit across from her ex in court, bringing her anxiety level "from an eight to a six." Becoming a survivor, then, is in part about mastering a controlled type of embodiment that can maintain equilibrium in the cruel, anxiety-producing institutional contexts in which women find themselves as they try to put their lives together after abuse. Trauma workers want to help victims develop mastery over their bodily reactions so that they can perform survivorhood convincingly in punitive settings. This is what focusing on "triggers," "reactions," and somatic "release" can bring: a newly regulated body that is able to manage the difficult labor of survivorhood. In this way, domestic violence agencies are key sites where women learn about the embodied performances they'll need to execute in order to become good survivors.

While body-based trauma approaches lead to the individualization of suffering and to pathologizing victims' bodies, I also found that these approaches sometimes allow workers to retain feminist goals, since these paradigms are loose and nontechnical. As Nora explained, sometimes a client's "treatment goal" is just to be able to have dinner with her family. Such a goal does not register on the rubric of trauma treatment and checklists, but Nora prioritizes it anyway. "How do we break that down into steps that we're monitoring? What does it take to eat dinner together?" Here, Nora *articulates* the clinical approach of step-by-step goalsetting to the feminist framework of self-determination, manipulating a clinical protocol in order to meet her client's goal. While domestic violence organizations are saturated in the therapeutic gaze, workers also use trauma in clever ways to put feminist goals in clinical guise. After all, many trauma workers (like Nora) have feminist commitments. Their interpretations of clinical demands, therefore, sometimes subvert those very demands.

Because domestic violence agencies are sites of a new kind of trauma expertise in formation, there is leeway for this kind of subversion. Still, Nora is an exception in the landscape of domestic violence care. Even when clinical interventions are "soft," they typically create new investments in the survivor body. Victims are understood to be dysregulated at a deep, cellular level, in need of therapeutic interventions that target the body. The body continually reenacts trauma, making regulation very labor intensive. Trauma workers face pressure to execute these interventions so that they can say they are using "evidence-based" protocols. Trauma creates new expert investments in the temporal trajectory of recovery, and therefore also in a normative "survivor body."

SELF-CARE

A key part of cultivating a survivor body is developing "self-care" strategies to manage the stresses of domestic violence, which are ongoing and full of slow bureaucratic harms. Trauma workers are also encouraged to adopt self-care strategies as part of their jobs. Survivors and trauma workers are asked to employ these techniques to reduce their anxiety in stressful institutional environments that are unlikely to provide them long-term material stability. Trauma workers, then, must also learn how to embody trauma, *how to become legible* to ideologies of psychic injury and recovery. ICADV issued this advice to service providers: "It is normal that helpers experience Vicarious Trauma. . . . You should establish a 'self-care plan' that will help you remain healthy. . . . The best type of role models for children exposed to domestic violence are those who are healthy themselves."[38] Just as trauma discourses redeem the victim from her bad behavior, "self-care" does some absolution work for the domestic violence field: it is the trauma worker's individual responsibility to stay "healthy" and break the cycle of trauma between the helper and the client.

Cassi's domestic violence agency exhibits many of the contradictions embedded in discourses of self-care. A familiar ritual took place when I visited her organization in the Chicago suburbs. I pulled up in my car to an agreed-upon intersection, called the agency, and they verified my identity before giving me the address and entry instructions. Cassi, one of the directors, greeted me warmly at the front door, offering to give me a tour of the shelter before our interview. The building is large and beige, sort of like a house—but it feels more like an institution than a home. When I walked inside, there was a waiting area with curfews posted (10 p.m. every night) and mandatory group meeting times listed in bright, bold lettering. The intake room had an enormous television with live footage from security cameras all around the building, giving the space an eerie feeling of surveillance. Cassi showed me the support group rooms, which felt homey—packed with shabby floral couches and rocking chairs. She walked me through the upstairs resident rooms, where a handful of women were sitting around eating breakfast and chatting while their kids played ping pong. We walked through the TV room, where a gigantic couch had recently been donated by a professional sports team. Cassi joked that the couch was uncomfortable, so we both flopped into it and laughed, struggling to get back up off the oversized cushions.

Like many domestic violence organizations, Cassi's agency feels like an institution, complete with curfews and security cameras, but it also has a touch of "home"—overstuffed couches, food smells, and diaper bags strewn about. Women who come to the shelter don't want to be there. Shelters are horribly stressful: food and bedtime rules are infantilizing, communal living is disorderly, required meetings feel coercive and inconvenient, and women are usually in the midst of significant familial and financial upheaval by the time they arrive, feeling depleted and angry. Domestic violence shelters are a last resort. For the women staying there, every other option has fallen through and they have become homeless. Cassi is in the difficult position of trying to offer women safety and healing—while also requiring them to attend groups they may not want to attend, to work on goals and service plans, to look for work and childcare and housing, and to keep their locations hidden from friends and family.

The women staying at Cassi's shelter have to work toward meeting their material needs during their stay, but they are also expected to participate in "trauma-informed" support groups where they learn about emotional self-reflexivity. Trauma workers like Cassi try to make this kind of therapeutic work feel "survivor centered"—part of which involves teaching women how to engage in "self-care." Shelter residents live under the gaze of security cameras and endure scheduled mealtimes, but they are also asked to pay attention to their own needs and desires, their autonomy and self-worth. Trauma work is indeed paradoxical.

"Self-care" is one of the most popular ways that trauma paradigms have become part of the daily routine of the domestic violence agency. I heard the language of self-care over and over again when I was doing fieldwork. I use the language of self-care myself when I answer hotline calls. Usually, in the context of *feminized* spaces like domestic violence agencies, "self-care" means something like deep breathing, yoga, meditation exercises, mindfulness activities, and other gendered body projects like pedicures, baths, and massage. While some agencies have "self-care support groups," others schedule "self-care days," and almost all agencies ask clients to write some version of a "self-care plan." In Cassi's agency, self-care is sometimes used to encourage relaxation techniques like deep breathing during support groups. Other times, self-care is offered as a "spa day" complete with manicures. Alexis, a trauma worker at a different agency, uses stones labeled "Body," "Mind," and "Spirit" that each woman picks up at the beginning of group sessions to describe how she's taking care of each piece of herself. A focus on the body as a site of self-care is explicit, as Alexis and other trauma workers ask women to develop plans for keeping their bodies regulated and their minds "relaxed."

Self-care strategies are usually nontechnical—meaning, they don't involve clinical expertise—and trauma workers try to provide women with techniques they can use while in court or while dealing with child services. Self-care strategies are supposed to help women manage the labor of survivorhood. Alexandra shows her clients apps on their smartphones that they can use for guided meditation and nature sounds. Natalie asks her clients to write down a favorite song that they can hum to themselves when they get "triggered" and their "brains aren't thinking." Because discourses of trauma construct survivor's bodies as inching out of control at all times, self-care techniques focus on "calming" the nervous system and redirecting physiological responses. In this way, trauma interprets women's bodies and behavior as out-of-control—but also as recoverable via simple strategies targeting common bodily responses to stress.

As they teach these techniques to their clients, trauma workers are also expected to care for their own bodies and brains. Program directors frequently talked to me about research on "secondary" or "vicarious" trauma. Kim explained: "If you are in this work and you are not taking care of yourself, and you're not positioning yourself and your staff to respond in a healthy way to the crises that you see every day, you cannot respond appropriately." Kim suggested incorporating practices like tai chi into staff meetings. Other program directors described using deep breathing techniques during staff check-ins or creating "self-care rooms," where staff can recline on a yoga mat for thirty minutes during the workday. Domestic violence victims are asked to "take care of themselves" so as not to be revictimized, but workers too, are responsibilized for their trauma. If staff are given yoga mats and meditation time, are organizations then absolved of responsibility for labor issues such as low pay, meager vacation time, inadequate supervision, and worker burn-out? In this context, "burn-out" becomes a problem of the heroic but overworked employee, rather than a structural problem that the anti-violence field must redress on a larger scale.

Through self-care, workers and survivors alike are asked to develop what Foucault calls "technologies of the self," preparing themselves for emotionally draining labor in stressful conditions with limited material supports.[39] According to Foucault, technologies of the self are ways in which we "transform" ourselves in order to attain "happiness, purity, wisdom, [and] perfection."[40] "Technologies of the self" make us responsible for "acquiring certain attitudes" and bodily comportments so that we can optimize ourselves.[41] As such, we appear as "free subjects" who can work on ourselves to "live a good life."[42] In the words of Italian philosopher Giorgio Agamben, technologies of the self "bind [the individual] to his own identity and consciousness and, at the same time, to some external power."[43] Technologies of the self, importantly, obscure the workings of such an external power, making it appear as if we are all "free to choose."[44] Therapeutic programs are especially dense sites for technologies of the self. Self-care *appears* liberatory, teaching us how to make time for our own needs. Self-care makes it seem like survivors could improve their lives with just painted nails and avocado face masks. But "self-care" is an individualized interpretation of feminist self-help and empowerment philosophies: it asks women to take responsibility for what their communities—and the state—fail to provide.

This is not to say that trauma workers shouldn't teach clients strategies aimed at regulation and calming. Sometimes "self-care" techniques are the only thing that workers can really offer, especially when the bus cards have all been used up that month and there are no more apartments available in the transitional housing program. Trauma workers do not have the resources to provide long-term, intensive therapy, *nor* can they typically provide robust material supports like permanent housing or good jobs. "Self-care" asks women to take care of themselves in a context of depleted resources. As Melinda Cooper argues, self-care transforms what should be the responsibility of the welfare state into the responsibility of the private self.[45] Self-care strategies also encourage a sense of feminine indulgence, pampering, and middle-class norms of healthy embodiment. In this sense, one of the ways that agencies like Cassi's resolve the tension between their coercive institutional realities and the empowering home space they seek to provide is by asking clients and workers alike to *absorb the work of survival into their own bodies and minds*, rather than demanding that such a burden be met by institutions.[46]

PRODUCING SURVIVORS

As state service provision is transformed through the trauma revolution, our basic understandings of victimization and recovery also transform. Because trauma relies on neurobiological theories of the body and brain, suffering is made somatic and permanent. In the context of the therapeutic state and its privatization of suffering, trauma helps translate the complex, structural needs of domestic violence victims into needs that are "administerable."[47] Trauma makes suffering quantifiable and documentable. Workers execute complex types of labor in order to cultivate a new style of expertise that can satisfy the demands of medicalized service systems *and* the historically feminist philosophies of domestic violence agencies.

Trauma is useful in the domestic violence agency because it responds to the requirements of quantification and professionalization, bringing forth women's psychologies and bodies for expert evaluation, allowing workers to explain women's behavior via signs and symptoms. Domestic violence victims' behaviors are reinterpreted as trauma reactions rooted in neural pathways and bodily dysregulation. A penetrating therapeutic gaze is introduced into this historically feminist space, resulting in several transformations: (1) trauma workers manipulate the boundary of diagnosis to manage their professional liminality; (2) the victim body is imagined as internally dysfunctional; (3) "soft" forms of clinical intervention and "self-care" strategies seek to transform the victim body into a survivor body. Those same strategies also target the worker's body, making trauma into a technology of wellness that obscures stressful working conditions.

Trauma is imagined to be liberating in the context of the domestic violence agency because it is not explicitly coercive, does not demand absolute conformity—plus it can sometimes speak the language of structural harm.[48] But trauma also recasts all of victims' behaviors and modes of embodiment as attempts to *survive trauma*. It recasts workers' frustrations with long hours, low pay, and inadequate support as "vicarious trauma" that can be resolved with individualized techniques. Trauma explains everything a woman says and does—even the way she moves and breathes—within one, expansive framework. In this way, trauma tethers the category "survivor" to individualized, biologized epistemologies and interventions.

The result of these transformations is *not* an omniscient clinical gaze that fully reconstitutes workers, clients, and organizations. Rather, feminist logics of care, empowerment, and self-determination continue to find expression through trauma frameworks. Trauma workers use feminist philosophies of care to soften clinical approaches, to push back against diagnosis, and sometimes to take up subversive professional positions. Thus, "trauma" takes a unique form in domestic violence agencies, even though "trauma-informed" approaches are spilling out across the therapeutic state.

Trauma is reconfiguring the way dependency is imagined, the way social services are conceptualized and delivered—but the meanings and consequences of these shifts depend on the institutional context and social movement history upon which they unfold. Feminism in the domestic violence agency has not disappeared—*it has been remade into the expert work of processing and producing survivors.* Importing trauma into the domestic violence agency therefore reconstructs domestic violence victims as a new class of somatic and psychological sufferers. And as a group, they need "intervention." In fact, trauma institutionalizes therapy as the solution to women's problems—even though therapeutic programs *actually* rely on victims' ability to narrate and perform good survivorhood, a set of labor-intensive practices I take up in the next chapter.

PART II Surviving

Surveying

4 Becoming Legible

"I bounce back quick. Because I have to." This is how Brenda, a thirty-four-year-old Black woman, explained the effects of domestic violence on her life, the pressure to show that she is turning her life around and moving forward. Like many of the women I interviewed, Brenda has no time to waste because she is caught up in the confusing bureaucratic tangle that accompanies victimization. Speaking quickly but calmly during our interview, Brenda jumped between stories about therapy appointments, child services meetings, and court hearings—as if to demonstrate, rhetorically, how much work it takes to juggle the seemingly endless demands of these institutions. First things first, Brenda wants to put her abuser in prison. Surprisingly, the state's attorney agrees and has pursued felony domestic violence charges against Brenda's abuser. On the witness stand, Brenda must prove that she is a domestic violence *victim*, recounting in horrific detail the time he held her captive for days in a family member's bedroom and gave her broken ribs and black eyes, forcing her to perform fellatio on him while she went in and out of consciousness. Brenda narrates these events in order to present evidence that she has been the victim of a violent crime. In court, Brenda emphasizes her fear and subordination, sitting across the room from her abuser, participating in a legal ritual that many victims say is as traumatizing as the violence itself. Brenda's job in court is to make herself into an unquestionable "victim."

Second, Brenda wants to get her children back from state custody. On another day of the week, Brenda must attend group and individual counseling sessions during which she works on becoming a *survivor*. Her Department of Children and Family Services (DCFS) caseworker checks Brenda's pill bottles to ensure she is taking her medication, evaluates Brenda's counseling attendance, and reviews reports from Brenda's therapist. Brenda must further demonstrate her commitment to therapeutic progress by holding down a steady job and securing a lease on a satisfactory apartment. Though Brenda herself has never been the aggressor, she must show that she is on a "better path" so that the state will return custody of her children. Performing survivorhood—active psychological improvement—is Brenda's task in these institutional settings. Demonstrating respectable motherhood is key to this performance of survivorhood.

Understandably, Brenda feels frustrated by these institutional requirements. She told me, "It's like every time I finish something, they'll come with something new. . . . I just finished all the [parenting] classes and everything, and now they want me to do family therapy. But my kids' counselors said they're not ready for family therapy." Despite her hard work and compliance, Brenda struggles to make sense of the various expert demands on her life. She described the violence itself as merely a rehearsal for the hardships of these institutional tasks. Still, Brenda told me, like she tells her counselors, that this experience has made her stronger, that she will get her children back and put the violence behind her. Nonetheless, Brenda struggles to "bounce back" while working two low-wage jobs, navigating a shared and precarious housing situation, all the while commuting to multiple counseling sessions each week. Brenda, like many women who have experienced domestic violence, is working hard to become legible as a survivor amid punitive, confusing institutional pressures and crippling material deprivations.

This chapter exposes how women are expected to perform survivorhood, or psychological betterment, in order to receive much-needed resources. Paradoxically, going through the institutional rituals of "healing" often obstructs genuine healing. That's because the labor of survivorhood is replete with contradictions. First, as Brenda's story shows, the demands of survivorhood are wielded inside or alongside punitive systems like child services: confusingly, women face pressure to demonstrate psychological independence and "resilience" while undergoing forced involvement in systems that undermine their autonomy. Second, while becoming "survivors," women face institutional pressure to convince authorities that they are also legal "victims." State bureaucracies require that women demonstrate legal victimization, but it turns out that women are *actually* granted resources contingently based on performances of survivorhood, or therapeutic wellness. Women must therefore figure out how to execute seemingly incommensurate performances of victimhood and survivorhood simultaneously. Finally, survivorhood is contradictory such that women are supposed to "recover" even though the material conditions of their lives often worsen after leaving their abusers.

These contradictory realities highlight the processual nature of domestic violence: the experience of abuse is rarely "wrapped up" by leaving a violent relationship. Rather, abuse is characterized by ongoing struggles with institutions, experts, abusers, and identities. The contradictions of survivorhood outlined above shape women's efforts to make rights claims based on their experiences of violence, often drawing them into a labor-intensive relationship with the state, its privatized services, and its expert knowledges. The women I interviewed learned how to perform "good" survivorhood—through racialized and classed performances of respectable motherhood, for example—in order to make themselves legible to institutions. In so doing, many also refashioned their identities and made long-term rearrangements to their intimate lives.

HIDDEN GEOGRAPHIES OF GOVERNANCE

Sociologists have long studied how people learn to fit themselves into the complicated bureaucratic systems of the state, using categories—such as "victim"—over which they have little control. Women who have experienced domestic violence come into contact with various branches of what we may broadly call the "welfare state" when they seek resources during and after abuse. These interactions with the state shape their performances of deservingness, sense of self, embodiment, and intimate attachments. As such, the study of governance—or how the state regulates and manages people's conduct—is key to understanding the terms through which women become legible as survivors.[1] As a site of citizenship, the welfare state coerces marginal subjects into "redeeming" themselves in order to receive aid, often through forced involvement in therapeutic programs. For example, Lynne Haney shows how carceral programs transform poor women into "healthy" citizens by reorienting their desires toward motherhood and middle-class lifestyle norms.[2] Studies of governance shed light on the institutional scaffolding that coerces marginalized subjects into normative performances of self and family.

However, governance scholars have focused almost exclusively on mandatory systems. Beginning with survivors' stories reveals that, in fact, women—especially poor women—are subject to governance across an array of quasi-mandatory systems that regularly fall outside of sociological attention. Domestic violence services are not "mandatory" in the way of carceral programs. Nonetheless, domestic violence survivors make little distinction between services that are mandatory and those that are "suggested." Both kinds of programs *feel* mandatory. It is my goal to expand our understanding of governance to include this quasi-mandatory state infrastructure, which operates as a kind of underground disciplinary apparatus. This apparatus, in the case of domestic violence, is organized by trauma discourses and a gendered demand for psychological improvement— a temporal trajectory from "victim" to "survivor." I borrow Hester Parr's phrase, "hidden social geographies" to identify these semi-mandatory spaces of governance and identity formation.[3]

While scholars and policy makers often imagine that the state governs primarily through carceral institutions (like prisons) and public aid offices (welfare checks and food stamps), there is actually a vast complex of private, nonprofit organizations that provides publicly funded services to marginalized populations.[4] This "shadow state" is in fact what welfare *is* in the United States.[5] Community organizations such as senior centers, youth development programs, employment services, childcare—and domestic violence services—administer a significant amount of state-funded aid.[6] More than 20 percent of federal social provision dollars are spent on these kinds of organizations.[7] Yet they operate in a way that is "obscured and distant" to the public eye.[8] These organizations "represent the welfare state to its citizens" without *seeming* to be part of the state at all.[9] Further, nonprofit organizations like domestic violence agencies have played an increasingly central role in American life since the 1970s. From 1974 to 1996, when neoliberal policies stripped down welfare provision, federal funding to nonprofit organizations increased from $23 billion to $175 billion.[10] The number of nonprofit providers increased by 125 percent between 1977 and 1997.[11] The growth of the anti-violence field has more or less followed these trends, making it an important sector of "the delegated state."[12]

These privatized services have also become more therapeutic over time—what Nina Eliasoph calls a "recovery industry."[13] Rather than providing material assistance, the "shadow state" administers aid based on the coercive therapeutic premise that "socially marginal groups practice appropriate behaviors" by learning how to "empower" themselves.[14] "Once motivated by material concerns and issues of economic equality, [service organizations] now focus on culture, environment, morality, lifestyle issues."[15] Therapeutic governance operates under the radar, *normalizing* social actors by convincing them it is their job to better themselves.

Class and race are foundational to this style of governance. While middle- and upper-class people can *purchase* therapeutic privacy and choice, the poor are presumed to require psychological intervention when they seek assistance.[16] They are encouraged to work toward "wholesale personal and family reconstruction."[17] This is a deeply intimate kind of governance: racialized and classed understandings of appropriate sexuality, gender, and parenthood are embedded in programs, such that compliance means meeting state-defined standards of private life.[18] The therapeutic state is also feminized, since women are the primary beneficiaries of such services.[19] Social needs are interpreted as problems of the pathological mother, who must help her family *redeem* itself from structural disadvantages.[20]

Further, the growth of the therapeutic state is related to the expansion of professional psychology. These kinds of programs are usually staffed by counselors and therapists instead of bureaucrats or activists.[21] Sociologist Teresa Gowan describes how health professionals have taken hold of the "homelessness industry" such that clients now learn to explain their experiences of housing insecurity through "sick talk."[22] Many such institutions espouse a mix of therapeutic and punitive discourses. This mix has advanced most rapidly through institutions like drug courts, where coerced "treatment" is the norm.[23] While "the therapeutic" emerged as a modality of state punishment in the 1990s, hybrid therapeutic-penal systems are increasingly common and include anti-violence programs such as domestic violence courts.[24]

Further, what Haney calls "institutional intersectionality" increasingly defines people's experiences of interacting with the state, such that they have to become clients of multiple systems at the same time.[25] Incarceration, welfare provision, health care, and child services constitute overlapping "satellite states."[26] Rather than shrinking the state, decentralization actually expands governance into new spaces.[27] Women are subject to special kinds of familial discipline at the intersection of these systems, often premised on the idea that they need to redeem themselves from their "dependency" on the state or on "bad" men.[28]

Because of their distinct history as feminist organizations, domestic violence services have historically retained a certain level of autonomy from these systems. But this is hardly the case today, especially in urban centers like Chicago. Domestic violence counseling is increasingly "prescribed" by judges and social workers as a kind of "cure" for domestic violence. Domestic violence victims are more likely than ever to find themselves in domestic violence support groups as part of DCFS requirements or a judge's "suggested" interventions. All of this happens while domestic violence organizations pitch their services as "optional." Domestic violence services therefore make up part of the *hidden social geography* of the state, which operates beneath mandatory systems but is nonetheless an important site of citizenship.[29] Surviving domestic violence requires that women develop new material and symbolic attachments to the state by attending therapeutic programs.

For example, the domestic violence court in Chicago is a one-stop-shop for legal issues related to intimate violence. Victims go to 555 West Harrison Street (figure 13) to file orders of protection, to attend criminal proceedings, and to meet with legal advocates. Since 1999, the court has also housed a trauma clinic for children on its top floor. While in court, victims' children can be evaluated by a licensed therapist. As Rekha Mirchandani

Figure 13. Cook County Domestic Violence Courthouse, Chicago, Illinois. Photo by Ayla Karamustafa.

observes, domestic violence courts are a curious mix of technocratic court logics and feminist values.[30] Today, this means that discourses of trauma and survivorhood are omnipresent. Though women are interpellated into court as legal victims, the expectation that they attend professional counseling is pervasive. Therapeutic professionals and their expert languages inundate the building. *This* is the geography of traumatic citizenship.[31]

Domestic violence agencies and their clinical employees therefore play an important role in the "juridical-administrative-therapeutic" apparatus of the state, rearticulating women's marginality and suffering in the language of trauma.[32] For example, domestic violence organizations pay the salaries of the legal advocates who work on the ground floor of the courthouse. Judges, lawyers, and social workers regularly "recommend" that women go to domestic violence organizations for counseling, even if this is not an official stipulation of women's cases. Women are often told by family lawyers that it will help their case if they see a therapist, to show that they are in "recovery" from abuse. Women seeking US residency documents through domestic violence laws face pressure to demonstrate psychological improvement, and their progress is conveyed in a letter to immigration authorities. But the most ardent promotor of a therapeutic "cure" for domestic violence is DCFS. Many domestic violence victims are involved in DCFS because the home is deemed unsafe when male violence is discovered, or because they are charged with some version of "failure to protect" when their children witness abuse.[33] Therapy, especially offered by domestic violence agencies, is a central feature of the institutional sites that women traverse after abuse.

For example, a U-VISA, if granted, can give an undocumented domestic violence victim up to four years of legal residency and an opportunity to petition for a green card. The visa application requires that women help police and prosecutors pursue legal action against the abuser, effectively making victims into accessories of the carceral state. The application also requires a personal narrative, police reports, and evidence of injury from medical experts. At first glance, this seems like a straightforward "victimization" document. Women have to prove that they're legal victims. However, I came to learn that women must also demonstrate *survivorhood* through this paperwork. The U-VISA requires a letter, typically from a clinical therapist, that the victim has experienced significant suffering but is on the path to recovery. Therapists told me that they use the language of "trauma" over and over again in the letter, granting psychiatric authority to women's suffering. Typically, victims are asked to attend domestic violence counseling for at least three months so that they can receive such a letter. Survivorhood is then demonstrated through the clinician's testimony of the victim's "good" character, which may include evidence of attending domestic violence support groups, English language classes, even children's report cards from school. As Roberta Villalón reveals in her ethnography of the domestic violence visa process, workers help victims selectively based on who they think can effectively navigate these systems: the promise of citizenship is therefore doled out contingently based on sexual, maternal, and class-based norms of victimization and recovery.[34] The state may grant some necessities like employment authorization to undocumented victims, but only "on the basis of their traumatic past," which must be effectively communicated in visa paperwork.[35] In this way, women seeking U-VISAs must mobilize whatever cultural capital they have to demonstrate that they are legal victims *while also* attending counseling to show that they are "becoming" survivors. Survivorhood is an implicit but powerful requirement of this system.

So, while domestic violence services are imagined to be optional, most of the women I interviewed encountered them as part of this quasi-mandatory state apparatus. In fact, the majority of the women I interviewed were involved in multiple types of therapy at the same time. Many were in the support group because it was a stipulation of their efforts to gain legal residency, and even more became involved in a support group because it was "suggested" they do so as part of an ongoing family court case. The women I interviewed often learned critical skills from trauma workers and support group members about how to pitch themselves as "good survivors" in punitive systems. Domestic violence workers act as brokers of legibility for victims—brokers of the cultural capital that comes with identifying as a "survivor"—teaching them how to use expert language like "trauma" as they navigate adjacent institutions.[36] While survivorhood is rooted in the "experiential capital" that comes from surviving violence, "experience" does not magically transform into capital.[37] Rather, experiences of violence must be made legible to experts: *pitched* through narratives and embodied performances. Survivorhood is an institutional performance through which domestic violence victims integrate (or reintegrate) themselves into the state, as well as into more diffuse forms of social and political belonging. By participating in domestic violence programs, women earn cultural capital as "survivors," an identity that matters for access to resources but that is taken up and embodied in ambivalent ways.

LEGIBILITY AS PROCESS

Legibility as a worthy victim and a good survivor is not automatic. As the U-VISA shows, paperwork is needed. Consistency of a therapeutic narrative is required. Organizational skills, time off work, and money to pay lawyers are all necessary. Simone provided a visual of this type of labor when she described the months after she left her abuser: "I think those eight

months I walked around, I had the same briefcase and it had all my medical files in there, it had every police report in there, it had my order of protection in there, and I'd walk around with this briefcase like this [*clutches
bag to chest*]. And I would literally walk around . . . holding it tight to my
chest." Simone carried with her the documentation that would translate
her confusing experiences with her ex-husband into something legally and
therapeutically recognizable. Her domestic violence story would never be
just a set of words, arrived at haphazardly; it was a bulky briefcase with
complicated, bureaucratic paperwork, nearly fused to her body, compiled
into one story only through Simone's labor of making herself available to
various expert systems and practicing their rituals of legibility.

For Simone, legibility was not a moment of recognition, but an ongoing
and labor-intensive process. However, sociologists often understand legibility to be achieved through a straightforward moment of interpellation,
when subjects are "seen" by the state. State categories are presumed to
recruit citizens into them: "The process of recruitment necessarily rests
on the effective mobilization of subject positions—that is, identities and
discourses made available to actors. When these subject positions reso-
nate, emotionally as well as cognitively, they enlist people in certain social
categories."[38] Interpellation accounts for how social actors are called
forth into categories. However, interpellation is a rather blunt analytic
tool, often imagined as a preordained *fit* between subject and structure.
Interpellation—especially in Althusser's terms—is *given* by structure.[39]
The position already exists, and the subject is called forth.

But in reality, the process of interpellation is just that—a process. It
must be practiced and embodied. As sociologist Anna Korteweg explains,
interpellations have to be *strategized*—interpreted and transposed into
different contexts.[40] Critique and resistance may arise therein.[41] Subjects,
especially those who do not fit the right way into given categories, may
turn away from the interpellating call, sidestep the work of fitting themselves into harmful categories, or critique a given identity framework.[42]
Identification is always a site of struggle rather than a mechanistic "calling
forth."[43] Women who have to fit themselves into state categories, in fact,
constantly evaluate and reinterpret the messages given to them.[44] For the
women I interviewed, the process of becoming legible as good survivors
and worthy victims involved webs of systems and experts that sometimes

recognized them but also regularly failed to recognize them, making a "moment" of fit impossible to identify.

Women who experience domestic violence are not interpellated as survivors in a consistent and straightforward way; rather, they *work to make themselves legible* to the politics of survivorhood. Women perform survivorhood in response to institutional pressures that are often messy and ill-defined. Authorities may only have a vague idea of what kind of performance is "good" in a given context. Survivorhood, as a category of state legibility, is produced at the *interface* of women's needs, practices, and institutional performances—and the categories to which they must attach themselves. Interpellation as a survivor is also replete with feelings of disjuncture and dissatisfaction because subjectivity is itself a site of struggle.[45]

For example, Tina, a thirty-five-year-old Black woman, talked to me extensively about her struggle with the "victim" label: "I just don't want to be the victim. . . . I always want it to be like I've got it together, I'm handling this. . . . Because most people know me as being loud, boisterous, very independent, speaking my mind, things like that. And for them to know that I was in a domestic [violence] relationship . . . to me it shows a sign of weakness." For Tina, the cost of assuming a victim identity in order to access anti-violence services is incredibly high. It means labeling herself as "weak," although she has been supporting her children on her own for years, enduring ongoing stalking and harassment from her ex, and working a full-time job while attending nursing school. "Victim" imperils her hard-fought identity as someone who *endures*, someone who can "handle it."

But for Tina, the victim label *also* imperils her careful performance of survivorhood. Performing as a survivor is in part about demonstrating organizational skills and control over the paperwork and bureaucratic processes associated with legal victimization. Tina's abuser continues to harass her at home, forcing her to call the police regularly. When the police come to the house, Tina has to select the correct legal file from the pile of paperwork, arranged by year, and present it calmly to the officers. She must prove her victimization (order of protection document) while simultaneously performing a survivor self (organized folders, calm demeanor). Tina is invested in a survivor identity and told me several times throughout our interview that she sees herself as "independent." Because she is involved in a child custody battle with her abuser, this survivor identity helps give Tina legibility in court, making her the got-it-together parent. Tina uses the language of victimization to tell her domestic violence story and to interact with the police, emphasizing injury, while she also represents herself as a capable, "recovered," and economically stable parent. One of the central ways she executes this latter task is by attending two kinds of therapy and making sure her daughters see a therapist weekly.

Tina told me she was tired so many times during the interview that I lost count: tired of thinking about the court case every day, tired of keeping the legal documents organized, of having to take time off work to show up in court. Tired of her own story. "I'm still dealing with it, and it's been almost six years. And I'm still dealing with it. I just feel like my life is ruined. Like, I messed up so bad. . . . I blame me. I know it's really not my fault, but . . . I don't know. I just feel like quitting at times and giving up." The hardships of institutional legibility, combined with ongoing fear of her ex, force Tina to fight for a legal status that she does not even want to claim. For Tina, legibility is not a moment of recognition, not a straightforward process of being "seen," but a years-long endeavor that involves state categories, confusing webs of therapeutic and legal programs, and an ambivalent struggle for identity.

TELLING DOMESTIC VIOLENCE STORIES

In order to become legible as survivors, women typically have to excavate the domestic violence story from their larger life stories and package it in a therapeutic narrative. To complicate things, most of the women I interviewed speak from a social situation of unreality in which their abusers and various institutions have countered their claims of suffering and violence and have marked them as criminals, "sluts," bad mothers, and liars. Survivors of domestic violence must seek recognition precisely through their stories of failed recognitions; they must seek social intelligibility through experiences of deliberate social invisibility. Domestic violence stories are not simply available but must be *worked for*.

Adriana is a twenty-two-year-old Latina woman who has survived two violent relationships. Adriana carefully pieced her domestic violence story together through years of counseling, and she used that story of abuse to get her order of protection, to get a divorce granted, and to submit her US residency documents. When I asked her if it was difficult to talk about the abuse when she started counseling, she told me no, because she had already been "prepped." Having been through a therapeutic program in high school, Adriana knew the drill: "When you go to counseling, you get into this routine of focused conversation. Only talking about the things that you're really supposed to be talking about. Don't talk about your best friend's boyfriend who did this to your best friend." For Adriana, as for other women I interviewed, talking about their experiences and emotions in this "focused" way, eschewing non-relevant details, is part of learning how to become a survivor of domestic violence.

In addition to learning how to "do" therapy, Adriana had to prove, beyond any doubt, that she was a victim. When she went to civil court, the judge asked her: "What happened? Tell me what happened on this date, and then tell me what happened on this date." Adriana knew how to talk about domestic violence in this way because her counselor had already asked her to write out each violent incident with a date next to it, coaching her into formulating a victim narrative for court. Adriana learned to deploy a carefully constructed account of legal victimization, complete with police reports, while also performing a "survivor" self for the judge. This survivor self is someone who has her story pieced together and can demonstrate that she attends therapy regularly. Adriana's legibility in court—as victim, good citizen, good mother—depends on executing both legitimate victimization *and* calm, cool, collected survivor.

The women I interviewed also described learning how to talk about their experiences in an emotionally "respectable" way. When I asked Fabiola how she felt when she started going to counseling, she told me, "I'm learning [how to have] that conversation. I was feeling like, I need the help. . . . It was not easy to talk, but I did it." For Fabiola, counseling was about learning how to have a specific type of conversation, one in which she learns how to string a narrative together. After she learned about domestic violence, Fabiola told me she ran around telling everyone about the abuse, even strangers. She was so excited to have a name for what she lived through that she could not stop talking about it. Over time, she learned that this was not a good idea, and in her words, she became more "in control of her emotions."

Women also have to learn how to translate their narratives across institutional sites. Gwyn got so tired of retelling her story that she typed it up, made copies, and handed them out to the judge and lawyers each time she got called back to court. "Between the second and third public defender [I was assigned], I wrote myself a statement. . . . I actually have a really good memory but, you know, by the fourth or fifth person you talk to, your brain starts to go all in a muddle. Just read the piece of paper." Gwyn carries these documents around with her in a fanny pack, enclosed in a hard, plastic case alongside a copy of her order of protection. Gwyn's strategy speaks to the fatigue that women experience when they have to pitch their stories to authorities for evaluation over and over again. But, for Gwyn, the narrative itself is also strategic: in her typed story, she emphasizes the frequency and duration of her therapy attendance, making sure the judge knows that she takes her son to regular appointments. Attending therapy distinguishes Gwyn from her ex-husband, who—to her dismay—has never attended therapy. Gwyn uses therapy attendance as legitimacy: she proves her victimization by carefully explicating each violent event on paper, and then she pivots the narrative toward her family's therapeutic progress.

Becoming a survivor, then, is in part about creating and communicating a (respectable) narrative of victimization and recovery. This often requires using expert, medicalized language. Rosalyn, for example, reminded me several times throughout our interview that "her body remembers" the trauma of domestic violence. "I believe that that last time my daughter's father picked me up and threw me on the ground, I heard a crack. When I got up, it didn't feel like anything was broken, but you know how adrenaline is. I've had low back pain ever since. Then I got an MRI a couple years ago . . . and they said I have four bulging disks. . . . So, then I wondered. Now I have a lot of knee pain. I'm only thirty-four. . . . I think . . . the body [does] remember." *The Body Remembers* is the title of a popular book about trauma by psychologist Babette Rothschild, a book that Rosalyn's domestic violence counselor uses during support group to teach clients about trauma.[46] For Rosalyn, telling a recovery narrative involves using the expert language of trauma theory. She picks up this phrase in order to explain that she cannot just "get over" domestic violence: the harms of abuse and institutional entanglements stick with her, get inside her. Recovering from trauma, for Rosalyn, is an ongoing project of body and soul.

Medicalized language of therapeutic recovery plays an important role in the way women navigate institutions. But this language also matters for how women relate to their own experiences, becoming a valuable discourse of self-making. Betsy is a sixty-eight-year-old woman who recently left her husband of forty years because of emotional and financial abuse. Leaving her husband has resulted in financial upheaval for Betsy, and she is on her own for the first time since she was a very young woman, living in a studio apartment that she recently had to evacuate due to a bedbug infestation. For Betsy, realizing that what she experienced could be called "domestic violence" has been revelatory, and she referred to domestic violence throughout our interview as her "diagnosis." Before we even sat down for our interview, Betsy explained that domestic violence is a recent "diagnosis" and she is still figuring out how to talk about it. She told me she didn't know where to begin the story. Should she talk about the good years early in the marriage? Her adult children's reactions to the divorce? Throughout the interview, Betsy asked me if I agreed with her "diagnosis" of domestic violence. She has to do a lot of reflective work to make this diagnosis stick to her past experiences, and she seeks ongoing validation from those she perceives as experts along the way. Betsy is managing her diagnosis by attending support groups and seeking out "self-care" exercises such as acupuncture and massage.

The kind of expert, medicalized language that Betsy uses to describe her experiences is especially valuable for educated women from middle-class backgrounds who have the resources to pick it up and use it effectively—such as Gwyn and Betsy. The language of therapy makes sense to them and they are able to wield it effectively in settings like courts. After all, the therapeutic self is a middle-class self, unencumbered by material deprivations that would impede "recovery." In this sense, the "survivor" is a classed figure who can engage convincingly in medicalized explanations and wellness practices. Rosalyn even told me that learning how to make "green smoothies" and "choosing peanuts over chips" has been a key part of transforming her life after abuse. In other words, middle-class norms of health and embodiment are part of Rosalyn's training in survivorhood.

For women who do not have class or educational privilege, survivorhood often feels desperately out of reach, though the same norms of therapeutic recovery are imposed. With a narrative of survivorhood comes pressure to transform psychologically, whether or not the conditions at hand offer any means of transformation. Maria L. describes this push to overcome the past via a domestic violence story:

> I always cried and said, "This isn't life. Why was I born?". . . My head would hurt [and I'd say], "Why did this happen?" But when I told them [at the domestic violence agency], I cried and the counselor said, "Don't cry. It's over. It's done with. All you had to do was tell us everything because so many things have happened [to you]. It's difficult. But that's done [now]." But every time that I remember all that, I feel anger. My head hurts and I start to ask, "Why did this happen to me?" So it's like I'm living it, like it was yesterday or a week ago that this all happened. I can't forget all that has happened to me.

Maria L.'s domestic violence counselor encourages her to focus on the future, to leave the past in the story. Maria L. wants to accomplish this but cannot quite execute it. She is plagued by "why" questions about her abuse. Her head still hurts, making it impossible to perform psychological transformation. Maria L.'s domestic violence narrative is lacking something. She's left feeling that she is failing in a trajectory of recovery. And that's because, for Maria L., the part of her story that plagues her most deeply involves leaving her three small children behind in South America to accompany her abuser to the United States. Nonetheless, the language available to Maria L. to make sense of her experiences requires that she pretend the violence is behind her, though she remains separated from her children years later, even after a failed $20,000 border-crossing attempt.

The domestic violence is *supposed* to be the worst part, and leaving that behind is *supposed* to be transformative. For Maria L., however, the violence of migration and borders exacerbates and exceeds the boundaries of interpersonal violence. She expresses a sense of frustration and failure—bouts of headaches—in part because her narrative of psychological recovery from *domestic* violence cannot capture her other experiences of violence and marginality, which are structured powerfully by the immigration system. While Maria's narrative of domestic violence offers her institutional legibility and state resources—hopefully a U-VISA—her immigration story can offer no such aid on its own. Maria L., then, is forced to make these multiple tragedies hang together via a story about overcoming domestic violence, a story that fails to capture the multiple economies of violence that shape her life. Maria must learn to prioritize her husband's violence toward her because *that* is the story that brings institutional currency, allowing her to submit an application for US residency under domestic violence laws.

For Maria L., extracting the domestic violence portion of her story means denying the violent impact of the border on her life, and she faces pressure to tell a therapeutic narrative that does not match her struggles. Her experiences of "legal violence" via immigration policies and detention centers are intense and ongoing.[47] Her domestic violence story therefore fails to offer her any sense of triumphant survivorhood. For many women, the pressure to tell a therapeutic narrative with a beginning and a promising end—and their disappointment that they cannot tell it properly—causes them to blame themselves for abuse.

TELLING SELF-ESTEEM STORIES

While learning to tell a domestic violence narrative is the first step in performing survivorhood, women also learn to use the language of self-esteem to make themselves convincingly "recoverable." Trauma workers told me that state officials and other authorities love to hear that victims have improved their self-esteem. For this reason, domestic violence workers sometimes coach women into using that language on forms and evaluations. "Self-esteem" helps grant women legibility as suffering *but* recoverable.

"Self-esteem" also makes survivorhood even more paradoxical, such that women are encouraged to acknowledge that the abuser was the one acting badly, and yet *they* still need to do self-work—the implication being that perhaps something was just a little wrong with them too. This therapeutic labor is feminized: the discourse of low self-esteem marks women as inward-turning victims of pathological femininity.[48] While men are constructed as hedonistic and immature in therapeutic programs, women are wrought as sufferers of "dependency" who need to focus on emotional autonomy.[49] As Jessica Wyse has found, women's work to "rehabilitate" themselves must be focused on restraining their affect, establishing "boundaries," and avoiding emotional "triggers" such as new romantic relationships.[50]

Women who have experienced domestic violence frequently do self-esteem exercises as part of support groups. Counselors assign exercises aimed at building self-esteem, encouraging women to practice "self-care" and emotional reflexivity. Luz, a fifty-four-year-old Latina woman, describes one such exercise:

> They gave us a mirror . . . [to] look at ourselves and maybe write how we feel today or how was our week. We had to take the mirror and . . . decorate it. And then they go, "Okay it's your turn to look in the mirror." . . . And when I turned, I'm like, oh my god, you know, how many years had passed and I did not look in the mirror? At that point, I found out I never looked in the mirror. . . . Like fifteen years, something like that, I never looked at myself. Then . . . I looked at myself and I saw me. I saw the pain. . . . I saw how I stopped taking care of myself. [*pause*] I saw my eyes. I saw inside me.

Luz's counselor used a literal reflection exercise to prompt women to turn their analysis inward. The women in the group were encouraged to "take care" of themselves once again—the assumption being that they had neglected this task. For Luz, this exercise was valuable. She learned how to think about her needs and desires after years of what she describes—in clinical language—as "masking" and "numbing." Luz's "self-esteem" emerged as something that was hiding inside all the time.

However, because many women encounter support groups involuntarily, they also learn to use the language of self-esteem strategically to appease institutions that demand recovery narratives. Margaret, a fifty-one-year-old white woman, sarcastically explained her motivations for attending support group: "To help my self-esteem, because apparently I have low self-esteem. I have a lot of confidence, but apparently not good self-esteem." Through her support group, Margaret has learned that her self-esteem is the problem. Though she does not *feel* she has low self-esteem, she knows she must tell a narrative indicating that this is indeed the case.

Margaret also feels compelled to separate her anger at her husband from her anger at the systems that have intervened in her life. After a minor physical incident with her husband, Margaret called the police and they came to the house. They told her that if she did not get an order of protection against her husband, they would call DCFS. She kicked her husband out, went to the courthouse in the morning, and was granted an order of protection. However, when she checked her phone after leaving the courthouse, she already had messages from a DCFS caseworker. The police had called already, despite their promises to give her twenty-four hours.

Margaret has not spoken with her husband since the incident and is performing her DCFS tasks with painstaking dedication. The first task that Margaret has been asked to perform is to attend a domestic violence support group. In the group, she feels that while the focus is on abusive men, the real enemies in *her* story are the police officers who lied to her and the DCFS system itself. Margaret told me, "I'm just so pissed at the whole system. I guess I'm not really mad yet, mad at my husband. I'm more mad at myself. Still kind of dumbfounded, wishing, feeling stupid, because you'd think at my age, I should've ... done something different so we wouldn't be at this point." Though DCFS has labeled her situation one of domestic violence, Margaret feels that her husband's problems have mostly to do with his heroin addiction, and that he has never been particularly abusive.

This is one of the contradictions of survivorhood at work: Margaret is transforming her life to become a "survivor" according to DCFS demands, using the language of domestic violence even though other injustices are more pressing, and the primary terms she is given to explain the situation are those of "self-esteem." Rather than empowering her, the language of self-esteem leaves Margaret feeling "stupid" and responsible for the violence. Further, the stakes of Margaret's legibility as a domestic violence survivor are high. Once her DCFS caseworker determines that therapeutic progress has been made, Margaret's "reward" for legibility will be granted: she will be able to continue parenting her child without state surveillance.

This process of transformation is especially fraught for Margaret because she feels guilty about her supposed lack of psychological progress, a common refrain throughout interviews. For example, Simone told me, "Because I've been in therapy for so long ... I feel like I should be over some of this stuff by now. But I'm just learning how to navigate my new life." After years of abuse, Simone kicked her abuser out of the home they lived in with their two children. As a result of this decision, Simone faced financial devastation, while her husband maintained his high-paying job and family money, promptly buying a new house nearby. Simone navigated food stamps and other public assistance for the first time, undergoing a dramatic financial destabilization as now the sole wage earner in her house. While the "new life" after leaving an abuser is supposed to be better—psychologically transformative—it is often actually characterized by financial destitution, loss of social networks, lengthy court battles, and new stressors associated with living alone and being a single mom. Domestic violence is processual and leaving is rarely a circumscribed "event" that marks an easier chapter. Unfortunately, the primary language for navigating this "new life" is one of healing and recovery, sidelining acknowledgment of structural obstacles. Simone feels she is failing because the systemic obstacles in her way are made invisible under the umbrella of psychological language that permeates her life.

The stakes of "self-esteem" are steepest for women who are highly system-involved. Alma is a forty-year-old woman who immigrated to the United States with her abuser when she was twenty-seven, pregnant with their first of four children. He was first violent when they had only been dating a couple of months. After beating her, he kept her locked in the house for several days until her injuries healed, fearing she would go to the police. The abuse continued for nearly ten years after they came to the United States. Alma's husband would not allow her to have a cell phone, to learn English, or to seek residency documents. "He would hit me. I had to take it because otherwise he would send me back . . . take me to Immigration." When she bought cell phones secretly, he found them and held them underwater until they stopped working. He frequently threatened to call ICE on her, and he raped her when he found packed suitcases hidden around the house. When she called her parents on the phone, he listened in from the other receiver. To escape, Alma asked her children to tell their teachers at school what was going on, even though she feared doing so would lead to her deportation. DCFS became involved and Alma lost custody of her children for two years.

DCFS demanded that Alma see an individual therapist *and* attend a domestic violence support group. Alma's therapist told her she was "trapped in a ball" of depression and low self-esteem. During the relationship, her self-esteem was "on the floor." Alma described pain in her back from years of hunching over and refusing eye contact with men. Alma told me that now she can hold her head up, that she's getting to know who she is, something she never had a chance to think about before. Alma believes that because of her depression, she *let herself* be abused. It was not just that he "dominated" her, she told me, but that she "let him" do so. In fact,

DCFS therapeutic requirements require that Alma take up this position: in order to show that she has transformed her life and can parent on her own, Alma must show psychological improvement. She must, as Maria L. put it, become "cured" of the abuse.

Alma told me her story as she made sense of it through therapy and support groups: a past, depressed self who let herself be abused by a man who had complete control over her. Her story is what Joseph Davis identifies as a typical survivor narrative, wherein the therapist works to "authorize and structure the client's rejection of old self-understandings and the appropriation of new ones."[51] This is the paradigm of subjectivity through which Alma is expected to "govern herself."[52] Despite this more or less scripted *psychological* narrative, the *infrastructural* changes that Alma made to her life in order to survive were enormous: she got a second job, secured her own apartment, hired a private lawyer, took parenting classes, learned how to use a bank, took English classes, and established a new network of friends who don't know her abuser. Yet Alma locates her transformative work in overcoming an internalized state of "depression." The contradictions of survivorhood are evident yet again: Alma survived abuse by rebuilding her material life, but the symbolic tools offered to her to make sense of the abuse are those of self-esteem, minimizing her structure-building labor. Further, Alma's guilt about her past self is saturated with feelings of failed motherhood, amplified by DCFS's insistence that she take parenting classes and attend therapy in order to resume caring for her children. For Alma, telling a domestic violence story means locating the causes of abuse in symptoms, sidelining the structural labor she executed to escape and reunite her family.

Often, the language of self-esteem works to obscure the real sources of harm in women's lives. For Ebony, learning that what she experienced could be called "domestic violence" made her look back on her former self as "not right." Ebony told me, "I wasn't eating. I was too depressed and unhappy in my relationship; that's why I wasn't eating. . . . It's like, I couldn't enjoy my food. . . . I put on this façade or whatever like I was happy, but really deep down, I was torn up inside and depressed. I wasn't right." Ebony was physically trapped by her abuser, who would not allow her to work, own a car, have friends, or keep her own money. She stayed at home with her children and relied on neighbors for rides to the grocery store and money to buy diapers. Ebony's entrapment was compounded by the fact that she could not return to her mother's home: the housing projects where she grew up had been torn down, her community scattered. Abandoned by social safety nets, Ebony attempted to escape her relationship by having her boyfriend arrested after he pushed her out a third-story window. The police refused to accompany him to the apartment while he collected his things after release. While in the apartment, with the police waiting downstairs, Ebony's boyfriend slammed her head into a nail on the wall, leaving her with a gash on her forehead that required twenty-seven stitches. Ebony explained the pain of this experience through the language of depression: it was she who "wasn't right." Ebony herself becomes the locus of pathology, rather than the systems that failed to protect her.

In this way, producing a domestic violence story—a therapeutic narrative—is also a process of self-responsibilization. Survivorhood conceals a paradox with which victims of domestic violence must wrestle: it is acknowledged that domestic violence is not your fault, but you must work on yourself nonetheless. Mariposa explains these pressures: "I don't have any reason to be sad. I don't know why sometimes I am. I feel ashamed. I say, oh come on! How come you are sad if you are in a good place, in a good country, your kids are doing what they want to do?" Mariposa is supposed to have overcome, to be happy—a *survivor*—even though her new life is lonely and disappointing. Though she learned how to tell a narrative of survivorhood, Mariposa worries it is not genuine. She blames herself for its failure. In this way, the language of self-esteem often leads women to feel "stuck" because they have not made a temporal transition to triumphant survivorhood. Self-esteem discourses may help women navigate institutions, but those same discourses also tend to amplify feelings of guilt and to obscure women's structural labor. Indeed, women are encouraged to believe that their own lack of psychological gumption—rather than their structural vulnerabilities—is to blame for domestic violence in the first place.

ILLEGIBILITY, PART 1

Many women's stories are filled with feelings of confusion, frustrating holes in memories, or a sense of being pushed outside the bounds of wellness and recovery. Women experience these forms of dissonance because survivor and victim identities are difficult to achieve, contradictory, and often unwanted. Many of the women I interviewed felt devastated by what they perceived as their lack of psychological progress, even though the material conditions of their lives stayed the same or worsened after leaving their abusers. This disjuncture between the promises/demands of therapeutic progress and their material realities often makes women illegible as good survivors: they literally cannot *afford* to become survivors.

Diamond had only recently become involved in domestic violence services when I met her. She often referred to herself as depressed, as having anxiety disorder, and as suffering from PTSD. Like Gwyn and Betsy, Diamond has a college degree and uses medicalized language with seeming ease, punctuating her narrative of abuse with clinical descriptions like "flashbacks" and "fight or flight." However, at one point during our interview, Diamond became frustrated with herself for not being able to give me a chronological narrative of the abuse. "I was very, very, very depressed. I don't even remember a lot of my life. I feel like there's snapshots." For Diamond, these snapshot memories are impediments to improving her life. Lacking a clear victimization story feels like a personal failing. Diamond believes that therapy, by now, should have transformed her into someone who can produce clear, sharp stories—a survivor.

"It's a year later and still I sometimes literally feel like he's next to me. Sometimes I have bad dreams that he's trying to kill me. They say it's PTSD. . . . It feels very, very real. I know that it's because my body and my mind [are] trying to process that whole trauma." Diamond told me that she sees herself more as a victim than a survivor because she still has these symptoms. She does not think she has "overcome" the abuse—even though she left her abuser, refused his financial support, has a full-time job, a new apartment, and is raising two small children on her own. Diamond is struggling financially in these new circumstances and keeps a strenuous schedule packed with work, commuting, day care pickups, and therapy appointments.

Diamond believes that once she can tell a better narrative, she will exhibit signs of recovery and recognize herself as a true survivor. But when will survivorhood be achievable for Diamond, who does not have the financial resources to bracket work and housing struggles in order to focus on "recovery"? Diamond's financial situation has worsened since leaving her abuser, making it difficult for her to "overcome," mired as she is in new material hardships. Her childcare network has also weakened since leaving her abuser—who provided some childcare—and since breaking off contact with her mother, who took her abuser's side when Diamond left him. The pressures of psychological transformation feel especially overwhelming because Diamond's material circumstances cannot actually support a psychological transformation. Still, she remains hopeful: "I'm in the acceptance stage. Okay, these two guys abused me. Alright. I'm healing. It hurts sometimes, but I'm going to get through it."

The last time I saw Diamond, she had arrived late to the domestic violence agency for her therapy appointment and was upset with me—in my role as a volunteer—for following agency rules and canceling the session. She frequently missed appointments due to her work and childcare schedules. The structural obstacles in Diamond's life impeded her from engaging in formal practices of survivorhood. That day, Diamond, understandably frustrated, stormed out of the agency and drove away. Last I heard, Diamond had dropped out of services and lost touch with her counselors. Diamond was a popular client, and everyone at the agency was concerned about her. I can't help but think that the pressures of a victim-to-survivor transformation forced Diamond to leave the program, since she kept falling through the cracks of institutions and attributing those failings to herself rather than to the structure of care. The dissonance that Diamond experienced between her lived reality and the survivor narrative she so desired was perhaps more than she could bear.

PERFORMING RECOVERY

Survivorhood is not just about *individual* interpellation, but interpellation as a mother and a sexual subject, as a bearer of the family's health and well-being. As part of their therapeutic projects, women who have experienced domestic violence must produce narratives about their families of origin and their children, their partners, and their sexual histories. Making oneself legible as a domestic violence survivor across institutions is feminized labor: becoming a head of household, managing children's distress and therapeutic interventions, reflecting on one's own family of origin for signs of the "cycle of violence," seizing one's health as a project of the self. Women who have experienced domestic violence must become "independent" and "empowered," especially in relation to motherhood. Traumatic citizenship requires normative and respectable performances of family life.

For example, women typically take their children to therapy as part of their efforts to demonstrate good survivorhood. "Recovery" is often performed *through* motherhood, an identity that is itself jeopardized by the processual nature of domestic violence. Women are expected to take their children to therapeutic appointments in order to ensure that they will not repeat the "cycle of violence," becoming perpetrators or victims themselves. Women face pressure to cultivate an "intensive mothering" style rooted in professional therapeutic interventions, watching their children for signs of trauma and demonstrating to institutional authorities that they are mitigating psychological risk to their children.[53] Tina, for example, insists that her daughters see therapists at the domestic violence agency *and* at school, not only because she worries about their mental health, but also so that she can show she is a committed parent in court. Many of the women I interviewed came to domestic violence counseling because they were told that their children needed therapy. Margaret, for example, was required by DCFS to attend domestic violence counseling *alongside* her daughter. Other women were encouraged by mental health providers to take their children to therapy due to the traumatic risks of being a "child witness" to domestic violence. This therapeutic labor is not just executed *on behalf of* children, but on the terrain of the mother-child relationship.[54] As Fabiola told me, it is her job to "close the cycle of violence" by ensuring she has not passed "bad lessons" on to her daughter.

Further, the experience of domestic violence amplifies maternal surveillance, especially through family court and DCFS. For many women, the stakes of performing therapeutic mothering are very high because they are already assumed—because of race and immigrant status, for example—to be incompetent mothers. As Alisa Bierria and Colby Lenz describe, some women are marked by race, class, and nationality as "hyper-culpable mothers" in domestic violence situations.[55] Aware of their hyper-culpability, survivors use therapeutic services to "make up for" their stigmatized statuses. Even for women not experiencing DCFS or court surveillance, therapeutic motherhood matters: women actively fear these systems and feel they must guard against potential state intrusion in their lives. DCFS is a nearly constant, haunting presence for poor women and women of color, even if they have never interacted with a child services caseworker.[56] Women learn to preempt these potential intrusions by "doing all the right things"—which, for them, includes putting their kids in therapy.

For example, Fabiola is a thirty-four-year-old Latina woman whom I met through her domestic violence support group in Chicago. Fabiola met her daughter's father when she was twenty-five while he was on vacation in her hometown in Mexico, where they had a "beautiful romance." He convinced her to move to the United States and promised to make her a legal resident through marriage. However, as soon as Fabiola picked up her life and moved, the relationship began to sour. Her boyfriend became mean and possessive. He told her that he "didn't like fat girls" and pressured her to lose weight after she gave birth to their child. He revealed that he did not intend to marry her and threatened to abandon her without papers, without a home, without a job, and now with two children. His threats to call ICE were constant. He began calling her "bitch" and "prostitute," humiliating her in public by calling out to men on the street and asking if they wanted to have sex with her. He had expensive affairs and lied about it. Fabiola's isolation, combined with her emotional attachment to her partner, meant that she stayed with him for years: "[It gets to the point where] you think it's normal to have someone to hit you, to scream at you or to call you names. When your boyfriend . . . is calling you names and you love him, you cannot say nothing to your family because you love him." One night, he strangled Fabiola and threatened to kill her. This time she left, and in retaliation, he began to aggressively seek full custody of their daughter.

Fabiola was eventually awarded primary custody and generous child support, and she attributes her success in the court system to her counselors at the domestic violence agency. She explained the importance of going to counseling: "You can fall again. It's like when you're drinking and you quit, you start over again. . . . You can let another person hit you, to treat you bad." Fabiola feels that her support group kept her psychological reactions in check—keeping her "sober." She told me, "If you don't go to these groups . . . when you get a new boyfriend, you can repeat the process." She explained that the support groups helped her become a "healthy girl." The centrality of substance abuse language in domestic violence agencies—imported via trauma frameworks—is evident in Fabiola's description. The idea that domestic violence is a "chronic condition" that requires therapeutic management is widespread and mimics the logic of addiction treatment programs.

Fabiola talked to me a great deal about her process of "healing," about the deep breathing techniques she learned in the support group. She told me that these techniques keep her body "calmed down" so that she does not have to take pills for anxiety, which she insists would make her look "crazy" to the courts. Fabiola explained that she learned how to be a "survivor" in the support group—someone who smiles and addresses healing actively, refusing to be one of those women, she said derisively, who is "still a victim." During one of our interviews, Fabiola walked me around her apartment to show me the positive artwork and affirming phrases she tapes to the walls (figure 14). Her mirrors remind her to smile, her refrigerator reminds her to embrace life, and her cupboards remind her that her family is beautiful.

Embodying psychological recovery, "empowerment," and happiness are important to Fabiola, and I learned over the course of our interviews that failing to perform survivorhood convincingly carries considerable risks for her. She explained:

> Sometimes you forget about cleaning the house or doing your bed or doing the things that have to be in order. . . . [The court] can tell you a social worker is going to come. So you need to take care of yourself. Think clear. 'Cause sometimes we [domestic violence victims] are crying. [Then they say], you can't handle how to take care of your kids because you're crying and I think you need to go to see the doctor and need to take pills, maybe. These things make you afraid. . . . Don't answer questions that they don't ask. Don't talk too much because whatever you say, they're going to write everything. Clean the house. . . . Then make sure you don't have anything bad in the refrigerator.

Fabiola learned to make herself into a survivor as she moved through the family court system. Her domestic violence counselor helped her navigate these requirements, telling her what the social workers would

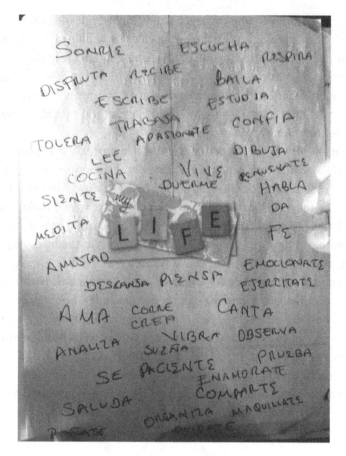

Figure 14. Fabiola's artwork. Photo by author.

expect from her, giving her tips on how to pitch her story to the lawyer and the judge so that they would see her as a devoted mother, "recovered" from domestic violence as if it were a disease. Fabiola learned to avoid medication, to control her emotions and bodily reactions, and to communicate "wellness" by tidying up her house and displaying affirmational phrases. The stakes of Fabiola's performance are especially high because her status as a proper mother is already imperiled by her ethnic and immigrant status.

Fabiola's experiences reveal the risks associated with a failed performance of survivorhood. After all, Fabiola has to survive in systems biased against her. To compensate, she emphasizes her "wellness." It became clear to me, as Fabiola showed off her art projects, that she had created them to impress the social workers who used to visit her home. But by the time I met Fabiola, it had been more than a year since there was any real threat of such a visit. Still, Fabiola had become attached to this survivor self, to a wellness identity. It came to feel very genuine to her. Fabiola now takes up the "survivor" identity actively and creatively. She even started a photography self-portrait project on Facebook focused on "being a survivor."

Still, taking up an identity rooted in expert medicalized frameworks is risky. Consider Fabiola's fear that the judge in her custody case might learn that she needs anxiety medication. Domestic violence victims fear mental health systems and diagnoses because their use of those services is regularly used against them by abusers in court. The women I interviewed navigated a serious double bind related to the mental health system, wherein they are expected to attend *counseling* but are pathologized for seeking mental health *treatment*. Someone like Fabiola is supposed to admit that she is suffering and needs recovery, but *not suffering too much*, not in need of *too much recovery*, lest she lose respectability as a good mother. Striving for legibility as a good survivor via therapeutic systems is full of these kinds of pitfalls.

In general, women feel the pressures of psychological improvement and respectable motherhood simultaneously—indeed, psychological improvement should be performed *through* respectable motherhood—and when these pressures become too much to bear, they blame themselves. The language of trauma, self-esteem, depression, and recovery train women to take on this personal responsibility. Carla, a thirty-year-old Latina woman, told me a story about her milk drying up while nursing: "[People tell me], 'You overcame [domestic violence] by yourself, without help. . . . You alone did it.' I do feel tough. But inside I still felt weak. I still wasn't right. My girl, I didn't even breastfeed her for a month because I dried up. I felt that I was failing even my daughter. . . . I'm not giving her a part of me. I'm leaving her exposed to the world." Though Carla knows she is strong—a survivor—she also knows that this label cannot capture what she is *really* experiencing. Despite identifying as a survivor, she feels that her body is too weak to nurture her child, and she blames herself for being a bad mother. If she is strong, why can her body not provide sustenance?

If she has overcome "on her own," why is she "failing" at motherhood? Critical gaps are exposed here: between discourses of survivorhood and the lived experience of surviving abuse, which involves dealing with ongoing harassment, single motherhood, and financial loss after leaving a dual-income household. Carla feels a disjuncture between the survivor identity and the realities of survival.

For both Fabiola and Carla, motherhood is newly fraught after abuse. Both women blame themselves for not protecting their children from the ugly realities of being a woman in the world. Such feelings of guilt and self-blame are compounded by institutions that surveil and pathologize their motherhood. Even for Carla, who was not enduring institutional surveillance when we met, the pressure to perform recovery via maternal respectability is intense because she fears DCFS and court involvement in her life. After leaving abusive relationships, women often live in fear that their abusers will take them to court for child custody and that clinicians will evaluate their maternal fitness. In many cases, their abusers spent years threatening them with precisely this scenario. For Fabiola, performing psychological wellness by keeping her house clean and her bed made is key to performing respectable motherhood. Carla, on the other hand, exposes the failings of survivorhood to provide her any real help as a mother. She is *supposed* to feel better, but she feels ill-equipped. For the women I interviewed, the pressure to perform survivorhood through maternal respectability often feels devastating, since no amount of psychological "recovery" will allow them to achieve an idealized image of maternal success.

ILLEGIBILITY, PART 2

Despite their hard work, not all women who have experienced domestic violence are able to tell convincing stories, to perform recovery and respectability to authorities, to become legible as good survivors. The stakes of these failures are high. For women who are working hard to become survivors at the nexus of multiple powerful institutions, illegibility may mean that resources are denied or withheld. For example, I accompanied Susan, a thirty-two-year-old Black woman, to the courthouse downtown to get an order of protection after her new boyfriend punched her and threw her into a wall. During the assault, she lost consciousness twice and her boyfriend knocked out three of her teeth. Susan was frantic but determined as we pored over paperwork together on the busy first floor of the domestic violence courthouse.

I naively assumed that the court appearance would go well. I had interviewed Susan several months prior: she was in a counseling group, talked about herself as a "survivor," and had just secured a long-awaited Section 8 housing voucher. As Susan told me during our first interview, "I'm a domestic violence survivor. I feel like that was one of the things that I had to go through to become the woman that I am today." But as we were filling out the paperwork together, I realized things had changed. Susan could barely put the recent assault into words—even though she knew the language of domestic violence well, having spent years in support groups. When we finally got inside the courtroom, Susan spoke to the judge in unintelligible outbursts. It became clear that she was no longer attending her domestic violence support group. She was visibly high and unable to answer the judge's questions about where her children were and when the violent incidents had taken place.

After less than ten minutes, the judge denied Susan's request for an order of protection, stating that Susan hadn't proven that she was in an "emergency" situation. From my perspective, the situation was clearly an emergency, but Susan hadn't been able to communicate this in convincing language on forms or in the courtroom. I later found out that Susan had dropped out of her support group because she was so embarrassed that her new boyfriend had become violent. As a result, Susan had no one to help her *translate her story into a victim narrative* for court before she showed up that day. Further, she could not demonstrate that she was attending domestic violence services to "get help" like a good victim/survivor does. Even though Susan was visibly injured and met the legal requirements of victimization, she could not make herself legible as *worthy* in court. The transformed conditions of her life could not sustain her performance of survivorhood, and she could no longer tell a convincing story of abuse and recovery. As a result, Susan lost access to crucial resources.

Further, Susan had heard that her landlord was making complaints to the city about her boyfriend, jeopardizing her housing voucher. Susan knew that in order to keep her voucher, she would have to reenroll in the housing office's domestic violence program, which would give her extra time and protections based on her victim status. Susan was not sure she would be able to handle this extra bureaucratic hurdle, though. She talked to me instead about moving to the suburbs, leaving Chicago to escape her abuser, abandoning her voucher. She was afraid to be in that apartment anyway, since her boyfriend knew how to sneak in. Before we parted ways, Susan promised me that she would call her counselor from the domestic violence agency to reapply for an order of protection, but I wasn't sure she would or could. Susan described a sense of transformation, but not a sense of recovery. "Once I went through this, I saw people turn their backs on me. I was like the outcast over something that I really didn't do. Or [they] blamed me. That just made me feel like a different person. I feel very different. I really wish I could go back to the girl I was before this. But you never can. And you never will. You never will trust or [have] happiness. . . . Physically, mentally, emotionally. It transforms you."

This is the only transformational narrative left for Susan, who feels abandoned despite years of therapeutic work related to domestic violence. Being abused by a new partner sent her into something of a tailspin, in part because Susan felt it was her fault for getting into "another" abusive relationship. Of course, the material conditions of Susan's life offered her little safety, few resources to avoid being abused again. And her inability to pitch herself as a worthy victim and as an organized survivor meant that she wouldn't get any added safety in the form of a court order. Rather, Susan is left to sort out the pieces from scratch—to go back to counseling and put her story together once more, to reapply for housing, to work toward seeing herself as a successful survivor all over again. In the meantime, Susan's illegibility in court put her at risk of further violence *and* left her feeling empty and defeated: bereft of recognition.

REFUSING SURVIVORHOOD

Violence, especially when perpetrated by a trusted partner, provokes a profound destabilization of meaning. Everyday routines become sites of fear and insecurity, comforting expectations of family and community become unmoored, and sources of love become sites of humiliation. Yet, for the women I interviewed, experiences of domestic violence are also bound up with the "discovery" of their own abuse, with their acquisition of a system of meaning for naming violence. Domestic violence therefore involves both destabilized meanings and acquired meanings; it is about unlearning cultural lessons about sexuality and love and family—and then learning a new symbolic system through institutionalized narratives and performances of survivorhood, performances that require new and different kinds of investments in family and identity. I have focused on how these processes of loss and recognition take shape through a quasi-mandatory welfare state apparatus that combines therapeutic and punitive systems.

Still, the categories of "victim" and "survivor" are replete with blurred boundaries. The bureaucrats who ask for recovery narratives often only have a vague understanding of what they are looking for. Domestic violence workers often help women perform recovery in superficial ways only to appease other institutions. Domestic violence victims and workers alike use the language of "trauma" in loose and nontechnical ways. All of these gray areas sometimes allow women to secure resources even without "good" performances of survivorhood. But the gray areas also create cracks that women fall through. In fact, women's overwhelming experience of survivorhood is one of dissonance—expressed through feelings of frustration and self-blame—because survivorhood misrecognizes structural harms for psychological failings.

Nevertheless, women's attempts to become legible as survivors may also make new things available for telling and feeling, becoming sites of transformative sensemaking and practice. We can see this, for example, in Luz's use of the self-esteem exercise to value herself as a woman. Becoming a "citizen-subject" is, after all, an *active* process that is about belonging to something, a process that is never closed.[57] When a woman names, classifies, and narrates her experiences of abuse, she reaches for something new.[58] Categories of legibility—victim, survivor, trauma, therapy, recovery—may take on new meanings when they become part of everyday life. Technologies of the self "permit individuals to effect by their own means or with the help of others . . . operations on their own bodies and souls."[59] This is engagement, not rote interpellation.[60]

Survivorhood therefore becomes the means through which domestic violence agencies help women *engage* as new kinds of citizens. This language may offer them resources and cultural capital, even as it forces them to conform to new norms. Women who have experienced domestic violence confront those norms differently depending on race, class, sexuality, nationality, and ability: they are unequally positioned in survivor discourse and have unequal resources for engaging with the state.[61] Survivorhood is therefore both "enabling and annihilating."[62] I have focused on the ways in which women's intersecting structural vulnerabilities—race, motherhood, immigrant status—shape the type of labor they have to perform in the institutions surrounding domestic violence.

Still, some women may refuse traumatic citizenship entirely. It is critical to attend to these refusals of legibility, which are also labor intensive. Several of the women I interviewed refused to tell domestic violence stories that would satisfy the demands of institutions. For some women, the labor of survivorhood was not worth the resources on offer. For others, performing survivorhood simply felt exhausting and exclusionary. Some women face less pressure to tell survivor stories because they are not dependent on the institutional configuration outlined in this chapter. Nanette's reasons for resisting a survivor narrative are multiple.

When I met Nanette, she was staying in her daughter's living room, helping to care for her three grandchildren and recovering from a flareup of one of the health problems that punctuate her life. Throughout our interviews, Nanette, who is a fifty-eight-year-old Black woman, confidently evaded my attempts to get her to tell a chronological story about domestic violence. When I asked about her boyfriend's verbal abuse, she talked instead about her mother's death ten years ago. When I asked about what happened after a violent incident with her son's father, she told me a lengthy story about a stint in jail when she was in her thirties, where she watched a woman commit suicide. And throughout our many interviews, Nanette returned again and again to the story of her adult son, recently released from prison only to be shot and killed in front of a currency exchange three months before our first interview.

Though Nanette and I talked extensively about domestic violence, *these* were the events, the deaths, that of course dominated her everyday life. Domestic and sexual violence are integral to each of Nanette's tragic stories: to her son's birth and childhood, to her decision to live with her mother before her death, and to her arrest and the drug use that precipi-tated it. And yet, domestic violence fades into the interstices of the other forms of violence—constitutive of them, but less frequently the source of Nanette's consternation, rage, and sorrow. Nanette has attempted to make sense of the intersecting forms of structural and interpersonal violence in her life through participating in Alcoholics Anonymous (AA) and other substance use programs—both mandated and optional. Through pro-grams such as these, Nanette has learned to reach back into her past and discover her then-self through the lens of addiction.

What AA has *not* allowed her to do is to make sense of the patterns of abusive men who have held her hostage and assaulted her, and the police and mental health systems that have made her feel irrational and invis-ible. This sensemaking and self-making work she has had to do on her own, and only recently through occasional visits to a domestic violence support group. And while Nanette likes the group, she has no concrete need to attend, and she is critical of the messages that the counselors provide. She explained that women really need help *after they leave that room*, where their abusers are "lurking around corners," promising to help with next month's rent and to put food on the table, services that the sup-port group does not provide.

Of course, when Nanette told me her story in what she called "bits and pieces," she was not doing so simply because she forgot the chronology. She was resisting my attempt at the professional mutation of her experi-ences into a trauma narrative, resisting my push to translate her suffering into something bureaucratically legible.[63] When she spoke about intimate violence, she was more likely to do so through the oblique entry point of her health and embodiment. When I visited her the second time, Nanette described her hospitalization the previous weekend for chronic urinary tract infections. In a whisper, Nanette told me that she believes her UTIs are the result of two rapes she experienced as a young woman. The doc-tor told her she needed surgery, and when she resisted, telling him she'd already had too many surgeries, he said, "Then one more shouldn't make a difference." Nanette shook her head as she told me, "They just want to cut. Chop, chop, chop."

For Nanette, the sexual violence inflicted on her body is linked to the dehumanization she experiences in the medical system, as well as to physical sensations of pain in her pelvis, which make it difficult for her to sit. When I asked her how she thinks domestic violence has affected her overall, she told me a story about her uterus dropping out when she was thirty-two, how it actually came out of her body. She believes this happened because she was abused so frequently, that she had been "jumped on" too many times and her body couldn't hold itself in anymore. This is connected, she explained, to her current lack of desire to have sex with men. She feels guarded around men and thinks they all share a "dark, dirty secret."

Despite her refusal to tell a survivor narrative, Nanette explicated abuse through the language of addiction and through stories about her health and body. Nanette's method of storytelling suggests that male violence has targeted and injured precisely her embodied symbols of femininity (her uterus), that those injuries have long-lasting effects on her desire, and that the institutions (medicine) to which she must address these injuries cannot possibly apprehend them. Nanette's refusal of narrative is caught up in her embodiment, expressed in ways she can show me are *real*. Nanette makes meaning not through a story of psychological transformation, but through locating suffering in and on the body itself; not by describing the aftermath of rape, but by telling me about her current sexual abstinence; not by calling herself a survivor, but by lifting up her shirt to show me hysterectomy scars. By refusing a psychological narrative, Nanette also refused to isolate her experiences of domestic violence. Instead, she layered state violence, medical violence, and interpersonal violence on top of each other, stitched them together, and then asked me to look right at where stitches cut into flesh.

In this way, Nanette forced her audience to bear witness to the intersection of symbolic and physical violence, as well as to the ways in which violence is embedded across powerful institutions. Structural and interpersonal violence are, after all, not separate events, but co-constitutive processes.[64] Violence is often indirect and systemic, but it also shows up as real harm in everyday life.[65] For most of the women I interviewed, violence was not a set of criminal incidents, but something more diffuse that permeated multiple spheres of their lives. Sometimes it was a pain felt in the body for years to come.[66]

Nanette did not *need* to tell a story of overcoming because she was not asking for resources. She was not seeking legibility in state programs.

She'd been through the rigmarole in addiction services and had no need to become legible as a domestic violence survivor. But it's not as if that lack of institutional pressure offers Nanette some sort of *freedom*. Even when women face little pressure to comply with survivorhood, their stories are punctuated with silences and erasures. Several times, women waited until the third hour of the interview to tell me in hushed tones they had been raped as teenagers, an experience they knew was part of their "domestic violence story" but which still *felt* separate, unintegrated. Their whispered disclosures speak loudly about silences that extend well beyond the scene of service programs.

Still, I think Nanette's message is clear: domestic violence is not a set of violent incidents, but an ongoing process of navigating coercive men, institutions, experts, and categories. Perhaps the fact that Nanette did not need to become legible as a survivor means that she was better equipped to link these multiple levels of violence together, refusing a linear story of suffering and overcoming. Perhaps. That might be too optimistic. As women's forestalled disclosures indicate, violence is still experienced as a profound kind of silence. Even when women are coached into telling narratives of survivorhood for institutional legibility, their stories are saturated with dissatisfaction and dissonance. With silences. For Nanette and others, the process of establishing personhood and citizenship after intimate violence is full of whispers, full of experiences that *won't fit*. Women's attempts to become legible, and even their refusals of legibility, are haunted by a more inchoate social reality that we must strain to hear.

5 Gaslighting

> Power can be invisible, it can be fantastic, it can be dull and routine. It can be obvious, it can reach you by the baton of the police, it can speak the language of your thoughts and desires. . . . It can cause bodily injury, and it can harm you without seeming ever to touch you.
>
> Avery Gordon (1997)

> When you're in domestic violence, you think it's always like that. But reality is not like that.
>
> Alma, forty years old, Latina

Women who have experienced domestic violence often describe their relationships as altered states of reality. This altered reality is: (1) manufactured by abusers, and (2) reinforced by institutions. First, abusers do and say things to try to make victims seem and feel as if they are losing their minds, as if their perceptions of reality are wrong—*gaslighting* them. Second, institutional authorities regularly deny and minimize women's experiences of abuse. Women who have experienced domestic violence struggle to become legible to institutions because their abusers construct them as irrational *and* because institutional authorities minimize psychological forms of abuse. Abusers' "crazy-making" tactics make the experience of domestic violence illegible to institutions and, often, to women themselves. In order to understand what it takes to become legible after domestic violence, we must forge a deeper, more sociological understanding of what abuse really looks like: gaslighting, I argue, should be considered the core of domestic violence.

Recent quantitative data provide evidence that "crazy-making" strategies are an incredibly common feature of domestic violence. A survey conducted by the National Domestic Violence Hotline in 2014 asked twenty-five hundred adult women hotline callers about their experiences of coercion.[1] In response to the question, "Do you think your partner or ex-partner has ever deliberately done things to make you feel like you are going crazy or losing your mind," 73.8 percent answered positively. And in response to the question, "Has your partner or ex-partner ever threatened to report to authorities that you are 'crazy' to keep you from getting something you want or need," over 50 percent of callers answered "yes." The descriptive results of this survey are staggering: *nearly three-quarters* of this sample experienced gaslighting and over half identified gaslighting as an obstacle to accessing supports. Quantitative evidence therefore suggests that casting women as "crazy" is key to male violence.

Susan gave a striking and devastating description of gaslighting:

> You feel like it's actually witches out here. It will get to the point that you feel like that. Like, did this person hypnotize me or drug me? I had a self being before I got with him. . . . I made more decisions, and I knew myself. When a person abuses you to the point where you don't know yourself no more, that's mental abuse. . . . [It] got to the point that I wanted him to hit me, to get it over with. . . . One time [I] jumped at him [so that] he can hit me and get it over with. . . . 'Cause the worst part was messing with my head. . . . Because . . . all I had was my head. So it's like I made a choice between physical and mental. . . . I could get me a job and have surgery and fix my outer being, but I could never fix my inner being.

Susan's ex-partner spent many years abusing her physically and psychologically. Though he is in prison, she knows that once he is released, he will come for her. Seven years after leaving, he still calls the house from prison to "talk to the kids" and insists on speaking with her instead, indifferent to the court orders that bar him from doing so.

Susan talked about her ex's "crazy-making" tactics mostly in terms of "flipping the script," meaning that he changed stories and events to make it seem like she was the abuser. Psychologist Jennifer Freyd has referred to this strategy as DARVO, or "deny, attack, and reverse victim and offender," a tactic that erodes victim credibility in the face of powerful authorities.[2] Susan's abuser denied that abusive events happened at all, despite her visible injuries. He told the children that she was "crazy," followed Susan when she left the house, monitored her text messages, and called her friends to check up on her. After all that, he would insist that *she* had jealousy problems. Susan's quote above, which references witches and drug-altered realities, suggests the "spectral" nature of gaslighting, in which one's sense of reality becomes haunted by external invasions and inexplicable distortions.[3] Susan told me many times, "Domestic violence comes with a lot of confusion." She came to doubt her sense of reality, to believe his manipulations as he cut her off from loved ones who could have provided her with a different narrative. Susan's abuser insisted that she was a "crazy bitch" who was intent on keeping him to herself, using stereotypes about Black women's aggressive sexuality to fuel his gaslighting campaigns. Susan's words further suggest that gaslighting may increase physical violence, since women in abusive relationships may provoke physical abuse in order to "get [the psychological part] over with."

Susan's sense of lost reality was exacerbated by her abuser's manipulation of police and legal systems to his advantage. She described an incident when she called the police after an assault: "The police talked to me. Then [my ex was] like, [*in a fake concerned voice to Susan*] 'You know I wasn't doing that. You know that. Did you hear me? Are you blanking out? What's wrong?' He'll make eye motions with me, like are you going crazy and everything?" When Susan was telling the police what happened, her abuser interceded and made it seem as if she were making up the story, as if she were an unreliable witness, suggesting that she had delusions or was too unstable to understand what had happened. Susan's credibility with the police was already in jeopardy because she had called them so many times: "It got to the point where the police didn't believe me because I kept going back. Like, fifteenth time it happened and they was called, they were like, 'You're the problem. Something wrong with you now.'" Susan experienced "crazy-making" from her abuser, then, in the context of police abandonment. He used this loss of institutional credibility to exacerbate her isolation.

Susan's abuser manipulated event narratives, accused her of being a "crazy bitch," isolated her, and used the police against her in order to unravel her social and psychic context. I found throughout my fieldwork that abusers relied on the refrain of "crazy bitch" alongside manipulations of institutional authority in order to assert that women are unreliable witnesses to their own experiences. This insistence that women cannot offer credible testimony is the core of gaslighting and is rooted in the association of femininity with irrationality. Gender intersects powerfully with race and class here, such that Susan's social positioning as a poor, Black woman made her exceptionally unreliable to police. Susan's abuser leveraged this lack of credibility against her to rob her of authorities who would corroborate her experiences and protect her from future violence.

What Susan's story makes clear is that we must attend to invisible violences: forms of abuse that are rooted in the spectral, in the construction of femininity as irrational. This kind of abuse crosses interpersonal and institutional realms, enrolling powerful authority figures in the "crazy-making" process. In this chapter, I show how gaslighting, or "crazy-making" tactics, draw from and reinforce women's social vulnerabilities—around gender, race, sexuality, and legal status—and complicate their ability to become legible as good survivors. I also explore how women reclaim their own rationality in the face of this kind of power. For example, Susan described her experiences of abuse in bodily terms: she has chronic pain in her neck and back, she "hurt[s] all the time" and feels weak, she needs to smoke cigarettes to calm down, she feels a "shake in [her] body" that won't go away. For Susan, as for many of the women I interviewed, describing the effects of abuse via physical ailments helps her show that the harms of gaslighting are *real, verifiable, and persistent*.

WHAT IS GASLIGHTING?

Gaslighting is characterized by psychological manipulations aimed at undoing another's social context and sense of reality. I define gaslighting as a set of attempts to make the other in an intimate relationship seem or feel "crazy" by creating what Kathleen Ferraro calls a "surreal" social environment.[4] Gaslighting derives its name from a 1944 film directed by George Cukor.[5] *Gaslight* tells the story of Paula (Ingrid Bergman) and her new husband, Gregory (Charles Boyer), who isolates her and makes her believe she is insane. His eponymous tactic is to dim and brighten the gaslights and insist she is imagining it. The goal is to undermine Paula's sense of self and everyday life, to confuse and distort her reality such that she must accept his imposed reality in place of her own.

Gaslighting is a newly popular term used to describe the mind-manipulating strategies of abusive people—both in politics and interpersonal relationships.[6] Though its mechanisms may *appear* psychological, gaslighting is sociological: it is the result of structural and cultural conditions that set certain people up to be irrational and non-credible.[7] Gaslighting affects domestic violence victims' lives in dramatic ways—robbing them of social context, a sense of reality, institutional supports, and social networks—because abusers mobilize gender-based stereotypes, structural inequalities, and institutional vulnerabilities against them to manipulate their realities. Ferraro describes abuse as "surreality," showing how abusers distort victims' perceptions of everything from minor details of everyday life to the entire biographies of their partners.[8] Similarly, Emma Williamson describes domestic violence as "unreality," since abusers consistently try to determine the boundaries of victims' realities.[9] While gaslighting is rarely theorized explicitly in the intimate partner violence literature, these kinds of tactics emerge regularly in scholars' descriptions of abuse.

In my interviews, women across racial and economic backgrounds identified abusers' attempts to make them seem or feel "crazy" as central to the control and entrapment they experienced.[10] Gaslighting is not an "add-on" to physical abuse. Rather, *gaslighting is the glue that holds patterns of physical abuse, name-calling, control, and isolation together.* Gaslighting attacks women's realities, constructing them as irrational, robbing them of a consistent sense of self and social environment. Gaslighting tactics are also amplified by powerful institutions, such as law and mental health, that deny women credibility and autonomy.

Theorizing gaslighting is tricky because this is a shadowy form of power. Gaslighting operates on the terrain of unreality and unrepresentability, shaping women's lives in ways that are disorienting and deadly but that often escape the social scientific gaze. The women I interviewed experienced routine, gender-based attacks on their credibility and rationality, but they struggled to name those attacks as "abuse."

Avery Gordon argues that power functions through "spectral" effects and ghostly presences, through the almost-but-not-quite-there qualities of social domination.[11] Gaslighting works in such a ghostly way. There is not a measurable presence of violence; rather, an absence is created where women's credibility and knowledge of their realities should reside.

Author Debbie Weingarten writes, "When people ask about the marriage, it is as though I have rocks in my mouth. *Psychological abuse is the absence of shape.*"[12] When power is shapeless, the experience of abuse puts obstacles in the way of speech and recognition ("rocks in my mouth"). Many of the women I interviewed told me that they wished their abusers had used *more* physical violence because this would have made their experiences legible as "real abuse." Physical abuse would give them something to claim, something tangible. Psychological manipulation, on the other hand, targets something ineffable. Maria S. told me, "This is why it was so difficult for me . . . to admit that I was abused. For so many years. Because he never really beat me up. He held me, grabbed me, strong, but not slapping or anything. But what he did, I don't know if I'm gonna get back. And I know if he had bashed my face, I could have a face back. But what he took from me, I don't know if I'm ever gonna get back. . . . It's my soul."

Because gaslighting is invisible and difficult to tell a story about, it also affects victims' ability to become legible in institutions.[13] For example, women described feeling that court officials and police were more likely to believe men's stories because, in Gwyn's words, her abuser was skilled at "telling a good story." Abusers intercede in women's attempts to become legible to institutions, undermining their credibility by making them seem "crazy." Brenda's abuser pressured her to drink alcohol so that she would forget temporal sequences of events and lose respectability in court. "He got to the point where he was trying to make me drink. I don't drink [anymore]. So [in] court . . . he told them that I was an alcoholic and that I'm bipolar." His attempts to make Brenda seem unstable were implicitly supported by DCFS mandates, which require Brenda to take medication for her supposed bipolar disorder—a diagnosis she received while in a previous violent relationship—even though she does not experience bipolar symptoms. Brenda doesn't take the medication because it makes her sleep all day, a side effect she can't afford because her schedule is packed with work and counseling appointments. When she meets with her DCFS case-worker, Brenda is required to bring her prescription bottles to show she is taking her medication. What she actually does is flush the pills down the toilet. She told me, "I don't believe the diagnosis [is] true." Brenda's abuser weaponized her institutional precarity to undermine her in court and slash at the credibility of her story.[14] The gaslighting routines that characterized Brenda's intimate relationship are mirrored in the surveillance she experiences in DCFS, mental health, and legal systems.

In these ways, gaslighting tactics render women's accounts silly, exaggerated, overly emotional, and unfathomable. As such, it is imperative to understand the role of institutions in gaslighting, since victims often depend on powerful institutions to document their experiences of discrimination and violence. As the stories presented in this chapter reveal, gaslighting erodes women's abilities to make credible claims in institutions. This invisibility contributes to a broader sense of unease, mistrust, and displacement that women struggle to articulate in the language of violence.

FEMININITY AND IRRATIONALITY

Women are "systematically haunted" by the association of femininity with irrationality—we live in the wake of that stereotype and continue to feel its effects.[15] The idea that women are overly emotional and lack reason is built into the fabric of our social world. This association is integral to constructions of the feminine body and feminine emotion.[16] Women regularly experience abjection from the realm of reason—as in being cast outside the bounds of reason—in interpersonal relationships, at work, in powerful institutions like courts, and in everyday interactions.[17] The persistent, mundane link between femininity and irrationality is of concern to me because it is the cultural association that underlies gaslighting.[18]

The history of psychiatry and psychology, for example, consistently reinforces the association of femininity with irrationality: "Depictions of women's emotions as out of control and irrational compared to men's have been key in the historical construction of feminine emotion. . . . Men have historically been seen as rational beings with the ability to control their emotions, but women's emotion has been seen as 'dangerously unregulated.'"[19] Women's emotions have been constructed not only as unregulated but also as childish. Stephanie Shields explains, "The combined effects of mere emotionality and comparative lack of intellectual competence ... were believed inevitably to handicap women, both in terms of exercising 'mastery' of the home and in achieving in the public sphere outside it."[20] Further, irrationality and lack of emotional control are racialized and classed. Shields argues that theories of emotion developed in the 1800s propped up whiteness as the vanguard of emotional civilization, while non-white women were assumed to lack emotional nuance and restraint—"slaves" to their base instincts.[21] Claims to controlled emotions are claims to status and power.[22]

Women's "irrationality" has also been associated with their reproductive capabilities, including hysteria, in the context of what Ehrenreich and English called psychology's "ovarian takeover" of women's personalities.[23] Ellen Herman argues that the postwar United States was rife with anxieties about women's renewed independence, ramping up psychological discourse about women's inability to exercise rational decision-making.[24] Jonathan Metzl shows that Valium and Prozac were created to temper cultural anxiety about the changing role of women by drugging their out-of-control instincts.[25] For Metzl, women represent the threat of *lack* in medical and psychiatric history—there is an emptiness where reason and rationality should reside.[26] Unregulated emotion and irrationality are therefore key historical symbols of femininity, and medicine is a central site of this symbol's reproduction.[27]

This symbolic structure has important effects: for example, women are regularly cast as noncredible in medical institutions when they talk about their pain and embodiment. As Kristin Barker argues, "When women's corporeal certainty cannot be confirmed in biomedical terms, they discover they no longer feel confident about what is real and what is not. . . . What is scary is that when the sureness of the body is called into question, so too is reality itself."[28] These dynamics—long explored in literature on gender and medicine—read very much like gaslighting, since women's realities are denied by associating them with lack of bodily know-how. As I will show, domestic violence victims experience the weight of these pathologies directly when they interact with mental health systems.

But the persistent association of femininity with irrationality is also part of intimate violence itself. Kristin Anderson and Deb Umberson's interviews with male perpetrators of domestic violence indicate that abusers minimize women's use of violence against them and describe women as ridiculous, overwrought, silly, and irrational.[29] Micro-regulations of feminine performance—such as clothing—are key to abuse, suggesting that women are cast as childish, and femininity itself becomes an object of control.[30] Abusers further regulate women's bodies by controlling access to birth control and abortion.[31] Research with male perpetrators demonstrates that abusers tend to hold traditional gender-role ideologies.[32] These abusers refer to their partners as "crazy bitch," a common refrain in my research as well.[33] Women report being encouraged by their abusers to think of themselves as "stupid" and "crazy."[34] Williamson recounts the story of an abuser who broke his wife's arm on their honeymoon and then told friends and family that she was walking drunkenly in high heels when she fell and injured herself.[35] Feminine performance (clothing) and carelessness (drinking) became his weapons as he successfully drew on the association of femininity with irrationality to "flip" the story. The dynamics of abuse therefore function, at least in part, through ideologies that associate femininity with irrationality.

This chapter documents the social dynamics—such as stereotypes of irrationality—that give gaslighting its power *and* it explores how gaslighting shapes women's efforts to become legible to institutions. But this chapter also reveals that, despite its invisibility, women *do* manage to tell stories about gaslighting. Women make their experiences of psychological abuse real by describing their suffering as *bodily harm*. By narrating psychological abuse through bodily ailments, the women in this study "seized upon that which had been used against and denied them," reclaiming their rationality.[36] Women worked hard to show that they were *not* in fact irrational. They used physical ailments to make these kinds of claims, making gaslighting verifiable in/on the body. Surviving gaslighting requires that women learn how to survive in *bodies marked by irrationality*—often in bodies further marginalized by race and class. Survivors use evidence of somatic suffering to render their experiences of gaslighting visible and knowable, to produce bodies that have been "dis-abled" by abuse. Bodies, in this way, become key to women's reconstruction of themselves as rational subjects.

THE SOCIAL DYNAMICS OF GASLIGHTING

The women I interviewed described their abusers "twisting" reality, flipping the script, creating a feeling of "the Twilight Zone," "manipulating," "messing with," and "controlling" their minds, and "changing the facts." Ebony's partner would steal her money and then tell her she was "careless" about finances and had lost it herself. Adriana's boyfriend hid her phone and told her she had lost it, in a dual effort to confuse her and disable her from communicating with others. Jenn described her ex-boyfriend as a "chameleon" who made up small stories to confuse her, like lying about what color shirt he had worn the day before to make her feel disoriented. Luz told me, "He was so astute. When things happened, he would turn it around and make it seem like something else was going on." When Jaylene's boyfriend pushed her, he yelled, "Look what you made me do. . . . You're crazy." Emily described her ex-husband stealing her keys so that she could not leave the house and then insisting she had lost them "again."

Across racial and socioeconomic backgrounds, women identified a hostile atmosphere of confusion and distortion that affected their sense of reality. For example, when I asked women about their partners' abusive tactics, they often described being called a "crazy bitch." This phrase came up so commonly during interviews that I began to think of it as the literal discourse of gaslighting. Gaslighting systematically constructs victims as "crazy," destabilizing their realities. This can take many forms, but what's consistent is the association of femininity, feminine embodiment, and female sexuality with irrationality, unreasonableness, exaggeration, and carelessness. It is easy enough for abusers to use tactics that rely on the idea that women are "crazy," since those tools are readily at hand in dominant culture.

For example, Britney's abuser put her down for not having a college degree and made her out to be unintelligent and unreasonable. "I felt like I was being reprimanded. I was sitting there, and he was just walking in circles [around me], cursing me out. Anything I said, he would start throwing in these big words. . . . I [felt] like I needed a dictionary. But he would do that all the time. And then he would double back and say, 'Are you understanding what I'm saying? . . . You need to work on your vocabulary.'" He also began playing what many in the domestic violence field call "mind games." He went into the basement and turned off the power to the house whenever Britney wanted to do something on her own, like watch TV. He broke her phone. Britney told me that she "always [felt] confused" during their relationship. "I think he would on purpose try to confuse me." He insisted that she needed to improve her IQ because every point she made in an argument was "crazy," while his own (often physically violent) behavior was rational. Slowly, Britney began to feel unhinged: "I was always questioning my state of mind. I was just like, am I losing it?"

Eventually, these "crazy-making" dynamics became physical. Britney had to call the police when her ex-husband restrained her on the ground while yelling "You need to calm down! You need to calm down!" He made it seem like he *needed to be physically violent* because she was so irrational. Britney's ex was wearing his army uniform when the police came. The police let him off the hook, giving him what Britney called a "brotherly" scolding, telling him, "You know better." Afterward, the violence escalated. The last day they lived together, Britney and her ex got into a yelling match. It ended when he held her underwater in the bathtub, insisting that he was simply trying to "calm her down." He gave her two black eyes while trying to keep her underwater; he still has scars on his face from where she gouged him with her fingernails as she fought her way out of the tub. Afterward, he barricaded the door to the bathroom and wouldn't let her out "until she calmed down." Britney's neighbors called the police, and he was arrested, this time without question.

Labeling women's reactions "crazy" ranges from belittling tactics and violent outbursts, as in Britney's case, to public campaigns. For example, Simone referred to her abuser's sustained attempt to delegitimize her as "the crazy narrative." After she left him, Simone's ex-husband convinced his family that she was "crazy" and attacked her sanity relentlessly during divorce and child custody proceedings. Simone described how her abuser's tactics found traction in court:

SIMONE: He said all sorts of terrible things about me in the divorce
         papers . . . like I had orgies at the house, which isn't true. I am
         not that way at all. [*pause*]

PAIGE: He was trying to discredit you?

SIMONE: Yeah. Like, that I'm absolutely crazy and I can't be around the kids. It was terrible. [He would say] that adulterous women run in my family. . . . He would say, "Be a mother." Because he would always be saying that I'm not a good enough mother.

Simone's husband hacked into her social media accounts during the divorce and wrote public posts that made her appear unstable. He accessed her bank accounts and moved money around randomly in order to confuse her and make her appear financially careless. He intentionally used tactics that evaded police attention, convincing others that she was "crazy" and leaving her little legal recourse to challenge him. Simone's abuser embedded his attacks on her sanity in attacks on her sexuality and motherhood, claiming that she had "orgies" and was therefore not fit to be a mother. In this way, Simone's experiences of gaslighting played on her existing social vulnerabilities, such that her failings of respectable motherhood and her sexuality became justifications for her abuser's claims that she was "crazy." Simone had recently come out as bisexual, suggesting that he sought to mobilize a stigmatized sexual identity against her to make her seem unstable. These tactics also ruptured Simone's ability to rely on institutions like the law to sort out what was done to her, since her abuser manipulated the divorce process to eviscerate her credibility. As a result of these manipulations, Simone now has to share joint custody of her children with her abusive ex-husband.

As Simone's experiences demonstrate, gaslighting could not exist without inequities in the distribution of social, political, and economic power—especially around gender and sexuality. The existing grooves of social inequality provide footing for gaslighting strategies. The reciprocal play between psychological manipulation and social inequality is precisely what makes this form of violence so devastating. Gaslighting targets women's social vulnerabilities, making them into weapons.

In fact, some of the women I interviewed did not experience direct physical violence from their partners at all. This does not mean that their relationships were not violent, but that physical violence was not *necessary* to keep them isolated and controlled.[37] In general, women felt that psychological abuse was more devastating, more insidious, and more consistent than physical violence. "Crazy-making" routines—which include fractures to social networks, to helping institutions, to a consistent sense of self and others, to a reliable sense of reality, and to a narrative of events—often make physical force unnecessary. They yoke together incidents of abuse into an overall pattern of fear, insecurity, and lost reality.

For example, Maria L. describes how her ex-husband's gaslighting tactics drew on her lack of financial know-how: "When I separated [from my husband], I was really dumb. . . . I'm seeing a counselor for Latina women and she tells us that we shouldn't call ourselves dumb or crazy. [But] my whole paycheck was his. I didn't have a bank account. I didn't know how to use the bank. . . . He had his bank account and took care of everything. Every check I handed over to him." Maria's husband's financial abuse was rooted in his efforts to convince her she was "dumb" and "crazy." If Maria L. had been raised middle-class, had family on which to rely for money, or had grown up understanding banks in the United States, his efforts to make her feel "dumb" and "crazy" about finances would not have been so effective. He prevented her from controlling her own finances and then convinced her she was too stupid and unreliable to do it anyway. Inequalities around class and gender set the context for gaslighting, and abusers regularly manipulate those kinds of vulnerabilities in order to isolate and control their partners.

Attacks on women's sexual respectability also play a major role in gaslighting strategies. Rosa, a forty-one-year-old Latina woman, explains how her ex-husband would invent tales of her infidelities and try to convince her they were true:

> He'd make things up that didn't happen. Sometimes he'd tell me things like, "A cousin saw you at X place and that you were with someone." Things like that. I'd get upset and tell him, "Bring him. Bring him to my face and we'll see if it's true." I didn't do anything and wasn't at such place. But he'd make things up. . . . He'd say that I was crazy and all that. . . . I told him that I wasn't crazy, that he was the crazy one. Obviously, he would start everything and then make me feel [like I started it]. . . . Sometimes I did feel confused.

Rosa's ex-husband tried to convince her that she was cheating on him, a constant accusation that obsessed him. He used these stories to justify following Rosa when she left the house and beating her physically when she came home. Rosa had to constantly defend herself against his version of events, which was also a defense of her own sexual respectability.

It was common for the women I interviewed to have to defend their sexual reputations against their abusers' outrageous accusations of infidelity. Cultural ideas about women's dangerous, unruly sexuality—especially stereotypes surrounding Black and Latina women's "bad girl" sexualities—underlie attempts to unmake their realities.[38] Jaylene, a twenty-three-year-old Latina woman, explained to me that her partner calls her a "ho" and insists that she needs psychiatric help. He pressures her to drink alcohol and then calls her "slut" when he thinks she has drunk too much. Jaylene's boyfriend embeds his accusations that she is "crazy" in attacks on her sexuality. He talks about her old boyfriends and invents stories about her continued interest in them, stories against which Jaylene is forced to defend herself in order to avoid violence. Throughout our interview, Jaylene insisted, "I'm not the crazy one."

Fabiola explained the relationship between sexuality, crazy-making, and gender very clearly: "Every man has a different way to make the girl feel like she's crazy or she's the bad one." Being "bad" and being "crazy" are closely linked in the gendered power dynamics that Fabiola lays out. Assumptions about women's promiscuity or sexual pathology undergird abusers' attempts to construct them as unreliable and untrustworthy. Fabiola's ex-boyfriend would tell her she was "nasty" and "sick" after they had sex, even after pressuring her into being intimate. Fabiola's sense that she was "bad" was amplified by the fact that she had immigrated to the United States and remained separated from friends and family. "He said, 'You are crazy. No one loves you. You are here with me. You don't have anyone else here.'" When Fabiola tried to leave her boyfriend, he threatened to "prove" she was crazy in court so that she would lose custody of their daughter. Similarly, Maria S.'s ex-husband told her she was too sexually open, that she did not know how to behave properly as a wife "in this country." Like Fabiola, Maria S.'s ex-husband constructed her as a sexual deviant and a cultural outsider at the same time.

These examples show that manipulation of women's immigrant status is central to gaslighting. Abusers seize on women's devalued legal statuses in order to further their isolation and sense of displacement. For example, Liz, a twenty-seven-year-old Latina woman, endured persistent insults and threats from her husband, who told her repeatedly that no one would want her because she was undocumented. He even convinced her he had cancer so that she would stay with him, inventing doctors' appointments and faking bouts of illness from chemotherapy. Because she was afraid of becoming involved in the health care system, she was too isolated to figure out his lies. Liz and Fabiola were already living precariously as undocumented women and their abusers' manipulations took on the flavor of these existing structural vulnerabilities. Their partners robbed them of social belonging, security of self and place, institutional legibility, and the very sense of being rights-bearing persons.

Women of color face increased vulnerabilities around police and courts, especially when abusers mobilize stereotypes about Black women's "aggressive" and "jealous" personalities against them. Rosalyn, a thirty-four-year-old Black woman, told me stories about her abuser undermining her credibility in front of police, relying on stereotypes of Black women as innately aggressive. She described an altercation on a busy street that led to police involvement: "By the time I get to a place where I can [stand] up, the police are on top of me, talking about, 'Stop before we tase you.'. . . [My ex] was very charming. . . . He's like, 'You know she crazy. That's my baby momma. . . . She just mad 'cause, you know, we can't get back together.'" In this case, Rosalyn's abuser convinced the police that *she* was the aggressor, and the police arrested her, an experience more common for Black women than other groups.[39] After this incident, Rosalyn could not return home and was forced to flee to a domestic violence shelter in the suburbs to avoid her abuser. Rosalyn's ex then told their friends and family that she was "crazy," using social media to poison her reputation.

Rosalyn told me she began to believe his version of events because he was so outspoken about the idea that she had lost her mind and was desperately trying to get him back: "It's funny because sometimes I still think I'm crazy. . . . Because I feel like I had to have been [crazy] to let him get in and then stay in. Maybe he was right in some ways, I wonder." Rosalyn's abuser ruptured her institutional legibility, denying her a rightful victim status, her grounds for legal protection, as well as her grounds for empathy among friends and family. This tactic spread outward across their shared social networks and left Rosalyn alone, doubting her own sanity.

Tina, also a Black woman in her thirties, provides another example of the intersecting dynamics of gaslighting, race, and the legal system. She explained what happened when she and her ex were arguing at the courthouse while the child representative—an official responsible for mediating their child custody arrangement—looked on:

> I was always being called crazy. Even when [the child rep] had me cornered in the hallway with him, and my kids' father goes, "I never punched you, though." He says that. "I never blacked your eye. I never punched you." And I looked at the child rep, and I was like, "I'm leaving." I was like, "I can't. He feels like since he never punched me in the eye or busted my lip that it wasn't abuse." And when he said that at that time, I was so done. And for [the child rep] to not respond to that, I was . . . I was baffled. I was like, "He's admitting the abuse to you, and you let it go. You're not doing anything. Right over your head." He said nothing.

The child representative went on to participate actively in her abuser's manipulations of the story, asking Tina to apologize to her ex for her "role" in the abusive relationship. Though Tina's ex pulled hair out of her scalp, slammed her against walls, strangled her so hard that her feet left the ground, and broke her furniture and computers, he believed he was "non-violent" because Tina never had a black eye. The abuse was so severe that Tina's abuser has been prosecuted multiple times on felony domestic violence charges. It was easy enough for Tina's abuser to convince the child representative that she was exaggerating and "crazy," undermining Tina's dedicated attempts to retain full custody of their children. Tina's presumed irrationality was more legible to this court official than her ex's violence. The lack of institutional language for domestic violence outside of "black eyes" made Tina's experiences invisible, and her desperation to keep her children was read as "crazy."

As these examples indicate, women's structural vulnerabilities—gender, immigrant status, race, sexuality—create the terrain upon which men's gaslighting tactics become successful. Race and class matter enormously for how gaslighting strategies take shape, especially in powerful institutions where women of color and undocumented women experience fear and lack of autonomy. Gender and sexuality are also central. Abusers' use of "crazy bitch" to delegitimize women suggests the ongoing and effective association of "crazy-making" tactics with femininity itself, especially around the threat of female sexuality. The cultural link between femininity and irrationality allows gaslighting to become both successful and devastating, making it a core feature of domestic violence. While I have shown here how institutions like courts become part of gaslighting routines, I focus in the next section on the role of the mental health system in exacerbating "crazy-making" dynamics.

THE MENTAL HEALTH SYSTEM

The mental health system anchors and amplifies gaslighting tactics in at least two ways. First, abusers weaponize women's use of mental health services to cast them as unstable, as incapable of testifying to their experiences. For women who have disabilities or vulnerabilities around mental health status, gaslighting is especially dangerous because abusers are able to "prove" that they are "crazy"—or at least to control them with such threats. Second, mental health providers frequently lack an understanding of abusive relationships and contribute to abusers' construction of women as irrational by overmedicating them and denying the significance of abuse in women's lives. This is not the result of a few bad therapists; rather, it is rooted in the authority, expertise, and individualized epistemologies of the mental health field. For example, mental health providers might assume that women have participated in creating abusive "dynamics," "systems," or "processes" in their relationships: therapists regularly construct abusive relationships as "bad relationships" in which both parties are at fault. Lisa Larance and her colleagues show that women in abusive relationships tend to find couples counseling unhelpful and victim-blaming—though they often attend counseling as a "symbolic performance" in order to buy time before leaving.[40]

Further, mental health providers often locate the causes of abuse inside women's psyches rather than in the structural conditions of their entrapment. And because mental health systems are authoritative, women's own explanations are frequently erased when they seek help. The women I interviewed were especially fearful of the mental health system because of its *power to define maternal fitness*—a power that abusers regularly invoke to intimidate women. The mental health system therefore becomes a key site of power in gaslighting dynamics.

Margaret described her husband's threats to take their children away from her if she saw a therapist after the birth of their second child: "I think the worst thought I ever had was, right after I had [my son], I felt worthless. . . . I thought I should just go away, and he should get a better mom. So that's when I think I started talking to [my husband] about it, and that's when he said, 'You go [to a therapist] and I'll prove you're nuts. Go ahead.'" Margaret's husband prevented her from getting help for what she now labels postpartum depression, an experience that she was forced to struggle through alone. Margaret's husband used the stigma of mental health to keep her trapped and weak, isolated from potential institutional resources.

Luisa's abuser also used threats related to the mental health system to manipulate her. He made a consistent effort to convince Luisa that she was "crazy," and he was so committed to this project that he forced her to schedule an appointment with *his* psychiatrist to ask for antidepressants. He regularly pressured her to use drugs (marijuana and cocaine) and to drink alcohol, and Luisa believes he drugged her with anti-psychotic medication to force her to engage in bondage sex. Luisa once had to go to a clinic for perplexing blisters on her vagina that he gave her—from extended intercourse with objects—while she was in and out of consciousness. Afterward, when Luisa told him she was going to leave him, he threatened to bring her underwear to her workplace and tell her boss what a "whore" she was. Luisa felt she was the problem because she was an immigrant and did not understand the ways of American relationships. He used to call her a "fucking immigrant" as well as "crazy." Luisa explained, "And I always was staying, staying, staying, being hurt and stay, stay, stay because I was thinking it was my fault. Because of the fact that I don't understand."

Luisa's perception that his behavior was normal was exacerbated by her status as an immigrant, as well as by his constant manipulation of her memory of events. In one early episode, he pressured her into drinking alcohol and then provoked her into an argument, later claiming that she assaulted him and was acting "crazy" all night. Luisa did not remember becoming violent herself, but she eventually came to believe that she could not trust her own memories of the evening. Luisa's boyfriend used this incident against her every time she tried to leave, telling her he would expose her as the real abuser. Abusers' attempts to recast victims as the primary abusers is a key tactic in the creation of "surreality."[41]

Though Luisa's doctor told her she did not need antidepressants, her ex-boyfriend forced her to take his prescription pills, insisting that she needed them because of "women's issues." "I noticed that sometimes he used to give me small pills, he was saying because I have menstruation. He was blaming on me, every time I wanted to end the relationship, he was saying it's because of me because I have [an imbalance] in my hormones." Luisa's boyfriend relied on the idea that women are inherently unstable to perpetuate her confusion and dependence on him, using medication to construct her as psychotically female. His insistence that she *could not trust herself* was connected to his construction of her as worthless and unknowledgeable because she was an immigrant.

When Luisa began plotting seriously to leave her boyfriend, she found a therapist and started seeing him secretly. She told him about the sexual practices that made her uncomfortable and about her boyfriend's constant threats and stalking each time she tried to leave. Luisa describes how her therapist responded:

> [He said] that I have to breathe and he would teach me some exercises [for] breathing. And he said for me to go deep inside of me and find "the real [Luisa]." And I was explaining to him that every time I try to leave this guy, this guy would follow me, would send me a lot of crazy messages, won't leave me alone . . . that I was scared. He was trapping me, things like that. The psychologist didn't get it, that I was in the cycle of being abused. . . . He didn't help me. And it was a hundred and forty dollars I had to pay.

Understandably, Luisa resented her therapist's implication that all she needed to do was breathe deeply. It was after this incident that Luisa's boyfriend kidnapped her and held her captive in a hotel room for nearly twenty-four hours while he raped her, strangled her, and beat her. Luisa knew she was right to be afraid of her boyfriend, and she also knew that no amount of deep breathing would help. It's unlikely that Luisa's therapist could have prevented this episode of brutal violence. And he probably lacked training in domestic violence. Still, Luisa's experience points to the problems with clinical interventions that ignore women's structural vulnerabilities and the power imbalances embedded in abusive relationships.

Relatedly, three of the women I interviewed were institutionalized as an indirect result of domestic violence. Adriana and I spent most of our time together talking about her experiences in a psychiatric institution while she was a teenager. Adriana's high school years were characterized by nearly constant social upheaval. When she was thirteen years old, she ran away from home and became involved with a twenty-one-year-old man with whom she lived for several years. He was psychologically abusive, physically violent, and deeply controlling. He did not like her going to school, so he pressured her to skip class and monitored her whereabouts. He dictated what she wore, what she ate, and who she talked to. Because she missed so much school at his demand, Adriana faced expulsion. Adriana's guidance counselor noticed her distress and recommended that she be sent to a psychiatric hospital in lieu of being expelled. Adriana's parents agreed, and she was sent to a juvenile psychiatric facility for three months.

While in the hospital, Adriana's doctors diagnosed her with manic depressive disorder and forced her to take medication. She often refused, but each refusal resulted in the addition of three days to her stay in the hospital. She was not yet fourteen years old at the time. Adriana described her interactions with the psychiatrists:

> Everything that was going on in my life was due to the abuse that I was receiving from my boyfriend. He took me out of my house, he was stopping me from going to school. Maybe at that time, I couldn't conceptualize it as abuse, but it was clear that when I would talk to them about what was going on with him, that all my problems were rooted in him. *But every single time that we were in group therapy or something, they would be like, "Stop talking about him. This is about you."*

Adriana got in trouble for talking about her boyfriend and was treated as if she were an infatuated child, even though her statements were clear evidence of his control and manipulation. It took Adriana years to understand that, in this way, her therapists contributed to the environment of "surreality" that saturated her relationship, making her doubt and blame herself.

When she finally got out, Adriana's hospitalization worsened her boyfriend's entrapment of her. "When I got out of the hospital, he was like, 'I fucking told you that you were insane! What type of person gets locked up in a hospital? How crazy are you!'" Adriana's boyfriend used her hospitalization against her to destroy her credibility *and* to amplify his controlling and "crazy-making" tactics. Adriana told me, "He would lose my phone on purpose and then he would tell me it was me who lost my phone. And then he'd say, 'You're so fucking careless, you see how you are?'. . . It was always me. Of course, it was always me." Dependent on her boyfriend for money and housing, Adriana's life was replete with the fractures to her reality that her boyfriend invented to maintain control of her. During this time, Adriana's boyfriend also publicly reprimanded her for having an abortion—for "killing his baby"—and used this incident to convince Adriana's friends that she was a liar, that she was manipulating him, and that she was sexually toxic. Adriana therefore lost access to her only social networks. Gaslighting tactics are often accompanied by abusers' attempts to poison women's reputations in shared social networks so that they remain isolated, stuck in the topsy-turvy world of the abuser.

During our interviews, Adriana connected the "symptoms" for which she was treated in the hospital directly to her boyfriend's abusive behavior: "I hated taking medication. I thought it was stupid. I didn't need it. You could tell right away. I was only [in the hospital] because . . . I was in an abusive relationship. You can't fix abusive relationships with medication. . . . They gave me Trazadone. I was taking it at night to help me sleep. Which was stupid because the only reason I couldn't sleep was because I felt like he was gonna sneak in my window at night." Adriana was afraid of her boyfriend sneaking through her window because he frequently did so. In fact, manipulating her sleep was one of his central "crazy-making" tactics. When she moved back in with her parents, Adriana's boyfriend dropped her off at 11:00 p.m. every day, forced her to stay on the phone with him until 2:00 a.m., and called her again at 6:00 a.m. to tell her what she should wear to school (sweatshirts, so that no one would "look at her"), before picking her up and driving her to school. It was nearly impossible for Adriana to do homework, to talk to friends, to spend time with her parents, or even to watch television. She was tired all the time because he would keep her awake at night to make her lose focus and lower her guard. Staying awake was Adriana's learned survival tactic—a survival tactic for which her psychiatrists pathologized and medicated her. Adriana's experiences in mental health systems thereby exacerbated her experiences of psychological abuse. As a fourteen-year-old girl with little support at home or at school, Adriana had few resources with which to resist her psychiatrists or her abuser, though she managed to do both frequently (by refusing medication, by staying on the school's campus all evening, by seeking an abortion). Adriana lived in a state of insecurity and deprivation that was heightened by her involvement in the mental health system, an institution that came to operate as an intersecting site of violence in her life.

Elaina, a thirty-two-year-old white woman, was also hospitalized—for depression, a diagnosis she believes is not "real," but is rooted in her situational experiences of domestic violence. Rather than giving her information on domestic violence or emotional abuse, however, her therapists gave her literature on "co-dependence" and suggested that she attend Co-Dependents Anonymous. Elaina now laughs about this: "I started to read [the pamphlet], and I was like, 'Yeah *he is* co-dependent. I don't know where *I* fall into this.'" That Elaina's experiences of abuse were recast as a problem with *her*, that she "loved too much" and was overly dependent on men, reveals her psychiatrists' lack of attention to the power imbalances in her relationship. The very discourse of co-dependence exposes the feminization of the problem of domestic violence: male violence is recast as lovesick feminine irrationality.

Elaina is not the only woman I interviewed who was told by experts that she was "co-dependent." Maria S., a forty-nine-year-old woman from South America, was also encouraged by a therapist to attend Co-Dependents Anonymous. Though "co-dependence" was a pop psychology favorite in the 1990s—against which anti-violence feminists waged public campaigns—it has never been included in the DSM. The term is closely related to dependent personality disorder, which is an official psychiatric diagnosis characterized by submissiveness and excessive fear of abandonment. Despite the lack of official diagnosis for "co-dependence," the term retains popular currency, particularly via the book *Women Who Love Too Much* by Robin Norwood, a bestseller many times over.[42] Maria S. handed me this book during one of our interviews and told me it helped her understand her own role in the abusive relationship. The central claim of Co-Dependents Anonymous, and books like Norwood's, is that women sacrifice themselves in relationships to a pathological degree, creating unhealthy patterns of dependence on their partners. Because Maria S. and

Elaina had therapists who misrecognized the power imbalances in their relationships, "co-dependency" became their quasi-medicalized explanation. Rather than exploring abusers' behaviors or the cultural schemas that excuse them, discourses of "co-dependency" insist that women actively construct the oppressive dynamics of their relationships because they are *too feminine.*

Even more common than being labeled with personality disorders, many of the women I interviewed were prescribed medication that they did not believe they needed. Emily, a sixty-two-year-old Black woman, struggles with doctors who she believes are constantly over-medicating her. Emily described domestic violence very succinctly as an effort to "control your mind." During one of our interviews, Emily walked over to the closet and pulled out a box of medications (figure 15), an archive of the various drugs she has been prescribed over the past 10 years. She told me the doctors will not look at "what's been done" to her—they only meet with her for fifteen minutes and prescribe something new, at a higher dosage.

Emily does not believe that her ongoing distress is a result of a disorder; rather, she believes her experiences of gaslighting continue to disable her. For example, her abuser would do small things to manipulate her mind, like hide the keys when she tried to leave for work and claim she had lost them. "I would rather a lot of times for him to hit me. Because after a while, the pain . . . you know, you take somebody and go [*smack*]. [But] somebody keep on messing with your mind every day, every day . . . [*trails off*]." For Emily, physical abuse was episodic, while psychological abuse was unyielding. Emily feels that the only remedy ever offered to her has been medication, and she is not interested.

Some of the women I interviewed also rejected medication because they felt it actively contributed to their abusers' efforts to construct them as "crazy." Tina, for example, felt that a diagnosis would be dangerous because she faces ongoing custody battles with her ex and cannot afford to have the courts view her as "crazy." Tina described her complex negotiations with her primary care doctor around this issue:

> She was trying to label me with depression. . . . But I'm just like, let me read what you're writing. She goes, well, no no no. And I'm like, yeah. I'm not owning that. I won't own up to it. I'll just find other ways that's an outlet. And I end up telling my therapist. And she's like, well maybe that's a good

idea. She was all for it too. And I'm just like, no. Why is meds the answer? That is not the answer. I'm not crazy. It's just, I'm having a hard time juggling everything by myself. It's just life right now. Life is tough right now. I'm not gonna let you put labels on me and just have me medicated. 'Cause it made me really sleepy. I was forgetting things.

Tina felt she needed to protect herself from an official diagnosis of depression, in part because she recognized that she was not really "depressed," but simply struggling with the stress of leaving her abuser, with the processual nature of domestic violence: financial chaos, working multiple

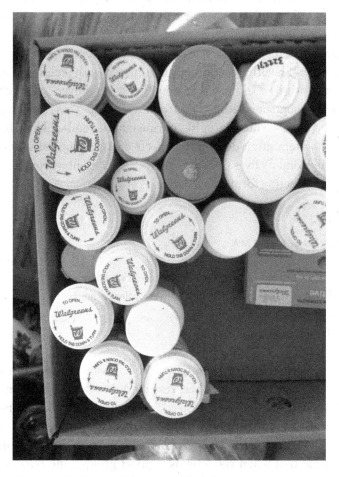

Figure 15. Emily's medicine. Photo by author.

jobs, moving homes, stalking, orders of protection, custody battles, and single parenthood. But Tina also felt that the medication contributed to her sense of lost reality, making her lose focus. She must remain vigilant, she believes, because any slip-up with her kids will be used against her in court. For Tina, the forgetfulness caused by anti-depressants endangered her performance of good survivorhood.

Overall, women's experiences with the mental health system suggest that gaslighting tactics are embedded in the inequities of this system: *women often experience mental health interventions as extensions of psychological abuse* and exacerbations of their lack of control over reality. Women of color and poor women fear these systems because of their power to define maternal fitness and custody arrangements, sites where medication and diagnoses are regularly used against them. More generally, the mental health system is often saturated with feelings of fear and uncertainty, with well-founded anxiety that control over one's well-being can be lost to someone with letters after their name. This fear compounds gaslighting tactics. Thus, the epistemic inequalities embedded in the mental health system often deepen the effects of psychological violence and coercion in women's lives. In what follows, I explore how women respond to these intersecting forms of violence.

EMBODYING TRAUMA

> Violence under patriarchy is not theoretical. The memory
> of it lives in my body, like it lives in countless other bodies.
> It forms its own tissue and knots.
> Mackintosh, 2019

Yesenia is a forty-seven-year-old Latina woman who was living in a group housing program when I met her. Yesenia didn't tell me a chronological story about domestic violence. Instead, she explained that she suffers from spider veins in her legs, flat feet, a misaligned spine, headaches, pain in her face, and fibrosis—all of which she attributes to intimate violence. Yesenia told me that when she attends support groups, she refuses to "tell her story." She explains to the social worker, "I can't do it." Instead, she describes the health effects of abuse on her body, using the language of chronic pain, rooting harmful experiences in her embodied reality. Yesenia has tried to talk to doctors and psychologists about her history of sexual abuse, but it never works out. She jumped around to several domestic violence programs that gave her short-term help but couldn't find her permanent housing. Talking about diffuse forms of bodily pain—rather than telling a story about her complicated history of physical, sexual, and psychological abuse—is a technique of survivorhood that allows Yesenia to *insist on the reality of the abuse she has endured* while navigating institutions that fail to help and hear her.

When violence is unreadable *as* violence and women lack a clear language of sensemaking around it, they may—like Yesenia—enroll their bodies in projects of testimony. As anthropologist Miriam Ticktin reveals, victims use accounts of illness and physical suffering in order to render alienation *visible*.[43] Sociologist Cecilia Menjívar shows that women use illnesses and somatic suffering as expressions of structural inequality.[44] Scholars of embodiment have theorized the way social ruptures get written on or absorbed into the body.[45] Some forms of power are more like a haunting than a presence, so they may be best expressed through physical unease and bodily pain.[46]

The women I interviewed received little institutional recognition for their experiences of gaslighting. Institutions tend to prioritize visible, physical injuries. Even in sociology, we rely on a legalistic understanding of abuse that overemphasizes physical assaults. Evan Stark traces the roots of this "injury model" to feminists' credibility work in the 1980s, when activists needed to prove that domestic violence was a "real" crime.[47] The white woman with the black eye, or the passive woman shrinking away from a stereotypically aggressive man, became the paradigmatic images of domestic violence.[48]

Images like the *Ms* magazine cover shown in figure 16, representing unquestionable physical victimization, were key to legislative efforts and public campaigns, and they remain the most convincing displays of domestic violence today, both in courtrooms and in the public imagination. Through the injury model, the abused female body became an object of public fascination and revulsion, a terrifying symbol of masculinity gone awry, of quintessential (white) feminine victimization. Indeed, sociologist

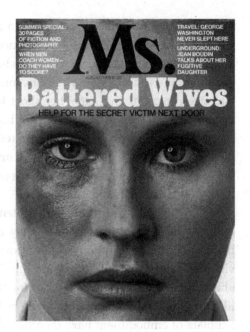

Figure 16. Ms. magazine cover, 1976.
Reprinted by permission of *Ms.*
magazine, © 1976.

Barbara Sutton describes violence as the *expectation of visibility*, of a body marked by atrocity.[49] The *Ms. Magazine* cover typifies this expectation and shows how injury itself becomes something of a fetishized object, making invisible the underlying mechanisms of abuse that escape the reach of the camera.[50]

Despite this obsession with physical injury, women who have experienced domestic violence consistently report vague pains and ongoing health problems that are untraceable to physical injuries. Clinicians note that domestic violence victims exhibit health problems characterized by nonspecific complaints: they report "general" declines in health and describe issues like headaches, stomach problems, and pain in their limbs.[51] The National Intimate Partner and Sexual Violence Survey (see table 1) indicates that women who have experienced rape, stalking, and intimate partner violence are more likely to have chronic pain, headaches, and difficulty sleeping.[52] Researchers and clinicians are often perplexed by these symptoms and typically attribute them to issues like "psychosomatic reactions" or the "traumatic sequelae" of abuse.[53]

Table 1   Prevalence of Physical and Mental Health Outcomes among Those with History of Rape or Stalking by Any Perpetrator or Physical Violence by an Intimate Partner

	Weighted %		
Health Outcome	History	No History[1]	p value[2]
Asthma	23.7	14.3	<.001
Irritable Bowel Syndrome	12.4	6.9	<.001
Diabetes	12.6	10.2	<.001
High Blood Pressure	27.3	27.5	n.s.[3]
Frequent Headaches	28.7	16.5	<.001
Chronic Pain	29.8	16.5	<.001
Difficulty Sleeping	37.7	21.0	<.001
Activity Limitations	35.0	19.7	<.001
Poor Physical Health	6.4	2.4	<.001
Poor Mental Health	3.4	1.1	<.001

1. No history of rape, stalking, or intimate partner physical violence
2. p-value determined using chi-square test of independence in SUDAAN™
3. Non-significant difference
SOURCE: National Intimate Partner and Sexual Violence Survey, CDC, 2010

But I think we should also understand these symptoms as attempts to *claim* experiences of violence that are invisible. This doesn't mean that these symptoms are not "real," but rather that they're rooted in conditions of structural and symbolic violence. By explaining their experiences of gaslighting and psychological manipulation via physical ailments, victims of domestic violence *make real and visible* the effects of abuse on their lives. In so doing, they produce a body that has been "dis-abled" by abuse, allowing them to transform invisible ruptures into identifiable outcomes. Explicating their experiences through the physical body is one strategy, among others, that women use to survive in *bodies marked by irrationality*.

Maria S.'s ex made her feel "crazy" all the time. He cheated on her and then accused her of psychotic jealousy when she confronted him with proof of the affairs. He convinced her she was imagining things. She wished he had physically assaulted her, she told me, because that type of abuse would have been "more compatible with reality." Instead, she could never figure out if she was *actually* being abused. During our second interview, Maria S. began telling me about the fibroids in her uterus, which she believes grew because of gaslighting. "I have five fibroid tumors in my uterus. . . . Everything doubled or tripled in size. So, I'm not pretending or joking. *It's a reality*. My doctor . . . she's shocked: how can that happen? How can, in one year? They tend to grow, but slowly. She said she's never seen something like that." For Maria S., her fibroids testify to the reality of abuse, providing clear evidence of harm when cultural scripts about violence will only validate physical injury.

The body is a material site of violence *and* a site of symbolic sense-making around abuse. Many of the women I interviewed described feeling fractured and alienated from their bodies. Because the effects of abuse often fall outside what is visible and verifiable, women explicate those effects at the level of the corporeal and sensory. When women describe psychological abuse through physical manifestations like fibroids, they produce a different kind of body than the one they had before, a body that has endured chronic uncertainty and insecurity, a body that has been made "heavy with meaning."[54] Women capture gaslighting's ghostly qualities by producing a physically harmed body, "a re-articulation of subjectivity that takes place through physical changes."[55] After suffering gaslighting and institutional silencing, the women I interviewed found ways to reclaim their rationality through stories of physical transformation.

Nevaeh put it bluntly when she told me, "Things don't ever go right back where they were." Nevaeh feels that her body has changed permanently as a result of abuse. Her abuser stomped on her toes to keep her in place so that she could not run away while he hit her. Her feet have never really gone back to the "right" place. Nevaeh told me this story about her toes, but she was also speaking more profoundly: "Before I became a victim, I was so hard and rough on the outside. I wouldn't break a tear for nothing in the world . . .[but] since I've been a victim, since I've overcome and had to overcome, I'll cry at anything." Here, Nevaeh connects the distortion of her toes and her transformation into a more empathetic person to her experiences of violence. Abuse has forced her to occupy a different body, a body that is physically and emotionally changed. Gaslighting and other forms of abuse have altered her body—its capacities and its physiology.

Nevaeh also explained that she suffered multiple miscarriages because her relationship was so toxic. In fact, many of the women I interviewed attributed miscarriages to domestic violence. Occasionally, miscarriages were caused by physical violence to the abdomen and surrounding area, a common site of violence for pregnant women in abusive relationships.[56] Susan, for example, had a miscarriage in her bathroom after her abuser punched her in the stomach. Other women attributed their miscarriages to gaslighting, imagining psychological abuse as a type of poison that invades the womb. Fabiola explained, "I believe that stress can kill a baby. And I still think that if I wasn't in the situation like the way that I was . . . I would never . . . lose the baby." Betsy also believes the poisonous environment of her marriage contributed to her miscarriages, and she blames herself for allowing those feelings to seep inside her body: "I fed my fear, anxiety, frustration, sadness, disappointment . . . all those things which were not [normal]." Some women believe that psychological abuse made their bodies quite literally toxic.

When I asked survivors if they felt domestic violence had affected their health in general, almost all of them said yes. Often, they would then list a series of health problems that they associated with abuse. Here is Rosa's response:

PAIGE: Do you feel that domestic violence has affected your health overall?

ROSA: I think it has, because I had depression. I also gained a lot of weight for the same reasons: the violence, the emotional [abuse]. I have diabetes, and I think it's hereditary but I [got it]. It affected me because of the life I was leading with him. I'd take as much as three pills for diabetes because of that life. It affected me because I was feeling bad emotionally and because of the diabetes which I had really high. I had to take many pills.

Rosa mentions weight gain, diabetes, depression, and overmedication, suggesting that domestic violence has overwhelmed her bodily systems. She also suggests that her genetic predisposition for diabetes was activated by abuse. For Rosa, the body becomes an important site of explication for the ongoing, invisible effects of abuse on her life. Martha made similar claims, telling me that the abuse gave her a "spastic colon," "all sorts of gastrointestinal issues," that she "couldn't lose weight," had no "energy," and carried the stress of the relationship "in her shoulders." These ailments make *real* the years of abuse that Martha experienced, which she has long struggled to identify in the language of "violence," since physical abuse was never her abuser's primary tactic.

The women I interviewed also frequently talked about how abuse cut them off from the operations of their bodies. Maria S. described her body becoming absent from her: "I would have lost my body [if I stayed with him]. . . . Because it's a violence, in a way, against my own self." Maria S. described the relationship as a kind of embodied self-violence, suggesting that psychological abuse would have eventually severed self from soma. Elaina told me that her abuser regularly pressured her to drink alcohol in an attempt to control her, which contributed to a "state of up and down" and feelings that she could not "focus" during day-to-day life. Both women experienced fractures in their bodily self-knowledge.

Adriana gave a vivid description of this sensation:

It felt like I didn't know how my body was working. It really felt like . . . my body was just gonna faint and shut down on me. One, because of the lack of sleep, because I would stay up on the phone with him till 3:00 in the morning, until he made sure I was exhausted, until I was falling asleep on the phone, [then] he would hang up on me. So it was because of the lack of sleep. He would call me at 6:00 in the morning and I had to be up already. It was because of the amount of stress that you live under. I don't know how my brain could survive in that situation. So it definitely affected my health. I always felt like I was gonna pass out. Just all the time.

Psychological manipulation left Adriana physically weak and alienated from her body. Maria S. similarly describes herself as "wandering around lost" during the abuse, as if she were in a fugue state: "My brain kind of shut down." This sense of the body's alienation or collapse points to the deep exhaustion involved in surviving psychological abuse. These descriptions also highlight the utility of the body for describing the invisible violences of gaslighting.

Like Rosa, many women described bodily alienation through issues around their weight, through a sense of lost control over the size and shape of the body. For example, Jaylene used her weight to mark her boyfriend's control over her. She explained, "When I met him, I wasn't a supermodel or anything, but I liked my body." Jaylene's body became a problem for her boyfriend, who told her that it was inappropriate for her to be skinny because it would make her seem too "available." Jaylene told me, "So I kind of let myself go. And I wouldn't take care of myself, even to the point where my mom . . . would call me ugly. . . . 'Cause I wouldn't get ready, I wouldn't put makeup on, I wouldn't do exercise or anything. I would just eat and eat." Jaylene used food as a way to deal with her boyfriend's jealous and control- ling behavior, but even this was not self-initiated: "He would tell me, eat, eat, eat! And I would eat. Like, he would always buy me McDonald's and I would take it. . . . He even tells me right now, he's like, 'Oh my chubby . . . I like you like this.'" Jaylene's boyfriend manipulated her body directly, attempting to transform it into his possession, ostensibly undesirable to other men. His manipulations of her body were rooted directly in the threat of her sexuality. Other women described similar manipulations in which their boyfriends encouraged them to gain weight or lose weight, to wear more conservative clothing, or to stop wearing makeup. These experi- ences contributed to a sense that their bodies were not really their own, to a feeling of alienation from their physical selves.

Jenn laughed about the material manifestations of abuse: "Through the verbal and mental abuse, I got depressed and then I stopped taking care of myself. Overeating. Stress eating. I gained a lot of weight in a short period of time. He even gave me gray hairs. It's so funny, the few gray hairs that I have, I can honestly say that each one of them popped up right after an altercation with him [*laughs*]." Like many women, Jenn blames herself for gaining weight, explaining that she "stopped taking care" of herself. However, for Jenn, the abuse transformed her daily life such that even the task of eating was not under her control. Saddled with sole responsibility for the children, Jenn barely had time to shower during the years she was with her abuser, much less to cook the healthy meals she desired. For Jenn, the ghostly qualities of abuse become visible through her gray hairs, providing (tongue-in-cheek) proof of the corporeal effects of violence. In these examples, women's social precar- ity and isolation become "real" when explicated through the language of embodiment. The toxicity of psychological abuse and control reveals itself in or on the body. Survivors piece together different systems and objects, including the body, in order to reconstruct the reality of their experiences.

Mariposa explained the sensations she started to feel when having fights with her boyfriend: "When I have some troubles with [him] I start feeling pain. . . . I learned how to notice the changes because when I was young I didn't notice anything. I think your body never hurts [when you're young]. But when you are a little bit older, you start learning how your body language is. When I have anxiety, I get pain in my back." Mariposa uses her body to mark invisible experiences of harm. Mariposa believes that this pain in her back will always be with her, that it is not amenable to logics of "fixing" or "cure." A different body has been produced through abuse, one that she must manage in a new way. Her previous body, the one she had before, is no longer available, since that was a body about which she "didn't notice anything."

In these examples, women describe the body as a site of ontological unsettling, violence, and rupture, but also as a site of sensemaking around the shadowy aspects of abuse, around forms of violence that are unknowable through normative means (visible, legal, medical). The body is not offered here as a transcendental site of redemption, but as a material effect of "crazy-making" strategies—*and* as a means for knowledge production around spectral aspects of power. Of course, this sensemaking work is also deeply gendered, as stories about body size and miscarriage attest. Women reclaim the rationality of their bodies by describing gendered somatic ailments as *outcomes* of violence.

When institutions or popular discourses deny women the ability to make legible their experiences of gaslighting and other types of psychological abuse, they may develop alternate strategies for knowing and testifying. This is not to say that women engage with the world through an essentializing, feminized descent into the body. Rather, women who have experienced domestic violence theorize their bodies as sites of rupture when expert discourses fail them. Their theories of embodiment and health are not pure or even necessarily resistant—in fact, women often learn this language through trauma paradigms that posit abuse as "stored" in the body. Still, their theories of embodied rupture insist on the *reality* of gaslighting and its institutional erasures. Women's theories of embodied harm demonstrate a kind of knowledge production from the margins that reaches beyond institutionalized discourses of victimization, survivorhood, and recovery.

CAPTURING THE GHOST

By focusing on gaslighting, I have tried to illuminate the "crazy-making" structure of gender-based violence—even as it attempts to turn away from empirical analysis. Gaslighting is "spectral" in the sense that it is largely unrecognized and denies credibility to those who experience it. This form of abuse is effective when mobilized in the context of victims' existing structural vulnerabilities. For example, poor Black women may experience gaslighting around their interactions with police. Women with mental health needs are particularly susceptible to gaslighting in psychiatric systems, where they are "epistemologically vulnerable."[57] Undocumented women are vulnerable to gaslighting because they are cut off from institutional supports and reliant on dangerous intimate relationships to retain or secure legal status. Thus, while gaslighting is ghostly, it is structured by objective systems of inequality, by cultural stereotypes about irrational femininity, and by patterns of institutional discrimination.

Understanding the spectral nature of gaslighting helps explain why women use their physical health and embodiment as sites of explication. Describing the ongoing effects of violence via headaches, miscarriages, back pain, and general unwellness *concretizes* a confusing and shadowy experience, making "unreality" verifiable. The persistent insecurity caused by gaslighting bars women from straightforward explanations of their suffering. Women typically cannot document their experiences of domestic violence with photographs of injuries. In response, then, women *produce a body that has been transformed by abuse*. This production of a body dis-abled by violence subtly resists institutional practices that privilege physical abuse over psychological abuse, even as it reinscribes medicalized ideas about trauma. Women's stories of bodily pain should therefore be understood as an implicit critique of the institutional configuration surrounding domestic violence. In conditions of institutional erasure, women invent new ways of making themselves legible as survivors. Discourses of health, even the sensations and postures of the body, become important to these bids for legibility.

Understanding gaslighting as a central source of women's injury, suffering, pain, and inequality requires speaking in a different language, one that is attentive to "confused relations, opaque memories, and ruptured belongings."[58] As Veena Das has argued, pain is not a reference to an inner state, but *a claim demanding acknowledgment.*[59] Domestic violence is characterized by a form of power that is processual, built into the shadows of authoritative institutions, a type of power that tilts women's realities while denying them institutional means of apprehending those realities. This type of power is not easy to speak about, despite women's complex negotiations for survival. Attending to the deep and costly labor of this negotiation is perhaps one move toward acknowledgment.

6 Surviving Heterosexuality

For Julie, a forty-seven-year-old white woman, the topic of sexuality is rife with anxiety. When I interviewed her, she described her marriage as sexually abusive. Her husband demands sex from her and then insults and badgers her for days if she refuses. When she says no, he begins masturbating next to her, often when she cannot leave the room, forcing her to participate in his sexual acts. He claims that if he does not ejaculate regularly, he will get sick: "He would say I had to have sex with him because of his medical condition." If Julie consents to his sexual demands, she feels violated and depressed afterward, knowing she has only acquiesced in order to avoid emotional and verbal abuse. Julie started coming to the domestic violence support group where I met her because she was having panic attacks each time she pulled into her driveway, knowing she would have to see her husband.

This is not how marriage was supposed to be. Raised and married in an Evangelical community, Julie and her husband both based their hopes for social success on creating the ideal heterosexual nuclear family. They went into insurmountable debt in order to purchase a big, beautiful house in the suburbs. Because of the abuse, Julie now feels that these dreams have come crashing down on her, that they were a sham to begin with. Julie's sense of self has been undermined as a result of these ruptured dreams. She told me that if she wants to "rebuild" her life, she will have to get away from her husband's sexual demands, to rediscover herself on her own terms. Julie's despair about the failed promise of the heterosexual nuclear family is connected to her feelings of violated sexuality. Julie ended our interview by telling me that she has to remake her life in order to reclaim any notion of family, belonging, and sexual fulfillment. In her words, "I've spent way too much time analyzing him and not building my own life." Through therapeutic programs, Julie learned not only that her husband's behavior is abusive, but also that too much "dependency" on him is detrimental to her psychological health. She must orient her life away from him in order to regain a sense of self. Like many of the women I interviewed, Julie described surviving abuse as a process of deconstructing cultural ideologies about the nuclear family, romantic love, and intimate attachments.

In this chapter, I explore how the experience of intimate violence changes women's relationships to heterosexuality and the nuclear family, to sexual citizenship, even to their sense of themselves as sexual beings. Sexuality is not a "private" matter, but a set of norms and behaviors associated with powerful systems of compulsory heterosexuality, gender, race, and class.[1] Sexuality is "a cultural artifact that reflects the social conditions of any given historical moment."[2] But it is an artifact that is also transformed by social actors over the life course—a contested, gendered site of meaning making and social practice.[3] For the women I interviewed, sexuality and family became sites of change after violence. Abuse often violates women's sexual identities and their sense of themselves as strong women. Further, survivors often feel that their homes and families have been ruptured as a result of abuse—that their houses have been made into prisons, their families into failed promises. The experience of intimate violence transforms women's relationships to home and to the nuclear family ideal. As such, surviving violence often means that women have to break with what Mimi Schippers calls the "regimes of normalcy" in heterosexual culture.[4]

To complicate things, navigating the therapeutic programs I've described throughout this book *also* changes women's relationships to heterosexuality and romantic partnership. When women participate in anti-violence programs, they learn that feeling sexual desire and finding new partners is not "good" survivor behavior. Women face pressure to downplay or hide their sexual relationships in order to perform good survivorhood. They learn to search for "red flags" among potential partners and to distrust their sexual or romantic instincts. In so doing, they also blame themselves for their "victim" sexuality. The dynamics of domestic violence itself therefore *combine with* these lessons of sexual respectability, prompting women to reorient their sexuality after abuse. Borrowing José Esteban Muñoz's term, I show how these pressures cause women to *disidentify* from the social norms and cultural promises of heterosexuality.[5]

Disidentifying from the ideological structure of heterosexuality means that women remake their sexual subjectivities and relationship practices after abuse, often in ways that defy cultural norms. I am not suggesting that women who have experienced domestic violence *reject* heterosexuality, but rather that they formulate new goals and practices related to sexual intimacy and the family. After all, even when social actors resist sexual norms, they do not "escape" those norms.[6] Heterosexuality, like other social institutions and cultural ideologies, is a site of both "identifications and antagonisms," of struggle.[7] To borrow language from Jennifer Hirsch and Shamus Khan, the women I interviewed revised their "sexual projects"— their sexual goals and self-making—after experiencing intimate violence.[8] In response to abuse *and* in response to therapeutic programs, women refocused on their own sexual autonomy; some refused to bear children and many created new rules for future relationships. They often came to question the idea that a heterosexual, reproductive lifestyle should be the "gold standard" by which they measure their success.[9] This chapter reveals how, after surviving violence, women may revise what it means to be a sexual citizen, disidentifying from cultural messages about protective masculinity and heterosexual "success," reimagining ideals of home and family.

HETEROSEXUALITY AND HOME

Sexual Citizenship

This book has explored the gendered nature of state governance— especially how gendered norms of deservingness intersect with race and class. But *sexuality* is also key to the distribution of state resources and to political belonging. As historian Margot Canaday shows, the US government helped *produce* the heterosexual-homosexual binary by regulating homosexuality, using sexual categories to determine who could access benefits.[10] Sexual behaviors have long been "bureaucratized" as part of state power.[11] Implicitly and explicitly, the state has used sexual categories to define citizenship, even when psychiatric and legal definitions of "normal" and "abnormal" sexuality did not yet exist.[12]

And as Diane Richardson argues, the straight, middle-class, white nuclear family is the quintessential model of "good" citizenship.[13] State policies and programs reinforce this norm through child services requirements about what constitutes a healthy family, through fatherhood programs that promote marital monogamy, and through adoption laws, to name a few examples.[14] Programs like these cultivate the value of monogamous heterosexual marriage as a kind of "civilizing influence" on poor families.[15] After all, states are "interpretive entities that define the ideal attributes and characteristics of parents and spouses."[16] Heterosexual familial norms are also fundamentally racialized. Raka Shome writes, "The logic of whiteness . . . underwrites all (hetero)gendered narratives of national belonging."[17]

These ideals of heterosexual familism are not just abstract representational projects: they shape concrete program requirements. As sociologist Jennifer Randles shows, promoting heterosexual marriage and responsible fatherhood simultaneously is a "package deal" in state programs.[18] Bill Clinton's 1996 welfare reform emphasized the role of "strong families" (read: married, heterosexual nuclear families) in good citizenship, "shaping men for taking on long-term affective commitments to their children and a heterosexual spouse."[19] Dorit Geva calls this "nuclear family governance."[20] Good citizenship is also therefore reproductive citizenship: it involves the promise of social "success" through childbearing in a nuclear family.[21] Even when same-sex couples are allowed entry into this formulation, it is through a normative grid of kinship that centers the traditional two-parent, middle-class household.[22] Monogamous marriage and parenthood remain central to imaginaries of good citizenship, success, and livelihood.[23] All of these observations have led feminist theorist Sara Ahmed to argue that, in fact, social and political belonging *is itself heterosexual.*[24]

Sexual citizenship therefore refers to the sexual norms embedded in rights claims, state recognition, and national belonging.[25] Sexual citizenship norms appear, for example, in the ubiquitous cultural images that place the heterosexual nuclear family at the center of what it means to be a good American. As Steven Seidman writes, "Citizenship involves not only juridical enfranchisement but *symbolic incorporation into a national community.* Individuals aspiring to the status of citizen must claim to possess the psychological, moral, and social traits that render them good and warrant their integration."[26] Sexual citizenship is defined not only by cultural values, images, and expectations centered around the heterosexual nuclear family but also by monogamizing institutions—like welfare and parenthood programs.[27] As feminist and critical race scholars have long insisted, the normative "family" is a key representational technology through which modern power is exercised.[28] In this chapter, I explore how women who have experienced domestic violence interact with these norms.

Heterosexual arrangements and performances help secure rights, resources, and belonging. But domestic violence programs teach different kinds of sexual lessons. After they have experienced abuse, women learn that they should *abstain* from new relationships. Their "dependency" on men is made into a problem of the self—and women learn, implicitly and explicitly, that they should focus on becoming "independent" instead. To borrow the words of Ellen Scott and her colleagues, domestic violence victims are cast as having "dangerous dependencies."[29] Survivors should apply themselves to personal therapeutic recovery and to their children's mental health. They should definitely *not* focus on men. Here, being a good sexual citizen means guarding against potential sexual risk. Victims of domestic violence are presumed to have failed, in both sexual and familial terms, and so they must work to recuperate themselves.[30] Even the U-VISA process forces women to violate normative heterosexual arrangements, since victims are required to assist police in criminalizing men who are often the fathers of their children, rupturing the nuclear family unit.

The expected lessons of social citizenship are inverted here: state programs do not enforce heterosexual monogamy but rather "independence" from bad (racialized/other/violent) men. Thus, while the sexual citizenship literature imagines heterosexuality to be a stabilizing institution necessary for belonging and resources, all of this works differently for women who have experienced domestic violence. Heterosexual intimacy has become *destabilizing.* Women therefore learn to pivot their goals away from heterosexual monogamy in order to become good survivors. For victims of domestic violence, we cannot assume that heterosexuality means normativity, safety, and inclusion.[31]

The Institution of Heterosexuality

Heterosexuality is not simply a category by which to mark people's identities and sexual behaviors. Rather, it is an ideological and material structure that is central to gendered social life.[32] Heterosexuality is foundational to gender-based economic distribution, as well as the distribution of desire and emotion. In Adrienne Rich's formulation, heterosexuality is a political institution that is *compulsory*, such that heterosexual desire and social arrangements have been "forcibly and subliminally imposed on women."[33] In this sense, the consequences of compulsory heterosexuality are gendered: in the words of sociologist Chrys Ingraham, heterosexuality cements the unequal sexual division of labor as the "natural" order of things.[34]

Nevertheless, heterosexuality is not "stable," even if it is hegemonic.[35] The very existence of domestic violence reveals that heterosexuality is always failing by transforming into an exploitative dynamic rather than a scene of cultural and economic security. The queer approach I take in this chapter regards heterosexuality as an unstable social institution that requires subjective and cultural work for its reproduction. As sociologist Jane Ward notes, "The amount of psychic and cultural labor extended to produce and enforce heterosexual identification and procreative sexuality suggests that heterosexuality . . . [is] a psychic and social accomplishment, an institution, and a cultural formation."[36] That heterosexuality is a powerful social institution does not mean that its dominance is ensured— it must be reproduced through interactional (i.e., assuming straightness), affective (i.e., desire and social validation), cultural (i.e., wedding rituals), and structural (i.e., opposite sex "complementarity") mechanisms.

And indeed, the rewards of sexual normativity are not evenly distributed. For Black women, heterosexual partnership and parenthood with Black men is saturated with stereotypes of deviance and failure.[37] Race, gender presentation, class, and nationality shape the degree to which social actors are allowed to reap the benefits of heterosexuality. As Julie Bettie shows, working-class girls' heterosexual identities are forged in relation to their class experiences and often have little in common with upper-class girls' sexual identities.[38] And while Latina girls are subject to heteronormative lessons in school and family life, those lessons are complicated by the good girl/bad girl dichotomies that construct Latina girls' sexuality as dangerous.[39] Race is deeply "harnessed" to sexuality and sexual politics.[40] Black women are not even supposed to *have* sexuality, really. As Evelyn Hammonds writes, "Black women's sexuality is often described in metaphors of speechlessness, space, or vision, as a 'void' or empty space that is simultaneously ever visible (exposed) . . . this always already colonized black female body has so much sexual potential that it has none at all."[41] Something like heterosexual *normativity* is therefore out of reach for racially marginalized women.[42] Susila Gurusami shows that Black women are aware of their perceived sexual deviance and engage in hypervigilance in order to avoid state intervention in their families.[43] The promises and rewards of heterosexual normativity are deeply stratified by race and class.

Despite this, queer theory tends to represent heterosexuality as a *comfort*. Being straight is about feeling at home. Queerness, on the other hand, is about not coming home.[44] Meanwhile, heterosexuality is hospitable to those who can conform. Ahmed argues, for example, that heterosexuality orients social actors toward procreation and the heterosexual family, which feels natural and easy: homey.[45] We develop a heterosexual habitus by orienting our lives around the nuclear family and reproductive desire. For Ward, "The child learns to repeat the sensations, gestures, and practices that orient him or her toward heterosexuality—e.g. ways of relating and communicating that are premised on a gender binary in which 'opposites attract.' This ongoing repetition is the very process that sustains heterosexual selfhood."[46] Here, Ahmed and Ward are interested in how heterosexual orientation creates familiarity with "how the social is arranged."[47] Heterosexuality allows for engaging with the world in a "natural" way.[48] But what happens when heterosexuality and the nuclear family become violent and disorienting rather than "homey"?

Disidentifying

This contradiction between heterosexual "success" (the ideological structure of heterosexuality) and the violent realities of heterosexuality (male violence) forces women who have experienced domestic violence to struggle on the terrain of sexuality. It turns out that even straight-identified women "have" sexual citizenship, which is a site of contradiction and unease.[49] For the women I interviewed, heterosexuality often transformed into a set of troubled attachments, not because of queer desire, but because of violence and exploitation. As Ward writes in *The Tragedy of Heterosexuality*, assumptions about the "ease of heterosexuality" often mask the "gendered suffering produced by straight culture."[50] Indeed, I find that life-altering experiences like domestic violence may change how social actors respond to the interpellating call of heterosexuality.

Muñoz argues, for example, that minority subjects often sidestep interpellation when dominant culture makes them Other.[51] For Muñoz, resistance is not about *rejecting* ideology. Rather, resistance means identifying *with* and *against* at the same time: disidentifying. Disidentifying involves taking what has been foreclosed and holding onto it.[52] This requires picking up terms of identity and using them differently. It is interpellation "with a difference." Disidentification is enabled by the fact that we are continuously hailed across different ideological systems, sometimes in contradictory ways.[53] This is not about "winning," escaping, or rejecting dominant terms. Rather, disidentifying is about survival, about opening the possibility for a different kind of identity.[54] "Disidentification is the third mode of dealing with dominant ideology, one that neither opts to assimilate within such a structure nor strictly opposes it; rather, disidentification is a strategy that works on and against dominant ideology."[55] Muñoz uses the concept of disidentification to theorize subjects who are nonnormative—queer-identified people, for example. But how could disidentification apply to those who technically "fit" into heterosexuality, in this case, to heterosexual-identified women who have experienced domestic violence?

In this chapter, I ask how women who have experienced domestic violence deal with heterosexual norms and expectations. I show that survivors often *disidentify* from heterosexual norms and practices after experiencing abuse. They enact heterosexual citizenship differently. For the women I interviewed, heterosexuality was no longer a stable ground from which to make claims for belonging, to secure rights and resources, or to rebuild familial life. Women who have experienced domestic violence have to *disidentify* in order to make heterosexuality survivable.

This kind of disidentification has two components. First, women perform abstinence and sexual respectability in therapeutic programs in order to get what they need. They learn that their "dependency" is a problem, so they disidentify from the promises of heterosexual nuclear family success—for example, by becoming abstinent or rejecting romantic relationships. Second, women disidentify from cultural ideologies of heterosexuality and reproduction because those ideologies have become violent and disorienting. As Muñoz argues, when dominated subjects encounter a normative cultural representation—like the heterosexual nuclear family—they may turn sideways toward that representation because they have already "failed" to fit.[56] They do not reject those representations altogether, but they "recycle" and "rethink" them.[57] Women who have experienced domestic violence may refuse to bear children, refuse to engage in new intimate relationships—or they may create new goals outside the promise of the nuclear family, rewriting the rules of their intimate partnerships. As I'll show, motherhood may become an important site of disidentification as women distance themselves from heteronormative expectations of reproductive womanhood. In this sense, women turn away from normative heterosexual membership, opting instead for a slantwise position. Disidentification is therefore both a survival strategy *and* a key part of becoming legible as a good survivor.

In what follows, I show how abusers' use of spatial entrapment, isolation, and jealousy make heterosexuality and the nuclear family into problematic objects for victims. I then show how therapeutic programs pressure women to discipline themselves sexually in order to perform as good survivors, making abstinence part of survivorhood. These two sets of pressures—constraining abusive dynamics and the asexual expectations of therapeutic programs—prompt women to disidentify from ideals of heterosexual citizenship, belonging, and identity.

ENTRAPMENT

The experience of intimate violence is spatial. It is embodied. Women often experience abuse as a *problem of space*. Indeed, existing research suggests that women's primary experience of domestic violence is one of isolation, a kind of imprisonment in the private sphere.[58] Being in an abusive relationship means living in an environment of constraint. Getting out of the relationship often involves dramatic spatial rearrangements—leaving a beloved house, a childhood neighborhood, even a city. Leaving means learning how to orient differently toward others and toward the social world. *Re*-orienting—a process rather than a "moment." I'll show that these experiences often cause women to question the "private" nuclear family as a site of success, belonging, and fulfillment. Home and family come to feel uncertain and dangerous. Heterosexual romance feels like a lie. Entrapment within heterosexual monogamy and the nuclear family may cause women to question the ideological promises of those institutions.

Kathy, a fifty-one-year-old white woman, described her boyfriend's favorite abusive tactics: holding her down by the wrists or forcing her to stand by herself in the corner of the apartment. Both tactics constrain Kathy's bodily movements, her freedom to move about in space. They also humiliate her. Kathy's boyfriend is the bus driver along the busy road she takes to and from work. When he does not want her to go to work, he simply refuses to let her on the bus. He will not let her buy a car, insisting that she is too sickly to drive on her own—in fact, he uses her chronic illness against her constantly to make her feel dependent on him. Kathy's boyfriend often objects to her outfit choices and refuses to let her leave the house if she is wearing something "inappropriate." Kathy described several incidents in which her boyfriend became angry while driving and pulled over on the expressway, pushing her out of the car into busy traffic. Kathy was forced to walk home for several miles on the shoulder of the suburban highway, cars whizzing by at seventy miles per hour. Kathy's abuser uses tactics like these to make public space menacing so that she remains trapped in the home.

Kathy talked about these moments as disorienting. She felt the relationship was cutting her off from the world, and she reminisced about living in Colorado on her own when she was in her twenties, when she could "look out the window and see horses and mountains." She told me that she craves that kind of "peace and tranquility" every day. Kathy wants to leave her boyfriend, but she does not make enough money to get by without him and she fears she would not be able to manage her health conditions on her own. Like many of the women I interviewed, Kathy talked about her world becoming smaller and smaller over the course of the relationship. Not only has her mobility been curtailed, but the circle of people with whom she is allowed to communicate has also shrunk. This feeling of shrinking space is familiar to Kathy, since her ex-husband used to follow her to work and sit outside in his car, making sure she did not talk to other men. In both situations, Kathy's social space became dangerously circumscribed. Over and over again, women told me stories about their engagement with the outside world being violently cut off by their partners, being forced to turn inward, becoming accustomed to keeping their eyes and head bent downward.

Delma, for example, wasn't allowed to talk with neighbors because her husband would accuse her of sleeping with them: "I couldn't even say hi to a neighbor because I'd already slept with the whole world." Delma describes her life as a "circle" that kept shrinking the longer she stayed with her husband. When she brought family over to the house, her husband would get drunk and embarrass their guests, even calling their family friend a "fag" during one visit. When I asked Delma how she survived the loneliness of those years, she told me she became used to it. "You don't turn crazy. But you're isolated in such a way that [you don't] reach out to the world." Rosa also used the circle metaphor to describe her relationship, telling me, "It's better to leave a relationship like that because your world is *only* that. It's a circle that you're inside of and you can't see what surrounds you. . . . You're [trapped] inside that circle." For most women, that circle is defined by the physical space of the home, which loses the promise of family and safety. In this way, abusers demand that women orient *solely* toward the ideological space of heterosexuality—making that space dangerous and isolating.

Delma went on to explain that the isolation stays with her, even after leaving: "I'm giving you two hours today, but I never last talking to anyone more than twenty minutes. I begin to get nervous. . . . As of right now I don't have friendships. If I go upstairs to talk to my friend, I talk, but I don't talk. You get me? When I was young, I was very talkative. . . . Now the few people I talk to, I talk to for five to ten minutes and I get desperate and that's as much as I can stand them." Delma's experience of domestic violence not only stunted her social space, but also her friendships, the conversations that might have broadened her sphere of belonging. Abuse caused long-term shifts in her intimate attachments and sense of community.

Like Delma, many women described an involuntary, inward turn to their personalities. Liz told me that she used to be "joyful" and "joke around" with family members, but her husband was jealous. He would take her home early from family gatherings and quiz her about each conversation, asking why she was laughing so much. Liz's personality retreated as her social space was cut off: "I lived in a world where I had no friends. After I moved in with him, I didn't go out with anyone. I was dedicated to him, my house, my daughter." Following patterns already outlined in this book, Liz's abuser used guilt, sexual accusations, and manipulation to shrink her social world. She became completely oriented toward her home and family, highlighting the intersection of spatial confinement strategies with ideologies of wifely, domestic heterosexuality. Similarly, Rubi talked about how her boyfriend would hit her in the face before family events so that she would be too ashamed to attend. "He was always very *encerrado* [closed up]. He didn't want to go to parties, go to any places. So I was always alone." Like her partner, Rubi was forced to become "closed" in her orientation toward the social world. Many women felt this kind of possessiveness was romantic at first—*he wants me all to himself*—only to feel suffocated and scared later on.

Some women also experienced the isolation and entrapment of domestic violence as a larger sense of disorientation. Diana, a thirty-nine-year-old Latina woman, explained: "I came here [to the domestic violence organization] because . . . I felt disorientated. . . . When I arrived here, I didn't know what to do. I just wanted to cry. I didn't know where I was going, what to do. I felt like [I needed] a compass. I felt desperate. . . . Do I leave or do I go? What do I do?" Diana described driving around in her car, lost and confused, not being able to get her bearings. This feeling was compounded by the fact that Diana had immigrated to the United States recently before the abuse started. Her partner's tactics of isolation and surveillance amplified her sense of being misplaced via the migration process. Being forced to orient toward the home and toward a heterosexual relationship can make the outside world feel bewildering, as women are cut off from the resources of public life and social networks.

Carla described race and nationality as compounding factors in her isolation: "All the people in the surrounding homes were all white, or Americans. I didn't know who to reach out to help. I didn't want to involve other people, because I thought that if I went and knocked at someone's door and tell them to call the police and he found out they were the ones that called [*trails off*] . . . I just didn't want to involve them." In a social space defined by whiteness, Carla felt unsafe asking for help, so she stayed inside the house. The racial dynamics of her neighborhood kept her oriented inward, transforming the "success" of finding a home in a "good" neighborhood into a kind of prison. Through this imprisonment, Carla began to feel differently about the promises of the heterosexual nuclear family— and she wanted only to escape.

But escaping also involves spatial reorientation, which can be equally disorienting. Nevaeh explained, "After the baby, I [got] completely out of Dodge. No one ever heard from me again. I didn't care to go around in the old neighborhood or meet the old family, or the friends that we knew. I started my life over brand new, just me and [my son]. I knew that in order to get away from [my abuser], I had to scratch the board. . . . You have to give up the life you knew and the life you had." Because abuse is a spatial experience of entrapment, the process of leaving requires transforming and uprooting precisely that space. Nevaeh left her apartment, her lifelong friends and family neighborhood, and the support system in which she had long been embedded.

Hope, on the other hand, explained that she executed a gradual leaving process, taking jobs farther and farther away from her husband's house so that she could begin building a life without his surveillance. She told me that the freedom of long drives to and from work, of establishing herself in a new neighborhood and talking with new coworkers, gave her the strength to leave. For Hope, leaving meant inching away from the family home.

Other women described orienting away from heterosexual partnership— and its presumed "success"—as a process of learning how to make ends meet as a single woman. Mariposa told me that it was "nice to stay alone with myself" in her apartment, a space of independence that she had never known before. Martha and Delma both described the spatial reorganization of their homes after they kicked their husbands out. For the first time, rather than hiding in their rooms at night, their teenage children started to spend time in the living spaces. Delma explained that her children used to close their bedroom doors and wait to hear the first slap or broken bottle, phones in hand to call the police. Now that she is a single mother, the doors are always open.

Despite labor-intensive efforts to orient away from their abusers, however, many women endure ongoing surveillance and spatial control. Diana, for example, is forced to live with her abusive ex-boyfriend because neither of them can afford their own apartment. She told me, "He'll still call me [asking], 'What are you doing?' Or when I leave work and I can't answer calls because I'm driving, he'll text, 'Are you at home yet? Who are you with?'" Despite leaving the relationship, Diana is trapped by economic constraints, forced to endure her ex's ongoing control of her mobility. Elaina also described constant fear of spatial invasion from her ex-boyfriend, since his primary abusive tactic was to follow Elaina and her family members in his car. For some women, despite sustained attempts to reorient their lives away from their abusers, material circumstances and ongoing harassment keep their social spaces circumscribed.

Space is a critical and overlooked factor in abusive relationships: often, it becomes difficult or impossible for victims to inhabit space comfortably, to move around in public space, to extend outward toward others. I've borrowed from Ahmed's queer reading of phenomenology here to emphasize the "orienting" dynamics of abuse, showing how *spatial constraint and unease can prompt distrust toward ideologies of the heterosexual nuclear family*.[59] The narrowing of social space may bring nuclear family ideals and even heterosexuality itself into view, exposing them *as ideologies*. The experience of entrapment may transform the meaning of home, the promises of nuclear family citizenship. The space of the home becomes prisonlike and the romantic promises of heterosexual coupledom become sinister. Thus, the spatial surveillance that characterizes domestic violence may result in ideological confrontations with heterosexuality.

RED FLAGS AND RESPONSIBILITY

As I've shown, the entrapping dynamics of abuse may prompt women to develop new relationships to heterosexual nuclear family ideals. But when they participate in therapeutic programs, women also learn that healthy survivorhood means being single. Therapists, social workers, and other experts regularly suggest—sometimes gently, sometimes not so gently—that women orient their lives *away* from men. Some domestic violence housing programs have rules that require victims to abstain from living with new partners while in the program, and women staying in emergency shelters are not allowed male guests. The institutional configuration surrounding domestic violence targets women for sexual discipline. Often, these messages reinforce women's feelings of failure about their own sexuality. Though infrequently discussed in the intimate partner violence literature, sexuality is an important site of stigma for victims. Just as women learn to hold themselves responsible for their psychological states before and during abuse, they also learn to blame themselves for the supposedly deviant sexuality that propelled them into an abusive relationship and kept them there. Racialized and class-based narratives of the dysfunctional family amplify this blame, as women often believe they have participated with their abuser in creating a pathological home. Managing their sexuality in the future—safeguarding against "unhealthy" relationships—therefore becomes integral to survivorhood.

A comment that Alma made as she was leaving our interview stands out from my fieldwork. As she walked out the door, Alma turned to my research assistant and me and warned, "Be careful of men!" We all laughed. Despite her smile, Alma was quite serious, and she called out her warning to us again before disappearing down the fluorescent hallway of the domestic violence agency. Similarly, Mariposa feels cautious about getting serious with her current boyfriend, even though he wants to marry her, and she told me several times throughout our interview that I should be careful of men, that I should be suspicious of them. The risks for Alma and Mariposa are high: becoming involved in a second abusive relationship would mean that they would have to blame themselves even more deeply for the abuse, that they were truly pathological. Being "re-victimized" would mean more systems involvement, potential exposure to DCFS or other punitive programs. Heterosexual intimacy has become a landmine for both women. Because domestic violence victims are responsibilized for their abuse through narratives of recovery, sexuality is a dangerous site of potential failure.

Maria L. described a similar situation: she is in love with a man who is good to her, but they cannot live together because she is being monitored by immigration authorities. Because her daughter was recently returned to her care from a detention center at the border, Maria L. cannot afford to *have* a sexual identity while undergoing state surveillance and custodial uncertainty. It would be dangerous for her to seem "dependent" on a man, since the experience of domestic violence has already called into question her ability to be independent. Stigmatized for being bad at relationships or sexually pathological, survivors of domestic violence are often made to feel as if they should not be starting new relationships at all. Good motherhood and survivorhood are rendered incompatible with sexuality. Performing sexual control and abstinence is part of the labor of survivorhood.

Being dragged through the family court system by an abuser also amplifies the threat of sexuality. Of the women I interviewed, those with minor children felt the most pressure to perform abstinence as part of their survivorhood, suggesting that sexual and maternal respectability intersect profoundly in women's efforts to become good survivors. For example, Fabiola refused to date until after she gained full custody of her daughter. Tina's new relationship of almost three years ended because her boyfriend wanted to have a child. Because Tina's ex had controlled her by keeping her pregnant, Tina saw her new boyfriend's request to become a father as a deal-breaker. "With every relationship I'm thinking about, I always stop it. I don't let it go longer. I'm looking for signs and things like that. There's no trust. So I do feel like I'm gonna probably be alone for the rest of my life because of it." For Tina, the danger of prolonging a relationship that may replicate any aspect of her abusive past is simply not worth it. Because she must perform maternal respectability meticulously in the family court system, Tina knows she cannot afford any intimate slipups, and she certainly cannot afford to become a single mother again. Performing survivorhood and navigating the institutional pressures of respectable motherhood have forced Tina into long-term transformations of her intimate life.

Nearly a mandate when it comes to women involved in DCFS and family court, keeping men out of their lives is also important for women involved in "softer" services like domestic violence support groups, in which they report feeling discouraged from talking about new relationships. This is especially true when the "new relationship" is with the former abuser. Emma, a twenty-four-year-old white woman, felt conflicted about getting back together with her daughter's father, who was her abuser. When she told the support group about giving him another chance, she did not, in her words, "feel the love" from the group. The other women shook their heads and told her she was making a mistake. The therapist who leads the support group didn't say anything to defend her, and Emma felt judged by her silence. Still, Emma holds firm. It's her decision, she told me, not theirs. Susan also described hesitating to talk about a new relationship in support group. She sensed that the group leader and the other women would think it was inappropriate to talk about her boyfriend, even though she considered these women her friends. Susan and Emma both understand that there is a deep and often implicit pressure to be *independent* from heterosexual relationships in order to be a good survivor.

Women in support groups also learn about "red flags." After participating in anti-violence services, the women I interviewed described seeing male violence all around them, feeling the need to protect themselves against constant onslaughts. Elaina described how this feels when navigating everyday life: "Even the other day, I went shopping and this man, random man, joked that he was following me. And it just had me all freaked out for the rest of the day." Rather than lamenting this skeptical orientation toward men, Elaina told me that she values it because it will help her navigate future relationships, teaching her how to detect "patterns of abusive behavior." For Elaina, any interaction with men is potentially problematic. She has developed a watchful reorientation toward heterosexual attachments, toward even the possibility of a sexualized interaction.

For some women, attention to red flags means swearing off romantic relationships altogether. I first noticed this pattern when, while collecting demographic information in interviews, I asked women if they had current sexual or romantic partners. Many women laughed derisively at my question, as if to say, "Are you kidding me?" Luz described men as "vultures" and told me that, as a survivor of childhood sexual abuse, she would never let another man into her house. Liz told me that since surviving an abusive relationship, she would not expose her two daughters to a man who might not "respect them." Rosalyn explained that all men exhibit red flags if you look carefully: "Anything, it's a red flag. If you're cheating, that means you gonna start cheating and get mad, and then you're gonna hit me. I don't know what you're doing: you say you at work, but I don't believe anything anymore. . . . It's like once this thing happens, how do you get rid of them? . . . Once they feel like they possess you, they own you, you're theirs, there is no getting out of there." Rosalyn detects male violence everywhere now that she has learned about abusive patterns. Mariposa, similarly, explained that being a survivor has given her a "weakness detector" that goes off around men. Disidentifying from heterosexuality, then, involves disidentifying from the romantic promises of protective masculinity and focusing instead on its potential violence.

Other women talked about disidentifying from heterosexuality through the language of celibacy and abstinence, refusing the possibility of dating or becoming intimate again. Emily explained that abusive relationships drove her to alcohol and drugs, and celibacy has been her only peace. She says that abusive men "stick out like a sore thumb," and that when men try to approach her, she tells them, "I see you for who you are. I'm not fooled by you." For Emily, the perils of heterosexuality are not just found in experiences of violence, but also in substance use. Having been through multiple addiction programs, Emily feels that the only way to maintain her sobriety is to pivot her life away from heterosexuality, retaining total independence. A city housing voucher helps her do this, since she can now afford to live on her own without a partner.

Still, many of the women I interviewed subverted these demands by downplaying the seriousness of their intimate relationships or by hiding their sex lives from support group leaders and other institutional authorities. It often took multiple interviews before women told me about new relationships or sexual desires. The first time I interviewed Maria S., she said she found all men "repulsive." However, when I returned to Maria S.'s apartment several weeks later, she admitted that she had recently slept with a man she liked, her first sexual encounter after leaving her husband. She felt like she was starting to "be alive again" through this relationship. But she also warned him that she only wants "the good side" and that her life will never be in a man's hands again. Despite anxiety about men, Nanette also recently began a new relationship. During our third interview, Nanette told me she had had sex for the first time in six years. She enjoyed the closeness, but like Maria S., Nanette wants to keep her distance. She refuses to let him stay overnight in her apartment. Both Maria S. and Nanette reveal that sexuality is a site through which the ambiguities of survivorhood are felt and confronted. Feelings of anxiety about men circulate together with desire to develop relationships over which they have some control. Neither Nanette nor Maria S., however, have minor children. Thus, their relative freedom from maternal surveillance allows them more flexibility in their sexuality. Legibility as a "good" survivor is lower stakes: both women can afford some *illegibility* in their performances of survivorhood, since they are less dependent on institutions for survival.

On the one hand, women are forced to hide, downplay, and pathologize their sexualities in order to appear as good survivors and to claim resources. On the other hand, some women admitted to longings for new relationships, or disclosed in hushed voices that their new relationships were more serious than they appeared. Though some women created intimate connections amid disciplinary institutional demands, other women rejected heterosexual relationships. In both cases, lessons about the dangers of heterosexuality *sometimes* become tools through which women exert sexual autonomy, questioning the cultural promises of heterosexual "success." In this way, women do not reject heterosexuality in order to claim citizenship after abuse, nor do they reassert themselves as normatively heterosexual subjects; rather, they disidentify from heterosexual citizenship norms, pivoting their goals and hopes for their futures away from partnership with men. While therapeutic programs encourage abstinence as a form of survivor respectability, women enact those norms in complex ways: *slantwise*.

DISIDENTIFYING: HETEROSEXUALITY

So far, I've shown that women alter their relationships to heterosexuality in response to the institutional pressures of survivorhood *and* in response to the spatial dynamics of violence itself. This includes a shift away from the cultural promises of heterosexual romance and from the material arrangements of a male-female, two-parent household. Disidentifying is not about rejecting heterosexuality, but about pivoting within heterosexual arrangements in order to remake sexual subjectivity. Here, I show how women disidentify from normative heterosexuality by avoiding spaces defined by heterosexuality, questioning cultural narratives of heterosexual romance, and creating new rules for their intimate partnerships.

Britney provided an eloquent example of this kind of disidentification. After she left her husband, Britney feared that others would see her as "just another" single Black mother:

> I don't have a ring anymore. It was more like my identity [that was the problem]. Just being okay with being a single mom. I was fine with being without him, but . . . how does this look now? . . . I did not like family functions. I was invited to a Memorial Day barbecue or something. And it was just a bunch of mommies and dads and kids. And I was just like, oh god. It was a big storm that day, I remember. I was like, oh thank you, thank you. Kids, come on, storm's coming. [We gotta go.] Oh god. I'm the only one without a spouse. I gotta go. That was just . . . it was hard. It was hard.

For Britney, being without a partner meant that racialized stigmas surrounding motherhood came crashing down on her. Idealized images of the heterosexual nuclear family—around which family events tend to revolve—began to feel alienating.[60] Britney was doubly affected by fears of Black maternal stigma and nuclear family failure. Britney also refused to date anyone new, fearing that letting a man into her home would undo the self-work she had accomplished in therapy. Orienting her life away from her husband did not simply mean leaving *him*; it also meant refashioning her identity around single motherhood. She began to disidentify—avoiding family functions and refusing to date—with spaces defined by heterosexuality.

Other types of disidentification focus less on the nuclear family and more on the ideological promises of heterosexual romance. Susan told me that since leaving her abuser, she began instructing her children on the dangers of romance narratives. She always believed that her abuser kept her isolated because he loved her so much, buying into the idea that if a man loves you, you should belong to him. She now sees what she calls "the reality:" that the romantic narrative underlying abusive dynamics is a trap. She told me:

> I want [my children] to tap into reality. Especially when they're . . . having boyfriends, girlfriends. Because I see that they think it's like the TV. And it's so sad that the Disney Channel parades being boyfriends and girlfriends at

a young age. When really a child shouldn't even be having their mind on that. But you know, I wish I could change things, but that's the way the world is moving. . . . So what I need to do is also tap into reality myself. And if I tap into reality, then I could try to steer them.

Susan transformed her ideas about heterosexual romance after leaving her abuser, getting in touch with "reality" and defying the Disney fantasy. While she used to give men the benefit of the doubt, she now "tests" them by making them mad and waiting to see if they will become violent. She explained that if they pass her test and do not hurt her, she knows she can date them. Susan acknowledged that this ritualistic "testing" of men is risky, but she feels it's necessary to protect herself. This is Susan's method of disidentified sexual citizenship—approaching intimate relationships as always already steeped in violence, teaching her children to abandon the promises of idealized heterosexual romance. She does not "buy into" the promise of heterosexuality anymore, though she still dates men and hopes to fall in love.

Other women described the process of relinquishing idealized images of the nuclear family as painful. Diana told me, "I thought we were having a child, a happy home, like princesses do. . . . I thought we were going to lead a life in peace. . . . I work and he works. [After the abuse started], I couldn't even look in the mirror because I felt like no one would ever want to look at me. . . . [He'd say], 'You're fat. Who's going to pay attention to you? Who'd want to go out with you?'" Diana described the dissolution of her fantasy of living like a "princess" in the successful folds of the nuclear family. She also described the painful loss of material stability from a dual-earning household. This failed promise was wrapped up in the fear (which he instilled) that she would never find anyone else. This fear kept her trapped, forcing her to continue investing in their relationship even after she knew it was hurting her.

Giving up this dream of a perfect nuclear family was devastating for Diana. She no longer sees heterosexual partnership as a bright promise for the future. She learned, instead, to pivot away from heterosexual partnership, rebuilding her life around different hopes: "I've learned to first place myself before others. It's important to be happy first before making others happy. . . . Sadly my situation, I'm stuck. [I need to] save enough to move out by myself. My goal is to go through all that process and . . .

continue therapy and complete everything and not leave things half done. . . . To find my compass and know what to do." Diana has found new kinds of independence by deciding she doesn't need a man, but she also now faces the reality of raising her son alone on a paltry income earned from restocking supplies in a warehouse in the suburbs. Her therapeutic programs encourage her to find "independence," though the material means of such independence remain maddeningly out of reach.

Luz explained how she guards her relationships from becoming too close: "I'd rather just have friends and that's it. . . . If some friendship kind of turned a little bit closer, then bye, I can't talk to you no more. . . . That's it, nope, bye. No, no, no, I can't do that, I can't do that. It's just safer like that." Luz told me she can tell just from a man's tone of voice if he is capable of becoming "aggressive." For Luz, pivoting away from heterosexuality means having male friends but keeping them at arm's length, maintaining single motherhood and paying for her apartment by herself. But this kind of self-protective work is possible only because heterosexuality has become both visible and perilous. The promises of a tranquil, "successful" heterosexual life have been violently disrupted, and women sometimes respond by pivoting away from heterosexuality altogether, orienting their futures around a different set of expectations. Delma, for example, takes a practical approach to heterosexual relationships and cheerfully explained that she likes it when her male friend does household chores for her like "cleaning the fish tank," but she does not allow him to stay overnight.

Nevaeh told me she had been abstinent since she gave birth to her son six years ago. "I don't want to be involved, because I know what happens with it. If I am involved, it'll have to be my husband, or someone that I know will be there for the long haul. Because we're gonna have to work together." Nevaeh still desires a male partner, even a husband, but she refuses to orient her life around that promise. The jig is up, so to speak. She made that mistake with her son's father, idealizing the relationship and the image of them working together as coparents, despite his brutal violence and his refusal to support her financially by marrying her. As Nevaeh reveals, disidentified sexual citizenship does not have to mean rejecting marriage, but something more like "identification with a difference."[61] Nevaeh still hopes to be married but vows that she'll make the rules this time, making sure they're "working together."

Even Ebony and Rubi, both married since leaving their abusers, have transformed their orientations toward heterosexuality. Married to the man who helped her escape from her abuser many years ago, Ebony still struggles to make her husband understand the ongoing effects of domestic violence on her life: "[Domestic violence] is always gonna be with me. It's like baggage with me. . . . Sometimes my husband don't want to understand. That I can't just zip this out of my mind. It's always gonna be there. It's planted. . . . When you married me, you married the whole package." As a survivor of abuse, Ebony finds that she has to navigate heterosexual partnership differently than she did before. Violence has shifted the terms of her relationship with her husband. Ebony is therefore tasked with remaking both her *and* her husband's expectations surrounding heterosexual partnership.

Rubi described a similar situation: "I've developed a barrier so that [my husband] isn't attached to me and whenever he wants to leave my life, he can leave. . . . I've become a very bitter person, a very angry person and a person that . . . doesn't allow anyone to hurt me. Sometimes, my husband won't do anything and I'm already on the defensive. I can't recuperate the [Rubi] that I was before." Rubi articulates here the difficulties of developing new relationships after surviving violence. She has transformed her expectations of romance and intimacy, insisting on her own independence and the need to persevere as a single mother should her husband choose to leave. Rubi pivoted away from some of the ideals of heterosexual marriage *in order to be married*; this disidentification complicates her marriage but makes her feel safer. Rubi and Ebony both disidentify from heterosexuality *from within the institution of marriage*, admitting that they are transformed as heterosexual subjects, unable to fit normative models of wifely contentment. They do not disavow a sexual subjectivity associated with heterosexual marriage, but they attest that the work of rebuilding a nuclear home life is rife with new obstacles.

It is the disjuncture between the *ideologies* of heterosexuality and lived experiences of the *violence* of heterosexuality that prompts disidentification.[62] Women feel a fracture between the promises of heterosexuality and its treacherous reality, which causes them to disidentify when they are hailed, again and again, into the ideological structure of heterosexuality. Remaking sexual subjectivity after violence requires a slantwise approach to heterosexuality, or a process of breaking off from its normative arrangements. For the women I interviewed, heterosexuality no longer feels "like home."[63] It is pockmarked and menacing. Women's experiences of violence bring the institution of heterosexuality into view—its precarity, its instability, the masculine privilege that comes with it. However, questioning heterosexual ideals often forces women into a painful reworking of their intimate lives, leaving them feeling lonely, as if they have failed in their social contracts to be happy and reproductive citizens.

DISIDENTIFYING: REPRODUCTION

While heterosexual reproduction is supposed to fulfill the promises of sexual citizenship, domestic violence victims often experience pregnancy and motherhood as imprisoning. Pregnancy coercion and reproductive violence are increasingly well-documented phenomena, as domestic violence victims report their abusers tampering with their birth control, limiting their access to abortion, lying about or refusing condom use, and/or pressuring them to have children.[64] Being in an abusive relationship increases women's risk of sexually transmitted infections, dangerous pregnancies, and poor infant health outcomes.[65] Several of the women I interviewed told me that at least one of their children was the result of their partner raping them. These experiences of violence surrounding reproduction, pregnancy, and birth are significant, since the promises of procreation and the biological family are bedrocks of heterosexual citizenship. While disidentifying from heterosexual reproduction may be painful, women also reported that refusing reproduction can be liberating. Women may disidentify from sexual citizenship by questioning the role of children in creating an ideal home and/or by using birth control secretly. In this sense, motherhood (or refused motherhood) is a site through which women distance themselves from abusive men and even from heterosexuality itself.

Women's experiences of birth control sabotage and manipulation were extensive. Kathy's ex-husband refused to let her use birth control and called her a prostitute for wanting it. He once removed her birth control device in the process of raping her. When Brenda got the birth control patch and told her boyfriend that it was a nicotine patch, he demanded to see the box it came in and then ripped it off her arm. Carla's husband forced her to have her IUD taken out and called her a prostitute for having one. Jaylene secretly uses the birth control ring while her boyfriend pressures her to have a child with him. L. L.'s husband barred her from using birth control and repeatedly forced himself on her while she was still in recovery from childbirth. While L. L. was fearful of her husband's sexual aggression, she described being even more afraid of having another child. Cloaked in cultural promises of romance and feminine fulfillment, pregnancy and childbearing often turn violent for domestic violence victims, causing them to disidentify from the heterosexual nuclear family as a site of social success.

For the women I interviewed, this type of control over reproduction was part of the "everyday" of domestic violence. Some women did not even bother mentioning the level of reproductive coercion they experienced until I asked them explicitly about their health. Other women talked about pregnancy as the worst kind of entrapment, since it yoked their lives to their abusers' lives more strongly, making it impossible to leave. Some women were forced to return to their abusers upon discovering a pregnancy, needing the material support of his income, housing, or childcare. Susan told me:

> When I wound up pregnant and went back to him, I just felt like . . . I felt like it was a loss for me . . . [*voice drops*] 'cause I felt like he would always follow me. . . . He took me to the abortion clinic, and they told me, no you're too far along. And so I wind up having my daughter. And I just cried and cried and cried. In front of the abortion clinic. He was like, "Get your ass in the car!" Pulling me by my hair and everything else. For someone who wanted to have a baby, this should be a happy time. Instead it was like, I don't know, like I couldn't do nothing right.

Susan discovered she was pregnant and tried to have an abortion, but she relied on her boyfriend for transportation and money. He refused to drive her to the clinic and kept her locked inside the house for more than a month. By the time she persuaded him to take her in for a "check-up," she was too far along to have the procedure. Susan wanted to regain control by having an abortion, to seize her body back. When she was denied this, she felt her life collapsing. The ideological structure of the heterosexual nuclear family became very visible to Susan through this experience, and she described shifting her feelings about partnership and parenthood afterward. More specifically, she began to understand that her partner didn't really *want* children—he just wanted to control her.

Other abusers used financial pressures and stigma around single motherhood to keep women trapped. Margaret cried when she told me that she loves her children but wishes she'd never had them: they kept her tied to her abusive ex-husband for too many years. The women I interviewed often felt regret about having children—though they also felt deep shame about that regret.[66] Still, Alma told me that if she were to be born again, she would never have children. Because her husband sabotaged her attempts at birth control, when she became pregnant for the fifth time, she thought she was doomed to stay with him forever. Instead, her coworker helped her sneak away to get an abortion. Alma described this as the most liberating moment in her life. Afterward, she started to tell people about the abuse and to lock the door when her husband came home drunk. For Alma, disidentifying from reproduction was essential to the process of leaving her husband, as she pivoted away from her role as dutiful wife/mother in order to survive.

Disidentifying from heterosexual reproduction also often means that women have to remake their sexual subjectivities. As in Alma's case, sometimes seizing control of reproductive technologies allows this to happen. Ebony, for example, had her tubes tied secretly after she gave birth to her second child. She knew her boyfriend would beat her if he found out, but she also knew that if she had another baby, her chances of leaving would vanish. Having her tubes tied also allowed her to have sexual relationships with other men, which gave her some respite from his control and abuse. Through the sexual independence brought by this procedure, Ebony began to fashion new types of relationships that made her feel in control of her future. Indeed, several women told me that part of their escape strategy was to begin using birth control secretly.

Megan's husband forces ovulation tests on her and follows her hormonal cycle in minute detail. She told me he is "tracking her body" in order to get her pregnant, which makes her feel helpless. Despite wanting a child herself, Megan is avoiding pregnancy until she can plot how to leave him. She needs to save more money and make a plan for moving across state lines with a baby. By sabotaging his surveillance of her ovulation and maneuvering to get some control back over her body, Megan disidentifies from the heterosexual nuclear family even as she plans for motherhood. Megan is actively transforming her plans for motherhood, but in a way that is certainly *not* a rejection of a heterosexually reproductive future.

Pregnancy and reproduction are sites of heterosexual disidentification and "self-making" because they are flashpoints for multiple tensions.[67] Most of the women I interviewed faced the arduous task of rerouting their lives away from a two-parent household, a difficult maneuver because male partners and their extended families are often caregivers for children or provide other essential financial support. While disidentifying from reproduction often means taking control of one's body, it also might mean having to raise children with little support. Disidentifying from heterosexuality may involve rejecting the association of motherhood with good citizenship, but it may also involve facing social devaluation as a single mother. Distancing oneself from heterosexual normativity, then, is not distinct from the paradoxes of survivorhood already outlined in this book. Disidentifying is a set of strategies that women execute when no available, redeeming, or transformative discourses of sexual subjectivity are offered to them. Disidentifying from heterosexuality after violence is a learned survival tactic, one that may still yield heterosexual and reproductive futures—just enacted differently.

SLANTWISE

Part of my effort in this chapter is to challenge the widespread, asexual depiction of domestic violence survivors in research on intimate partner violence. Existing literature tends to reproduce the assumption that women should be abstinent in order to be "good" survivors. The stories presented in this chapter reveal that surviving violence is not simply about gender and the family, but also about heterosexuality and sexual subjectivity. When women survive abuse, they navigate fraught relationships to their sexual desires, their sense of home, and their familial identities. It turns out we've been missing a lot by ignoring the role of heterosexuality in women's experiences of domestic violence.

In fact, women often experience domestic violence as failed sexuality. Many women asked, "What's wrong with me?" because they fell in love with a partner who became abusive. Some women used the language of failure explicitly: Gwyn told me, "Something's a little wrong [with me]." She referred to herself as "Failure [Gwyn]." Or as Diamond said, "I graduated early from high school, so I was always a nerd. But I failed when it came to men." While we can attribute this language to larger victim-blaming narratives, there is also a structural critique at work here: women understand that the promises of heterosexuality have failed *them*. Women who have experienced domestic violence often feel these "failures" as a deep loss, and I do not intend to read them as liberating, queer adventures. Rather, my intention is to show that even when heterosexuality becomes violent and imprisoning, women manage to recraft sexual and familial identities by disidentifying from heterosexuality and nuclear family ideals. These are not necessarily "happy" reorientations—they are survival strategies.

When the ideological contradictions of heterosexuality are felt and experienced, women may imagine different types of relations to men and reconfigured spaces of the nuclear family. For some, this means rejecting promises of heterosexual familial "success." For others, this means approaching heterosexuality with a new sense of no-bullshit wisdom. Many women still seek heterosexual partnerships, but they approach those partnerships with a new drive for autonomy and a different set of expectations around feminine complementarity to the masculine ideal. Some women distance themselves from motherhood in order to escape abusers and put up barriers against hegemonic masculinity. In these ways, women do not construct entirely new frameworks for their sexual subjectivities, but they pursue a different approach to heterosexuality and nuclear family citizenship. Experiences of intimate violence and survivorhood sometimes give women the resources to *reinterpret* the hail of heterosexuality.[68] This is what I mean by disidentification: women continue to engage with cultural promises of the heterosexual nuclear family, but they take a different approach toward fulfilling those promises.

By focusing on women's experiences of violence and their participation in therapeutic programs as the turning points in their relationships to heterosexuality, I show that it is not only queer desire that produces queer reorientations. Heterosexuality produces its own ruptures and bad feelings, which women seize upon to remake some of its patterns in their lives. While queerness is typically thought of as a site of difference, I have shown that *heterosexuality* may also be a site of difference and subversion.[69] We must take seriously that heterosexual identifications may be nonnormative. There is analytic danger, in fact, in treating heterosexuality as unified, as having a near-natural ideological cohesion.[70] There is volatility in heterosexuality, even though it is hegemonic. My analysis has shown that, in fact, heterosexuality continuously produces its own possibilities for disidentification, since its ideological promises conflict with its violent realities in women's lives. Surviving this conflict requires that women take up a new relationship to heterosexuality, practicing it differently, refashioning their sense of belonging and their imagination of social success and fulfillment.

Conclusion

TRAUMATIC CITIZENSHIP

> The fight wasn't just to survive bodily, though that could
> be intense enough, but to survive as a person possessed
> of rights, including the right to participation and dignity
> and a voice. More than to survive, then: to live.
>
> Rebecca Solnit (2020, 4)

Martha, a fifty-one-year-old white woman, was excited and emotional when I interviewed her at the large dining room table in her suburban home. She had recently left her husband and was new to the support group where we met. For the first time in her life, Martha was busy searching for free therapy services, scoping out the best food pantries, and applying for food stamps and other state assistance. Near the end of our interview, Martha told me: "I am a victim of domestic abuse. Not a survivor yet. I'm working on becoming one. When I started [support] group, I [was] a victim of domestic abuse. Now I'm a victim working on being a survivor. . . . You don't go to school for this. You don't take a class on how to get over being a victim. You don't take a class to even *know* you're a victim. . . . You learn how to cook an egg. You don't learn how to do this. . . . I'm not a survivor yet." When I pressed her to explain what she meant by "survivor," Martha told me she didn't feel like she had overcome the abuse because going to divorce court still felt like "ripping open surgical staples." Survivorhood, for Martha, will have to be deferred until a later date, until she reaches a promised stage of psychological overcoming—and gets her divorce papers signed.

Martha senses that the court will be more likely to believe that her marriage was abusive if she and her children are attending therapeutic programs at a domestic violence agency. Martha attends the support group strategically to show that she has been a victim. But she also goes because she feels she needs the help. Martha finds therapeutic programs to be empowering and eye-opening—but also quasi-mandatory and labor intensive. To achieve a sense of resilience after abuse and to get what they need from state bureaucracies, women learn to seek out therapeutic programs and perform psychological improvement. Martha, like the other women I interviewed, is engaged in a kind of traumatic citizenship—or telling stories about trauma and performing recovery in order to become legible within powerful systems. This book has explored the pleasures, the power, and the dangers of these therapeutic transformations in antiviolence politics and in women's intimate lives.

Traumatic citizenship is indeed an intimate process.[1] For domestic violence victims, rights and recognition are claimed through face-to-face interactions, storytelling, and embodied practices like therapy attendance. Traumatic citizenship is not a *thing* achieved in a moment of recognition, but an ongoing social practice.[2] In Charles Tilly's formulation, citizenship is a set of "mutual, contested claims between agents of states and members of socially constructed categories."[3] The very possibility of making such claims has been created by feminist activism.[4] When women demand recognition as "victims" and "survivors," they participate in histories of feminist struggle. Through these processes of claims making, women create attachments to systems and institutions. Citizenship is not membership, then, but a power-laden *relation*.[5] Foucault describes it as a "field of relationships."[6]

Rape and domestic violence are recognized as gender-based crimes for which victims deserve protection and resources. However, as Poulami Roychowdhury points out, "women who claim rights face retaliation, ill health, and social isolation," as well as uneven enforcement of their rights by authorities.[7] It turns out to be very complicated and onerous to secure rights and resources based on an experience that is fundamentally exclusionary, an experience for which victims themselves are blamed and pathologized. Citizenship emerged as a question for me when almost all the women I interviewed described feeling "shocked" the first time they experienced violence from an intimate partner.[8] Women typically experience intimate abuse as a rupture of their social context and sense of equality. Even if they had experienced male violence before, women described violence from trusted partners as intense betrayals. Domestic violence violates their ideas about romantic love, family, community, and the home—as well as their sense of themselves as strong, capable women. Women expect to be treated as relative equals in their relationships, and the experience of violence severs them from that sense of equality. Further, abused women's mobility and autonomy are severely circumscribed over the course of their relationships, curtailing their ability to participate equally in their families and communities.

In this sense, *intimate violence is itself a violation of citizenship*. As Evan Stark writes, domestic violence is an "offense to liberty that prevents women from freely developing their personhood, utilizing their capacities, or practicing citizenship."[9] I draw from sociological work on "social" or "substantive" citizenship to understand this type of violation.[10] Social citizenship is different from formal citizenship, which references one's status as the legal member of a nation-state. Social citizenship refers instead to economic and social security, centered around issues such as work, education, health, and quality of life.[11] It is concerned with the responsibilities of the welfare state to provide the means through which everyone can share in social life.[12] The experience of domestic violence cuts victims off from their communities and from key social institutions like work and education. Martha, for example, lost access to her beloved church community as a result of the abuse. Some of the women I interviewed dropped out of school to appease their abusers, others lost their jobs, some were unable to participate in community programs, and almost all lost access to social networks. Victims of domestic violence simply do not have equal freedom to move about and participate in everyday life. This is what it means to talk about abuse as a violation of citizenship.

Expanding the concept of social citizenship, Evelyn Nakano Glenn defines "substantive citizenship" as recognition by others and a sense of belonging in a political community.[13] Substantive citizenship is of central concern for understanding domestic violence, since women often have to work hard to install themselves in an imagined community of other victims and survivors when they seek help. When women access resources after abuse, they learn how to engage in *traumatic citizenship*, to tell stories about trauma and participate in therapy in order to get what they need.[14] Because intimate violence violates women's citizenship and cuts them off from the resources of social life, when they leave or try to leave, they have to plug themselves into various institutions in order to reclaim citizenship and put their lives back together. This process of reclaiming citizenship, I have shown, is increasingly structured by professional therapeutic interventions and discourses of traumatic victimization and recovery.

Scholars have shown that being able to tell stories of suffering matters for claiming rights and resources.[15] E. Summerson Carr reveals that clients in addiction programs are forced to engage in "scripting," or parroting narratives about future recovery in order to gain cultural capital in therapy, court, and welfare systems.[16] This kind of narrative labor—telling the *right* kind of story, a *recognizable* story—is often the only way "out." Didier Fassin and Richard Rechtman argue that testimony of traumatic suffering is increasingly important for such claims, since trauma purports to offer a trans-contextual "truth" about the human condition.[17] But truth cannot be achieved through telling alone. Rather, I have shown that trauma stories must be *performed and embodied* via motherhood, sexuality, race, and class.[18] Respectable performances make victims "translatable" to the "networks of responsible actors empowered to manage" them.[19]

The concept of translation suggests that citizenship and belonging are "in motion," that access to recognition requires ongoing labor across webs of institutions and experts. To capture these dynamics, I have focused on the concept of legibility. Legibility refers to the desire to be seen and acknowledged, but also to what is lost when we have to use the limiting categories handed to us. As the women in this book have shown, *becoming legible through performances of trauma and recovery is itself traumatizing.* Women are situated across structures of inequality that complicate their interpellation as trauma survivors, and as a result, they often feel dissonance when they seek legibility. Becoming legible is not a moment of recognition, but an ongoing process of learning how to tell therapeutic stories, how to perform respectable motherhood, pivoting away from the ideological promises of heterosexuality, and using alternative discourses of health and embodiment. Becoming legible is disciplinary and multi-sited. It is open-ended. Legibility provides things but it is characterized by loss.

In an anonymous letter written to the Massachusetts Coalition of Battered Women Service Groups in 1981, "Jane Doe" told her story of abuse for the first time, writing "I have tried several times to hand compose this letter but it wouldn't come properly. The writing was shaky. The typing is not very good either, although I am a good typist. The truth is that I am emotional about what has happened to me because *it is so much more real than I can ever describe.*"[20] Jane Doe makes several important points about legibility here. First, legibility may be written in a "shaky" hand: one may be unsure of one's categorization, may doubt one's ability to perform correctly, or may feel fearful about what such recognition will expose. The process of becoming legible involves uncertainties, pauses, and tremulous performances. Second, one's body may falter when attempting to become legible, betraying the ability to communicate. Becoming legible, after all, often requires an able, normative body and self.[21] Finally, Jane Doe tells us that her experience is "more real" than the words she can write, suggesting the inadequacies of language to capture lived experience, an excess of reality that cannot be contained in categories.

Theorizing legibility requires that we pay attention to the "shakiness" and betrayals of interpellation *and* to the possibilities generated by social recognition. Another woman's story of abuse, written to ICADV in the 1990s, speaks to these possibilities: "Through individual and group counseling . . . for the first time I didn't feel alone. For me, it was a new beginning, and I started setting goals. First, get out of the situation. Then I hired a lawyer and filed for divorce. I also got my order of protection, barring him from the home. . . . I started attending group sessions and my individual counseling on a weekly basis. . . . I could feel myself starting to grow. . . . I do matter, and I am alive!"[22] For this woman, a terrifying and obscure experience has become legible to herself and others. Legal recognition is conferred through telling her narrative in court. Cultural and institutional legibility are conferred through the support group setting. Finally, this exclamation—"I do matter, and I am alive!"—is the heart of legibility. The process of forcing one's (invisible) experiences into the public sphere materializes a new self (literally: "I *matter*"), a sense of belonging and identity, even of renewed life.

Still, the process of becoming legible is not holistic. What had to be left out of this woman's narrative in order for the courts to recognize her as a good victim? Which parts of her suffering did she expel so that she would be read as worthy? Were there other women applying for orders of protection that day who didn't get them? Achieving legibility is replete with erasures. But there is also the reprieve of having a language for something previously unnamable, the feeling of kinship with other survivors, the empowering sense of institutions giving a name to a "private" experience. This kind of reprieve takes work—it is labor-intensive—because the categories of "victim" and "survivor" do not allow for an open field of possibilities, but a set of expertly defined constraints.

In many ways, then, this book explores subject formation, a dynamic process that takes place at the intersection of ideology and desire. Traumatic citizenship is rooted in *relations* and *attachments* between women and systems. From getting a visa to securing an order of protection to having one's story heard in support group, emotional and material relations are constantly generated between women and state programs. Survivors are not "created" through social welfare systems. Rather, survivorhood is forged at the intersection of women's needs/desires and the systems that bear down on them. In this sense, while the terms of traumatic citizenship are imposed on women "from above," discourses of trauma, victimization, and survivorhood become part of women's everyday lives, their deeply held identities, their maternal practices, their romantic relationships, their relationships to their bodies. Trauma and survivorhood, as capacious languages of suffering and resilience, radiate across women's lives.

FAILURE

And yet, what women *get* when they become legible as survivors is rarely enough to recover even what they had before domestic violence decimated their social, financial, and psychological resources. Women may be able to reclaim emotional stability through counseling, perhaps a sense of belonging with other women in support group, and hopefully some resources like temporary housing. But they typically do not secure long-term, stabilizing resources that would help them escape the social and economic precarity that made them vulnerable to intimate violence in the first place. As Sarah Haley writes, the intersection of state abandonment with intimate abuse creates "structures of captivity and abjection" that shape women's lives even after they "leave."[23] Celeste Watkins-Hayes reminds us that personal transformations are really only possible when structural conditions are improved.[24] Most of the women I interviewed did not experience much improvement in their structural circumstances, despite their committed participation in state-funded, therapeutic programs.

This thin infrastructural support means that women learn to take personal responsibility for their continued suffering and abandonment. The failings of systems are recast as the internalized effects of "trauma." There is a great deal of invisible maternal labor embedded in this process of responsibilization. As Fabiola told me: "I learned at [the domestic violence agency] that domestic violence happens most of the time because it's a cycle. It comes from your ancestors, from your older families. I think. . . . These kinds of groups help . . . another person [see] that they're like me. [They're] a survivor. So, we close the cycle. We bring our kids to the therapies. We bring our kids to do healthy activities and teach them that it's not right to scream. We [want to] scream sometimes, but we need to control our feelings, our emotions." Here, Fabiola describes the maternal labor that saturates traumatic citizenship: she must teach her children how to control their emotions and *she* must take responsibility for not "repeating the cycle" of abuse. In fact, Fabiola wants to scream, but survivorhood requires emotional self-discipline—for herself and for her children.

Like Fabiola's suppressed desire to scream, women's labors of survivorhood are rife with forestalled longings, absences, and failures. These kinds of frustrations are compounded by the fact that women experience gaslighting and other forms of abuse *that are themselves a kind of absence*, that are confusing to name and invisible to others. Further, the experience of intimate violence changes women's relationships to heterosexuality and the nuclear family, often in ways that feel disorienting and depressing, cutting them off from once-comforting cultural expectations. The survivor story is simply not enough to account for all of these violences and their rippling effects.

In this sense, survivorhood demands a redemption narrative that often conceals women's rage and disappointment. As another woman wrote to ICADV in the 1990s, "Am I a 'SURVIVOR'? I guess to the extent that I am still alive. . . . I'd like someone to tell me. . . . WHERE ARE MY RIGHTS? Where is my right to get on with my life, to not continue to be financially devastated at the hands of this man?"[25] This type of indignation, this demand for material resources, is more or less illegible under the politics of trauma. This woman's capitalized questions speak volumes about the effects of this illegibility.

In fact, what becomes clear from listening to women's stories is precisely the unclarity of it all. The victim-to-survivor story is attractive because it has a clear temporal trajectory. She's on a better path. She is now "deserving." But, of course, women who have experienced domestic violence often use violence and manipulation themselves—to survive abuse, yes, but also to wield some power in institutions. We want there to be a victim so innocent, so blindingly pure, that she could turn any story into a narrative of good and evil, of triumphant overcoming. As psychologist Janice Haaken explains, the survivor's ability to mobilize support depends on the "dramatic power of [her] trauma story."[26] We want a crystalline temporality: causes X, effects Y. It is my job in this book to offer a set of explanations for intimate violence and the hushed violences of the bureaucracies that surround it. But the story I'm telling is also disingenuous in the clarity it tries to offer. What really happens is more amorphous. Intimate violence is often paradoxical and confounding at its core. Even in this book, we want there to be a story of progress and redemption. But often, no one is saved, finally.

REDEMPTION

> Victims exist in a society that tells us our purpose is to be an
> inspiring story. But sometimes the best we can do is tell you
> we're still here, and that should be enough.
> Chanel Miller (2020, 312)

One of the only intelligible stories we're allowed to tell about gender-based violence is of a past, violated self that uses expert therapeutic intervention to open, resiliently, into a new future. This story and performance of self—this path to survivorhood—can do amazing things: it can create new capacities for emotional reflexivity, it can help women understand the role of gender-based oppression in their relationships, it can link families to caring professionals. Survivorhood also offers new forms of identification.

And an identity, especially one forged through marginalization and stigma, is never *just* an identity. As Evelyn Hammonds writes, identities are "discursive and material terrains where there exists the possibility for the active production of *speech, desire,* and *agency*."[27] Survivorhood, even though it is an expert medicalized discourse, does make its offerings.

For example, as we were wrapping up our interview, I asked Mariposa, a forty-six-year-old Latina woman, what she'd like her pseudonym to be. Quickly, she answered "Mariposa" because it means butterfly in Spanish. She told me that, like butterflies, domestic violence victims undergo a "metamorphosis" when they survive abuse. Mariposa explained that her own consciousness has transformed since leaving her boyfriend. She had a "mental break," she told me, when he threw her into a refrigerator. Afterward, she found a domestic violence support group in her neighborhood and it became her "medicine." She began reading self-help books and meditating. Mariposa used therapeutic language and practices to enact a transformation in the self, a transition from "victim" to "survivor."

And yet, despite all her self-work, Mariposa told me that she remains frustrated and angry since leaving her boyfriend. She has a new outlook, she says, but she feels confused about everything that has happened to her. Her story of metamorphosis—though genuine to her, unquestionably *real*—has not allowed her to recover financially from this relationship, to pay her medical bills, or to convince her teenage children to move back in with her. Mariposa's story of psychological recovery fails to capture the ongoing material effects of domestic violence, which ripple through her life without a language of redemption to capture them.

Even though it promises a redemptive identity, then, survivorhood is unsatisfying because it offers little in the way of material supports. Further, survivorhood is part of an institutional apparatus that disciplines women into telling certain kinds of acceptable stories and engaging in respectable performances of self and family. This story isn't really an *option*—it is mandatory and normative. Its compulsory nature is subtle, however, such that the victim-to-survivor paradigm feels like self-discovery. In fact, *good feelings* of "overcoming" are often the only things on offer while interacting with slow, cruel bureaucracies and skeptical authorities.

The survivor paradigm is not only full of such disappointments, but it is exclusionary: some women cannot or will not tell such stories. Because their lives cannot follow an upward trajectory, survivorhood forces some women onto a plane of abjection. They may be denied resources, or they may just be seen as "bad victims" who don't deserve our care. Women blame themselves for these exclusions because the failures of "recovery" are understood to be personal rather than structural.[28] For the women I interviewed, the harms of abuse are regularly compounded by the institutions set up to help them, by the stories and performances demanded of them when they seek support. It is for these reasons that we should think of intimate violence as *processual*.

Theorizing the processual nature of abuse requires paying attention to the identities and performances that women develop as they move through therapeutic bureaucracies.[29] I have shown that when women seek domestic violence counseling after abuse, when they fight for child custody in courts or with DCFS, when they apply for visas or seek mental health treatment, they take on new roles as traumatized citizens. Therapeutic programs reshape women's relationships to the state, as well as to their families, bodies, sexualities, and sense of self. Claiming the status of "victim" or "survivor" is experienced at deep and ambivalent levels of the self, and it is an ongoing process that for many women seems to have no end, despite promises of a redemptive finale.

SURVIVOR POLITICS

Nonetheless, the politics of trauma have the potential to be more open-ended than all of this, to be rooted in a social context that enables self-determination. Survivorhood *could* be (and sometimes is) forged in communities rather than in professional networks of therapeutic expertise, in political commitments and chosen identities. As many domestic violence leaders hope, the concept of trauma *could* capture structural and psychological harms together. As it stands, however, trauma is embedded in a professionalized circuit of experts who are presumed to know more than the women they serve. Trauma is enmeshed in state funding mechanisms over which anti-violence activists long ago ceded control. As Mimi Kim explains about the criminalization of domestic violence, "Each successful demand for criminalization . . . weakened feminist autonomy, diminishing its power and presence within a field increasingly occupied by hybrid institutions."[30] "Survivor" is not free-floating; it is part of a complex infrastructure that is increasingly medicalized and professionalized. This book is not an argument *against* survivor identities, but rather, an effort to begin extracting survivorhood from a political economy of deservingness tied to professionalized networks of expertise.

After all, second-wave feminists' imaginings of what they could offer domestic violence victims were limited: they thought they could empower women by offering a place to stay for a few days and a support group of other women. But the women who showed up at their doors were poorer and had more complex problems than activists could have imagined. Women arrived having been abandoned by the state *and* having suffered generations of racial violence, police harassment, poverty, addiction, and discrimination in mental health systems. Feminists focused too narrowly on counseling victims, criminalizing abusers, and collaborating with social service systems. They thought they could negotiate with the state while preserving the grassroots spirit of early programs. However, negotiations became trade-offs—and together, feminists and state actors transformed the movement into a victim services branch of the penal and welfare states. The result, today, is an overwhelming focus on psychological victimization and recovery.

I'm not saying that we should abandon therapeutic services. Everyone should have access to quality therapy if they want it. But we cannot expect anything like genuine empowerment to emerge from professionalized therapeutic offerings—especially when participation is coerced. Trauma workers know this. They are saddled with the seemingly impossible task of helping women "become" survivors with only meager resources to offer in one-hour time slots. The solutions imagined by feminist activists are therefore increasingly out of joint with the material realities of women's lives. And women who have experienced domestic violence suffer the consequences of those miscalculations.

But of course, women do figure out how to *survive*, how to make meaning and rebuild—even on this exclusionary terrain. As Claire Decoteau writes, "People's everyday trajectories—the ways in which they strive and thrive—constitute a radical form of politics in their own right."[31] As women make bids for traumatic citizenship, they piece together new stories and

explanations that help them navigate what's to come. And beyond therapeutic narratives, women actually *do* overcome, executing all sorts of feats
to survive. Ebony fled Illinois and married an older man for protection.
Nevaeh left her neighborhood and all her friends so that she would not
run into anyone connected with her abuser. Adriana started a relationship
with a man from a more powerful gang in order to escape the grips of her
first boyfriend. Brenda left Chicago with five children and learned a whole
new social service and education system in her new home. Diamond had
her toddler's first and last name changed so that her abuser could not
find them. *This* is the labor of survivorhood, and this kind of labor gives
women resources and strategies that exceed therapeutic discourses.

And in fact, wanting, demanding, and claiming recognition as a survivor is an important kind of politics. As feminist theorist Sara Ahmed
explains:

> The struggle for recognition can be about having access to a good life. It
> can be about wanting inclusion in the structures that have been oppressive,
> wanting inclusion in the very structures that remain predicated on the dis-
> possession of others. But that's not the only story. The struggle for recogni-
> tion can also come from the experience of what is unbearable, what cannot
> be endured, when you lose your bearings, becoming unhoused. The
> struggle for recognition can be a struggle for an ordinary life . . . in making
> an ordinary life from the shattered pieces of a dwelling, we tell. We dwell,
> we tell.[32]

The juxtaposition that Ahmed sets up between "dwelling" and "telling"
is instructive for thinking about domestic violence, an experience that
literally and figuratively "unhouses" women, forcing them—willingly
or not—into a process of "telling." While telling is certainly no guaran-
tee of being rehoused, it is nonetheless required in order to achieve
legibility. Still, what if one cannot "tell" correctly? What if one's telling
is unintelligible to listeners? What if what one seeks to tell is unutter-
able, unreal, inexplicable? In this book, I have tried to suggest answers to
some of these questions, revealing the limits of therapeutic frameworks
for offering a "political map" of a better life.[33] These limits show up in
conditions of structural vulnerability and the "pernicious dichotomy" of
victim/survivor.[34] Despite such limits, Ahmed's words suggest a kind of
willfulness—being in a place, demanding to be heard—that can also be

found in the stories of the women I interviewed, an insistence on picking up the tools offered and using them to craft new forms of being and knowing. *To resist erasure*, after all, is precisely what survivors of domestic violence know how to do. This is hard-won knowledge. And this refusal to disappear—women's insistence that they will not be swallowed up by coercive men and institutions—is the heart of their stubborn bids for legibility.

Methodological Appendix

People often ask me if interviewing domestic violence survivors is difficult. If it's emotionally draining to listen to women's stories. Even though these kinds of questions make me uncomfortable, I have to admit that there are challenges to this kind of interviewing. Sometimes I was stoic while women cried. Sometimes the women I interviewed were stoic and I cried in the car on the way home. There were times when we both sat in silence for long stretches, waiting for anger or other emotions to pass. The lines between empathy and pity and fear for someone's safety can feel icky. I often agonized over my role as a researcher and wondered how I could "share" women's stories the way they wanted me to. I struggled over how much of their stories to include in this text, over what Barbara Sutton describes as the tension between presenting "horror show" narratives about violence versus "sanitized" accounts.[1]

But mostly, conducting these interviews was a joyful experience because the women I interviewed were funny, sarcastic, smart, thoughtful, curious, and yes, sometimes very pissed off. The trauma of domestic violence does not devour a whole complex life and personality. I focus on violence in this book because I believe—and the women I interviewed also believe—that to *not* talk about gender-based violence is to "cede power."[2] If one has the capacity to listen to these stories and still go on with one's day, with one's life, then I think it's necessary to do that listening. This book engages in a long history of feminist insistence that we should be loud about precisely the things that masculine culture tries to convince us are "private" problems. But let us not cede power, either, by allowing trauma and violence to overtake the whole story, to subsume everything that can be said or imagined about a person.

Writing about other people's traumas can feel heavy, however, because as a sociologist I cannot present women's stories in some pure, untranslated form. Not at all. One of the tasks of ethnography is to tell a story, to build a "believable world" that the reader will accept as factual.[3] Inevitably, I take women's stories and put them into my own larger explanation of what's happening. Those of us who observe and record have the power to define.[4] We cannot make believe that our task as researchers is simply to "give voice to the voiceless." We are situated, instead, in what Patti Lather has called the "ruins" of the Western feminist ethnographic enterprise, which disallows us from pretending we are benevolent storytellers.[5] I have not always been able to foreground the things that women cared most about telling me. I let the interviews go where they went and asked follow-up questions, but let's be clear that my own knowledge production agenda has prevailed here. Certainly, I have aimed to center marginalized standpoints. I have sought a grounded approach that builds theory from women's experiences. I have tried to trace women's silences as their own type of knowledge. But ultimately, I decided to tell a story about legibility, trauma, and survivorhood—whether or not that's the story women wanted me to tell. I have tried to remain accountable to women's struggles for self-representation, knowing that such struggles are open-ended. But I'm sure my failures are many, and that they weigh more than I know.[6]

I cannot pretend, either, to have told a complete story—though I have tried to approach this research in a multi-sited, multilevel way. Postmodern and critical approaches to social science have rightly insisted that we cannot read our data as a whole archive of a person, a history, or a meaning system. Rather, researchers should allow for contradictions, silences, and incompleteness. Selves are "split," always caught between systems of difference.[7] Rather than arriving at some existing "truth," the interview process is full of fractured and partial representations. Donna Haraway instructs us to take "splitting, not being" as the privileged perspective in feminist research.[8] My approach has "split" the data across several sites—archives, professional observations and interviews, and life story interviews with survivors—and refused a centered subject position for my interviewees. I have focused on women's performances of self, their ambivalent relationships to identity, their shifting attachments to expert systems, and their intersecting social exclusions. Resisting the subject's fixity helps clear a way for seeing women's lives *across* events, meanings, and experiences that we might not usually theorize in tandem.

To argue for a "split" methodology does not mean, however, that we should relinquish the social scientific task of building knowledge about real social structures—their violence and their endurance. It is my contention that we can do this best by moving back and forth between "macro" historical and institutional stories and "micro" stories about everyday life and interpersonal harm. What I offer, then, is an epistemology of intimate violence that begins from the subjective and analyzes structures through their webs of feeling and meaning. It is a process that Lila Abu-Lughod refers to as an "ethnography of the particular," which requires reading across narratives of lived experience to elucidate structural conditions.[9] Understanding the subjective becomes the condition of possibility for theorizing the objective—a link that is also captured in the very concept of legibility, which analyzes intimate performances and identities *in relation to* expert knowledge and institutional requirements.

At the "micro" level, this book investigates how women make meaning with, resist, or simply confront survivorhood via their experiences of violence and help-seeking. At the "macro" level, this book analyzes the relationship between feminist politics, the state, and psychological expertise. In order to establish links between these levels of analysis, I conducted archival research on feminist activism, interviews and observations with domestic violence professionals, and life story interviews with women who have experienced domestic violence.

My archival research took place at four sites, all of which focused on the history of feminist anti-violence activism in the United States from the early 1970s through the 2000s. At these archives, I had access to the founding documents of shelters and political coalitions, letters among activists, national coalition meeting minutes, brochures and flyers, federal funding documents, policy statements, and the like. I supplemented these materials by conducting interviews with veteran activists and by listening to longtime activists' recorded life-story interviews in the archives. Luckily for me, feminist anti-violence activists were faithful archivists in their own right, compiling extensive bibliographies on domestic violence during the 1970s, thereby providing rich insights into extant knowledge about violence against women during those early years. With the help of a research assistant, I also created an original archive of Congressional hearings about domestic violence from 1978 to 1985 in order to analyze feminist participation in state policy making during this critical period.

The first archival site I visited was the "Voices of a Movement" collection at DePaul University, which catalogs the history of the Illinois Coalition Against Domestic Violence, founded in Springfield, Illinois, in 1978. This collection gave me a glimpse into local and regional organizing, allowing me to move beyond typical histories of feminist activism that linger on the coasts. The second archival collection I visited was the Violence Against Women collection at Smith College, which documents anti-rape and domestic violence work since the 1960s. I have to admit this was my favorite archival experience: Sylvia Plath went to Smith College, and I got to sit in a room surrounded by her original manuscripts while I pored over activists' papers for days on end—quite honestly a dream come true.

Third, I visited Denver, Colorado, to explore the collections of the National Coalition Against Domestic Violence (NCADV), founded in 1978. NCADV's organizational records are kept in hundreds of boxes in a storage unit to which I was given access. The staff at NCADV helped me schlep boxes from the storage unit to the office so I could do my work in a comfortable chair, rather than sprawled out on the storage unit floor. As far as I know, NCADV's extensive collections have not been used in published research, since they are not officially archived. Finally, I conducted research at Harvard's Schlesinger Library in a collection entitled "Papers of Susan Schechter, 1961–2005." Susan Schechter was a feminist activist and clinical professional who meticulously documented her participation in the anti-violence movement. Her 1982 book on the politics of the movement remains a foundational text.

Doing archival research allowed me to trace feminists' knowledge production, organizing, and policy-making strategies through four decades of movement building. But archives are imperfect and "split" in their own ways. These archives reflect the knowledge that movement leaders thought was important enough to save, and much of the time, archives reflect the voices of prominent organizational leaders while excluding lesser-known activists, volunteers, and community members. Because the organizational leaders who gained power throughout the 1980s were mostly white, educated, straight women, the voices of women of color, poor women, and lesbian activists—especially after the mid-1970s—are less present. Similarly, after the 1980s, survivors' voices are rare. These erasures reproduce inequities in our understanding of the movement, silencing important knowledge producers. But I also fear that because archives reflect large-scale organizing efforts, they also erase histories of radical organizing in small-scale coalitions. I am oriented toward state policy making and professionalization in this book not only because these efforts are related to my research questions, but also because the archives tell *those* stories instead of other stories. As A.K.M. Skarpelis writes, "If documentary practices are historically particular, we cannot infer the presence or absence of a phenomenon based on surviving documentation alone. We need to understand the ecosystem of record production, including the specific prerogatives of organizations generating and preserving them, to gain insight into normative and moral preoccupations."[10] Because most of the documents I used were produced by widely known organizations, their contents reflect the interests of those groups. In reality, anti-violence organizers came from diverse backgrounds and engaged in diverse strategies for social change. They still do.

To capture the contemporary domestic violence field, I studied local domestic violence organizations and programs in Chicago, drawing from interviews and observations with therapists, anti-violence workers, and policy leaders. Interviews were semi-structured and usually took place at the interviewees' workplaces, or occasionally at a coffee shop or restaurant. There are four types of professionals included in this group: (1) clinical therapists in domestic violence organizations, $N = 12$; (2) program directors in domestic violence organizations, $N = 18$; (3) trauma therapists who specialize in violence against women, $N = 6$; (4) domestic violence policy leaders, N = 19. By interviewing both therapists and policy professionals, I uncovered a range of active discourses in the field—reflecting both policy and direct service issues—providing richness to the data and validity checks across institutional locations.[11] I approached domestic violence professionals through a "purposive sampling" method in which participants were selected because of their experience and deep knowledge of the field.[12] When I was volunteering in organizations or attending anti-violence events, I also conducted dozens of informal interviews about these topics that are not included in my "N."

By separating domestic violence "professionals" from domestic violence "victims" in my interview sample, it is not my intention to impose a clear distinction between these groups. Nor do I want to suggest that domestic violence professionals are the "doers" of knowledge and domestic violence victims its recipients. In fact, most domestic violence workers have little control over their jobs. Workers are constrained by organizations and often hurt by clients. They rarely receive the mentorship or supervisory support they need. When I was conducting research at a national domestic violence organization in 2016, the office assistant sat with me and asked questions about my research. She told me, in a whisper, that she herself was a victim of domestic violence, that her husband had attacked her and landed her in the hospital. I asked why she was whispering. She told me that she had never told anyone at the agency: this was the first time she was telling her story inside the walls of that office. She said she didn't know why, but that maybe it felt unprofessional to talk about it. Her hushed voice and lowered eyes devastated me. I experienced her silence and her professional precarity as a kind of collective shame. The divide between "us" and "them," "professionals" and "clients," is incredibly powerful in domestic violence organizations today—and such a dichotomy leads to silences such as this. Workers, too, are vulnerable to the medicalization and bureaucratization of domestic violence work.

I also spent years volunteering in domestic violence agencies, and during my fieldwork period, I attended professional meetings, trainings, workshops, and webinars recommended by my interviewees. The majority of this research was conducted in Chicago and nearby suburbs, which is a rich site for the study of domestic violence. Home to one of the first domestic violence shelters in the United States, Chicago has a long history of anti-violence activism and more than fifteen domestic violence shelters and service organizations are located in the city and nearby suburbs. I developed relationships with many of these agencies, interviewing their staff, attending trainings, and visiting their support groups to recruit participants. Chicago is also home to the National Center for Domestic Violence, Trauma, and Mental Health (NCDVT), a research and policy organization dedicated to domestic violence and trauma. Led by psychiatrists and researchers, NCDVT has created a local environment in which the connections between trauma and domestic violence are at the forefront of anti-violence work. I developed relationships with NCDVT leaders and worked as a research consultant on their projects, allowing me insider knowledge about the relationship between feminism, domestic violence work, and trauma. I also traveled to cities around the Midwest and East Coast to interview national policy leaders and to visit organizations known for their trauma-informed programming.

Workers and policy leaders in the anti-violence field understand deeply the political tensions I explicate throughout this book—between grassroots feminism and professionalization, between social justice and medicalization, between victimhood and survivorhood. They strategize on behalf of their clients and offer much-needed services on this difficult terrain. I am indebted to domestic violence workers and policy leaders for showing me the grace it requires to hold tight to one's commitments while acknowledging these tensions—all while diving into another long day of work.

Finally, I conducted life story interviews with domestic violence survivors. I interviewed forty-three women, and I interviewed twelve of those women two to four times. Interviews typically lasted between two and four hours and were conducted in women's homes, at the agency where we met, or occasionally in my office or a public place. A few times, I accompanied women to other meetings or institutional settings, like domestic violence court. I met women through their support groups or through a referral from their domestic violence counselor. I had access to domestic violence agencies as a longtime volunteer and a state-certified domestic violence crisis advocate myself.[13] Spanish interpreters—recruited from my undergraduate Gender-Based Violence course—accompanied me when interviewees requested them. In the end, we conducted ten interviews in Spanish. All the women's names are pseudonyms that they chose for themselves at the end of our interviews.[14] See table 2 for their demographic details.

Because they attend support groups and other services, the women I interviewed were accustomed to talking about domestic violence. Nonetheless, I attempted to lessen the emotional burden of the interview by breaking it into two parts. In the first part, I asked general, open-ended questions such as, "Tell me a little bit about yourself." In the second part of the interview, I asked questions about women's interactions with medical, mental health, and legal systems, and about their own interpretations of domestic violence. By conducting life story interviews rather than narrowing in on women's experiences with abusive partners, I contextualize abuse in their life course and structural circumstances. Further, rather than imposing an existing framework, life story interviews allow for understanding women's experiences on their own terms, subverting traditional interview formats.

Risks were rarely but sometimes encountered when conducting interviews. On one occasion, we paused and restarted the interview several times so that a participant's children would not hear details of her story. On another occasion, a woman's husband—her abuser—was unexpectedly at home when I arrived for the interview, and we were forced to hastily relocate to a public library. In general,

Table 2   Survivor Demographic Characteristics, *N* = 43

Characteristic	Number	%	Characteristic	Number	%
Race/ethnicity			*Has children under 6 years old*	13	30
White	12	28			
Black/African American	11	26	*Immigrant status*		
Latina	17	40	U.S.-born	27	63
Mixed race	1	2	Documented immigrant	4	9
Arab	1	2	Undocumented (at time of abuse)	12	28
South Asian	1	2			
Family class background			*Length of abusive relationship*		
Poor or working class	29	67	Less than 1 year	1	2
Middle class	14	33	1–3 years	0	0
Primary means of "getting by"			4–6 years	4	9
Paid work only (FT/PT)	6	14	7–9 years	8	19
Child support	11	26	10+ years	16	37
Disability or other combined public assistance	18	42	Ongoing	4	9
			N/A or unknown	3	7
			Multiple of different length	7	16
Not working/family support	8	19			
Education			*Living situation*		
Less than high school	13	30	Rental	24	56
High school degree	11	26	Owns home	7	16
Some college or vocational	11	26	Section 8 rental	4	9
College degree	8	19	With family	6	14
Number of children			Housing program	2	5
No children	6	14	*Mean age*	41	
One child	6	14			
Two children	13	30			
Three children	12	28			
Four or more children	6	14			

however, conducting interviews in women's homes was warm and enjoyable. The home setting provided insights into how women reorganize their intimate lives after leaving abusive partners, and interviewing women at home often involved playing with their children and meeting their extended families, as well as long informal conversations over coffee or while lingering on the front stoop. I already had some rapport with many of the women I interviewed because they knew me as a regular volunteer in the domestic violence agency where we met. Interviewing women at the offices of domestic violence organizations also provided important context, since that setting often prompted women to talk more extensively about their interactions with helping systems.

Finally, my own race, class, and gender undoubtedly shaped this research. Various social identifiers cast me as a social worker or other type of professional when I was conducting interviews. The women I interviewed often perceived me to be an employee of the domestic violence agency—they may have seen me working as a volunteer there—or most often, as a therapist, despite my explanations to the contrary. Many of the women I interviewed thanked me afterward for what they felt like was a counseling session. I began to think of this moment as part of the interview routine: as they were leaving, women told me it was good for them to talk out their story, to help them "process" their feelings. Several women asked me if I agreed with their diagnoses. Some women asked for a second interview because there were still issues to "process." Many women asked me for legal advice or other resources, which I provided to the best of my ability or referred them to an advocate with more specialized knowledge.

That my participants perceived me as a therapeutic professional demonstrates my relative socioeconomic and professional power in the research relationship. But it also reveals something critical about the experience of becoming a domestic violence survivor today. Women's perceptions of me as a therapist—and the expert command they immediately assumed I had over their stories—reveals the centrality of "the therapeutic" in becoming a domestic violence survivor. Professional therapy is *so* fundamental to the institutions surrounding domestic violence that the women I interviewed often struggled to think of me as anything but a therapeutic expert. The way women interpellated *me*, then, also shaped this research. Inevitably, we are "knitted" into our own projects.[15] Despite the power I have to mold women's narratives by fitting them into my research agenda, *our* relationship—the one between me and the women I interviewed—also structures this book. These relationships helped me see, in fact, that legibility is a process of forming attachments to systems and to each other, attachments that don't disappear when the immediate experience of violence recedes. The women I interviewed were still embroiled in a process of making meaning about abuse and sorting out their institutional identities, and they recruited me into that process. The point is that we are all *affected*, though our sightlines remain partial and our stories incomplete.

Notes

1. Nevaeh is a pseudonym that this participant chose for herself, as are all survivors' and workers' names throughout this book.

2. Abusers' use of child custody cases to control and harass their partners is common. As Vivienne Elizabeth and her colleagues state, men "swap their fists for the system" (2012, 244) when they harass partners via custody battles. And actually, they often succeed in court. As a result, men may be excused from caretaking duties during the relationship only to be rewarded with "gender-neutral" and "equal" legal decision-making in custody arrangements. "The outcome for women in disputes over care and contact arrangements for their children is that men as fathers are able to engage in nonreciprocal exercises of power that have negative effects on the everyday lives of mothers and children" (243).

3. I use the imperfect term *domestic violence* throughout this book—which is not to say that the violence discussed here is contained in the private sphere or only occurs between partners who live together. The term *domestic violence* has been critiqued for focusing narrowly on cohabiting partners, and also for its heteronormative assumptions about couples and families. Some refer to "intimate partner violence" in an effort to be more inclusive. I use *domestic violence*—and often *intimate violence,* to include sexual violence—because it's recognizable to most people. It's also the more casual, everyday language of hotline calls and policy work. But I also find *domestic violence* to be the more

politicized term, whereas *intimate partner violence* is associated with medicalization and professionalization. In any case, terms are imperfect. What matters, I think, is acknowledging the politics of our choices.

4. NNEDV, 2020.

5. Bumiller, 2008; Durazo, 2006; Sweet, 2014, 2015.

6. This kind of psychiatric labeling takes place even when women lack access to high-quality therapeutic services (Humphreys and Joseph, 2004). In other words, trauma is a pervasive, medicalized language used to describe women's psychological vulnerabilities and their complex experiences of inequality, even when women are not offered formal resources with which to address those vulnerabilities. I will address this paradox most fully in chapter 4.

7. There is no doubt that people experience trauma—that structural, state, community, and intimate violence shape people's social and psychological worlds. Harmful experiences dramatically curtail our ability to participate equally in the social world. Those seeking therapeutic interventions should have them. Such care should be high quality. This book does not directly address the problem of mental health service quality and access, though it will touch on related themes throughout.

8. Nguyen, 2010; James, 2010. As the Foucauldian literature on "biological citizenship" (Petryna, 2003) and "biomedical citizenship" (Decoteau, 2013) demonstrates, the boundaries of citizenship in modern life are established through norms related to health and wellness. Social and political belonging—especially for those deemed too "dependent" on the state—is about demonstrating that you are "healthy" and "normal" (Decoteau, 2013; Rose, 1990). This may require making the claim to state authorities that you have suffered but can recover—using medical technologies and services (Rose and Novas, 2005). When rights are precarious, people have to tell stories about their suffering—often drawing from medical knowledge—and then "work on themselves" in order to access resources (Foucault, 1988; James, 2010; Petryna, 2003; Rose, 2007).

9. Laperriére, Orloff, and Pryma, 2019. The state has been preoccupied with women's "dependency"—as a question of welfare rights and resources—at least since the start of Aid for Dependent Children in the 1930s and its trajectory toward the Personal Responsibility and Work Opportunity Act of 1996, commonly known as "welfare reform" (Davis, 2012; Fraser and Gordon, 1994). Programs such as these have long sought to sort out "deserving" women from women who are *too* dependent on the state (i.e., nonwhite and immigrant women). They have also sought, since their inception, to bolster the heterosexual family as the symbol of normal social functioning, to protect against gender and sexual "confusion" by encouraging normative familial roles (Canaday, 2009, 96). The concept of dependency is itself feminized: men are supposed to be protected (as workers) from becoming dependent, and women are presumed to be dependent by nature but should not become "addicted" to state dependency. It is for these

reasons that feminist scholarship on the welfare state takes up the gendered, racialized, and sexualized construction of "dependency" as a central analytic project (Adams and Padamsee, 2001; Ferraro, 1996; Haney, 1996; Orloff, 2009). The very division of state programs into public and private spheres—that is, social security on the one hand, aid for mothers on the other hand—is gendered, premised on the assumption that men are workers while women have "private"-sphere responsibilities (Haney, 1996; Wacquant, 2009). In the new welfare state, women's "dependency" is increasingly wrought through the ostensibly blame-free framework of "trauma," which seeks to "empower" women to recover themselves (read: *not* to depend on the state or an abusive man) through body-based therapeutics.

10. Lara-Millán, 2017.

11. Gurusami, 2017, 3.

12. Cruikshank, 1999; Haney, 2010; Rose, 1999; Soss et al., 2011.

13. As Fergus McNeill (2019) argues, one of the characteristics of modern punishment is that it asks people to demonstrate self-control while providing them few opportunities to *actually* exercise control over their lives.

14. Naples, 2003.

15. Here, I draw from feminist theorists who have critiqued efforts at feminist recuperation, or the urge to make feminism good and positive rather than facing feminism's hard edges, its difficulties and failures (Berlant, 2011). Elizabeth Wilson argues that feminist efforts at reparation may themselves inflict harm, that instead we must be able to "stomach the fundamental involvement of negativity in sociality and subjectivity" (2015, 6). And as Rebecca Stringer (2014) argues, just because "victim" is a more or less "negative" formulation does not mean it cannot also be a powerful statement about inequality.

16. As Susila Gurusami (2017) argues, state programs invest implicitly in the idea of "redemption." She shows that formerly incarcerated women have to seek "redemptive" employment—for example, social work instead of stripping. Trauma narratives are involved here as well: redemptive employment requires women to "mobilize their traumatic histories for public service and wages" (2017, 19).

17. Haney, 2010; McKim, 2017; Miller, 2014; Kaye, 2019.

18. As Kelley Fong (2020) powerfully shows, child protective services surveil home and parenting practices through a range of techniques, many of which are (incorrectly) perceived as "helpful" by the third parties who instigate child services' involvement in families' lives.

19. Greenberg, 2019; Haney, 2010; Morgan and Orloff, 2017.

20. Suzanne Mettler (2011) reveals that when social programs are "submerged" in complex bureaucracies and private organizations, people do not know that their benefits come from the government at all. Indeed, surveys suggest that many people who rely on state assistance are not aware that those programs are provided by the federal government (37–47). Despite the popularity of social

programs, most people simply do not perceive them as "emanating from govern-ment" (39). Mettler argues that the "public" nature of this system is obfuscated by design, making citizens into passive and naive consumers rather than active constructors of public programs.

21. Soss et al., 2011, 10.

22. Mayrl and Quinn, 2017; Mettler, 2011; Rodríguez-Muñiz, 2017; Rose and Miller, 1992.

23. Greenberg, 2019; Lara-Millán, 2017.

24. Haney, 2010; Smith and Lipsky, 1993.

25. Garland, 2012, 104.

26. Rodríguez-Muñiz, 2017 (see also Lara-Millán, 2017).

27. See Haney, 2004, 349.

28. Garland, 2012, 23.

29. Auyero, 2012, 5.

30. The emphasis on "good," therapeutically informed motherhood makes domestic violence services distinct from other "trauma-informed" programs such as those found in addiction facilities. Allison McKim (2008) describes women in such programs being directed away from a focus on children to a focus on the self. They are supposed to "care-take" their self-concept, rather than someone else's (312). In domestic violence services, on the other hand, therapy is often explicitly directed toward the mother-child relationship, and policy leaders talk extensively about "parent-child psychotherapy." In domestic violence services, becoming a "survivor" means becoming oriented toward children's psychologi-cal development and improvement, alongside one's own—or perhaps as *evidence* of one's own.

31. Somers, 1994a.

32. Corrigan and Shdaimah, 2016, 429.

33. Dunn, 2004; Stringer, 2014.

34. Alcoff and Gray, 1993, 262.

35. Stringer, 2014, 18.

36. Roychowdhury, 2015.

37. Miller, 2020, 311.

38. Dunn, 2005, 2007.

39. Creek and Dunn, 2011, 312.

40. Dunn, 2004.

41. Whittier, 2018, 2.

42. Schwark and Bohner, 2019.

43. Stein, 2009, 2011.

44. Orgad, 2009, 141 (see also Alcoff and Gray, 1993; Hengehold, 2000; Naples, 2003; Ticktin, 2011).

45. Stringer, 2014, 5, 20.

46. Giordano, 2014.

47. Johnson, 2014, 32.

48. Boyle and Rogers, 2020. These findings also vary by race: Black women are less likely than other groups to use the "victim" label.

49. Thomas et al., 2015.

50. Dunn, 2001, 288. See also Laugerud (2019) on rape and trauma narratives.

51. Illouz, 2008.

52. Haney, 2010; Brush, 2003, 52.

53. Foucault, 1991, Haney, 2010, 7. In one of my favorite descriptions of the concept, Roderick Ferguson (2005) defines governmentality as the way in which power is activated through the *constitution* of agency, rather than through the evisceration of agency.

54. Orloff, 2009.

55. Orloff, 1996.

56. Brush, 2003, 9; Collins, 1998; Fraser. 1987.

57. McKim, 2014.

58. McKim, 2014, 445.

59. Haney, 2010.

60. McKim, 2008, 304 (see also Roychowdhury, 2015).

61. Brown, 1992.

62. Haney, 1996.

63. Althusser, 1971; Meadow, 2018. For Althusser, ideology—which serves the interests of the ruling class and the reproduction of capitalism—is that which recruits and transforms individuals into subjects. Ideological interpellation is the scene of social life. From Althusser, we have the famous moment of the police officer hailing the subject—"Hey, you there!" (1971, 174). The subject turns around and becomes a subject through that turning. He turns because "he has recognized that the hail was 'really' addressed to him, and that 'it was *really him* who was hailed'" (Althusser, 1971, 174). Interpellation means that the subject automatically recognizes their place within ideology. There are multiple recognitions here (Althusser says they are quadruple): subjects recognize each other, they recognize the central Subject (i.e., the law), they recognize their place in the system, and they recognize themselves. For Althusser, ideology has a "mirror structure": overlapping processes of recognition that produce the subject. For Judith Butler, we turn toward ideology because we *want* to become subjects: "The turn toward the law is not necessitated by the hailing; it is compelling, in a less than logical sense, because it promises identity" (1997, 108).

64. Butler, 1997, 113.

65. Subjects who fit the "wrong" way into social categories may experience these paradoxes of legibility *most* profoundly, since their interpellation may be injurious or they may be called forth as different, dangerous Others (Allen, 2011; Butler, 1997; Fanon, 1952; Muñoz, 1999). Recognition under conditions of domination may be desired, despite its risks, or it may be challenged directly, often at

the cost of having a livable/legible life (Butler, 2004). In any case, legibility is not fully and finally produced but is constantly remade and may be uncertain (Butler, 1990).

66. Giordano, 2014, 7.

67. Scott, 1998, 4. In Scott's words, "Certain forms of knowledge and control require a narrowing of vision. The great advantage of such tunnel vision is that it brings into sharp focus certain limited aspects of an otherwise far more complex and unwieldy reality. This very simplification, in turn, makes the phenomenon at the center of the field of vision more legible and hence more susceptible to careful measurement and calculation" (1998, 11). Scott's analysis of how states develop categories and bureaucratic processes to make society measurable is similar to Foucault's analysis of biopolitics as a set of knowledges and practices that allow the state to manage "the population" (1978). Scott's words point to the power of "simplifying" complex things for the purposes of large-scale management, a dynamic that is evident in "trauma." My analysis—while drawing on theories of how the state "sees" a population—goes beyond this formulation to analyze how people *interact* with those processes and categories, *making themselves legible* in ways that shape their identities and intimate relationships.

68. See Brubaker and Cooper, 2000.

69. Martel, 2017, 6.

70. Gill and Orgad, 2018.

71. Butler, 1997, 104. Philosophers and sociologists have long written about the role of legibility in the reproduction of social power. Bourdieu's notion of symbolic capital speaks to the two-sidedness of recognition: "Symbolic capital enables forms of domination which imply dependence on those who can be dominated by it, since it only exists through the esteem, recognition, belief, credit, confidence of others, and can only be perpetuated so long as it succeeds in obtaining belief in its existence" (2000, 166). Categories of recognition are powerful precisely because we believe in them and we want them—they allow us to participate in social life. The example Bourdieu provides is that the child makes a sacrifice (being "well-behaved") in exchange for social recognition from his parents. George Steinmetz (2006) argues persuasively that for Bourdieu, symbolic capital is just cultural capital in *recognized* form.

72. Bourdieu, 2000. In theorizing this dynamic of recognition, many sociologists and philosophers, including Bourdieu, have relied on Hegel's story of the lord and the bondsman. Hegel posits that self-consciousness can only arise through inter-subjectivity (1977). The self must be "mirrored" through the other. Self-consciousness is therefore consciousness of the other. Social life proceeds from this dialectic of recognition. As Frantz Fanon puts it, "[Man's] human worth and reality depend on this other and on his recognition by the other" (1952, 191). For Fanon, however, the colonial situation introduces a refusal of

recognition. The colonist's refusal to recognize him (a colonial subject) creates the "impossibility" (193) of full personhood. He *feels* erasure—he is socially undone—by the other's refusal. The colonized subject therefore loses his being-for-self and is forced to mime the colonizer. In this mimesis, he is not allowed to perform the opposite position in the dialectic and thus becomes "a negation" (197). Here, Fanon articulates the one-sidedness of legibility, its brutality and defacement in conditions of steep inequality. Being called forth as a marginal or subordinated subject requires distortion, contortion, and misrecognition. Earlier in the text, in an oft-quoted passage, Fanon is "recognized" by being called forth by a white child on the train—"*Maman*, look, a Negro!" (91). Rather than a form of social recognition, this is a violent interpellation. Fanon writes, "My body was returned to me spread-eagled, disjointed, redone, draped in mourning on this white winter's day. The Negro is an animal, the Negro is bad, the Negro is wicked, the Negro is ugly" (93). Social life is whiteness. Being hailed into such a configuration creates the sense of being taken apart limb from limb. Fanon describes the self-consciousness conferred through this interpellation as vulgar: interpellation into whiteness maims and mutilates him. Feeling this violence, Fanon tries to fight back, to oppose the white gaze through direct contestation. The white world denies him this revenge, the satisfaction of an *opposite* subject position: "I hailed the world, and the world amputated my enthusiasm" (94). The colonized is not allowed to call forth the world, to bring a new reality into being through opposition to the colonizer. Fanon is a French citizen, recognized as a legal subject—but only through a process of violent dismemberment that reconfigures him through the white gaze.

73. Connell, 2009.

74. Connell, 2009, 108.

75. Pfeffer, 2014, 12.

76. Stark, 2007.

77. This formulation draws from the pioneering work of scholars such as Kimberlé Crenshaw (1990) and Beth Richie (1996, 2012) on black women's experiences of domestic violence, as well as Cecilia Menjívar's (2011) work on intimate violence in Guatemala and on domestic violence among immigrant communities (Menjívar and Salcido, 2002; see also Roberta Villalón, 2010). I also draw from Jody Miller's (2008) work on intimate violence in the lives of African American teens, Claire Renzetti's (1988) work on violence in lesbian relationships, the Incite! Collective (2006), and many others. See also Armstrong et al. (2018) for a helpful overview of intersectional scholarship on intimate violence. I take very seriously Choo and Ferree's (2010) point that intersectionality should attend to co-constitutive forms of power and the social channels through which they operate—rather than simply to intersecting identity categories.

78. Merry, 2009, 3; Scheper-Hughes and Bourgois, 2004.

79. U.S. Department of Justice, 2016.

80. Stark and Hester, 2019. Recent research suggests that when the law includes factors like "coercion" and "control" in definitions of domestic violence, women are more likely to report abuse, in part because these definitions reflect their lived realities, which are characterized by violations to their autonomy, sense of reality, and mobility (Stark, 2007; Stark and Hester, 2019; Sweet, 2019b).

81. CDC, 2010; Tjaden and Thoennes, 2000.

82. Anderson, 2009; Kimmel, 2002; Reed et al., 2010; Stark, 2007.

83. Anderson, 2009; Ferraro, 2006; Reed et al., 2010; Schechter, 1982; Stark, 2007; Swan and Snow, 2006; Williamson, 2010.

84. Stark, 2007, 205.

85. Ferraro, 2006; Hardesty, 2002; Peled et al., 2000; Stark, 2007; Weisz et al., 2000. Over 40 percent of female homicide victims in the United States were killed by an intimate partner (CDC, 2018).

86. Brush, 2011 (see also Davis, 2012).

87. Bierria and Lenz, 2019, 91.

88. Women who use domestic violence shelters are the most vulnerable victims: they tend to experience the most frequent and severe abuse, they lack financial resources and social networks, and most come to shelters with dependent children (Glenn and Goodman, 2015).

89. Baker et al., 2003; Breiding et al., 2017.

90. Baker et al., 2010; Baker et al., 2003. Matthew Desmond's ethnography revealed that landlords evicted or threatened to evict their tenants 83 percent of the time when a domestic violence nuisance report was filed (2016). Most often, they evicted women victims rather than male perpetrators. Women's knowledge of housing precarity regularly prevents them from contacting police when they are in danger (Fais, 2008): "Keep quiet and face abuse or call the police and face eviction" (Desmond, 2016, 192).

91. "Leaving" is a strategic action and can take many different forms—everything from staying at a domestic violence shelter to sleeping in another room of the house (Larance et al., 2018) to moving in with extended family in a different state. Even among the women I interviewed who chose to stay with their partners, temporary moves to escape violence were common.

92. Many of the women I interviewed faced housing discrimination as single mothers, following documented trends in urban housing discrimination (Lauster and Easterbrook, 2011).

93. In general, micro-regulations of femininity are part of abusive tactics, such as controlling clothing choice, body size, and access to birth control and abortion (Anderson, 2009; Barber et al., 2018; Miller et al., 2010).

94. Though most domestic violence services are premised on a logic of separation, anyone who works in the domestic violence field will tell you that "leaving" does not mean "safety" (Goodmark, 2013). In a study of how domestic violence victims themselves defined safety, 20 percent reported a loss of social supports

when they left and 20 percent reported loss of financial supports (Thomas et al., 2015). Women tend to place housing concerns just as highly as physical safety concerns in their own needs assessments.

95. Watkins-Hayes, 2019, 154.

96. As Dana-Ain Davis notes about the role of welfare policy and victims' institutional entanglements, "While physical violence may create and sustain poverty, the structural violence of policy mandates sustains inequalities and inaccessibility to critical resources, leaving poverty unresolved" (2012, 183).

97. Petrosky et al., 2017.

98. Seim, 2020, 6.

99. Brush, 2000; Purvin, 2007; Riger and Staggs, 2004. Women who live in disadvantaged neighborhoods (Miller, 2008) and women of color (Richie, 1996, 2012; Scott et al., 2002) are more vulnerable to violence in general. They experience more economic and physical entrapment, less police protection, and more restricted mobility. Further, poor women face more barriers at the intersection of domestic violence and welfare policy (Scott et al., 2002). Low-income women face pressure to stay in abusive relationships or return to them when they hit welfare limits or fail to comply with difficult requirements. Applying for domestic violence protections within welfare policy often requires official documentation of victimization (which most women lack), leaving victims to choose housing, food, and childcare over safety (Purvin, 2007).

100. Waters et al., 2004.

101. Elizabeth et al., 2012; Richie, 2012; Scott et al., 2002; West and Rose, 2000.

102. There is also evidence that the stress associated with poverty compounds the social isolation of domestic violence to produce higher rates of PTSD and depression for marginalized women (Goodman et al., 2009). As Lisa Goodman and colleagues argue, the work of managing poverty is the work of managing both acute and chronic stressors, which are exacerbated by abuse.

103. Armstrong et al., 2018; INCITE!, 2006; Richie, 2012.

104. Glenn, 1999; Menjívar, 2011; Miller, 2008; Richie, 2012; Smith, 2005.

105. Goodman et al., 2009.

106. Richie, 1996.

107. As Deisy del Real (2019) shows, undocumented women are at increased risk of being exploited and demeaned by friends and family members—creating "power-dependent ties"—because of their precarious legal statuses.

108. Rapid increases in unemployment and financial stress at the household level have also been associated with increases in men's controlling behaviors over their partners (Schneider et al., 2016).

109. Coker, 2004; Richie, 2012.

110. Pishko, 2017; Richie, 2012; Sherman and Harris, 2015.

111. Richie and Eife, 2020.

112. Richie, 1996, 2012.

113. Villalón, 2010.

114. Goodmark, 2018, 123.

115. Varma, 2020, 3.

116. More information can be found in the appendix.

117. Chicago domestic violence agency data were released by ICJA to the author with permission.

118. Kimmel, 2002; Menjívar, 2011; Stark, 2007.

119. About 10 percent of women in the United States report being stalked by an intimate partner, and this percentage is higher for women who have already been abused and tried to leave (CDC, 2018). A recent survey in the United Kingdom found that over 90 percent of women who called the police for domestic violence experienced post-separation stalking (Sharp-Jeffs et al., 2018; Stark and Hester, 2019). Further, as many as 55 percent of women report that leaving the relationship has resulted in new problems in their lives related to financial strain, housing instability, and child custody problems (Thomas et al., 2015).

120. Das, 2000, 205.

121. Soss et al., 2011; Wacquant, 2009.

122. See Varma, 2020, 13.

123. By a "queer approach," I don't mean that the women I interviewed identified as queer. Instead, I mean that my analysis takes heterosexuality as the *troubling thing to be explained*, and that my analysis centers experiences of disjuncture and misfitting within heterosexuality—acknowledging that heterosexuality is hegemonic, full of ruptures and violence, and may nevertheless remain a site of desire.

124. Ward, 2020. As Ward goes on to explain, this "tragedy" is almost impossible to express: "Straight people have few opportunities to grieve the disappointments of straight culture (the bad and coercive sex, the normalized inequities of daily life, straight men's fragility and egomania, straight women's growing disillusionment with men's fragility and egomania, the failed marriages, and coparenting that is really solo parenting ...) because how does one speak about the failure of the very system that defines people's success?" (2020, 115). This tension between the promises of heterosexual "success" and survivors' sense that heterosexuality has failed them is what I take up in chapter 6. In my view, this means that we must attend to survivors' subtle practices of *disidentification* from heterosexual citizenship.

125. Nguyen, 2010.

126. Merry, 2001.

127. Reich, 2005.

128. Tilly, 1995.

129. Nguyen, 2010; Tilly, 1995.

130. Sweet, 2019a.

131. Hengehold, 2000, 201.

CHAPTER 1. BUILDING A THERAPEUTIC MOVEMENT

1. Stark, 2007.

2. Bumiller, 2008, 3.

3. Tinker, n.d. Activist and movement leader Bonnie Tinker's files in NCADV archives include a letter she wrote about the history of the movement in which she described the foundations of the Portland shelter movement as a "joint effort of bar dykes and women's movement lesbians." She wrote that anti-violence activists and survivors were regularly dismissed by radical leftists as "social service workers," though they were really the ones doing the "work of the revolution."

4. Fleck-Henderson, 2017.

5. NCADV, 1978b.

6. Ms. Foundation, 1981.

7. As Nancy Whittier (2009) argues in her work on child abuse, organizations that combined a social change approach with criminal and psychological interventions were the most resilient over time. The important thing about anti-violence work is that even the most radical activists are often employees or even leaders of "mainstream" anti-violence organizations, which makes for an especially diverse set of political commitments present at any given moment in the field.

8. Halley et al., 2018; Kim, 2020; Orloff and Shiff, 2016.

9. Morgen, 2002; Nelson, 2011. This is not to suggest that all anti-state efforts ceased after these early years. As a diverse coalition, the anti-violence movement included anti-state activists throughout the 1970s and 1980s—including, for example, activists who engaged in direct protest against suspected rapists. As Catherine Jacquet states, "Reductionist narratives that equate feminist anti-rape activism with law reform alone neglect these powerful calls for action and obscure what was, and continues to be, a multifaceted and complex feminist antirape movement" (2016, 72).

10. NCADV archives reveal that the earliest Title XX funds from the Social Security Act allocated money to economically underserved populations for the purposes of "strengthening families" (US Department of Labor, 1978): these funds could only be used for services that included children, with an emphasis on counseling. Still, communication among activists also reveals that program requirements were loose and that they could essentially do whatever they wanted with the funds.

11. Stark, 2007.

12. NCADV materials available from the 1970s include, for example, a CETA binder on how to fund domestic violence programs through the Department of

Labor. Training materials instruct shelters to use CETA and Title XX grants, and they provide example language for grant applications. Materials indicate that since 1970, LEAA spent $15 million on programs related to "family crimes," including "sensitive crimes" such as rape and family violence. A grant was made by LEAA to the Center for Women in Policy Studies (1977) to create a clearinghouse on "intra-family violence," from which many of these documents are drawn.

13. Richie, 2012.

14. Christianson, 1978.

15. Bockman, 2012; Marwell, 2004; Whittier, 2009.

16. Hasenfeld and Garrow, 2012; Smith and Lipsky, 1993.

17. Cooper, 2017.

18. Schechter, 1982.

19. Brown, 2006; Cooper, 2017; Duggan, 2003. As Lisa Duggan (2003), Melinda Cooper (2017), and Elizabeth Bernstein (2012) argue, the decimation of the welfare state *had* to be complemented by the rise of "family values" because public programs were deemed detrimental, thereby reinstating "the family" as the preferred locus of political life.

20. President's Task Force on Victims of Crime, 1982.

21. Wacquant, 2009.

22. While VAWA provides funding for domestic violence service organizations, it also disproportionately funnels money toward criminal systems, prioritizing legal and criminalizing responses to abuse (Goodmark, 2013, 2018; Kim, 2020). Indeed, VAWA is the paradigmatic example of the anti-violence movement's investment in criminal responses to abuse (Richie, 2012).

23. For example, in 1979 congressional hearings on domestic violence, lawmakers insisted that "family violence" was a serious problem, but they did not want to bring "regulation and rulemaking" to a "private" matter (US House of Representatives, 1979). The bill was therefore proposed with seventy cosponsors but a clear insistence on "limited federal role." Every version of FVPSA that went through the House and Senate in 1984 specified that funds should provide for "shelter and related assistance" to victims and "technical assistance and training" for employees—never cash assistance (FVPSA, 1984).

24. Fraser and Gordon, 1994; Polsky, 1991; Rose, 1990; Soss et al., 2011; Whittier, 2009.

25. Polsky, 1991.

26. Whittier, 2018.

27. Alcoff and Gray, 1993; Bumiller, 2008; Naples, 2003.

28. I do not conceive of the carceral state (expanded through the promise of "saving" victims) and the welfare state as *separate* (see Wacquant, 2009). The case of domestic violence reveals that the expansion of criminal solutions for domestic violence occurred simultaneously with shifts toward medicalized therapeutic infrastructures. Victims of crime bills firmly incorporate social welfare program

language with criminalizing, penal language. Anti-violence activists were pivotal to both of these shifts, which occurred in tandem. The addiction field is an example of the increasing imbrication of the penal and the therapeutic state, wherein punitive sanctions are executed through therapeutic means, such as forced attendance of treatment programs in order to avoid jail time or to get children back from state custody (Kaye, 2019; McKim, 2017; Tiger, 2013).

29. Bumiller, 2008, xii.

30. Kim, 2020, 20; Richie, 2012 (see also Bernstein, 2012).

31. Sweet, 2015.

32. Fassin and Rechtman, 2009.

33. Bernstein, 2012.

34. Wolch, 1990.

35. Cooper, 2017.

36. Franzway et al., 1989; Outshoorn and Kantola, 2007.

37. NNEDV, 2020. The same 2020 report indicates that there are over eleven thousand needs requests each day that go unmet, the majority of which are for housing.

38. Labriola et al., 2012.

39. Franzway et al., 1989; Orloff and Shiff, 2016; Sawer, 2007.

40. Bumiller, 2008; Richie, 2012; Stark, 2007.

41. Here, I disagree with a simplistic reading of Nancy Fraser's (2013) oft-cited claim that second-wave feminists traded off their aims of *redistribution* in favor of a politics of identity and state *recognition*. Anti-violence activists—while they cared a great deal about identity and psychological oppression—always aimed for policies that would *redistribute* state money to programs for abused women. In Illinois, they even forced the state government to redistribute money from the marriage tax to domestic violence organizations, something of a radical statement about women's imprisonment in marriage. The question is *what kind of redistribution* was allowed. For anti-violence feminism, the possibilities of state redistribution were curtailed early on, since services fell in line with existing avenues of funding forged via criminal and therapeutic frameworks. The creation of a state-supported victim services infrastructure constitutes a kind of redistribution, though not necessarily a radical one. Further, feminist aims at redistribution were as stratified as their aims at recognition, since both privileged white heterosexual femininity as the locus of state legibility and public sympathy (Coker, 2004; INCITE!, 2006; Richie, 2000).

42. Orloff, 1993.

43. Orloff, 1996, 52.

44. Richie, 2000, 2012.

45. Bako, 1978.

46. Corrigan, 2013.

47. Schechter, 1982.

48. Schechter, 1982, 107.

49. Stevenson, 1970, 1.

50. Loseke, 1992; Stark, 2007; Tierney, 1982; Whittier, 2009.

51. Metzger, 1977.

52. Warrior, 1975.

53. Haaken, 2010.

54. Bako, 1978.

55. Sweet and Giffort, 2021.

56. Warrior, 1976, 2.

57. ICADV, 1982.

58. Cooper, 2017.

59. US Department of Justice, 1985, 15.

60. Whittier, 2018.

61. Whittier, 2009.

62. Berns, 2001; Coker, 2004; Durazo, 2006; Sweet, 2015. And as Beth Richie points out, activists' intersectional frameworks—wherein racial inequality, classism, and homophobia were understood to constitute the matrix of patriarchal violence—were *also* handed off in order for the movement to become a "legitimate player" in the state (2012, 77). The Women of Color Task Force of NCADV agitated in the 1980s for better representation in meetings and executive committees, demanding 50 percent women of color in such spaces. The WOC Task Force was outspoken against the movement's increasing involvement with the criminal legal system and insisted (presciently) that this relationship with police and prosecution would harm women of color and result in movement depoliticization. While women of color and lesbians founded many domestic violence organizations and wrote many of the first feminist statements against violence in the 1970s, their claims and their leadership were quickly marginalized. This marginalization would come to define the compromises that movement leaders were willing to make in the effort of state legibility in the 1980s and 1990s, as professionalized leaders became increasingly detached from intersectional feminist politics and from concerns about state co-optation (Richie, 2012).

63. Corrigan, 2013.

64. US House of Representatives, 1978.

65. US House of Representatives, 1978.

66. US House of Representatives, 1979.

67. US Senate, 1978.

68. NCADV, 1978a, 6.

69. This was especially true for hearings that included victim testimony (US Senate, 1978).

70. MacDonald, 1978.

71. NCADV, 1986.

72. As Evan Stark (2007) explains, many shelters were founded in mental health centers or churches and integrated clinical staff even in the 1970s.

73. Hasenfeld and Garrow, 2012, 311 (see also Marwell, 2004, 278).

74. Stark, 2007.

75. Smith and Lipsky, 1993, 85.

76. Providing further evidence for this assertion, Nancy Whittier (2016) makes a similar argument about VAWA legislative hearings in the 1990s: while carceral solutions won the day, feminist activists did not *themselves* engage such arguments. Rather, feminists made their arguments in structural and intersectional terms, but "law and order" discourses were the most legible to conservative politicians.

77. Cooper, 2017.

78. Duggan, 2003; Soss et al., 2011.

79. Rose, 1999; Soss et al. 2011.

80. Morgan and Campbell, 2011 (see also Smith and Lipsky, 1993).

81. Cooper, 2017, 18.

82. Bockman, 2012. As Bockman (2012) goes on to argue, neoliberal elites created their political movement by co-opting many of the spaces and discourses that were created by liberation movements. Scholars sometimes misread discourses of "self-sufficiency" and "empowerment" as neoliberal when they were *actually* born from ideals of radical collectivity.

83. Wolch, 1990, 28.

84. Isin, 2009; Morgan and Campbell, 2011; Smith and Lipsky, 1993; Soss et al., 2011.

85. Soss et al., 2011.

86. Ong, 2006a, 501.

87. Ong, 2006b; Fraser and Gordon, 1994.

88. Fraser and Gordon, 1994; Haney, 2010; McKim, 2017.

89. Ong, 2006b.

90. Foucault, 1988; Soss et al., 2011; Trattner, 1999.

91. Polsky, 1991, 3 (emphasis mine).

92. Herman, 1995.

93. Soss et al., 2011.

94. In general, what Andrew Polsky (1991) calls the "therapeutic sector" expanded after the Great Depression, as programs for single mothers and "needy children" were developed under the purview of the federal government. The development of the Children's Bureau and other federal programs for mothers during the 1930s shaped the availability of funds for early battered women's programs in the 1970s, since "single mothers" had already been carved out as a welfare group (Fraser and Gordon, 1994). The explicit goal of such programs was to bring mothers and children back to "normal functioning" despite the abnormalizing influences of poverty and urban life. Such programs continued

to expand throughout the 1950s and 1960s, especially after the Social Security Act amendments of 1962, which widened the reach of therapeutic interventions through public programs that had surveillance mechanisms (Herman, 1995; Polsky, 1991). Clients were expected to overcome an attitude of "dependency" (Fraser and Gordon, 1994; Polsky, 1991; Soss et al., 2011). Therapeutic professionals were central to such programs, and the influence of psychologists and other social scientists on public policy became especially pronounced in the 1960s, with notorious results such as the Moynihan Report (Herman, 1995). Ellen Herman (1995) points out that Moynihan's "tangle of pathology" language became the Johnson administration's official explanation for violence in the 1960s, reflecting the increasing imbrication of family violence discourses with public policy aimed at pathologizing Black families. Further, despite retrenchment of social service programs during the Reagan years, this human services infrastructure has remained powerful, making therapeutic "casework" an unquestioned approach to marginality (Chriss, 1999; Nolan, 1998): "Because the therapeutic has insinuated itself so deeply into how we view marginality, normalizing intervention has become a constitutive element in our ethic of care" (Polsky, 1991, 215).

95. Garland, 2012, 174.

96. Soss et al., 2011, 27 (see also Rose, 1990).

97. Cooper, 2017.

98. Wacquant, 2009.

99. Soss et al., 2011; Wacquant, 2009. As Jamie Peck argues, neoliberalism is a "mongrel model of governance" (2010, 106) that responds to its own contradictions and crises, reinventing itself in new political environments. The problematization of the American family was a convenient starting place for neoliberalism, then, because it allowed neoliberals to make the "dependent" single mother into a national problem and to reinstate the private family as the preferred fulfiller of political and social needs (Cooper, 2017). These discourses were appealing to neoconservatives who sought to use the state to promote marriage and repeal feminist gains. Neoconservative discourses and policies therefore shaped neoliberalism in profound ways.

100. Goodman, 1985.

101. NCADV, n.d.

102. Goodman, 1985.

103. ICADV, 1986.

104. Bockman, 2012; Cooper, 2017.

105. US Senate, 1978; US House of Representatives, 1984.

106. US Department of Justice, 1984, 63.

107. In this way, the report is also a harbinger of George H. W. Bush's "thousand points of light" praise for the charitable sector: a way to venerate private organizations as altruistic and efficient (even ethereal)—as opposed to inefficient and cruel government-run programs (Smith and Lipsky, 1993). The

voluntary sector was understood to champion "family values" and good, hard work (Wolch, 1990).

108. Brown, 2006; Cooper, 2017; Duggan, 2003; Puar, 2007.

109. US Department of Justice, 1984, 199 (emphasis mine).

110. Morgan and Campbell, 2011.

111. Cooper, 2017.

112. Cooper, 2017.

113. Whittier, 2018.

114. Schechter, 1983.

115. Ahrens, 1980.

116. ICADV, 1982.

117. ICADV, 1978.

118. In fact, FVPSA provides more direct service funds than VAWA, which prioritizes criminal interventions and prosecutorial systems.

119. US Senate, 1983; US House of Representatives, 1983.

120. US House of Representatives, 1984.

121. Schechter, 1989.

122. US Commission on Civil Rights, 1982, 41.

123. Weinig, 1979, 1.

124. PCADV, 1985.

125. PCADV, 1985.

126. Pence, 1985.

127. Importantly, this conciliatory form of engagement with professional psychology was built on more contentious forms of activism from the 1960s, wherein feminists protested outside APA meetings and presented lists of demands, shouting things like, "The psychiatric profession is built on the slavery of women" (Herman, 1995, 287–88).

128. Women's Aid Federation, 1984.

129. Sweet and Giffort, 2021.

130. US House of Representatives, 1978.

131. Women's Aid Federation, 1984.

132. Whittier, 2009.

133. Stark, 2007.

134. Haaken, 2010.

135. Ferraro, 1996.

136. Wolch, 1990.

137. US Department of Justice, 2002 (emphasis mine).

CHAPTER 2. THE TRAUMA REVOLUTION

1. The adoption of the trauma framework in social service systems can be traced, in part, to the popularity of a book by Maxine Harris and Roger Fallot,

Using Trauma Theory to Design Service Systems (2001), which argues that social service delivery often fails because systems attempt to treat trauma victims without addressing the trauma itself. Trauma also affects social service system workers via "vicarious" and "secondary" trauma.

2. Waggoner, 2017.

3. Lara-Millán, 2017 (see also Giordano, 2014; Miller and Stuart, 2017).

4. Fraser, 2013, 59.

5. Laperriére et al., 2019; Sweet, 2014, 2015.

6. Davis, 2005, 4 (see also Fassin and Rechtman, 2009).

7. Humphreys and Joseph, 2004.

8. Walker, 1985.

9. Walker, 1985.

10. Walker, 1985.

11. MPD was never included as an official diagnosis. A version of MPD, called "Self-Defeating Personality Disorder," was included in the appendix of the DSM-III-R in 1987. When the expert boundaries of the psy sciences loosened and broadened, there were also more opportunities for radical critiques of psychiatry, for example through the emergence of the anti-psychiatry movement in the 1960s and 1970s (Herman, 1995; Horwitz, 2002). Partially in response to these critiques—including feminist and anti-war critiques—psychiatry retooled its relationship to the category of "victim" in the 1980s and 1990s using the category of PTSD (Fassin and Rechtman, 2009; Young, 1997).

12. Leys, 2002; Young, 1997.

13. Bourke, 2012; Leys, 2002; Young, 1997.

14. Leys, 2002.

15. Young, 1997.

16. Horwitz, 2018; Young, 1997.

17. Young, 1997.

18. Young, 1997. The DSM-III's inclusion of PTSD marks an important phase in the biomedicalization of trauma, transforming it from a psychoanalytic "traumatic memory" to a disorder located in the brain. Thus, trauma became a biologized psychiatric *disease*, rather than an affliction of the unconscious, reflecting a major epistemic shift in psychiatry (Horwitz, 2018). As Derek Summerfield points out, through the biologization of PTSD, horrifying experiences of war were transformed into "technical problems" to be solved by counseling and pharmaceuticals (1999). The predominant view in contemporary psychiatry is that trauma is a medical disorder characterized by "psychobiological dysfunction" (Horwitz, 2018; Stein et al., 2007).

19. Fassin and Rechtman, 2009.

20. Fassin and Rechtman, 2009; Young, 1997.

21. Allard, 1991, 191; Bumiller, 2008; Mulla, 2014.

22. Walker, 1989, 4.

23. Walker's model argued that women victims developed "learned helplessness" over time, producing a "negative cognitive set" that made them incapable of defending themselves or leaving the relationship (1979, 53). BWS has enjoyed a great deal of cultural legitimacy since Walker coined the term, including widespread use in courtrooms, clinics, and the popular imagination (Ferraro, 2003; Rothenberg, 2003). According to Bess Rothenberg, it was the "most recognized" explanation for abuse until the mid-1990s (2003, 778). Part of its enormous success, Rothenberg argues, is that the term *syndrome* provides an aura of medical legitimacy.

24. Stark (2007) argues that the rise of PTSD and BWS in the 1980s provided a set of convenient, internalized explanations for "why women stay" and why they might kill their abusers. Because trauma theory emphasizes desperation, dependence, and depression, it invites jurors into a "rescue narrative" (139). Other scholars have noted that clinical descriptions of victims' behaviors are particularly compelling in court, providing lawyers and judges an explanation for oppression with simple reference to a "syndrome" (Bumiller, 2008; Ferraro, 2003; Rothenberg, 2002, 2003).

25. Stein, 2009.

26. Cole, 2007.

27. Walker, 1989, 64.

28. Walker's theory was based explicitly on findings from psychologist Martin Seligman's research on learned helplessness in dogs (1979).

29. Goodmark, 2013, 54–55.

30. Ferraro, 2003.

31. Fassin and Rechtman, 2009, 87.

32. Allard, 1991.

33. Stark, 2007, 153.

34. Richie, 2012.

35. Richie, 2000. Part of activists' motivation for using psychological theories in the legal setting was that victims could become "legitimate witnesses" in their own cases (YWCA Chicago, 1978). The Chicago YWCA in the late 1970s wrote, "Through psychological counseling and long-term supportive follow-up, it is hypothesized that rape victims will develop the understanding and stability required to proceed in the court system." While activists were critical of the assumption that victims *needed* expert intervention, they also hoped to "give victims their voices back" by coaching them to be credible witnesses. Lenore Walker herself, in defense of her theory, wrote that the syndrome is a "bridge in the legal system that does not let women talk for themselves in their own voices" (1990). Ironically, then, the justification for the involving psy experts in battered women's legal cases was that psychological analyses would allow women to have *more* autonomy over their stories. Here again, the domestic violence movement balanced precariously on the borders of psychological expertise and political analysis.

36. Leonard, 2019.

37. Didier Fassin and Richard Rechtman (2009) attribute the rise of the new field of "psychiatric victimology" in the 1990s to the advent of "trauma specialists" in professional psychology. The VA's specialization in PTSD bolstered the credibility of the disorder, making it an official category of government compensation (Young, 1997). In the early 1990s, new academic journals about traumatic victimology appeared, as did a plethora of books and international aid organizations focused on the topic (Fassin and Rechtman, 2009). Few histories of trauma have given feminists their due, however, as creators of trauma theory.

38. Herman, 1992. Herman's theories are referred to as "complex trauma" because they account for structural inequality, oppression, and the ongoing nature of trauma outside of a singular "event." Herman's book, *Trauma and Recovery: The Aftermath of Abuse—from Domestic Abuse to Political Terror* (1992) continues to influence domestic violence work, and many movement leaders described it in interviews as a turning point in the anti-violence movement.

39. Eyal, 2013.

40. Schechter, c. 1990s.

41. Durazo, 2006; Sweet, 2015.

42. FVPF, 1993.

43. Stark, 2007, 11 (see also Loseke, 1992).

44. Bracken, 2001; Horwitz, 2018.

45. Fassin and Rechtman, 2009.

46. Schechter, c. 1990s.

47. Still, evidence suggests that movement leaders were often ambivalent about trauma theory. The Wisconsin Coalition Against Domestic Violence published an article in 1990 that asked: "Post-Traumatic Stress Disorder: A label That Does Not Blame?," questioning the ability of trauma theory to offer a way out of victim-blaming (Saunders, 1990).

48. Schechter, 1991.

49. Schechter and Sugg, 1993.

50. Bourke, 2012, 44.

51. Gondolf, 1994.

52. Warshaw, 1996.

53. DVMHPI, 2002; DVTMH, 2003. For example, domestic violence leaders attended the 2001 "Reaching Underserved Trauma Survivors through Community-Based Programs" conference, which featured a mix of presentations on neurological trauma research, community-based services, counseling, therapy models, and racism (ISTS, 2001).

54. Gowan, 2010; McKim, 2017.

55. Davis, 2005, 136.

56. In fact, the expansion of the mental health professions after World War II was itself dependent on the discovery of "the family" as a locus of psychological

intervention—as was the expansion of the welfare state's brand of "neoliberal paternalism" directed at "needy," badly behaving families (Soss et al., 2011). The mental health system—that is, the federal government's creation of the NIMH in the 1940s—expanded dramatically after World War II, as veterans became out-patients and the state developed new training programs for clinicians (Herman, 1995). Clinical psychology emerged as a profession in the postwar period and increasing numbers of veterans and the upper-class public became patients of psychoanalysis (Horwitz, 2002). To keep up with demand for psy authority, new clinical professions—such as school guidance counselors—were developed. Clin-ical social work became the center of theories of humanistic psychology (Her-man, 1995). Nikolas Rose points out that the discovery of "the family" as a unit of analysis in the psy sciences was critical to these developments, as it allowed the "vocabularies of the therapeutic" to be deployed inside the home, inside schools, and in child services fields (1990, 214). As psychotherapeutic techniques spread across an increasingly diverse array of professionals—most of whom did not have medical degrees—the softer language of "counseling" replaced "therapy" in human services (Chriss, 1999).

57. National Advisory Council on Violence Against Women, 2000.

58. ICADV, 1998.

59. Warshaw, 2001.

60. Horwitz, 2002. As Horwitz (2018) rightly points out, the "trauma indus-try" was institutionalized over a surprisingly short period of time and never could have emerged without feminists' insistence on expanding DSM-IV PTSD crite-ria in 1994. Feminists worked to expand psychiatric criteria for the disorder to include events *subjectively* deemed "traumatic" by the patient. The "new" PTSD of the 2000s is characterized by an increasing focus on life events as opposed to childhood development, with the decline of Freudian psychoanalysis (Horwitz, 2018). Experimentation, biostatistics, and psychometrics are all part of this shift. More recent interest in biological markers for PTSD have bolstered its legitimacy (Pitman et al., 2012). PTSD now focuses largely on brain changes and is one of the fastest growing diagnoses in the United States (Horwitz, 2018). The expan-sion of trauma professionals throughout the 1990s massively expanded the legit-imacy of the disorder and its popular salience. Trauma has undeniably become its own profession and has incredible public resonance as a language of human suffering.

61. Bumiller, 2008, 64.

62. Davis, 2005,193.

63. Davis, 2005; Fassin and Rechtman, 2009; Illouz, 2008; Naples, 2003; Rose, 1990.

64. Schechter, 1982, 253.

65. Fraser and Gordon, 1994; McKim, 2017; Soss et al., 2011.

66. Bourke, 2012.

67. Stark, 2007, 76.

68. There are many ways to define "trauma." Typically, I follow my interlocutors in the domestic violence field by referring to psychiatric definitions associated with PTSD. These definitions refer to a constellation of symptoms such as: reliving the traumatic events through flashbacks or nightmares, avoidance or numbing, hypervigilance or increased arousal, irritability, and inability to sleep or concentrate (Horwitz, 2018; Humphreys and Joseph, 2004). However, uses of the term *trauma* in feminist circles typically extend beyond symptomology, highlighting ongoing traumatic events—such as domestic violence, rape, and child abuse (Herman, 1992). Trauma has also been associated with "insidious" forms of structural violence such as racism, allowing social justice–minded domestic violence workers to use *trauma* in a politicized way.

69. There are a number of professional degrees held by clinical therapists in domestic violence agencies. Most professionals in these agencies are licensed clinical social workers (LCSWs) and licensed clinical professional counselors (LCPCs), both of whom have master's degrees and are licensed by states to provide clinical therapy. There are also registered art therapists (ATRs) who have master's degrees and clinical licensure, and PsyDs (doctors of psychology), which is a professional doctoral degree in psychology.

70. Some agencies also receive emergency housing vouchers through the US Department of Housing and Urban Development (HUD), an important but less common source of federal dollars for domestic violence services.

71. FPC, 2013, 44.

72. US Department of Health and Human Services, 2012, 14393.

73. Giordano, 2014.

74. Star, 2010; Star and Griesemer, 1989.

75. FPC, 2013.

76. FPC. 2013, 7.

77. FPC, 2013, 10–15.

78. FPC, 2013, 45.

79. Center for Healthcare Strategies, 2017.

80. Espeland and Stevens, 2008; Merry, 2016; Timmermans and Berg, 2010.

81. Espeland and Stevens, 2008, 415.

82. Espeland and Stevens, 1996; Merry, 2016.

83. Bowker and Star, 2000.

84. Merry, 2016.

CHAPTER 3. ADMINISTERING TRAUMA

1. This is not to suggest, however, that Resilience has abandoned its politics. Organization leaders still galvanize members to engage in public protests and

to call legislators, political work that is actually quite rare among direct service organizations. The name shift, however, is significant for marking the broad reach of the trauma revolution in social services.

2. de Leon et al., 2015; Hall, 1996; Laclau and Mouffe, 1985; Slack, 1996.

3. I do not mean to suggest that there is one type of "feminism" to be found in domestic violence work. As I showed in chapter 1, more contentious forms of feminist activism—focused on patriarchy, racism, and structural change work—have long existed alongside more conciliatory forms of activism focused on providing care. It is always more accurate, really, to talk about "feminisms."

4. Whittier, 2009.

5. Medvetz, 2012, Herman, 1995; Illouz, 2008; Stein, 2011; Whittier, 2009.

6. Decoteau and Sweet, 2016; Eyal, 2013; Medvetz, 2012.

7. Medvetz, 2008, 10.

8. Varma, 2020.

9. Weiss, 2020.

10. Frickel and Moore, 2005.

11. Naples, 2003.

12. Foucault, 1973.

13. Foucault, 1973, 15.

14. Foucault, 1973, 122.

15. Foucault, 1973, 130.

16. Foucault, 1973, 112 (see also Lupton, 2002).

17. Haaken, 1996.

18. Ticktin, 2011.

19. Foucault, 1973, 10.

20. Ong, 1995.

21. Haney, 2010; Messner et al., 2015 (see also Martin, 2005).

22. EMDR is a trauma-specific psychotherapy treatment that asks participants to focus on an external stimulus—sometimes a light they follow with their eyes—while thinking about a traumatic memory. The client is asked to call forth memories while the therapist directs their attention to the stimulus. The client then follows the stimulus with lateral eye movements, a series of finger taps, or other repetitive bodily motions. The idea is that new associations are created in the brain through such motions, so that the memory no longer feels traumatic. The EMDR counselors I interviewed described it as a type of body work that can lessen the burden of traumatic memories without "talking" through details of events. Some studies find strong support for the efficacy of EMDR treatments above and beyond talk therapy, while other studies find similar efficacy (Rodenburg et al., 2009; Seidler and Wagner, 2006). EMDR is increasingly popular in anti-violence work because it engages a "somatic" theory of trauma.

23. Epstein, 1996; Klawiter, 2008.

24. Conrad, 2007; Zola, 1991.

25. One of the most extended critiques of the co-optation framework is Michelle Murphy's (2012) analysis of the women's health movement. Murphy moves beyond the paradigm of biomedicine-as-actor, focusing on what social movements do within, across, and through biomedical assemblages. Rather than inventing something novel and pure, feminisms "act on scales already in place" (104). Feminists also politicize and change those scales. For example, feminists used the Pap smear as a technique of grassroots self-help at the same time that this technology gained prominence in mainstream biomedicine. As Murphy contends, such entanglements constantly proliferate when feminists "seize" biomedical technologies in order to politicize them. For Murphy, feminist practices are mobile at their core, which means that acting on "women's issues" always involves moving across existing networks of power.

26. Illouz, 2008; Stein, 2011; Whittier, 2009. In medical sociology, theories of biomedicalization (Clarke et al., 2010) and the sociology of diagnosis (Jutel, 2014) deal with the instability of biomedical power and the production of hybrid knowledges. Rather than attending to professional dominance or definitional processes, biomedicalization analyzes practices and epistemic transformations "from the inside out" (Clarke et al., 2010, 2). Biomedicalization occurs through an emphasis on "health itself" as a moral value and a project of the self, which reconstitutes citizens as health consumers (Rose, 2007). Many scholars of biomedicalization focus on how biomedicine reshapes bodies around discourses of health, wellness, and risk. The sociology of diagnosis attends to the ways in which biomedical knowledge shapes the very categories through which we engage with institutions and experts. However, in theories of biomedicalization, the analytic focus is typically on biomedicine and the life sciences, while the sociocultural realm is the base structure upon which these processes unfold. For example, Clarke et al. write about the sociocultural realm as providing the "infrastructures on and through which biotechnology and biomedicine can be built" (2010, 22). Here, biomedicine is the mover, while social and cultural forces provide the underlying structure, the surface upon which biomedicine works, leaving it unchanged. I want to ask instead how we can attend to the contradictions inherent in biomedicine *and* in its oppositional discourses. Maren Klawiter (2008) develops a framework like this in her analysis of the social movement dynamics surrounding breast cancer. She argues that we should focus on *practices* of biomedicalization—rather than levels—in order to understand how disease frames, social movement narratives, and patient identities shift. In her analysis, processes of biomedicalization do not overtake social movements; rather, biomedicalization operates in a loose and dialectical relationship with social movement logics.

27. Decoteau, 2017; Epstein, 1996; Klawiter, 2008; Murphy, 2012.

28. Clarke et al., 2010; Decoteau, 2017.

29. Murphy, 2006; Murphy, 2012.

30. Hall and Grossberg, 1986, Laclau and Mouffe, 1985.

31. Articulation helps avoid two types of reductionism: (1) explaining everything according to a base structure; and (2) assuming unity between a structure and its ideology (Althusser, 1969; Hall and Grossberg, 1986). For this case, articulation helps avoid reducing everything to biomedical logics, assuming that biomedical logics are homogeneous and that they subsume feminist claims, and analyzing biomedical shifts as if they obliterate all other social formations. The tools that articulation offers for avoiding reductionism come from Althusser via the concept of overdetermination (Althusser, 1969; Hall and Grossberg, 1986), typically used to explain a rupture or historical shift. Althusser uses overdetermination to complicate the Marxist idea of basic class contradiction, wherein the essential contradiction between the bourgeoisie and the proletariat will be overcome through struggle and revolution. Althusser (1969) uses the case of the Russian revolution to argue instead that revolutions actually require *many* contradictions, an accumulation of contradictions. What may appear simple actually has multiple causes and is recursively linked to multiple levels of social life, to a conjuncture of historical events and significations (Laclau and Mouffe, 1985). For Stuart Hall, overdetermination offers a way to think about events, texts, or structures as determined by more than one social force and set of meanings (Hall and Grossberg 1986). Thus, articulation and overdetermination offer tools for conceptualizing cause as multiple and for understanding the elements of social formations that are moving and in tension, without losing the concept of a social whole: something that operates powerfully and with some sort of unity. With articulation, we have both unity and difference, both power and mitigations to that power, both conflict and assimilation.

32. Slack, 1996.

33. Messner et al., 2015.

34. Sweet, 2014, 2015.

35. And yet, there is also some evidence that this diagnostic boundary between domestic violence work and mental health work may be eroding entirely. As national domestic violence movement leaders repeatedly informed me, the Affordable Care Act, combined with threats to domestic violence funding, has changed the landscape: Medicaid and insurance reimbursement are on the horizon. Domestic violence agencies are increasingly partnering with health care systems to ask how they might bill victims' insurance in order to earn revenue, which would require official diagnosis.

36. Van der Kolk, 2015. Others include Babette Rothschild, Peter Levine, and Pat Ogden.

37. Haney, 2010.

38. ICADV, 2000.

39. Foucault, 1988.

40. Foucault, 1988, 18.

41. Foucault, 1988, 18.

42. Rose, 1990, 228.

43. Agamben, 1998, 11.

44. Rose, 1990, 228.

45. Cooper, 2017.

46. Most of us are all too familiar with the language of self-care. For those of us in the academy, even emails from university administrators are full of reminders to care for ourselves—just as domestic violence agencies encourage workers and survivors to do. It is not so much the language of self-care that is the problem here—in fact, I think we should understand "self-care" as a survival tool for those living and working in conditions of abandonment, stress, and invisibility. Activists have long talked about self-care as a radical form of body politics. What's unsettling is that *the institutions that create those harmful conditions* can pick up the language of self-care and offer it as a salve for their inaction. *Here you go, you're welcome.* This places the responsibility for better conditions on those in subordinate institutional positions, making "self-care" into an alibi, while unequal and exhausting institutional environments go unchanged.

47. Fraser, 2013.

48. Rose, 1990, 238.

CHAPTER 4. BECOMING LEGIBLE

1. Rose, 1999.

2. Haney, 2010.

3. Parr, 2000.

4. Allard, 2008; Eliasoph, 2011; Haney, 2010; Marwell, 2004; Small, 2006.

5. Morgan and Campbell, 2011; Wolch, 1990.

6. Allard, 2008; Marwell, 2004.

7. Marwell, 2004.

8. Greenberg, 2019, 10.

9. Smith and Lipsky, 1993, 3.

10. Marwell, 2004.

11. Hasenfeld and Garrow, 2012.

12. Morgan and Campbell, 2011.

13. Eliasoph, 2011 (see also Naples, 2003).

14. Schram et al., 2009 (see also Cruikshank, 2009).

15. Hasenfeld and Garrow, 2012, 309.

16. Reich, 2005.

17. Polsky, 1991, 4.

18. Randles, 2018; Reich, 2005.

19. For example, Temporary Assistance for Needy Families (TANF) is made up of about 90 percent women recipients, whereas the prison system incarcerates

about 90 percent men (Haney, 2004). This inversion has led scholars to theorize these branches of the state as gendered—the penal system being "masculine" and the welfare state being "feminine" (Wacquant, 2009).

20. Fraser, 1987; Rose, 1990.

21. Haney, 2010; Polsky, 1991.

22. Gowan, 2010 (see also Willse, 2015).

23. Carr, 2010; McKim, 2017; Tiger, 2013.

24. Haney, 2010; Nolan, 1998; Mirchandani, 2005.

25. Haney, 2018.

26. Haney, 2010.

27. Greenberg, 2019; Haney, 2018. Further, as John Halushka (2020) shows, decentralized governance means that clients must engage in a time-consuming and exhausting "runaround" in order to satisfy the various institutions to which they are subject. This institutional "runaround" may even become a kind of full-time job.

28. Gurusami, 2017; Haney, 2018; Scott et al., 2002.

29. Parr, 2000; Lake and Newman, 2002; Wolch, 1990.

30. Mirchandani, 2005 (see also Piehowski, 2020).

31. As Victoria Piehowski (2020) explains, domestic violence courts "co-locate" services such as housing, medical care, and immigration services *with* law enforcement and prosecutors. The result, she argues, is that "empowerment" discourses obfuscate the punitive work actually going on inside the court: "The therapeutic discourse submerges tensions inherent to prosecution, including its disparate impact on marginalized communities and its conflictual reception by feminist anti-violence activists" (3).

32. Fraser, 1987; Giordano, 2014 (see also McKim, 2017).

33. The prosecution of survivors using versions of "failure to protect" in the child welfare system is the paradigmatic example of how "judicial systems collude with battering," worsening victims' circumstances (Bierria and Lenz, 2019, 92). As Bierria and Lenz argue, "failure to protect" is best described as a *political ideology* rooted in heteropatriarchy and in structures of mass punishment and incarceration (2019).

34. Villalón, 2010.

35. Villalón, 2010, 38.

36. Small, 2006.

37. Watkins-Hayes, 2019.

38. Adams and Padamsee, 2001, 13.

39. Althusser, 1971.

40. Korteweg, 2003.

41. Decoteau, 2016; Wingrove, 1999.

42. Allen, 2011; Muñoz, 1999.

43. Hall, 1996.

44. Haney, 1996.

45. Biehl, 2005, 6.

46. Rothschild, 2000.

47. Menjívar and Abrego, 2012.

48. Merry, 2001.

49. McKim, 2014, 2017.

50. Wyse, 2013.

51. Davis, 2005, 16.

52. Davis, 2005, 16.

53. Hays, 1996.

54. Underman et al., 2017.

55. Bierria and Lenz, 2019, 92.

56. Reich, 2005; Roberts, 2002.

57. Isin, 2009; Das, 2007.

58. Biehl and Moran-Thomas, 2009.

59. Foucault, 1988, 18.

60. Though, as Lois McNay (1992) reminds us, Foucault's terms are often too individualized, disallowing a robust sense of collective unease or action.

61. Naples, 2003; Decoteau, 2013.

62. Giordano, 2014, 216.

63. Giordano, 2014; James, 2010.

64. James, 2010; Menjívar, 2011; Scheper-Hughes and Bourgois, 2004.

65. Menjívar, 2011.

66. Giordano, 2014; Menjívar, 2011; Scarry, 1985; Sutton, 2010.

CHAPTER 5. GASLIGHTING

1. Warshaw et al., 2014.

2. Freyd, 1997; Harsey and Freyd, 2020; Harsey et al., 2017.

3. Decoteau, 2008; Gordon, 1997.

4. Ferraro, 2006 (see also Sweet, 2019b).

5. Originally adapted from a 1938 play by Patrick Hamilton.

6. Dozens of online checklists instruct readers on the "warning signs" of gaslighting in their intimate relationships. Robin Stern's bestselling 2007 book *The Gaslight Effect* was released for a second edition in 2018. The *Guardian*'s Ariel Leve wrote an article in 2017 titled, "Trump Is Gaslighting America." Psychotherapist Stephanie Sarkis, whose popular book *Gaslighting* came out in 2018, makes a similar argument. Gaslighting was even made an official part of criminal domestic violence law in the United Kingdom in 2015 (Mikhailova 2018).

7. Sweet, 2019b.

8. Ferraro, 2006, 73.

9. Williamson, 2010.

10. My purpose in this chapter is not to reify a presumed natural distinction between "crazy" and "not crazy," or to suggest that losing one's sense of reality equates to dysfunction. Rather, I am interested in exploring how tactics of "crazy-making" flourish in the structural context of gender and intersecting inequalities. That these tactics exist does not mean they are successful, or that there is any such thing as "normality" or its opposite. Categories of normal, just like categories of insanity, are disciplinary devices and ensembles of authoritative knowledge (Sweet and Decoteau, 2018). In other words, I am not suggesting any natural, embodied, or lived referent for women as "crazy." Mental illness is always over-coded with femininity and racial otherness (Metzl, 2003, 2010). Further, mental illness (and the isolation and stigma that accompany it) exacerbates other structural forms of inequality, operating as a point of intersection in the exercise of social power.

11. Gordon, 1997; Das, 2007; Decoteau, 2008.

12. Weingarten, 2016 (emphasis mine).

13. Gaslighting attacks one's sense of reality *and* one's ability to testify to that reality. As feminist philosopher Kate Manne (2017) argues, misogyny works by seizing control of the narrative and decimating the capacity for victim testimony. Relatedly, Kate Abramson has argued that gaslighting is not about dismissing someone's claims or not taking someone seriously—rather, it involves making another person "not take *herself* seriously as an interlocutor" (2014, 2). This occurs, she argues, when women attempt to call out patterns of sexism. Women's knowledge of their own discrimination is often "deliberately thwarted" (6). The same can be said of racial discrimination. Feminist scholar Brittney Cooper has theorized the ways in which Black women's rage and anger has been rendered "crazy" and unstable, their bodies "angry" and out of control (2018). Indeed, Black feminist scholars have long been attentive to the ways in which presenting as *Black and feminine* makes one vulnerable to being labeled overwrought and difficult, especially when calling out injustice.

14. Brenda's abuser was still convicted of felony domestic battery, one of the few convictions among the abusers of the women I interviewed. Brenda's abuser kidnapped her and held her in an upstairs room for multiple days, beating her unconscious and sexually assaulting her repeatedly. Brenda escaped by climbing down out of a second story window. She required a long stay in the hospital to recover from her injuries, including two broken fingers, fractured ribs, a split ear, black eyes, and bites on her neck. Still, Brenda described this experience as mere preparation for her long fight with DCFS over custody of her children.

15. Sharpe, 2016.

16. Grosz, 1994, 4; Shields, 2007.

17. Sharpe, 2016, 14.

18. Feminist theorists in the 1960s and 1970s, especially French feminists, were interested in femininity's presumed *lack* of reason. Luce Irigaray wrote that while men's desires have been read as wisdom and truth, women's desires have been systematically repressed and stigmatized, transformed into madness and alterity (1977). While psychoanalytic feminists have analyzed women's lives through the lens of social repression and its production of madness, sociologists of gender have long argued that women are labeled deviant and "crazy" via processes of medicalization and criminalization. Women's experiences of subordination (and/or their attempts at liberation) are misrecognized as symptoms of madness and shuttled into deviance categories (Blum and Stracuzzi, 2004; Metzl, 2003; Schur, 1984).

19. Littlejohn, 2013, 847.

20. Shields, 2007, 106.

21. Shields, 2007.

22. In Ehrenreich and English's (1973) classic work, women's emotional "diseases" are always class based—for example, hysterical symptoms were reserved for upper-class women.

23. Ehrenreich and English, 1973.

24. Herman, 1995.

25. Metzl, 2003 (see also Metzl and Angel, 2004).

26. Metzl, 2003.

27. Jutel, 2010; Lorber and Moore, 2002.

28. Barker, 2009, 102.

29. Anderson and Umberson, 2001.

30. Anderson, 2009.

31. Barber et al., 2018; Miller et al., 2010.

32. Anderson and Umberson, 2001; Yamawaki et al., 2009.

33. Schrock et al., 2017.

34. Enander, 2010.

35. Williamson, 2010.

36. Hartman, 1997, 5.

37. Ferraro, 2006; Stark, 2007.

38. Garcia, 2012.

39. Richie, 2012.

40. Larance et al., 2018.

41. Ferraro, 2006.

42. Norwood, 1997.

43. Ticktin, 2011.

44. Menjívar, 2011.

45. Biehl, 2005; Bourgois and Schonberg, 2009; Decoteau, 2013; Sutton, 2010.

46. Gordon, 1997.

47. Stark, 2007.

48. In 1976, *Ms.* became the first magazine in the United States to feature an image of domestic violence on its cover.

49. Sutton, 2018.

50. Despite this emphasis on brutalizing physical assault, decades of social science research indicate that physical violence is *not* the most consistent, petrifying, or imprisoning aspect of domestic violence (Stark, 2007). Physical violence is part of establishing control, scholars note, but so are tactics such as emotional abuse, humiliation, and isolation (Anderson, 2008; Giordano et al., 2016; Hardesty et al., 2015; Johnson et al., 2014; Kimmel, 2002; Myhill, 2015; Reed et al., 2010; Stark and Hester, 2019; Tanha et al., 2010). Psychological abuse exerts control by micro-regulating victims' everyday lives, self-concepts, and sense of reality (Hardesty et al., 2015; Murphy and Hoover, 1999; Myhill, 2017; Piipsa, 2002). Research on intimate partner violence consistently shows that psychological control tactics are used more commonly and effectively by men against women (Hester et al., 2017; Kelly and Westmarland, 2016; Myhill, 2015; Tanha et al., 2010) and that they affect victims more negatively than physical abuse in the long term (Anderson, 2009; Dutton and Goodman, 2005; Ferraro, 2006; Hester et al., 2017; O'Leary, 1999; Strauchler et al., 2004).

51. Dutton and Goodman, 2005.

52. Black et al., 2010.

53. Sweet, 2014; Warshaw et al., 2009.

54. Mol, 2002, 10.

55. Giordano, 2014, 186.

56. Bacchus et al., 2003.

57. Decoteau, 2013.

58. Giordano, 2014, 59.

59. Das, 1996; Giordano, 2014; Scarry, 1985.

CHAPTER 6. SURVIVING HETEROSEXUALITY

1. Garcia, 2009, 212; Rich, 1980; Valocchi, 2005.

2. Connell, 2014, 16.

3. Carrillo, 2002; Connell, 2014; Richardson, 2007. See Pascoe (2007) for a more extended analysis of the relationship between gender performance and compulsory heterosexuality.

4. Schippers, 2016, 6.

5. Muñoz, 1999.

6. Butler, 1990; Connell, 2014, 21.

7. Ferguson, 2004, 3.

8. Hirsch and Khan, 2020.

9. Ward, 2020, 115.

10. Canaday, 2009.

11. Canaday, 2009, 4.

12. Canaday, 2009, 7.

13. Richardson, 1998.

14. Bell, 1995; Haney and March, 2003; Randles, 2013.

15. Randles, 2013, 869.

16. Haney and March, 2003, 464.

17. Shome, 2001, 324.

18. Randles, 2013, 882.

19. Geva, 2011, 26.

20. Geva, 2011.

21. Richardson, 2017; Richardson and Turner, 2001; Ryan-Flood, 2009.

22. Butler, 2002; Puar, 2007; Ryan-Flood, 2009.

23. Richardson, 2017.

24. Ahmed, 2006.

25. Epstein and Carrillo, 2014.

26. Seidman, 2001, 323 (emphasis mine).

27. Randles, 2013, 2018.

28. Smith, 2006.

29. Scott et al., 2002.

30. These findings echo what scholars have discovered about criminally involved women, who also experience sexual discipline in carceral programs, since they are presumed to have "failed" romantically and sexually (Wyse, 2013).

31. None of this is to suggest that queer people don't experience intimate violence from their partners. They do (Ristock 2002; Sokoloff and Dupont 2005). LGBQ+ people may also be more reluctant to seek help because their experiences are ignored or misunderstood in mainstream institutions. As I have emphasized throughout this book, gender is not the only context for intimate violence. Race, sexuality, gender presentation, and class intersect to set the conditions for entrapment. It is important, for example, to theorize same-sex relationship violence in the structural context of homophobia and heteronormativity (Renzetti, 1988; Sokoloff and Dupont, 2005; Bedera and Nordmeyer, 2020).

32. Butler, 1990; Calhoun, 1994; Rich, 1980; Rubin, 1975.

33. Rich, 1980, 653.

34. Ingraham, 1994. As such, monogamy (at least for women) is also integral to compulsory heterosexuality (Schippers, 2016).

35. Puar, 2007.

36. Ward, 2015, 29.

37. Cruikshank, 1999; Ferguson, 2004; Roberts, 2002.

38. Bettie, 2003.

39. Garcia, 2012.

40. Stoler, 1995, 9.

41. Hammonds, 2004, 305.

42. Allen, 2011; Espiritu, 2001; Garcia, 2012; Hammonds, 2004; Moore, 2011; Muñoz, 1999.

43. Gurusami, 2019.

44. Ferguson, 2004; Puar, 2007. One of the goals of queer-of-color critique, according to theorist Rod Ferguson, is to disrupt the liberal capitalist construction of the home as the quintessential "site of accommodation and confirmation" (2004, 3). The construction of the home as a space of heterosexuality, state legibility and normativity, welfare state capitalism, and nationhood is therefore important to queer critique. Indeed, the state enacts racial divides of citizenship by assigning heteronormativity to certain racial subjects and sexual perversion to Others (Ferguson, 2004; Puar, 2007). Queer theory argues that heterosexuality is a refraction of the state's racialized nuclear family household *and* associates heterosexuality with a homey experience of belonging and recognition.

45. Ahmed, 2006.

46. Ward, 2015, 31.

47. Ahmed, 2006, 18.

48. When we follow such lines, we achieve normativity, but we also give up the possibility of alterity, in a kind of melancholic loss (Ahmed, 2006; Butler, 1997). Compulsory heterosexuality, according to Ahmed, is a "straightening device" that also injures.

49. Canaday, 2009, 256.

50. Ward, 2020, 172.

51. Muñoz, 1999, 6.

52. In a kind of intentional melancholic incorporation, one decidedly incorporates what is refused by culture in order to make oneself a bad subject (Butler, 1997; Muñoz, 1999).

53. Wingrove, 1999 (see also Decoteau, 2016).

54. Muñoz, 1999, 31.

55. Muñoz, 1999, 11. Elizabeth Wingrove (1999) has also argued that the process of interpellation is ambivalent and split. Because interpellation is concerned both with structure (language) and the mechanisms of reiteration (ideological practice), it is not stable, but historically and practically contingent. For Wingrove (1999), ideologies have multiple constitutive sites, which makes them ripe for rupture through practice. For example, femininity is practiced across multiple, intersecting ideological spheres (i.e., citizenship, motherhood). Enacting femininity in different ideological systems requires the subject to reconfigure herself continuously. Political tensions arise from these reconfigurations. Ideologies may then be exposed as incoherent. Social actors transform the ideological structures in which they operate precisely because they are always acting *across* them (Decoteau, 2016). This is not necessarily deliberate resistance. We might

think of this as a set of disidentifications that takes place across intersecting sites of identity constitution. Large-scale interpellating structures conflict with daily performances, causing distortions that may be productive.

56. Muñoz, 1999.

57. Muñoz, 1999, 31.

58. Ferraro, 2006; Johnson, 2008; Stark, 2007.

59. Ahmed, 2006.

60. Ahmed, 2006.

61. Muñoz, 1999.

62. According to Muñoz, the process of disidentification arises from the experience of failed interpellations in the dominant public sphere: "What stops identification from happening is always the ideological restrictions implicit in an identificatory site" (1999, 7).

63. Ahmed, 2006.

64. Barber et al., 2018; Miller et al., 2010.

65. McCauley et al., 2014; Shah and Shah, 2010; Silverman et al., 2001.

66. Feelings of regret about motherhood are complicated and ambivalent because they defy cultural expectations: women often struggled to articulate their feelings about motherhood clearly in interviews, alternating between statements of regret and expressions of guilt.

67. Allen, 2011.

68. Allen, 2011.

69. Garcia, 2012; Stein and Plummer, 1996.

70. Valocchi, 2005.

CONCLUSION

1. I borrow traumatic citizenship from Vinh Kim Nguyen's (2010) notion of "therapeutic citizenship," which he uses to describe how confessing a positive HIV status became the only means through which people could access resources during West Africa's AIDS crisis. According to Nguyen, therapeutic citizenship arises when institutions can only grant resources to *some* people—"talking about oneself" then becomes the mechanism for being sorted into the group that can access care.

2. Somers, 1994b, 79.

3. Tilly, 1995, 6 (see also Isin, 2009; Somers, 1994b; Turner, 1993).

4. Glenn, 2011.

5. Isin, 2009.

6. Foucault, 1991, 55.

7. Roychowdhury, 2020, 5.

8. The handful of women who were not surprised had experienced abuse as children and therefore *expected* men in their families to be violent.

9. Stark, 2007, 4.

10. Glenn, 2011; Marshall, 1950; Somers, 2008; Turner, 1993.

11. Roche, 1992.

12. Lister, 2007; Marshall, 1950.

13. Glenn, 2011.

14. James, 2010; Nguyen, 2010; Petryna, 2003.

15. As Foucault teaches us, confession is itself a political technology. In *The History of Sexuality* (1978), Foucault argues that the Christian compulsion to "confess" sin—though it was intended to *hide* sexuality within the self and the church—has actually multiplied discourses on sex, expanding sexual categories and knowledge. Subjects are called upon to tell their sexual secrets, which does not expel sexuality from public discourse, but causes it to proliferate, as expert institutions (i.e., medicine) transform sex into an object of knowledge and regulation. The practice of confession makes sexuality appear innate—driven outward from the soul through telling—when it is actually a public discourse. Confession is a procedure for producing the myth of an internalized "truth" (Foucault, 1978, 58).

16. Carr, 2010. "Talk" is important to accessing citizenship. Through recovery programs, women are encouraged to "talk" themselves out of dependency. Erica James (2010) details how victims of political violence in Haiti learn to tell stories about interpersonal violence that are appealing to humanitarian organizations. Narrative labor is required for survival. But this labor is deeply normative, such that staking claims to citizenship through stories or through suffering bodies also extends state power into the body and psyche in new ways, forcing social actors to undergo symbolic violence in order to be recognized (Bourdieu, 1977).

17. Fassin and Rechtman, 2009.

18. Both of these points push back against the misperception that citizenship is public and abstract. What Ken Plummer (2011) calls "intimate citizenship"—wherein the private sphere is included in conceptions of citizenship—better describes women's experiences of violence and help-seeking (see also Orloff, 1993; Walby, 1994). Citizenship is intimately located and lived (Lister, 2007). Further, ideas about masculinity and femininity, the sexual division of labor, compulsory heterosexuality, and motherhood define how state resources and rights are granted (Orloff, 1996; Richardson, 1998).

19. Miller and Stuart, 2017, 537.

20. MCBWSG, 1981, 7 (emphasis mine).

21. Decoteau, 2013 (see also Underman et al., 2017).

22. ICADV, 1995.

23. Haley, 2016, 3.

24. Watkins-Hayes, 2019.

25. ICADV, 1995.

26. Haaken, 1996, 1083.

27. Hammonds, 2004, 312.

28. Sweet, 2019a.

29. Giordano, 2014; James, 2010; Petryna, 2003.

30. Kim, 2020, 267.

31. Decoteau, 2013, 238.

32. Ahmed, 2015.

33. Berlant, 2000.

34. Dunn, 2005.

METHODOLOGICAL APPENDIX

1. Sutton, 2018.

2. Greenberg, 2019, 192.

3. Visweswaran, 1994.

4. Smith, 2012.

5. Lather, 2012, 135.

6. Collins, 1990; Pillow, 2003; Smith, 2012.

7. Abu-Lughod, 2008.

8. Haraway, 1988, 586.

9. Abu-Lughod, 2008.

10. Skarpelis, 2020, 393.

11. Lofland et al., 2006.

12. Lofland et al., 2006.

13. Some support group leaders handed out information about my research and asked for volunteers to participate. Others invited me to attend their support groups, where I described my project and asked for participants myself. An interpreter accompanied me to Spanish-speaking support groups and interviews. Women were provided $40 cash per interview, as well as transportation costs, per Institutional Review Board guidelines.

14. I assured the women who participated of confidentiality, which was especially important because many of them were in the process of leaving their abusers and/or were involved in ongoing civil and criminal cases. Therefore, when necessary, some of the women's demographic details—such as country of origin—are omitted throughout the book.

15. Meadow, 2018, 238.

References

Abramson, Kate. 2014. "Turning up the Lights on Gaslighting." *Philosophical Perspectives* 28(1):1–30.

Abu-Lughod, Lila. 2008. "Writing against Culture." In *The Cultural Geography Reader*, edited by Timothy S. Oakes and Patricia L. Price, 62–71. New York: Routledge.

Adams, Julia, and Tasleem Padamsee. 2001. "Signs and Regimes: Rereading Feminist Work on Welfare States." *Social Politics: International Studies in Gender, State, and Society* 8(1):1–23.

Agamben, Giorgio. 1998. *Homo Sacer: Sovereign Power and Bare Life*. Stanford, CA: Stanford University Press.

Ahmed, Sara. 2006. *Queer Phenomenology: Orientations, Objects, Others*. Durham, NC: Duke University Press.

———. 2015. "Living a Lesbian Life." Feministkilljoys, February 26. https:// feministkilljoys.com/2015/02/26/living-a-lesbian-life/

Ahrens, Lois. 1980. "Battered Women's Refuges: Feminist Cooperatives vs. Social Service Institutions." Box 1 Folder 1. Sophia Smith Collection, Violence Against Women, Smith College.

Alcoff, Linda, and Laura Gray. 1993. "Survivor Discourse: Transgression or Recuperation?" *Signs: Journal of Women in Culture & Society* 18(2):260–90.

Allard, Scott. 2008. *Out of Reach: Place, Poverty, and the New American Welfare State*. New Haven, CT: Yale University Press.

Allard, Sharon Angella. 1991. "Rethinking Battered Woman Syndrome: A Black Feminist Perspective." *UCLA Women's Law Journal* 1:191–207.

Allen, Jafari. 2011. *¡Venceremos?: The Erotics of Black Self-Making in Cuba.* Durham, NC: Duke University Press.

Althusser, Louis. 1969. *For Marx, Volume 2.* London: Verso.

———. 1971. "Ideology and Ideological State Apparatuses (Notes toward an Investigation)." In *Lenin and Philosophy and Other Essays*, 127–86. Monthly Review Press.

Anderson, Kristin L. 2008. "Is Partner Violence Worse in the Context of Control?" *Journal of Marriage & Family* 70(5):1157–68.

———. 2009. "Gendering Coercive Control." *Violence against Women* 15:1444–57.

Anderson, Kristin, and Deb Umberson. 2001. "Gendering Violence: Masculinity and Power in Men's Accounts of Domestic Violence." *Gender & Society* 15(3):358–80.

Armstrong, Elizabeth, Miriam Gleckman-Krut, and Lanora Johnson. 2018. "Silence, Power, and Inequality: An Intersectional Approach to Sexual Violence." *Annual Review of Sociology* 44:99–122.

Auyero, Javier. 2012. *Patients of the State: The Politics of Waiting in Argentina.* Durham, NC: Duke University Press.

Bacchus, Loraine, Gill Mezey, and Susan Bewley. 2003. "Experiences of Seeking Help from Health Professionals in a Sample of Women Who Experienced Domestic Violence." *Health & Social Care in the Community* 11:10–18.

Baker, Charlene K., Kris A. Billhardt, Joseph Warren, Chiquita Rollins, and Nancy E. Glass. 2010. "Domestic Violence, Housing Instability, and Homelessness: A Review of Housing Policies and Program Practices for Meeting the Needs of Survivors." *Aggression and Violent Behavior* 15(6):430–39. doi: 10.1016/j.avb.2010.07.005.

Baker, Charlene K., Sarah L. Cook, and Fran H. Norris. 2003. "Domestic Violence and Housing Problems: A Contextual Analysis of Women's Help-Seeking, Received Informal Support, and Formal System Response." *Violence against Women* 9(7):754–83.

Bako, Yolanda. 1978. "Battered Women: Issues of Public Policy: A Consultation Sponsored by the United States Commission on Civil Rights, Washington D.C., January 30–31, 1978." Box 1 Folder 1, Articles and Papers 1975–1981. Sophia Smith Collection, Violence Against Women, Smith College.

Barber, Jennifer S., Yasamin Kusunoki, Heather H. Gatny, and Jamie Budnick. 2018. "The Dynamics of Intimate Partner Violence and the Risk of Pregnancy during the Transition to Adulthood." *American Sociological Review* 83(5):1020–47.

Barker, Kristin. 2009. *The Fibromyalgia Story: Medical Authority and Women's Worlds of Pain.* Philadelphia: Temple University Press.

Bedera, Nicole, and Kristjane Nordmeyer. 2020. "An Inherently Masculine Practice: Understanding the Sexual Victimization of Queer Women."

Journal of Interpersonal Violence 0886260519898439. doi: 10.1177/ 0886260519898439.

Bell, David. 1995. "Pleasure and Danger: The Paradoxical Spaces of Sexual Citizenship." *Political Geography* 14(2):139–53.

Berlant, Lauren. 2000. "The Subject of True Feeling." In *Transformations: Thinking through feminism*, edited by Sara Ahmed, Jane Kilby, Celia Lury, Maureen McNeil, Beverly Skeggs, 33–47. New York: Routledge.

———. 2011. *Cruel Optimism*. Durham, NC: Duke University Press.

Berns, Nancy. 2001. "Degendering the Problem and Gendering the Blame: Political Discourse on Women and Violence." *Gender & Society* 15(2):262–81.

Bernstein, Elizabeth. 2012. "Carceral Politics as Gender Justice? The 'Traffic in Women' and Neoliberal Circuits of Crime, Sex, and Rights." *Theory & Society* 41(3):233–59.

Bettie, Julie. 2003. *Women without Class: Girls, Race, and Identity*. Berkeley: University of California Press.

Biehl, João. 2005. *Vita: Life in a Zone of Social Abandonment*. Berkeley: University of California Press.

Biehl, João, and Amy Moran-Thomas. 2009. "Symptom: Subjectivities, Social Ills, Technologies." *Annual Review of Anthropology* 38(1):267–88.

Bierria, Alisa, and Colby Lenz. 2019. "Battering Court Syndrome: A Structural Critique of 'Failure to Protect.'" In *Politicization of Safety: Critical Perspectives on Domestic Violence Responses*, edited by J. K. Stoever, 91–118. New York: New York University Press.

Black, Michele, Kathleen Basile, Sharon Smith Breiding, Mikel Walters, Melissa Merrick, Jieru Chen, and Mark Stevens. 2010. "National Intimate Partner and Sexual Violence Survey: 2010 Summary Report." https://www.cdc.gov /violenceprevention/pdf/nisvs_report2010-a.pdf.

Blum, Linda M., and Nena F. Stracuzzi. 2004. "Gender in the Prozac Nation: Popular Discourse and Productive Femininity." *Gender & Society* 18(3):269–86.

Bockman, Johanna. 2012. "The Political Projects of Neoliberalism." *Social Anthropology* 20(3):310–17.

Bourdieu, Pierre. 1977. *Outline of a Theory of Practice*. Cambridge: Cambridge University Press.

———. 2000. *Pascalian Meditations*. Polity Press.

Bourgois, Philippe, and Jeffrey Schonberg. 2009. *Righteous Dopefiend*. Berkeley: University of California Press.

Bourke, Joanna. 2012. "Sexual Violence, Bodily Pain, and Trauma: A History." *Theory, Culture, & Society* 29(3):25–51.

Bowker, Geoffrey C., and Susan Leigh Star. 2000. *Sorting Things Out: Classification and Its Consequences*. Cambridge, MA: MIT Press.

Boyle, Kaitlin M., and Kimberly B. Rogers. 2020. "Beyond the Rape 'Victim'-'Survivor' Binary: How Race, Gender, and Identity Processes Interact to Shape Distress." *Sociological Forum* 35(2):323–345.

Bracken, Patrick. 2001. "Post-Modernity and Post-Traumatic Stress Disorder." *Social Science & Medicine* 53(6):733–43.

Breiding, Matthew J., Kathleen C. Basile, Joanne Klevens, and Sharon G. Smith. 2017. "Economic Insecurity and Intimate Partner and Sexual Violence Victimization." *American Journal of Preventive Medicine* 53(4):457–64.

Brown, Wendy. 1992. "Finding the Man in the State." *Feminist Studies* 18(1):7–34. doi: 10.2307/3178212.

———. 2006. "American Nightmare: Neoliberalism, Neoconservatism, and De-Democratization." *Political Theory* 34(6):690–714.

Brubaker, Rogers, and Frederick Cooper. 2000. "Beyond 'Identity.'" *Theory and Society* 29(1):1–47.

Brush, Lisa D. 2000. "Battering, Traumatic Stress, and Welfare-to-Work Transition." *Violence against Women* 6(10):1039–65.

———. 2003. *Gender and Governance.* Walnut Creek, CA: AltaMira Press.

———. 2011. *Poverty, Battered Women, and Work in US Public Policy.* Oxford University Press.

Bumiller, Kristin. 2008. *In an Abusive State: How Neoliberalism Appropriated the Feminist Movement against Sexual Violence.* Durham, NC: Duke University Press.

Butler, Judith. 1990. *Gender Trouble: Feminism and the Subversion of Identity.* New York: Routledge.

———. 1997. *The Psychic Life of Power: Theories in Subjection.* Stanford, CA: Stanford University Press.

———. 2002. "Is Kinship Always Already Heterosexual?" *Differences: A Journal of Feminist Cultural Studies* 13(1):14–44.

———. 2004. *Undoing Gender.* Psychology Press.

Calhoun, Cheshire. 1994. "Separating Lesbian Theory from Feminist Theory." *Ethics* 104(3):558–81.

Canaday, Margot. 2009. *The Straight State: Sexuality and Citizenship in Twentieth-Century America.* Princeton, NJ: Princeton University Press.

Carr, E. Summerson. 2010. *Scripting Addiction: The Politics of Therapeutic Talk and American Sobriety.* Princeton, NJ: Princeton University Press.

Carrillo, Héctor. 2002. *The Night Is Young: Sexuality in Mexico in the Time of AIDS.* Chicago: University of Chicago Press.

Center for Healthcare Strategies, Inc. 2017. "State and Federal Support of Trauma-Informed Care: Sustaining the Momentum." https://www.chcs.org/state-federal-support-trauma-informed-care-sustaining-momentum/.

Center for Women and Policy Studies. 1977. "Response to Intrafamily Violence and Sexual Assault: LEAA Releases Draft Guidelines for Family Violence

Funding." Box 1, Bonnie Tinker's Personal Files. National Coalition Against Domestic Violence.

Centers for Disease Control (CDC). 2010. "Intimate Partner Violence in the United States—2010." https://www.cdc.gov/violenceprevention/pdf/cdc _nisvs_ipv_report_2013_v17_single_a.pdf.

———. 2018. "Violence Prevention." https://www.cdc.gov/violenceprevention /intimatepartnerviolence/consequences.html.

Choo, Hae Yeon, and Myra Marx Ferree. 2010. "Practicing Intersectionality in Sociological Research: A Critical Analysis of Inclusions, Interactions, and Institutions in the Study of Inequalities." *Sociological Theory* 28(2):129–49. doi: 10.1111/j.1467-9558.2010.01370.x.

Chriss, James J. 1999. *Counseling and the Therapeutic State*. Piscataway, NJ: Transaction Publishers.

Christianson, Judy. 1978. "Coordination of the White House Meeting on Family Violence." Box 1, Bonnie Tinker's Personal Files. National Coalition Against Domestic Violence.

Clarke, Adele, Janet K. Shim, Laura Mamo, Jennifer Ruth Fosket, and Jennifer R. Fishman. 2010. *Biomedicalization: Technoscience, Health, and Illness in the U.S.* Durham, NC: Duke University Press.

Coker, Donna. 2004. "Race, Poverty, and the Crime-Centered Response to Domestic Violence: A Comment on Linda Mills's Insult to Injury: Rethinking Our Responses to Intimate Abuse." *Violence against Women* 10:1331–53.

Cole, Alyson Manda. 2007. *The Cult of True Victimhood: From the War on Welfare to the War on Terror*. Stanford, CA: Stanford University Press.

Collins, Patricia Hill. 1990. *Black Feminist Thought: Knowledge, Consciousness, and the Politics of Empowerment*. New York: Routledge.

———. 1998. "It's All in the Family: Intersections of Gender, Race, and Nation." *Hypatia* 13(3):62–82. doi: 10.1111/j.1527-2001.1998.tb01370.x.

Connell, Catherine. 2014. *School's Out: Gay and Lesbian Teachers in the Classroom*. Oakland: University of California Press.

Connell, Raewyn. 2009. "Accountable Conduct 'Doing Gender' in Transsexual and Political Retrospect." *Gender & Society* 23(1):104–11.

Conrad, Peter. 2007. *The Medicalization of Society*. Baltimore: Johns Hopkins University Press.

Cooper, Brittney. 2018. *Eloquent Rage: A Black Feminist Discovers Her Superpower*. New York: St. Martin's Press.

Cooper, Melinda. 2017. *Family Values: Between Neoliberalism and the New Social Conservatism*. Cambridge, MA: MIT Press.

Corrigan, Rose. 2013. *Up Against a Wall: Rape Reform and the Failure of Success*. New York: New York University Press.

Corrigan, Rose, and Corey S. Shdaimah. 2015. "People with Secrets: Contesting, Constructing, and Resisting Women's Claims about Sexualized Victimization." *Catholic University Law Review* 65:429.

Creek, S. J., and Jennifer L. Dunn. 2011. "Rethinking Gender and Violence: Agency, Heterogeneity, and Intersectionality." *Sociology Compass* 5(5):311–22.

Crenshaw, Kimberlé. 1990. "Mapping the Margins: Intersectionality, Identity Politics, and Violence against Women of Color." *Stanford Law Review* 43:1241–99.

Cruikshank, Barbara. 1999. *The Will to Empower: Democratic Citizens and Other Subjects.* Ithaca, NY: Cornell University Press.

Das, Veena. 1996. "Language and Body: Transactions in the Construction of Pain." *Daedalus* 125(1):67–91.

———. 2000. "The Act of Witnessing: Violence, Poisonous Knowledge, and Subjectivity." In *Violence and Subjectivity*, edited by V. Das and A. Kleinman, 205–25. Berkeley: University of California Press.

———. 2007. *Life and Words: Violence and the Descent into the Ordinary.* Berkeley: University of California Press.

Davis, Dana-Ain. 2012. *Battered Black Women and Welfare Reform: Between a Rock and a Hard Place.* Albany: State University of New York Press.

Davis, Joseph E. 2005. *Accounts of Innocence: Sexual Abuse, Trauma, and the Self.* Chicago: University of Chicago Press.

de Leon, Cedric, Manali Desai, and Cihan Tugal. 2015. *Building Blocs: How Parties Organize Society.* Stanford, CA: Stanford University Press.

Decoteau, Claire Laurier. 2008. "The Specter of AIDS: Testimonial Activism in the Aftermath of the Epidemic." *Sociological Theory* 26(3):230–57.

———. 2013. *Ancestors and Antiretrovirals: The Biopolitics of HIV/AIDS in Post-Apartheid South Africa.* Chicago: University of Chicago Press.

———. 2016. "The Reflexive Habitus: Critical Realist and Bourdieusian Social Action." *European Journal of Social Theory* 19(3):303–21.

———. 2017. "The 'Western Disease': Autism and Somali Parents' Embodied Health Movements." *Social Science & Medicine* 177:169–76.

Decoteau, Claire Laurier, and Paige L. Sweet. 2016. "Psychiatry's Little Other: DSM-5 and Debates over Psychiatric Science." *Social Theory & Health* 14(4):414–35.

del Real, Deisy. 2019. "Toxic Ties: The Reproduction of Legal Violence within Mixed-Status Intimate Partners, Relatives, and Friends." *International Migration Review* 53(2):548–70. doi: 10.1177/0197918318769313.

Desmond, Matthew. 2016. *Evicted: Poverty and Profit in the American City.* Broadway Books.

Duggan, Lisa. 2003. *The Twilight of Equality? Neoliberalism, Cultural Politics, and the Attack on Democracy.* Boston: Beacon Press.

Dunn, Jennifer. 2001. "Innocence Lost: Accomplishing Victimization in Intimate Stalking Cases." *Symbolic Interaction* 24(3):285–313. doi: 10.1525 /si.2001.24.3.285.

———. 2004. "The Politics of Empathy: Social Movements and Victim Reper-
toires." *Sociological Focus* 37(3):235–50. doi: 10.1080/00380237.2004
.10571244.

———. 2005. "'Victims' and Survivors': Emerging Vocabularies of Motive for
'Battered Women Who Stay.'" *Sociological Inquiry* 75(1):1–30.

———. 2007. "'Everybody Makes Choices': Victim Advocates and the Social
Construction of Battered Women's Victimization and Agency." *Violence
Against Women* 13:977–1001.

Durazo, Anna Clarissa Rojas. 2006. "The Medicalization of Domestic Violence."
In *The Color of Violence: The INCITE! Anthology*, 179–88. Cambridge, MA:
South End Press.

Dutton, Mary Ann, and Lisa Goodman. 2005. "Coercion in Intimate Partner
Violence: Toward a New Conceptualization." *Sex Roles* 52(11–12):743–56.

DVMHPI (Domestic Violence and Mental Health Policy Initiative). 2002.
"Risking Connections." Box 18, Folder 7 (Chicago), September 11–13, 2002.
Papers of Susan Schechter, 1961–2005, Harvard University Schlesinger
Library.

DVTMH (Domestic Violence, Trauma, and Mental Health). 2003. "Risking
Connections." Box 20, Folder 4, DHHS meeting, January 16–17, 2003. Papers
of Susan Schechter, 1961–2005, Harvard University Schlesinger Library.

Ehrenreich, Barbara, and Deirdre English. 1973. *Complaints and Disorders:
The Sexual Politics of Sickness*. New York: The Feminist Press.

Eliasoph, Nina. 2011. *Making Volunteers: Civic Life after Welfare's End*.
Princeton, NJ: Princeton University Press.

Elizabeth, Vivienne, Nicola Gavey, and Julia Tolmie. 2012. "'He's Just Swapped
His Fists for the System': The Governance of Gender through Custody Law."
Gender & Society 26(2):239–60.

Enander, Viveka. 2010. "'A Fool to Keep Staying:' Battered Women Labeling
Themselves Stupid as an Expression of Gendered Shame." *Violence Against
Women* 16(1):5–31.

Epstein, Steve. 1996. *Impure Science: AIDS, Activism, and the Politics of
Knowledge*. Berkley: University of California Press.

Epstein, Steven, and Héctor Carrillo. 2014. "Immigrant Sexual Citizenship:
Intersectional Templates among Mexican Gay Immigrants to the USA."
Citizenship Studies 18(3–4):259–76. doi: 10.1080/13621025.2014.905266.

Espeland, Wendy Nelson, and Mitchell L. Stevens. 1996. "Commensuration as a
Social Process." *Annual Review of Sociology* 24(1):313–43.

———. 2008. "A Sociology of Quantification." *European Journal of Sociology*
49(3):401–36.

Espiritu, Yen Le. 2001. "'We Don't Sleep around Like White Girls Do': Family,
Culture, and Gender in Filipina American Lives." *Signs: Journal of Women
in Culture & Society* 26(2):415–40.

Eyal, Gil. 2013. "For a Sociology of Expertise: The Social Origins of the Autism Epidemic." *American Journal of Sociology* 118(4):863–907.

Fais, Cari. 2008. "Denying Access to Justice: The Cost of Applying Chronic Nuisance Laws to Domestic Violence." *Columbia Law Review* 1181–225.

Fanon, Frantz. 1952. *Black Skin, White Masks*. London: Pluto Press.

Fassin, Didier, and Richard Rechtman. 2009. *The Empire of Trauma: An Inquiry into the Condition of Victimhood*. Princeton, NJ: Princeton University Press.

Ferguson, Roderick. 2004. *Aberrations in Black: Toward a Queer of Color Critique*. Minneapolis: University of Minnesota Press.

———. 2005. "Of Our Normative Strivings: African American Studies and the Histories of Sexuality." *Social Text* 23(3–4):84–99.

Ferraro, Kathleen J. 1996. "The Dance of Dependency: A Genealogy of Domestic Violence Discourse." *Hypatia* 11(4):77–91. doi: 10.1111/j.1527-2001.1996 .tb01036.x.

———. 2003. "The Words Change but the Melody Lingers: The Persistence of the Battered Woman Syndrome in Criminal Cases Involving Battered Women." *Violence Against Women* 9:110–29.

———. 2006. *Neither Angels nor Demons: Women, Crime, and Victimization*. Hanover, NH: Northeastern University Press.

Fleck-Henderson, Ann. 2017. "From Movement to Mainstream: A Battered Women's Shelter Evolves (1976–2017)." *Affilia* 32(4):476–90. doi: 10.1177 /0886109917718230.

Fong, Kelley. 2020. "Getting Eyes in the Home: Child Protective Services Investigations and State Surveillance of Family Life." *American Sociological Review* 85(4):610–38. doi: 10.1177/0003122420938460.

Foucault, Michel. 1973. *The Birth of the Clinic*. Routledge.

———. 1978. *The History of Sexuality, Volume 1: An Introduction*. New York: Pantheon.

———. 1988. *Technologies of the Self: A Seminar with Michel Foucault*. Amherst: University of Massachusetts Press.

———. 1991. *The Foucault Effect: Studies in Governmentality*. Chicago: University of Chicago Press.

FPC. 2013. "Trauma-Informed Approaches: Federal Activities and Initiatives, Federal Partners Committee on Women and Trauma." https://s3.amazonaws .com/static.nicic.gov/Library/027657.pdf.

Franzway, Suzanne, Diane Court, and R. W. Connell. 1989. *Staking a Claim: Feminism, Bureaucracy and the State*. London: Allen & Unwin.

Fraser, Nancy. 1987. "Women, Welfare and the Politics of Need Interpretation." *Thesis Eleven* 17(1):88–106.

———. 2013. *Fortunes of Feminism: From State-Managed Capitalism to Neoliberal Crisis*. London: Verso Books.

Fraser, Nancy, and Linda Gordon. 1994. "A Genealogy of Dependency: Tracing a Keyword of the U.S. Welfare State." *Signs: Journal of Women in Culture & Society* 19(2):309–36.

Freyd, Jennifer J. 1997. "Violations of Power, Adaptive Blindness and Betrayal Trauma Theory." *Feminism & Psychology* 7(1):22–32. doi: 10.1177 /0959353597071004.

Frickel, Scott, and Kelly Moore, eds. 2005. *The New Political Sociology of Science: Institutions, Networks, and Power.* Madison: University of Wisconsin Press.

FVPF (Family Violence Prevention Fund). 1993. "National Health Advisory Committee, Family Violence Prevention Fund." Box 31 Folder 8, Papers of Susan Schechter, 1961–2005, Harvard University Schlesinger Library.

FVPSA (Family Violence Prevention and Services Act). 1984. Pub. L. No. 2430.

Garcia, Lorena. 2009. "Now Why Do You Want to Know about That?" Heteronormativity, Sexism, and Racism in the Sexual (Mis)Education of Latina Youth." *Gender & Society* 23(4):520–41.

———. 2012. *Respect Yourself: Protect Yourself: Latina Girls and Sexual Identity.* New York: New York University Press.

Garland, David. 2012. *The Culture of Control: Crime and Social Order in Contemporary Society.* Chicago: University of Chicago Press.

Geva, Dorit. 2011. "Not Just Maternalism: Marriage and Fatherhood in American Welfare Policy." *Social Politics: International Studies in Gender, State & Society* 18(1):24–51. doi: 10.1093/sp/jxr003.

Gill, Rosalind, and Shani Orgad. 2018. "The Amazing Bounce-Backable Woman: Resilience and the Psychological Turn in Neoliberalism." *Sociological Research Online* 23(2):477–95. doi: 10.1177/1360780418769673.

Giordano, Cristiana. 2014. *Migrants in Translation: Caring and the Logics of Difference in Contemporary Italy.* Oakland: University of California Press.

Giordano, Peggy C., Jennifer E. Copp, Monica A. Longmore, and Wendy D. Manning. 2016. "Anger, Control, and Intimate Partner Violence in Young Adulthood." *Journal of Family Violence* 31(1):1–13.

Glenn, Catherine, and Lisa Goodman. 2015. "Living with and within the Rules of Domestic Violence Shelters: A Qualitative Exploration of Residents' Experiences." *Violence against Women* 21(12):1481–506. doi: 10.1177 /1077801215596242.

Glenn, Evelyn Nakano. 1999. "The Social Construction and Institutionalization of Gender and Race." In *Revisioning Gender,* edited by M. M. Ferree, J. Lorber, and B. B. Hess, 3–43. Walnut Creek, CA: AltaMira Press.

———. 2011. "Constructing Citizenship: Exclusion, Subordination, and Resistance." *American Sociological Review* 76(1):1–24.

Gondolf, Edward. 1994. "Letter to Susan Schechter." Box 35 Folder 5, Understanding the Relationship between Domestic Violence Services and Mental

Health Providers, National Resource Center on Domestic Violence, 1994–1996. Papers of Susan Schechter, 1961–2005, Harvard University Schlesinger Library.

Goodman, Ellen. 1985. "*For Better Times*, Vol. 4 No. 3 Fall 1985." Box 1 Folder 3. "*For Better Times*" 1985–1988. Voices of a Movement: Illinois Coalition Against Domestic Violence, DePaul University.

Goodman, Lisa A., Katya Fels Smyth, Angela M. Borges, and Rachel Singer. 2009. "When Crises Collide: How Intimate Partner Violence and Poverty Intersect to Shape Women's Mental Health and Coping?" *Trauma, Violence, & Abuse* 10(4):306–29. doi: 10.1177/1524838009339754.

Goodmark, Leigh. 2013. *A Troubled Marriage: Domestic Violence and the Legal System.* New York University Press.

———. 2018. *Decriminalizing Domestic Violence: A Balanced Policy Approach to Intimate Partner Violence.* Oakland: University of California Press.

Gordon, Avery. 1997. *Ghostly Matters: Haunting and the Sociological Imagination.* Minneapolis: University of Minnesota Press.

Gowan, Teresa. 2010. *Hobos, Hustlers, and Backsliders: Homeless in San Francisco.* Minneapolis: University of Minnesota Press.

Greenberg, Max A. 2019. *Twelve Weeks to Change a Life: At-Risk Youth in a Fractured State.* Oakland: University of California Press.

Grosz, Elizabeth A. 1994. *Volatile Bodies: Toward a Corporeal Feminism.* Bloomington: Indiana University Press.

Gurusami, Susila. 2017. "Working for Redemption: Formerly Incarcerated Black Women and Punishment in the Labor Market." *Gender & Society* 31(4):433–56.

———. 2019. "Motherwork under the State: The Maternal Labor of Formerly Incarcerated Black Women." *Social Problems* 66(1):128–43. doi: 10.1093/socpro/spx045.

Haaken, Janice. 1996. "The Recovery of Memory, Fantasy, and Desire: Feminist Approaches to Sexual Abuse and Psychic Trauma." *Signs: Journal of Women in Culture and Society* 21(4):1069–94.

———. 2010. *Hard Knocks: Domestic Violence and the Psychology of Storytelling.* New York: Routledge.

Haley, Sarah. 2016. *No Mercy Here: Gender, Punishment, and the Making of Jim Crow Modernity.* Chapel Hill: University of North Carolina Press Books.

Hall, Stuart. 1996. "Race, Articulation, and Societies Structured in Dominance." In *Black British Cultural Studies: A Reader*, edited by Houston A. Baker, Manthia Diawara, and Ruth H. Lindeborg, 16–60. Chicago: University of Chicago Press.

Hall, Stuart, and Lawrence Grossberg. 1986. "On Postmodernism and Articulation: An Interview with Stuart Hall." *Journal of Communication Inquiry* 10(2):45–60.

Halley, Janet, Prabha Kotiswaran, Rachel Rebouché, and Hila Shamir. 2018. *Governance Feminism: An Introduction*. Minneapolis: University of Minnesota Press.

Halushka, John M. 2020. "The Runaround: Punishment, Welfare, and Poverty Survival after Prison." *Social Problems* 67(2):233-50.

Hammonds, Evelynn. 2004. "Black (w)Holes and the Geometry of Black Female Sexuality." In *The Black Studies Reader*, edited by J. Bobo, C. Hudley, and C. Michel, 313-26. New York: Routledge.

Haney, Lynne. 1996. "Homeboys, Babies, Men in Suits: The State and the Reproduction of Male Dominance." *American Sociological Review* 61(5):759-78.

———. 2004. "Introduction: Gender, Welfare, and States of Punishment." *Social Politics* 11(3):333-62.

———. 2010. *Offending Women: Power, Punishment, and the Regulation of Desire*. Berkeley: University of California Press.

———. 2018. "Incarcerated Fatherhood: The Entanglements of Child Support Debt and Mass Imprisonment." *American Journal of Sociology* 124(1):1-48.

Haney, Lynne, and Miranda March. 2003. "Married Fathers and Caring Daddies: Welfare Reform and the Discursive Politics of Paternity." *Social Problems* 50(4):461-81. doi: 10.1525/sp.2003.50.4.461.

Haraway, Donna. 1988. "Situated Knowledges: The Science Question in Feminism and the Privilege of Partial Perspective." *Feminist Studies* 14(3):575-99. doi: 10.2307/3178066.

Hardesty, Jennifer L. 2002. "Separation Assault in the Context of Post-Divorce Parenting: An Integrative Review of the Literature." *Violence against Women* 8(5):597-625.

Hardesty, Jennifer L., Kimberly A. Crossman, Megan L. Haselschwerdt, Marcela Raffaelli, Brian G. Ogolsky, and Michael P. Johnson. 2015. "Toward a Standard Approach to Operationalizing Coercive Control and Classifying Violence Types." *Journal of Marriage & Family* 77(4):833-43.

Harris, Maxine, and Roger D. Fallot. 2001. *Using Trauma Theory to Design Service Systems: New Directions for Mental Health Services, Number 89*. San Francisco: Jossey-Bass/Wiley.

Harsey, Sarah, and Jennifer J. Freyd. 2020. "Deny, Attack, and Reverse Victim and Offender (DARVO): What Is the Influence on Perceived Perpetrator and Victim Credibility?" *Journal of Aggression, Maltreatment & Trauma* 29(8):897-916. doi: 10.1080/10926771.2020.1774695.

Harsey, Sarah J., Eileen L. Zurbriggen, and Jennifer J. Freyd. 2017. "Perpetrator Responses to Victim Confrontation: DARVO and Victim Self-Blame." *Journal of Aggression, Maltreatment & Trauma* 26(6):644-63. doi: 10.1080/10926771.2017.1320777.

Hartman, Saidiya. 1997. *Scenes of Subjection: Terror, Slavery, and Self-Making in Nineteenth-Century America*. New York: Oxford University Press.

Hasenfeld, Yeheskel, and Eve E. Garrow. 2012. "Nonprofit Human Service Organizations, Social Rights, and Advocacy in a Neoliberal Welfare State." *Social Service Review* 86(2):295–322.

Hays, Sharon. 1996. *The Cultural Contradictions of Motherhood*. New Haven, CT: Yale University Press.

Hegel, Georg Wilhelm Friedrich. 1977. *Phenomenology of Spirit*. Oxford University Press.

Hengehold, Laura. 2000. "Remapping the Event: Institutional Discourses and the Trauma of Rape." *Signs: Journal of Women in Culture & Society* 26(1):189–214.

Herman, Ellen. 1995. *The Romance of American Psychology: Political Culture in the Age of Experts*. Berkeley: University of California Press.

Herman, Judith. 1992. *Trauma and Recovery: The Aftermath of Abuse—from Domestic Abuse to Political Terror*. New York: Basic Books.

Hester, Marianne, Cassandra Jones, Emma Williamson, Eldin Fahmy, and Gene Feder. 2017. "Is It Coercive Controlling Violence? A Cross-Sectional Domestic Violence and Abuse Survey of Men Attending General Practice in England." *Psychology of Violence* 7(3):417–27.

Hirsch, Jennifer S., and Shamus Khan. 2020. *Sexual Citizens: A Landmark Study of Sex, Power, and Assault on Campus*. New York: W. W. Norton & Company.

Horwitz, Allan. 2002. *Creating Mental Illness*. Chicago: University of Chicago Press.

———. 2018. *PTSD: A Short History*. Baltimore: Johns Hopkins University Press.

Humphreys, Cathy, and Stephen Joseph. 2004. "Domestic Violence and the Politics of Trauma." *Women's Studies International Forum* 27(5–6):559–70.

ICADV. 1978. "Board Meeting Minutes." Box 3 Folder 1, Board Meeting Minutes 1978. Voices of a Movement: Illinois Coalition Against Domestic Violence, DePaul University.

———. 1982. *"For Better Times* Vol. 1, No. 2 Winter 1981–1982." Box 1 Folder 2. *"For Better Times"* Photocopies 1981–1984. Voices of a Movement: Illinois Coalition Against Domestic Violence, DePaul University.

———. 1986. "ICADV Minutes, Finance Committee." Box 8 Folder 9, ICADV Minutes, Committee, Finance. Voices of a Movement: Illinois Coalition Against Domestic Violence, DePaul University.

———. 1995. "For Better Times Newsletter, "Success Stories", Illinois Coalition Against Domestic Violence." Box 1 Folder 5. "For Better Times" 1995-2003. Voices of a Movement: Illinois Coalition Against Domestic Violence, DePaul University.

———. 1998. "Executive Director Statement, 'For Better Times.'" Box 2 Folder 1. Annual Reports—Five Year Repot (1978–1983); Ten Year Report and Anniversary 1978–1988. Voices of a Movement: Illinois Coalition Against Domestic Violence, DePaul University.

———. 2000. *"For Better Times*, Spring 2000." Box 1 Folder 6 *"For Better Times"* 1995–2003. Voices of a Movement: Illinois Coalition Against Domestic Violence, DePaul University

Illouz, Eva. 2008. *Saving the Modern Soul: Therapy, Emotions, and the Culture of Self-Help*. Berkeley: University of California Press.

INCITE! Women of Color Against Violence. 2006. *Color of Violence: The INCITE! Anthology*. Cambridge, MA: South End Press.

Ingraham, Chrys. 1994. "The Heterosexual Imaginary: Feminist Sociology and Theories of Gender." *Sociological Theory* 12(2):203–19.

Irigaray, Luce. 1977. *This Sex Which Is Not One*. Ithaca, NY: Cornell University Press.

Isin, Engin. 2009. "Citizenship in Flux: The Figure of the Activist Citizen." *Subjectivity* 29:367–88.

ISTS (International Society for Trauma Studies). 2001. "Reaching Underserved Trauma Survivors through Community-Based Programs." Box 17 Folder 16, December 6–9, 2001. Papers of Susan Schechter, 1961–2005, Harvard University Schlesinger Library.

Jacquet, Catherine O. 2016. "Fighting Back, Claiming Power: Feminist Rhetoric and Resistance to Rape in the 1970s." *Radical History Review* (126):71–83. doi: 10.1215/01636545-3594421.

James, Erica Caple. 2010. *Democratic Insecurities: Violence, Trauma, and Intervention in Haiti*. Berkeley: University of California Press.

Johnson, Lacy. 2014. *The Other Side: A Memoir*. Portland, OR: Tin House Books.

Johnson, Michael P. 2008. *A Typology of Domestic Violence: Intimate Terrorism, Violent Resistance, and Situational Couple Violence*. Boston, MA: Northeastern University Press.

Johnson, Michael P., Janel M. Leone, and Yili Xu. 2014. "Intimate Terrorism and Situational Couple Violence in General Surveys: Ex-Spouses Required." *Violence Against Women* 20(2):186–207.

Jutel, Annemarie. 2010. "Framing Disease: The Example of Female Hypoactive Sexual Desire Disorder." *Social Science & Medicine* 70(7):1084–90.

———. 2014. *Putting a Name to It: Diagnosis in Contemporary Society*. Baltimore: Johns Hopkins University Press.

Kaye, Kerwin. 2019. *Enforcing Freedom: Drug Courts, Therapeutic Communities, and the Intimacies of the State*. New York: Columbia University Press.

Kelly, Liz, and Nicole Westmarland. 2016. "Naming and Defining 'Domestic Violence': Lessons from Research with Violent Men." *Feminist Review* 112(1):113–27.

Kim, Mimi E. 2020. "The Carceral Creep: Gender-Based Violence, Race, and the Expansion of the Punitive State, 1973–1983." *Social Problems* 67(2):251–69. doi: 10.1093/socpro/spz013.

Kimmel, Michael. 2002. "'Gender Symmetry' in Domestic Violence: A Substantive and Methodological Research Review." *Violence against Women* 8(11):1332–63.

Klawiter, Maren. 2008. *The Biopolitics of Breast Cancer: Changing Cultures of Disease and Activism.* Minneapolis: University of Minnesota Press.

Korteweg, Anna. 2003. "Welfare Reform and the Subject of the Working Mother: 'Get a Job, a Better Job, Then a Career." *Theory & Society* 32:445–80.

Labriola, Melissa, Sarah Bradley, Chris S. O'Sullivan, Michael Rempel, and Samantha Moore. 2012. *National Portrait of Domestic Violence Courts.* New York: National Institute of Justice Center for Court Innovation). https://www .ncjrs.gov/pdffiles1/nij/grants/229659.pdf.

Laclau, Ernesto, and Chantal Mouffe. 1985. *Hegemony and Socialist Strategy: Towards a Radical Democratic Politics.* London: Verso.

Lake, Robert W., and Kathe Newman. 2002. "Differential Citizenship in the Shadow State." *GeoJournal* 2–3:109–20.

Laperriére, Marie, Ann Shola Orloff, and Jane Pryma. 2019. "Commodification, Vulnerability, Risk: Gendered Social Policy Developments in the United States, 1980–2018." *Journal of International and Comparative Social Policy* 35(1):41–58.

Lara-Millán, Armando. 2017. "States as a Series of People Exchanges." In *The Many Hands of the State: Theorizing Political Authority and Social Control,* edited by K. J. Morgan and A. S. Orloff, 81–102. Cambridge: Cambridge University Press.

Larance, Lisa Young, Spencer Garrison, and J. Lotus Seeley. 2018. "Strategically Stealthy: Women's Agency in Navigating Spousal Violence." *Affilia* 33(2):177–92. doi: 10.1177/0886109917738067.

Lather, Patti. 2012. *Getting Lost: Feminist Efforts toward a Double(d) Science.* Albany: State University of New York Press.

Laugerud, Solveig. 2019. "Narrating the Harm of Rape: How Rape Victims Invoke Different Models of Psychological Trauma." *BioSocieties.* doi: 10.1057 /s41292-019-00178-0.

Lauster, Nathanael, and Adam Easterbrook. 2011. "No Room for New Families? A Field Experiment Measuring Rental Discrimination against Same-Sex Couples and Single Parents." *Social Problems* 58(3):389–409.

Leonard, Samantha. 2019. "What Is the Work? And with Whom Are We Working? Relational Practices in the Intimate Partner Violence Field." *Affilia* 34(4):535–51. doi: 10.1177/0886109919868837.

Leve, Ariel. 2017. "Trump Is Gaslighting America—Here's How to Survive." *Business Insider,* March 18.

Leys, Ruth. 2002. *Trauma: A Genealogy.* Chicago: University of Chicago Press.

Lister, Ruth. 2007. "Inclusive Citizenship: Realizing the Potential." *Citizenship Studies* 11(1):49–61.

Littlejohn, Krystale E. 2013. "It's Those Pills That Are Ruining Me: Gender and the Social Meanings of Hormonal Contraceptive Side Effects." *Gender & Society* 27(6):843–63.

Lofland, John, David Snow, Leon Anderson, and Lyn Lofland. 2006. *Analyzing Social Settings*. 4th ed. Belmont, CA: Wadsworth.

Lorber, Judith, and Lisa Jean Moore. 2002. *Gender and the Social Construction of Illness*. Walnut Creek, CA: AltaMira Press.

Loseke, Donileen. 1992. *The Battered Woman and Shelters: The Social Construction of Wife Abuse*. Albany: State University of New York Press.

Lupton, Deborah. 2002. "Foucault and the Medicalization Critique." In *Foucault, Health, and Medicine*, edited by Alan Peterson and Robin Bunton, 94–112. New York: Routledge.

MacDonald, Sue. 1978. "Her Experience Means Help for Abused Wives." *Cincinnati Inquirer*, May 5.

Mackintosh, Sophie. May 22, 2019. "Feminine Weakness Is a Scam." *New York Times*. https://www.nytimes.com/2019/05/22/opinion/power-misogyny.html.

Manne, Kate. 2017. *Down Girl: The Logic of Misogyny*. Oxford: Oxford University Press.

Marshall, T. H. 1950. "Citizenship and Social Class." In *Class, Citizenship, and Social Development*, edited by S. M. Lipset, 65–123. Garden City, NY: Doubleday.

Martel, James R. 2017. *The Misinterpellated Subject*. Durham, NC: Duke University Press.

Martin, Patricia Yancey. 2005. *Rape Work: Victims, Gender and Emotions in Organization and Community Context*. New York: Psychology Press.

Marwell, Nicole P. 2004. "Privatizing the Welfare State: Nonprofit Community-Based Organizations as Political Actors." *American Sociological Review* 69(2):265–91.

Mayrl, Damon, and Sarah Quinn. 2017. "Beyond the Hidden American State: Classification Struggles and the Politics of Recognition." In *The Many Hands of the State: Theorizing Political Authority and Social Control*, edited by K. J. Morgan and A. S. Orloff, 58–80. Cambridge: Cambridge University Press.

MCBWSG (Massachusetts Coalition of Battered Women's Service Groups). 1981. "For Shelter and Beyond: An Educational Manual for Working with Women Who Are Battered." Box 2 Folder 7. Domestic Violence, National (Continued) and Regional (East), Massachusetts. Sophia Smith Collection, Violence Against Women, Smith College.

McCauley, Heather L., Rebecca N. Dick, Daniel J. Tancredi, Sandi Goldstein, Samantha Blackburn, Jay G. Silverman, Erica Monasterio, Lisa James, and Elizabeth Miller. 2014. "Differences by Sexual Minority Status in Relationship Abuse and Sexual and Reproductive Health among Adolescent Females." *Journal of Adolescent Health* 55(5):652–58.

McKim, Allison. 2008. "'Getting Gut-Level': Punishment, Gender, and Therapeutic Governance." *Gender & Society* 22(3):303–23.

———. 2014. "Roxanne's Dress: Governing Gender and Marginality through Addiction Treatment." *Signs: Journal of Women in Culture & Society* 39(2):433–58.

———. 2017. *Addicted to Rehab: Race, Gender, and Drugs in the Era of Mass Incarceration*. New Brunswick, NJ: Rutgers University Press.

McNay, Lois. 1992. *Foucault and Feminism: Power, Gender and the Self*. Malden, MA: Blackwell.

McNeill, Fergus. 2019. "Mass Supervision, Misrecognition and the 'Malopticon.'" *Punishment & Society* 21(2):207–30. doi: 10.1177/1462474518755137.

Meadow, Tey. 2018. *Trans Kids: Being Gendered in the Twenty-First Century*. Oakland: University of California Press.

Medvetz, Thomas. 2008. "Think Tanks as an Emergent Field." *Social Science Research Council*. http://ssrc-cdn1.s3.amazonaws.com/crmuploads/new _publication_3/%7BA2A2BA10-B135-DE11-AFAC-001CC477EC70%7D.pdf.

———. 2012. *Think Tanks in America*. Chicago: University of Chicago Press.

Menjívar, Cecilia. 2011. *Enduring Violence: Ladina Women's Lives in Guatemala*. Berekely: University of California Press.

Menjívar, Cecilia, and Leisy Abrego. 2012. "Legal Violence: Immigration Law and the Lives of Central American Immigrants. *American Journal of Sociology* 117(5):1380–421.

Menjívar, Cecilia, and Olivia Salcido. 2002. "Immigrant Women and Domestic Violence: Common Experiences in Different Countries." *Gender & Society* 16(6):898–920. doi: 10.1177/089124302237894.

Merry, Sally Engle. 2001. "Spatial Governmentality and the New Urban Social Order: Controlling Gender Violence through Law." *American Anthropologist* 103(1):16–29. doi: 10.1525/aa.2001.103.1.16.

———. 2009. *Human Rights and Gender Violence: Translating International Law into Local Justice*. Chicago: University of Chicago Press.

———. 2016. *The Seductions of Quantification: Measuring Human Rights, Gender Violence, and Sex Trafficking*. Chicago: University of Chicago Press.

Messner, Michael, Max A. Greenberg, and Tal Peretz. 2015. *Some Men: Feminist Allies and the Movement to End Violence against Women*. Oxford: Oxford University Press.

Mettler, Suzanne. 2011. *The Submerged State: How Invisible Government Policies Undermine American Democracy*. Chicago: University of Chicago Press.

Metzger, Mary. 1977. "What Did You Do to Provoke Him?" Box 1, Bonnie Tinker's Personal Files. National Coalition Against Domestic Violence.

Metzl, Jonathan. 2003. *Prozac on the Couch: Prescribing Gender in the Era of Wonder Drugs*. Durham, NC: Duke University Press.

——. 2010. *The Protest Psychosis: How Schizophrenia Became a Black Disease.* Boston: Beacon Press.

Metzl, Jonathan M., and Joni Angel. 2004. "Assessing the Impact of SSRI Antidepressants on Popular Notions of Women's Depressive Illness." *Social Science & Medicine* 58(3):577–84.

Mikhailova, Anna. 2018. "Theresa May Pledges to Tighten the Law on 'Gaslighting' Abuse." *Telegraph*, May 23.

Miller, Chanel. 2020. *Know My Name: A Memoir.* Penguin.

Miller, Elizabeth, Michele R. Decker, Heather L. McCauley, Daniel J. Tancredi, Rebecca R. Levenson, Jeffrey Waldman, Phyllis Schoenwald, and Jay G. Silverman. 2010. "Pregnancy Coercion, Intimate Partner Violence and Unintended Pregnancy." *Contraception* 81(4):316–22.

Miller, Jody. 2008. *Getting Played: African American Girls, Urban Inequality, and Gendered Violence.* New York: New York University Press.

Miller, Reuben Jonathan. 2014. "Devolving the Carceral State: Race, Prisoner Reentry, and the Micro-Politics of Urban Poverty Management." *Punishment & Society* 16(3):305–35. doi: 10.1177/1462474514527487.

Miller, Reuben Jonathan, and Forrest Stuart. 2017. "Carceral Citizenship: Race, Rights and Responsibility in the Age of Mass Supervision." *Theoretical Criminology* 21(4):532–48. doi: 10.1177/1362480617731203.

Mirchandani, Rekha. 2005. "What's So Special about Specialized Courts? The States and Social Change in Salt Lake City's Domestic Violence Court." *Law & Society Review* 39(2):379–417.

Mol, Annemarie. 2002. *The Body Multiple: Ontology in Medical Practice.* Durham, NC: Duke University Press.

Moore, Mignon. 2011. *Invisible Families: Gay Identities, Relationships, and Motherhood among Black Women.* Berkeley: University of California Press.

Morgan, Kimberly J., and Andrea Louise Campbell. 2011. *The Delegated Welfare State: Medicare, Markets, and the Governance of Social Policy.* Oxford: Oxford University Press.

Morgan, Kimberly J., and Ann Shola Orloff. 2017. "Introduction." In *The Many Hands of the State: Theorizing Political Authority & Social Control*, edited by K. J. Morgan and A. S. Orloff, 1–32. Cambridge: Cambridge University Press.

Morgen, Sandra. 2002. *Into Our Own Hands: The Women's Health Movement in the United States, 1969–1990.* New Brunswick, NJ: Rutgers University Press.

Ms. Foundation. 1981. "Ms. Foundation Domestic Violence Program Funding Meeting." Box 10 Folder 3. Papers of Susan Schechter, 1961–2005, Harvard University Schlesinger Library.

Mulla, Sameena. 2014. *The Violence of Care: Rape Victims, Forensic Nurses, and Sexual Assault Intervention.* New York: New York University Press.

Muñoz, Jose Esteban. 1999. *Disidentifications: Queers of Color and the Performance of Politics*. Minneapolis: University of Minnesota Press.

Murphy, Christopher M., and Sharon A. Hoover. 1999. "Measuring Emotional Abuse in Dating Relationships as a Multifactorial Construct." *Violence and Victims* 14(1):39–53.

Murphy, Michelle. 2006. *Sick-Building Syndrome and the Problem of Uncertainty*. Durham, NC: Duke University Press.

———. 2012. *Seizing the Means of Reproduction: Entanglements of Feminism, Health, and Technoscience*. Durham, NC: Duke University Press.

Myhill, Andy. 2015. "Measuring Coercive Control: What Can We Learn from National Population Surveys?" *Violence Against Women* 21(3):355–75.

———. 2017. "Measuring Domestic Violence: Context Is Everything." *Journal of Gender-Based Violence* 1(1):33–44.

Naples, Nancy. 2003. "Deconstructing and Locating Survivor Discourse: Dynamics of Narrative, Empowerment, and Resistance for Survivors of Childhood Sexual Abuse." *Signs: Journal of Women in Culture & Society* 28(4):1151–85.

National Advisory Council on Violence Against Women. 2000. "Ending Violence Against Women Campaign: U.S. Department of Justice and U.S. Department of Health & Human Services." Box 46 Folder 3, Papers of Susan Schechter, 1961–2005, Harvard University Schlesinger Library.

NCADV. 1978a. "Application for Federal ACTION Grant to Support NCADV." Box 1, Bonnie Tinker's Personal Files. National Coalition Against Domestic Violence.

———. 1978b. "Oregon letter." Box 1, Bonnie Tinker's Personal Files. National Coalition Against Domestic Violence.

———. 1986. "Steering Committee Meeting 1986." Steering Committee Box. National Coalition Against Domestic Violence.

———. n.d. "Response from the Department of Justice for Approval of a Brochure Produced by NCADV." Assorted papers. National Coalition Against Domestic Violence.

Nelson, Alondra. 2011. *Body and Soul: The Black Panther Party and the Fight Against Medical Discrimination*. Minneapolis: University of Minnesota Press.

Nguyen, Vinh-Kim. 2010. *The Republic of Therapy: Triage and Sovereignty in West Africa's Time of AIDS*. Durham, NC: Duke University Press.

NNEDV (National Network to End Domestic Violence). 2020. "14th Annual Domestic Violence Counts Report." https://nnedv.org/wp-content/uploads/2020/03/Library_Census-2019_Report_web.pdf.

Nolan, James L. 1998. *The Therapeutic State: Justifying Government at Century's End*. New York: New York University Press.

Norwood, Robin. 1997 [1985]. *Women Who Love Too Much*. Los Angeles: Tarcher.

O'Leary, K. Daniel. 1999. "Psychological Abuse: A Variable Deserving Critical Attention in Domestic Violence." *Violence and Victims* 14(1):3–23.

Ong, Aihwa. 1995. "Making the Biopolitical Subject: Cambodian Immigrants, Refugee Medicine and Cultural Citizenship in California." *Social Science & Medicine* 40(9):1243–57.

———. 2006a. "Mutations in Citizenship." *Theory, Culture, & Society* 23(2–3):499–505.

———. 2006b. *Neoliberalism as Exception: Mutations in Citizenship and Sovereignty.* Durham, NC: Duke University Press.

Orgad, Shani. 2009. "The Survivor in Contemporary Culture and Public Discourse: A Genealogy." *The Communication Review* 12(2):132–61. doi: 10.1080 /10714420902921168.

Orloff, Ann Shola. 1993. "Gender and the Social Rights of Citizenship: The Comparative Analysis of Gender Relations and Welfare States." *American Sociological Review* 58(3):303–28.

———. 1996. "Gender in the Welfare State." *Annual Review of Sociology* 22:51–78.

———. 2009. "Gendering the Comparative Analysis of Welfare States: An Unfinished Agenda." *Sociological Theory* 27(3):317–43.

Orloff, Ann Shola, and Talia Shiff. 2016. "Feminism/s in Power: Rethinking Gender Equality after the Second Wave." *Perverse Politics? Feminism, Anti-Imperialism, Multiplicity: Political Power & Social Theory* 30:109–34.

Outshoorn, Joyce, and Johanna Kantola, eds. 2007. *Changing State Feminism.* London: Palgrave Macmillan.

Parr, Hester. 2000. "Interpreting the 'Hidden Social Geographies' of Mental Health: Ethnographies of Inclusion and Exclusion in Semi-Institutional Places." *Health & Place* 6:225–37.

Pascoe, C. J. 2007. *Dude, You're a Fag: Masculinity and Sexuality in High School.* Berkeley: University of California Press.

PCADV. 1985. "Empowerment Counseling." Box 30 Folder 4, Empowerment counseling training curriculum, Pennsylvania Coalition Against Domestic Violence, ca. 1985. Papers of Susan Schechter, 1961–2005, Harvard University Schlesinger Library.

Peck, Jamie. 2010. "Zombie Neoliberalism and the Ambidextrous State." *Theoretical Criminology* 14(1):104–10.

Peled, Einat, Zvi Eisikovits, Guy Enosh, and Zeev Winstock. 2000. "Choice and Empowerment for Battered Women Who Stay: Toward a Constructivist Model." *Social Work* 45(1):9–25.

Pence, Ellen. 1985. "Interview with Lisa Leghorn." Box 6 Folder 5, Correspondence 1985. Papers of Susan Schechter, 1961–2005, Harvard University Schlesinger Library.

Petrosky, Emiko, Janet M. Blair, Carter J. Betz, Katherine A. Fowler, Shane P. D. Jack, and Bridget H. Lyons. 2017. "Racial and Ethnic Differences in Homicides of Adult Women and the Role of Intimate Partner Violence—United States, 2003–2014." *Morbidity and Mortality Weekly Report* 66:741–46. DOI: http://dx.doi.org/10.15585/mmwr.mm6628a1External

Petryna, Adriana. 2003. *Life Exposed: Biological Citizens after Chernobyl.* Princeton, NJ: Princeton University Press.

Pfeffer, Carla. 2014. "'I Don't Like Passing as a Straight Woman': Queer Negotiations of Identity and Social Group Membership." *American Journal of Sociology* 120(1):1–44.

Piehowski, Victoria. 2020. "Under the Punitive Aegis: Dependency and the Family Justice Center Model." *Punishment & Society*, November. doi: 10.1177 /1462474520972264.

Piipsa, Minna. 2002. "Complexity of Patterns of Violence against Women in Heterosexual Partnerships." *Violence Against Women* 18(7):873–900.

Pillow, Wanda. 2003. "Confession, Catharsis, or Cure? Rethinking the Uses of Reflexivity as Methodological Power in Qualitative Research." *International Journal of Qualitative Studies in Education* 16(2):175–96. doi: 10.1080 /0951839032000060635.

Pishko, Jessica. 2017. "She Didn't Want Her Boyfriend to Go to Jail. So They Sent Her to Jail Instead." *Cosmopolitan*, April 13.

Pitman, Roger K., Ann M. Rasmusson, Karestan C. Koenen, Lisa M. Shin, Scott P. Orr, Mark W. Gilbertson, Mohammed R. Milad, and Israel Liberzon. 2012. "Biological Studies of Post-Traumatic Stress Disorder." *Nature Reviews Neuroscience* 13(11):769–87.

Plummer, Ken. 2011. *Intimate Citizenship: Private Decisions and Public Dialogues.* Seattle: University of Washington Press.

Polsky, Andrew. 1991. *The Rise of the Therapeutic State.* Princeton, NJ: Princeton University Press.

President's Task Force on Victims of Crime. 1982. *Report: President's Task Force on Victims of Crime.* https://www.ovc.gov/publications/presdntstskforcrprt /87299.pdf

Puar, Jasbir K. 2007. *Terrorist Assemblages: Homonationalism in Queer Times.* Durham, NC: Duke University Press.

Purvin, Diane M. 2007. "At the Crossroads and in the Crosshairs: Social Welfare Policy and Low-Income Women's Vulnerability to Domestic Violence." *Social Problems* 54(2):188–210.

Randles, Jennifer M. 2013. "Repackaging the "Package Deal:" Promoting Marriage for Low-Income Families by Targeting Paternal Identity and Reframing Marital Masculinity." *Gender & Society* 27(6):864–88.

———. 2018. "'Manning Up' to Be a Good Father: Hybrid Fatherhood, Masculinity, and US Responsible Fatherhood Policy." *Gender & Society* 32(4):516–39.

Ray, Raka. 2000. *Fields of Protest: Women's Movements in India.* Minneapolis: University of Minnesota Press.

Reed, Elizabeth, Anita Raj, Elizabeth Miller, and Jay G. Silverman. 2010. "Losing the 'Gender' in Gender-Based Violence: The Missteps of Research on Dating and Intimate Partner Violence." *Violence against Women* 16(3):348–54.

Reich, Jennifer A. 2005. *Fixing Families: Parents, Power, and the Child Welfare System*. New York: Routledge.

Renzetti, Claire M. 1988. "Violence in Lesbian Relationships: A Preliminary Analysis of Causal Factors." *Journal of Interpersonal violence* 3(4): 381–99.

Rich, Adrienne. 1980. "Compulsory Heterosexuality and Lesbian Existence." *Signs: Journal of Women in Culture & Society* 5(4):631–60.

Richardson, Diane. 1998. "Sexuality and Citizenship." *Sociology* 32(1):83–100.

———. 2007. "Patterned Fluidities: (Re)Imagining the Relationship between Gender and Sexuality." *Sociology* 41(3):457–74.

———. 2017. "Rethinking Sexual Citizenship." *Sociology* 51(2):208–24.

Richardson, Eileen H., and Bryan S. Turner. 2001. "Sexual, Intimate or Reproductive Citizenship?" *Citizenship Studies* 5(3):329–38.

Richie, Beth E. 1996. *Compelled to Crime: The Gender Entrapment of Battered Black Women*. New York: Routledge.

———. 2000. "A Black Feminist Reflection on the Antiviolence Movement." *Signs: Journal of Women in Culture & Society* 25(4):1133–37.

———. 2012. *Arrested Justice: Black Women, Violence, and America's Prison Nation*. New York: New York University Press.

Richie, Beth E., and Erin Eife. 2020. "Black Bodies at the Dangerous Intersection of Gender Violence and Mass Criminalization." *Journal of Aggression, Maltreatment & Trauma* (March):1–12. doi: 10.1080/10926771.2019 .1703063.

Riger, Stephanie, and Susan Staggs. 2004. "Welfare Reform, Domestic Violence, and. Employment: What Do We Know and What Do We Need to Know?" *Violence against Women* 10(9):961–90.

Ristock, Janice. 2002. *No More Secrets: Violence in Lesbian Relationships*. New York: Psychology Press.

Roberts, Dorothy E. 2002. *Shattered Bonds: The Color of Child Welfare*. New York: Basic Books.

Roche, Maurice. 1992. *Rethinking Citizenship: Welfare, Ideology and Change in Modern Society*. Cambridge, MA: Polity Press.

Rodenburg, Roos, Anja Benjamin, Carlijn de Roos, Ann Marie Meijer, and Geert Jan Stams. 2009. "Efficacy of EMDR in Children: A Meta-Analysis." *Clinical Psychology Review* 29(7):599–606.

Rodríguez-Muñiz, Michael. 2017. "Cultivating Consent: Nonstate Leaders and the Orchestration of State Legibility." *American Journal of Sociology* 123(2):385–425. doi: 10.1086/693045.

Rose, Nikolas. 1990. *Governing the Soul: The Shaping of the Private Self*. London: Routledge.

———. 1999. *Powers of Freedom: Reframing Political Thought*. Cambridge: Cambridge University Press.

———. 2007. *The Politics of Life Itself: Biomedicine, Power, and Subjectivity in the 21st Century*. Princeton, NJ: Princeton University Press.

Rose, Nikolas, and Peter Miller. 1992. "Political Power beyond the State: Problematics of Government." *British Journal of Sociology* 43(2):173–205.

Rose, Nikolas, and Carlos Novas. 2005. "Biological Citizenship." In *Global Assemblages: Technology, Politics, and Ethics as Anthropological Problems*, edited by A. Ong and S. J. Collier. Oxford: Blackwell Publishing.

Rothenberg, Bess. 2002. "The Success of the Battered Woman Syndrome: An Analysis of How Cultural Arguments Succeed." *Sociological Forum* 17:81–103.

———. 2003. "'We Don't Have Time for Social Change:' Cultural Compromise and the Battered Woman Syndrome." *Gender & Society* 17(5):771–87.

Rothschild, Babette. 2000. *The Body Remembers: The Psychophysiology of Trauma and Trauma Treatment*. W.W. Norton.

Roychowdhury, Poulami. 2015. "Victims to Saviors: Governmentality and the Regendering of Citizenship in India." *Gender & Society* 29(6):792–816.

———. 2020. *Capable Women, Incapable States: Negotiating Violence and Rights in India*. Oxford: Oxford University Press.

Rubin, Gayle. 1975. "The Traffic in Women: Notes on the 'Political Economy' of Sex." In *Toward an Anthropology of Women*, edited by R. R. Reiter, 157–210. New York: Monthly Review Press.

Ryan-Flood, Róisín. 2009. *Lesbian Motherhood: Gender, Families and Sexual Citizenship*. New York: Springer.

Sarkis, Stephanie. 2018. *Gaslighting: Recognize Manipulative and Emotionally Abusive People—and Break Free*. New York: Da Capo Lifelong Books.

Saunders, Daniel. 1990. "Post-Traumatic Stress Disorder: A Label That Does Not Blame?" Wisconsin Coalition Against Domestic Violence, 1990. Box 71. Folder 1. Battered Women, Psychiatric/Behavioral Aspects, 1990–1991. Papers of Susan Schechter, 1961–2005, Harvard University Schlesinger Library.

Sawer, Marian. 2007. "Australia: The Fall of the Femocrat." In *Changing State Feminism*, edited by J. Outshoorn and J. Kantola, 20–40. London: Palgrave Macmillan.

Scarry, Elaine. 1985. *The Body in Pain: The Making and Unmaking of the World*. New York: Oxford University Press.

Schechter, Susan. 1982. *Women and Male Violence: The Visions and Struggles of the Battered Women's Movement*. Boston, MA: South End Press.

———. 1983. "Chicago/Springfield Talk." Box 11 Folder 5. Battered Women's Movement, Chicago/Springfield Talk—May 1983. Papers of Susan Schechter, 1961–2005, Harvard University Schlesinger Library.

———. 1989. "Letter." Box 26 Folder 7, Couples counseling article, research notes, and correspondence, 1989. Papers of Susan Schechter, 1961–2005, Harvard University Schlesinger Library.

———. c. 1990s. "Psychiatric Presentation of Abused Women." Box 21 Folder 6. Mental health training speeches, n.d. Papers of Susan Schechter, 1961–2005, Harvard University Schlesinger Library.

———. 1991. "Stages of Abuse." Box 50 Folder 6. Mental health training curriculum, 1991. Papers of Susan Schechter, 1961–2005, Harvard University Schlesinger Library.

Schechter, Susan, and Nancy Sugg. 1993. *Handbook on Family Violence for Healthcare Professionals: Women Victims of Domestic Violence.* Box 29 Folder 5. Papers of Susan Schechter, 1961–2005, Harvard University Schlesinger Library.

Scheper-Hughes, Nancy, and Philippe Bourgois, eds. 2004. *Violence in War and Peace: An Anthology.* Malden, MA: Blackwell.

Schippers, Mimi. 2016. *Beyond Monogamy: Polyamory and the Future of Polyqueer Sexualities.* New York: New York University Press.

Schneider, Daniel, Kristen Harknett, and Sara McLanahan. 2016. "Intimate Partner Violence in the Great Recession." *Demography* 53(2):471–505. doi: 10.1007/s13524-016-0462-1.

Schram, Sanford F., Joe Soss, Richard C. Fording, and Linda Houser. 2009. "Deciding to Discipline: Race, Choice, and Punishment at the Frontlines of Welfare Reform." *American Sociological Review* 74(3):398–422.

Schrock, Douglas, Janice McCabe, and Christian Vaccaro. 2017. "Narrative Manhood Acts: Batterer Intervention Program Graduates' Tragic Relationships." *Symbolic Interaction* 41(3):384–410.

Schur, Edwin M. 1984. *Labeling Women Deviant: Gender, Stigma, and Social Control.* New York: Random House.

Schwark, Sandra, and Gerd Bohner. 2019. "Sexual Violence—'Victim' or 'Survivor': News Images Affect Explicit and Implicit Judgments of Blame." *Violence Against Women* 25(12):1491–509. doi: 10.1177/1077801218820202.

Scott, Ellen K., Andrew S. London, and Nancy A. Myers. 2002. "Dangerous Dependencies: The Intersection of Welfare Reform and Domestic Violence." *Gender & Society* 16(6):878–97. doi: 10.1177/089124302237893.

Scott, James C. 1998. *Seeing Like a State: How Certain Schemes to Improve the Human Condition Have Failed.* New Haven, CT: Yale University Press.

Seidler, Guenter H., and Frank E. Wagner. 2006. "Comparing the Efficacy of EMDR and Trauma-Focused Cognitive-Behavioral Therapy in the Treatment of PTSD: A Meta-Analytic Study." *Psychological Medicine* 36(11):1515–22. doi: 10.1017/S0033291706007963.

Seidman, Steven. 2001. "From Identity to Queer Politics: Shifts in Normative Heterosexuality and the Meaning of Citizenship." *Citizenship Studies* 5(3):321–28. doi: 10.1080/13621020120085270.

Seim, Josh. 2020. *Bandage, Sort, and Hustle: Ambulance Crews on the Front Lines of Urban Suffering*. Oakland: University of California Press.

Shah, Prakesh S., and Jyotsna Shah. 2010. "Maternal Exposure to Domestic Violence and Pregnancy and Birth Outcomes: A Systematic Review and Meta-Analyses." *Journal of Women's Health* 19(11):2017–31. doi: 10.1089/jwh.2010.2051.

Sharpe, Christina. 2016. *In the Wake: On Blackness and Being*. Durham, NC: Duke University Press.

Sharp-Jeffs, Nicola, Liz Kelly, and Renate Klein. 2018. "Long Journeys toward Freedom: The Relationship Between Coercive Control and Space for Action—Measurement and Emerging Evidence." *Violence against Women* 24(2):163–85. doi: 10.1177/1077801216686199.

Sherman, Lawrence W., and Heather M. Harris. 2015. "Increased Death Rates of Domestic Violence Victims from Arresting vs. Warning Suspects in the Milwaukee Domestic Violence Experiment (MilDVE)." *Journal of Experimental Criminology* 11(1):1–20. doi: 10.1007/s11292-014-9203-x.

Shields, Stephanie A. 2007. "Passionate Men, Emotional Women: Psychology Constructs Gender Difference in the Late 19th Century." *History of Psychology* 10(2):92–110. doi: 10.1037/1093-4510.10.2.92.

Shome, Raka. 2001. "White Femininity and the Discourse of the Nation: Re/Membering Princess Diana." *Feminist Media Studies* 1(3):323–42. doi: 10.1080/14680770120088927.

Silverman, Jay G., Anita Raj, Lorelei A. Mucci, and Jeanne E. Hathaway. 2001. "Dating Violence against Adolescent Girls and Associated Substance Use, Unhealthy Weight Control, Sexual Risk Behavior, Pregnancy, and Suicidality." *JAMA* 286(5):572–79. doi: 10.1001/jama.286.5.572.

Skarpelis, A. K. M. 2020. "Life on File: Archival Epistemology and Theory." *Qualitative Sociology* (43):385–405.

Slack, Jennifer Daryl. 1996. "The Theory and Method of Articulation in Cultural Studies." In *Stuart Hall: Critical Dialogues in Cultural Studies*, edited by K.-H. Chen and D. Morley, 112–27. London: Taylor & Francis.

Small, Mario Luis. 2006. "Neighborhood Institutions as Resource Brokers: Childcare Centers, Interorganizational Ties, and Resource Access among the Poor." *Social Problems* 53(2):274–92.

Smith, Andrea. 2005. *Conquest: Sexual Violence and the American Indian Genocide*. Boston, MA: South End Press.

———. 2006. "Three Pillars of White Supremacy." In *Incite! Women of Color against Violence*, 66–73. Cambridge, MA: South End Press.

Smith, Linda Tuhiwai. 2012. *Decolonizing Methodologies: Research and Indigenous Peoples*. London: Zed Books.

Smith, Steven Rathgeb, and Michael Lipsky. 1993. *Nonprofits for Hire: The Welfare State in the Age of Contracting*. Cambridge, MA: Harvard University Press.

Sokoloff, Natalie J., and Ida Dupont. 2005. "Domestic Violence at the Intersections of Race, Class, and Gender: Challenges and Contributions to Understanding Violence against Marginalized Women in Diverse Communities." *Violence Against Women* 11(1):38–64. doi: 10.1177/1077801204271476.

Solnit, Rebecca. 2020. *Recollections of My Nonexistence*. New York: Viking, Penguin Random House.

Somers, Margaret. 1994a. "The Narrative Constitution of Identity: A Relational and Network Approach." *Theory and Society* 23(5):605–49.

———. 1994b. "Rights, Relationality, and Membership: Rethinking the Making and Meaning of Citizenship." *Social Inquiry* 19(1):63–112.

———. 2008. *Genealogies of Citizenship: Markets, Statelessness, and the Right to Have Rights*. Cambridge: Cambridge University Press.

Soss, Joe, Richard C. Fording, and Sanford F. Schram. 2011. *Disciplining the Poor: Neoliberal Paternalism and the Persistent Power of Race*. Berkeley: University of Chicago Press.

Star, Susan Leigh. 2010. "This Is Not a Boundary Object: Reflections on the Origin of a Concept." *Science, Technology, & Human Values* 35(4–5):601–17.

Star, Susan Leigh, and James R. Griesemer. 1989. "Institutional Ecology, 'Translations' and Boundary Objects: Amateurs and Professionals in Berkeley's Museum of Vertebrate Zoology, 1907–39." *Social Studies of Science* 19(3):387–420. doi: 10.1177/030631289019003001.

Stark, Evan. 2007. *Coercive Control: The Entrapment of Women in Personal Life*. Oxford: Oxford University Press.

Stark, Evan, and Marianne Hester. 2019. "Coercive Control: Update and Review." *Violence Against Women* 25(1):81–104. doi: 10.1177/1077801218816191.

Stein, Arlene. 2009. "Feminism, Therapeutic Culture, and the Holocaust in the United States: The Second-Generation Phenomenon." *Jewish Social Studies: History, Culture, Society* 16(1):27–53.

———. 2011. "Therapeutic Politics—An Oxymoron?" *Sociological Forum* 26(1):187–93.

Stein, Arlene, and Ken Plummer. 1994. "'I Can't Even Think Straight' 'Queer' Theory and the Missing Sexual Revolution in Sociology." *Sociological Theory* 12(2):178–87. doi: 10.2307/201863.

Stein, Dan J., Soraya Seedat, Amy Iversen, and Simon Wessely. 2007. "Post-Traumatic Stress Disorder: Medicine and Politics." *Lancet* 369:139–44.

Steinmetz, George. 2006. "Bourdieu's Disavowal of Lacan: Psychoanalytic Theory and the Concepts of 'Habitus' and 'Symbolic Capital.'" *Constellations* 13(4):445–64.

Stern, Robin. 2007. *The Gaslight Effect: How to Spot and Survive the Hidden Manipulation Others Use to Control Your Life*. New York: Harmony Books.

Stevenson, Judith. 1970. "Which Way to the Shelter? Which Way the Movement? OR Getting Up Off Our Rhetoric to Survive." Box 1 Folder 2. Domestic

Violence: General, Articles and Papers. Sophia Smith Collection, Violence Against Women, Smith College.

Stoler, Ann Laura. 1995. *Race and the Education of Desire: Foucault's History of Sexuality and the Colonial Order of Things.* Durham, NC: Duke University Press.

Strauchler, Orin, Kathy McCloskey, Kathleen Malloy, Marilyn Sitaker, Nancy Grigsby, and Paulette Gillig. 2004. "Humiliation, Manipulation, and Control: Evidence of Centrality in Domestic Violence Against an Adult Partner." *Journal of Family Violence* 19(6):339–46. doi: 10.1007/s10896-004-0679-4.

Stringer, Rebecca. 2014. *Knowing Victims: Feminism, Agency and Victim Politics in Neoliberal Times.* London: Routledge.

Summerfield, Derek. 1999. "A Critique of Seven Assumptions behind Psychological Trauma Programmes in War-Affected Areas." *Social Science & Medicine* 48(10):1449–62. doi: 10.1016/S0277-9536(98)00450-X.

Sutton, Barbara. 2010. *Bodies in Crisis: Culture, Violence, and Women's Resistance in Neoliberal Argentina.* New Brunswick, NJ: Rutgers University Press.

———. 2018. *Surviving State Terror: Women's Testimonies of Repression and Resistance in Argentina.* New York: New York University Press.

Swan, Suzanne C., and David L. Snow. 2006. "The Development of a Theory of Women's Use of Violence in Intimate Relationships." *Violence against Women* 12(11):1026–45. doi: 10.1177/1077801206293330.

Sweet, Paige L. 2014. "'Every Bone of My Body:' Domestic Violence and the Diagnostic Body." *Social Science & Medicine* 122:44–52. doi: 10.1016/j.socscimed.2014.10.014.

———. 2015. "Chronic Victims, Risky Women: Domestic Violence Advocacy and the Medicalization of Abuse." *Signs: Journal of Women in Culture and Society* 41(1):81–106. doi: 10.1086/681772.

———. 2019a. "The Paradox of Legibility: Domestic Violence and Institutional Survivorhood." *Social Problems* 66(3):411–27. doi: 10.1093/socpro/spy012.

———. 2019b. "The Sociology of Gaslighting." *American Sociological Review* 84(5):851–75. doi: 10.1177/0003122419874843.

Sweet, Paige L., and Claire Laurier Decoteau. 2018. "Contesting Normal: The DSM-5 and Psychiatric Subjectivation." *BioSocieties* 13(1):103–22.

Sweet, Paige L., and Danielle Giffort. 2021. "The Bad Expert." *Social Studies of Science* 51(3):313–338.

Tanha, Marieh, Connie J. A. Beck, Aurelio José Figueredo, and Chitra Raghavan. 2010. "Sex Differences in Intimate Partner Violence and the Use of Coercive Control as a Motivational Factor for Intimate Partner Violence." *Journal of Interpersonal Violence* 25(10):1836–54. doi: 10.1177/0886260509354501.

Thomas, Kristie A., Lisa Goodman, and Susan Putnins. 2015. "'I Have Lost Everything': Trade-Offs of Seeking Safety from Intimate Partner Violence." *American Journal of Orthopsychiatry* 85(2):170–80. doi: 10.1037/ort0000044.

Ticktin, Miriam I. 2011. *Casualties of Care: Immigration and the Politics of Humanitarianism in France.* Berkeley: University of California Press.

Tierney, Kathleen J. 1982. "The Battered Women Movement and the Creation of the Wife Beating Problem." *Social Problems* 29(3):207–20. doi: 10.2307/800155.

Tiger, Rebecca. 2013. *Judging Addicts: Drug Courts and Coercion in the Justice System.* New York: New York University Press.

Tilly, Charles. 1995. "Citizenship, Identity and Social History." *International Review of Social History* 40(S3):1–17. doi: 10.1017/S0020859000113586.

Timmermans, Stefan, and Marc Berg. 2010. *The Gold Standard: The Challenge of Evidence-Based Medicine.* Philadelphia: Temple University Press.

Tinker, Bonnie. n.d. "Untitled Letter." Box 1, Bonnie Tinker's Personal Files. National Coalition Against Domestic Violence.

Tjaden, Patricia Godeke, and Nancy Thoennes. 2000. *Full Report of the Prevalence, Incidence, and Consequences of Violence against Women: Findings from the National Violence against Women Survey.* US Department of Justice. https://www.ncjrs.gov/pdffiles1/nij/183781.pdf.

Trattner, Walter I. 1999. *From Poor Law to Welfare State: A History of Social Welfare in America.* New York: Simon & Schuster.

Turner, Bryan S. 1993. "Contemporary Problems in the Theory of Citizenship." In *Citizenship & Social Theory*, edited by B. S. Turner. London: Sage Publications.

Underman, Kelly, Paige L. Sweet, and Claire Laurier Decoteau. 2017. "Custodial Citizenship in the Omnibus Autism Proceeding." *Sociological Forum* 32(3):544–65. doi: 10.1111/socf.12348.

US Commission on Civil Rights. 1982. "The Federal Response to Domestic Violence." Box 1 Folder 9. Domestic Violence—General, National, Domestic Violence, National U.S. Commission on Civil Rights. Sophia Smith Collection, Violence Against Women, Smith College.

US Department of Health and Human Services. 2012. "Family Violence Prevention and Services / Grants to State Domestic Violence Coalitions." *Federal Register* 77(47):14393–401.

———. 2013. "Funding Opportunity Announcement for Family Violence Prevention and Services / Grants for Domestic Violence Shelters / Grants to Native American Tribes." *Federal Register* 78(69):21370–79.

US Department of Justice. 1984. *Attorney General's Task Force on Family Violence, Final Report.* Washington, DC: US Department of Justice.

———. 1985. *Surgeon General's Workshop on Violence and Public Health Report.* http://profiles.nlm.nih.gov/ps/retrieve/ResourceMetadata/NNBCFX.

———. 2002. "Remarks of Attorney General John Ashcroft, Annual Symposium on Domestic Violence." https://www.justice.gov/archive/ag/speeches/2002/102902domesticviolencesymposium.htm.

———. 2016. "Domestic Violence." https://www.justice.gov/ovw/domestic-violence.

US Department of Labor. 1978. "Letter from the Department of Labor, Field Memorandum No. 286-78. "CETA Funding of Activities to Aid Battered Women." Box 1, Bonnie Tinker's Personal Files. National Coalition Against Domestic Violence.

US House of Representatives. 1978. *Research into Violent Behavior before the Subcommittee on Domestic and International Scientific Planning, Analysis, and Cooperation.* Washington, DC: Government Printing Office.

———. 1979. *Domestic Violence Prevention and Services. Hearings before the Subcommittee on Select Education of the Committee on Education and Labor.* Testimony of Representative Lindy Boggs. Testimony of Representative Geraldine Ferraro. Washington, DC: Government Printing Office.

———. 1983. *Hearings on Domestic Violence before the Committee on Education and Labor, Subcommittee on Select Education.* Testimony of Bonnie Flynn, Sandra Crawford, Charles Gentry. Washington, DC: US Government Printing Office.

———. 1984. *Violence and Abuse in American Families. Hearing before the Select Committee on Children, Youth, and Families.* Ninety-Eighth Congress, Second Session, June 14, Washington, DC: US Government Printing Office.

US Senate. 1978. Testimony of Nancy Clinch, California Coalition, to the Senate Subcommittee on Child and Human Development of the Committee on Human Resources. Washington, DC: Government Printing Office.

———. 1983. *Crime Victims' Assistance Programs, Testimony of Senator Arlen Spector,* Committee on the Judiciary, Subcommittee on Juvenile Justice. Washington DC: US Government Printing Office.

Valocchi, Stephen. 2005. "Not Yet Queer Enough: The Lessons of Queer Theory for the Sociology of Gender and Sexuality." *Gender & Society* 19(6):750–70. doi: 10.1177/0891243205280294.

Van der Kolk, Bessel A. 2015. *The Body Keeps the Score: Brain, Mind, and Body in the Healing of Trauma.* New York: Penguin Books.

Varma, Saiba. 2020. *The Occupied Clinic: Militarism and Care in Kashmir.* Durham, NC: Duke University Press.

Villalón, Roberta. 2010. *Violence against Latina Immigrants: Citizenship, Inequality, and Community.* New York: New York University Press.

Visweswaran, Kamala. 1994. *Fictions of Feminist Ethnography.* Minneapolis: University of Minnesota Press.

Wacquant, Loïc. 2009. *Punishing the Poor: The Neoliberal Government of Social Insecurity.* Durham, NC: Duke University Press.

Waggoner, Miranda R. 2017. *The Zero Trimester: Pre-Pregnancy Care and the Politics of Reproductive Risk*. Oakland: University of California Press.

Walby, Sylvia. 1994. "Is Citizenship Gendered?" *Sociology* 28(2):379–95.

Walker, Lenore. 1979. *The Battered Woman*. New York: Harper & Row.

———. 1985. "Letter." Box 6 Folder 6. Correspondence 1985. Papers of Susan Schechter, 1961–2005, Harvard University Schlesinger Library.

———. 1989. *Terrifying Love: Why Battered Women Kill and How Society Responds*. New York: Harper & Row.

Ward, Jane. 2015. *Not Gay: Sex between Straight White Men*. New York: New York University Press.

———. 2020. *The Tragedy of Heterosexuality*. New York: New York University Press.

Warrior, Betsy. 1975. "Battered Lives." *The Second Wave*. Box 1, Bonnie Tinker's Personal Files. National Coalition Against Domestic Violence.

———. 1976. "Working on Wife Abuse." Box 2 Folder 7, Box 2: Domestic Violence, National (Continued) and Regional (East), Massachusetts. Sophia Smith Collection, Violence Against Women, Smith College.

Warshaw, Carole. 1996. "Domestic Violence and Mental Health: Developing Collaborative Models for Advocacy and Treatment." Box 35 Folder 3, Understanding the Relationship between Domestic Violence Services and Mental Health Providers, National Resource Center on Domestic Violence, 1994–1996. Papers of Susan Schechter, 1961–2005, Harvard University Schlesinger Library.

———. 2001. "Psychological Aspects of Women's Health Care: The Interface between Psychiatric and Obstetrics and Gynecology." Box 80 Folder 4, Domestic violence and mental health, 1996, 2000–2001. Papers of Susan Schechter, 1961–2005, Harvard University Schlesinger Library.

Warshaw, Carole, P. Brashler, and J. Gill. 2009. "Mental Health Consequences of Intimate Partner Violence." In *Intimate Partner Violence: A Health-Based Perspective*, edited by E. Mitchell, 141–71. New York: Oxford University Press.

Warshaw, Carole, Eleanor Lyon, Patricia J. Bland, Heather Phillips, and Mikisha Hooper. 2014. *Mental Health and Substance Use Coercion Surveys: Report from the National Center on Domestic Violence, Trauma, and Mental Health and the National Domestic Violence Hotline*. National Center for Domestic Violence, Trauma, & Mental Health. http://www.nationalcenterdv traumamh.org/wp-content/uploads/2014/10/NCDVTMH_NDVH_MHSU CoercionSurveyReport_2014-2.pdf.

Waters, H., A. Hyder, Y. Rajkotia, S. Basu, J. A. Rehwinkel, and A. Butchart. 2004. *The Economic Dimensions of Interpersonal Violence*. Geneva: Department of Injuries and Violence Prevention, World Health Organization. https://apps.who.int/iris/bitstream/handle/10665/42944/9241591609 .pdf;jsessionid=BE497E67C20D4B72657CDA558B779147?sequence=1

Watkins-Hayes, Celeste. 2019. *Remaking a Life: How Women Living with HIV/ AIDS Confront Inequality*. Oakland: University of California Press.

Weingarten, Debbie. 2016. "The Currency of Cars: How to Leave a Husband." *Longreads*. https://longreads.com/2017/04/18/the-currency-of-cars-how-to -leave-a-husband/.

Weinig, Irma M. 1979. "Help for the Battered Woman." Battered Women's Committee, Family of Woodstock, Inc. Box 1 Folder 4. Domestic Violence, General, Booklets. Sophia Smith Collection, Violence Against Women, Smith College.

Weiss, Benjamin R. 2020. "'Who Can We Tell Survivors to Call?' The Institutionalization of Criminal-Legal Interventions in a Domestic Violence Organization." *Social Problems* 67(2):270–85. doi: 10.1093/socpro/spz017.

Weisz, Arlene N., Richard M. Tolman, and Daniel G. Saunders. 2000. "Assessing the Risk of Severe Domestic Violence: The Importance of Survivors' Predictions." *Journal of Interpersonal Violence* 15(1):75–90. doi: 10.1177 /08862600001500106.

West, Carolyn M., and Suzanna Rose. 2000. "Dating Aggression among Low Income African American Youth: An Examination of Gender Differences and Antagonistic Beliefs." *Violence Against Women* 6(5):470–94. doi: 10.1177 /10778010022181985.

Whittier, Nancy. 2009. *The Politics of Child Sexual Abuse: Emotion, Social Movements, and the State*. Oxford University Press.

———. 2016. "Carceral and Intersectional Feminism in Congress: The Violence Against Women Act, Discourse, and Policy." *Gender & Society* 30(5):791–818. doi: 10.1177/0891243216653381.

———. 2018. *Frenemies: Feminists, Conservatives, and Sexual Violence*. Oxford University Press.

Williamson, Emma. 2010. "Living in the World of the Domestic Violence Perpetrator: Negotiating the Unreality of Coercive Control." *Violence against Women* 16(12):1412–23. doi: 10.1177/1077801210389162.

Willse, Craig. 2015. *The Value of Homelessness: Managing Surplus Life in the United States*. Minneapolis: University of Minnesota Press.

Wilson, Elizabeth A. 2015. *Gut Feminism*. Durham, NC: Duke University Press.

Wingrove, Elizabeth. 1999. "Interpellating Sex." *Signs: Journal of Women in Culture and Society* 24(4):869–93. doi: 10.1086/495397.

Wolch, Jennifer R. 1990. *The Shadow State: Government and Voluntary Sector in Transition*. New York: The Foundation Center.

Women's Aid Federation. 1984. "Letter." Box 6 Folder 5, Correspondence 1984. Papers of Susan Schechter, 1961–2005, Harvard University Schlesinger Library.

Wyse, Jessica J. B. 2013. "Rehabilitating Criminal Selves: Gendered Strategies in Community Corrections." *Gender & Society* 27(2):231–55. doi: 10.1177 /0891243212470509.

Yamawaki, Niwako, Joseph Ostenson, and C. Ryan Brown. 2009. "The Functions of Gender Role Traditionality, Ambivalent Sexism, Injury, and Frequency of Assault on Domestic Violence Perception: A Study between Japanese and American College Students." *Violence Against Women* 15(9):1126–42. doi: 10.1177/1077801209340758.

Young, Allan. 1997. *The Harmony of Illusions: Inventing Post-Traumatic Stress Disorder.* Princeton, NJ: Princeton University Press.

YWCA Chicago. 1978. "Grant Proposal: Rape Training." Box 4 Folder 3. Loop Center YWCA (Chicago), Correspondence, Schedules, Speeches, Etc. 1976–1978. Papers of Susan Schechter, 1961–2005, Harvard University Schlesinger Library.

Zola, Irving Kenneth. 1991. "Bringing Our Bodies and Ourselves Back In: Reflections on a Past, Present, and Future 'Medical Sociology.'" *Journal of Health and Social Behavior* 32(1):1–16. doi: 10.2307/2136796.

Index

Founded in 1893,
UNIVERSITY OF CALIFORNIA PRESS
publishes bold, progressive books and journals
on topics in the arts, humanities, social sciences,
and natural sciences—with a focus on social
justice issues—that inspire thought and action
among readers worldwide.

The UC PRESS FOUNDATION
raises funds to uphold the press's vital role
as an independent, nonprofit publisher, and
receives philanthropic support from a wide
range of individuals and institutions—and from
committed readers like you. To learn more, visit
ucpress.edu/supportus.